AF695751

Imperatives for Legal Education Research

In the last few decades, university teaching has been recognised as an activity which can be studied and improved through educational scholarship. In some disciplines this is now well established. It remains emergent in legal education. The field is rich with questions to be answered and issues to be raised.

This book provides the first overall review of legal education scholarship. The chapters outline the history of legal education research and provide a detailed analysis of the trends in areas of publication. Beyond this, the book suggests a typology for further conceptualising the field and a series of suggested paths for future research. The book originated from the 2017 UNSW conference 'Research in Legal Education: State of the Art?' It features internationally respected authors who bring their perspectives on how legal education – as a field of research – should be conceptualised. The collection is arranged into three themes. First, a historical view is taken of the emergence of legal education scholarship and its roots that predate modern educational theory. Second, the book provides overviews of the extant field of publications, highlighting areas of interest and neglect, and delineating the trends in current publication. Third, the book provides a set of suggested typologies for describing legal education research and a series of essays for future directions which both critique current approaches and provide inspiration for future directions.

The state of legal education research represents an authoritative introduction to the field, a set of conceptual tools with which to describe it, and inspiration for researchers to expand and grow research into legal education.

Ben Golder is an Associate Professor in the Faculty of Law at the University of New South Wales, Australia. He is the Law Faculty Associate Dean (Education). Ben teaches courses on law and social theory, on public law, and on the politics of human rights. His current research is into contemporary critiques of human rights discourse

Marina Nehme is a Senior Lecturer in the Faculty of Law at the University of New South Wales and a fellow of the UNSW Scientia Education Academy. Her teaching excellence has been recognized at the national and institutional level. She was formerly the Law Faculty Director of Learning and Teaching. Marina's research interests are in in corporate law, regulatory sanction and legal education.

Alex Steel is a Professor in the Faculty of Law at the University of New South Wales and a fellow of the UNSW Scientia Education Academy. His teaching excellence has been recognized at the institutional and national level. He was formerly the Law Faculty Associate Dean (Education) and is Acting UNSW Pro Vice Chancellor Education. His research interests are in the pedagogy and regulation of legal education, curriculum design and assessment practices, student wellbeing and teacher development.

Prue Vines is Professor of Law at the University of New South Wales and a fellow of the UNSW Scientia Education Academy. Her teaching excellence has been recognized at the institutional level. She is the Director of First Year Studies and incoming Law Faculty Associate Dean (Education). Prue's research is in tort law, particularly the impact of apologies on civil liability, Indigenous issues in succession law, and legal education, in particular the first year at university and student wellbeing.

Emerging Legal Education

Series Editors: Paul Maharg
Osgoode Hall Law School, York University, Ontario, Canada.
Meera Deo
Thomas Jefferson School of Law, San Diego, California, USA
Elizabeth Mertz
University of Wisconsin–Madison/American Bar Foundation, USA

Emerging Legal Education is a forum for analysing the discourse of legal education and creating innovative ways of learning the law. The series focuses on research, theory and practice within legal education, drawing attention to historical, interdisciplinary and international characteristics, and is based upon imaginative and sophisticated educational thinking. The series takes a broad view of theory and practice. Series books are written for an international audience and are sensitive to the diversity of contexts in which law is taught, learned and practised.

Other titles in this series:

The Moral Imagination and the Legal Life
Beyond Text in Legal Education
Edited by Zenon Bankowski and Maksymilian Del Mar

The Arts and the Legal Academy
Beyond Text in Legal Education
Edited by Zenon Bańkowski, Maksymilian Del Mar and Paul Maharg

Affect and Legal Education
Emotion in Learning and Teaching the Law
Edited by Paul Maharg and Caroline Maughan

Imperatives for Legal Education Research
Then, Now and Tomorrow
Edited by Ben Golder, Marina Nehme, Alex Steel and Prue Vines

Forthcoming:

Power, Legal Education, and Law School Cultures
Edited by Meera E. Deo, Mindie Lazarus-Black, Elizabeth Mertz

www.routledge.com/Emerging-Legal-Education/book-series/ELE

Imperatives for Legal Education Research

Then, Now and Tomorrow

Edited by Ben Golder, Marina Nehme, Alex Steel and Prue Vines

Routledge
Taylor & Francis Group
LONDON AND NEW YORK

First published 2020
by Routledge
2 Park Square, Milton Park, Abingdon, Oxon OX14 4RN

and by Routledge
605 Third Avenue, New York, NY 10017

First issued in paperback 2021

Routledge is an imprint of the Taylor & Francis Group, an informa business

© 2020 selection and editorial matter, Ben Golder, Marina Nehme, Alex Steel and Prue Vines; individual chapters, the contributors

The right of Ben Golder, Marina Nehme, Alex Steel and Prue Vines to be identified as the authors of the editorial material, and of the authors for their individual chapters, has been asserted in accordance with sections 77 and 78 of the Copyright, Designs and Patents Act 1988.

All rights reserved. No part of this book may be reprinted or reproduced or utilised in any form or by any electronic, mechanical, or other means, now known or hereafter invented, including photocopying and recording, or in any information storage or retrieval system, without permission in writing from the publishers.

Trademark notice: Product or corporate names may be trademarks or registered trademarks, and are used only for identification and explanation without intent to infringe.

Publisher's Note
The publisher has gone to great lengths to ensure the quality of this reprint but points out that some imperfections in the original copies may be apparent.

British Library Cataloguing-in-Publication Data
A catalogue record for this book is available from the British Library

Library of Congress Cataloging-in-Publication Data
Names: Research in Legal Education: State of the Art? (Conference) (2017 : University of New South Wales). | Steel, Alex, editor. | Golder, Ben, editor. | Vines, Prue, 1956– editor. | Nehme, Marina, editor.
Title: Imperatives for legal education research : then, now and tomorrow / edited by Ben Golder, Marina Nehme, Alex Steel and Prue Vines
Description: Abingdon, Oxon ; New York, NY : Routledge, 2019. | Series: Emerging legal education | "The book originated from the 2017 UNSW conference "Research in Legal Education: State of the Art?""—ECIP galley. | Includes bibliographical references and index.
Identifiers: LCCN 2019027865 (print) | LCCN 2019027866 (ebook) | ISBN 9781138387805 (hardback) | ISBN 9780429426070 (ebook)
Subjects: LCSH: Law—Study and teaching—English-speaking countries—Congresses.
Classification: LCC K100.A3 R47 2019 (print) | LCC K100.A3 (ebook) | DDC 340.071/1—dc23
LC record available at https://lccn.loc.gov/2019027865
LC ebook record available at https://lccn.loc.gov/2019027866

Typeset in Galliard
by Apex CoVantage, LLC

ISBN 13: 978-1-03-224050-3 (pbk)
ISBN 13: 978-1-138-38780-5 (hbk)

DOI: 10.4324/9780429426070

Contents

Contributors

Anthony Bradney is Professor of Law at Keele University. Between 2004 and 2006 he was Professor of Law at the University of Sheffield. In 2006 he was appointed Professor of Law at Keele University. He is a Senior Research Fellow at the Institute of Advanced Legal Studies. His research interests lie mainly in the fields of law and religion, legal pluralism, law and popular culture, law and literature, university legal education and judicial studies. He is the author of numerous books and articles on these topics.

Peter D. Burdon is Associate Professor at the Adelaide Law School. His most recent publications on legal education include 'Critical Thinking in Legal Education: Our Journey' (2013) 23(2) *Legal Education Review* 345–377 with G. Appleby and A. Reilly; 'Academic Resistance to the Neoliberal University' (2013) 23(2) *Legal Education Review* 379–401 with M. Heath; and 'Academic Resistance: Landscape of Hope and Despair' in A. Nocella II and E. Juergensmeyer (Eds.), *Fighting Academic Repression and Neoliberal Education: Resistance, Reclaiming, Organizing, and Black Lives Matter in Education* (Peter Lang Publishing, 2017).

Melissa Castan is Associate Professor and Associate Dean (Education) in the Law Faculty at Monash University, as well as Deputy Director in the Castan Centre for Human Rights Law. She is a Monash Education Fellow, and the National Editorial Convenor of the *Alternative Law Journal*, as well as serving as a current member of the executive committee of the Australasian Law Academics Association. Her teaching and research interests are Australian public law, constitutional law, Indigenous legal issues and human rights law, and she publishes regularly on matters of legal education. Her most recent books are education focused: *Federal Constitutional Law: A Contemporary View* (2019) with Professor Sarah Joseph, and *Public Law and Statutory Interpretation: Principles and Practice* (Federation Press, 2017) with Dr Lisa Burton Crawford, Dr Nina Boughey and Dr Maria O'Sullivan. She is also co-author, with Sarah Joseph, of *The International Covenant on Civil and Political Rights: Cases, Commentary and Materials* (2013).

Fiona Cownie is Professor of Law, Keele University, and an expert in the field of legal education. Her published research includes work on the purpose of the law school and on relationships between the academic study of law and vocational training as required by the legal professions. It also includes analysis of the ways in which law is taught, especially arguments about the importance of educational theory and philosophy to legal education. She has made a major contribution to debates about the academic staff who work in law schools; she has carried out extensive empirical research in this area, both in the UK and in Canada, and has written a monograph and a series of articles exploring different aspects of legal academic life. From 2013 to 2017 she was the Pro Vice Chancellor (Education and Student Experience) at Keele.

David Dixon is a Professor at UNSW Law, where he was Dean for ten years to mid-2016. He now teaches first year law students and conducts research on law in policing (particularly interrogation) and on legality in post-colonial contexts. His books include: *From Prohibition to Regulation: Bookmaking, Anti-Gambling and the Law; Law in Policing: Legal Regulation and Police Practices; Interrogating Images: Audio-visually Recorded Police Questioning of Suspects; A Culture of Corruption: Changing an Australian Police Service*; and (as co-editor) *The Integrity of Criminal Process.*

Kate Galloway is Associate Professor, Faculty of Law, Bond University. Her principal academic interests lie in property law and legal education. She is a nationally recognised law teacher, using research-informed approaches to teach property law and in designing and teaching subjects that offer students a future-focused view of legal practice. She publishes and presents both in Australia and internationally in academic, professional, and community contexts. Her work encompasses legal education, property – particularly land tenure, sustainability, social justice, and gender equality. She is the editor-in-chief of the *Legal Education Review* and is the Queensland editor of the *Alternative Law Journal.*

Ben Golder is Associate Professor and currently Associate Dean (Education) in the Faculty of Law, UNSW Sydney. He works at the intersection of legal and political theory and is an Associate Editor of the journal *Contemporary Political Theory*, a member of the Editorial Committee of the UK-based journal, *Law and Critique*, and a member of the Editorial Board of the *Australian Journal of Human Rights.* These posts capture both his teaching (in public law, legal theory and human rights) and research interests. His last book was on *Foucault and the Politics of Rights.* His most recent articles have been on human rights and metaphor and the concept of legal performativity, and his most recent public talks have been on the subject of how and why the contemporary university is killing the lecture.

Kristoffer Greaves is a Senior Lecturer and Deputy Director of Practical Legal Training at the University of New South Wales. He specialises in practice-based legal education teaching and research. His scholarly interests involve evidence-based approaches to practice-based legal education, scholarship of learning and teaching, and emergent legal professional and educational technologies.

Sally Kift is a Principal Fellow of the Higher Education Academy (PFHEA), a Fellow of the Australian Academy of Law (FAAL), and President of the Australian Learning & Teaching Fellows (ALTF). She has held several university leadership positions, most recently Deputy Vice Chancellor (Academic) at James Cook University. She is a national Teaching Award winner, a national Program Award winner and a national Senior Teaching Fellow on the First Year Experience. In 2010, she was appointed an Australian Discipline Scholar in Law. In 2017, she received an Australian University Career Achievement Award for her contribution to Australian higher education.

Tania Leiman is Associate Professor and Dean of Law, Flinders University. She has received national individual and team teaching excellence awards. She teaches *Law in a Digital Age* (which includes building AI legal apps to increase access to justice) and *Law in Action* (which includes a law reform clinic working on legal implications of emerging technologies). Her current research interests include future mobility solutions (primarily automated vehicles), disruption in the legal profession, artificial intelligence and legal tech, and the future of legal education. She is a member of the Australian Driverless Vehicle Initiative [*ADVI*]'s Policy & Risk Group.

Paul Maharg is Distinguished Professor of Practice – Legal Education at Osgoode Hall Law School, York University, Ontario, and Honorary Professor, ANU College of Law. He is also Visiting Professor at the Chinese University of Hong Kong Faculty of Law and Hong Kong University Faculty of Law. Over three decades he has published widely in the fields of legal education and professional learning design, and is a strong advocate of Open Access cultures in research and education. His specialities include interdisciplinary educational design, the regulation of legal education and the use of technology-enhanced learning at all levels of legal education. He was appointed a Principal Fellow of the Higher Education Academy (2015), HEA National Teaching Fellow (2011), and a Fellow of the *RSA* (2009). He blogs at http://paulmaharg.com.

Carrie Menkel-Meadow is Distinguished Professor of Law (and Political Science), University of California Irvine; and A. B. Chettle Jr. Professor of Dispute Resolution and Civil Procedure, Emerita, Georgetown University. She has won the Center for Public Resources' First Prize for Scholarship in Alternative Dispute Resolution three times (1983, 1990, and 1998), the American Bar Foundation Award for Outstanding Scholar (2018), and she won the Rutter Award for Excellence in Teaching at UCLA and the Frank Flegal Teaching Award at Georgetown (2006). She is the author of *Dispute Resolution: Beyond the Adversarial Model* (3rd ed. 2019); *Negotiation: Processes for Problem Solving* (2nd ed. 2014); *Mediation: Theory, Policy & Practice* (2nd ed. 2013); *Dispute Processing & Conflict Resolution* (2003), and over 200 articles.

Marina Nehme is a Senior Lecturer in the Faculty of Law at the University of New South Wales. She has just completed a term as Director of Learning and Teaching at UNSW Law. Her research interests include the use of enforceable undertakings and crowd equity funding. In 2011 she received a Citation for Outstanding Contributions to Student Learning from the Australian Learning and Teaching Council.

Alex Steel's legal education publications range across the pedagogy and regulation of legal education, curriculum design, assessment practices and student wellbeing. In criminal law, he focuses on aspects of white collar crime offences. He was part of the team that created the Smart Casual project (http://smartlawteacher.org), developing online professional development for sessional law teachers. He is a foundation member of the UNSW Scientia Education Academy. He is a consultant to the Australian Law School Standards Committee, the Law Admissions Advisory Committee and the Council of Australian Law Deans. He is a member of the member of the Executive of the Australasian Legal Academics Association and member of the Editorial Committee of the *Legal Education Review*. He has acted as Pro Vice Chancellor Education. He was previously Associate Dean (Education) of Law and co-convenor of the national Legal Education Associate Deans (LEAD) Network. He has numerous teaching awards including a Commonwealth Government Citation for Outstanding Contributions to Student Learning.

Prue Vines is Professor and Co-director of the Private Law Research and Policy Group at UNSW Law. She has been Director of First Year Studies there since 1996. She is a Fellow of the Australian Academy of Law, a UNSW Scientia Education Fellow and has received a UNSW Vice Chancellor's Teaching Award. Her research interests include torts and succession as well as legal education. In legal education she has been the author of a number of articles on teaching Indigenous issues in law school, running support programs for first year students (both academic and social) and on wellbeing of law students generally.

Julian Webb is Professor and Director of the Legal Professions Research Network, Melbourne Law School, University of Melbourne, and Honorary Professor of Law at the University of Exeter, UK. His long-term research interests focus on legal ethics and professional regulation, the political economy of legal education, and the design and regulation of legal education systems. He led the research phase of the national Legal Education and Training Review in England and Wales (2011–13) and was a consultant to the Comprehensive Review of Legal Education and Training in Hong Kong (2016–18). He is currently leading a multi-disciplinary research program, initially supported by the Melbourne Networked Society Institute, into the development, regulation, and organisational and epistemic effects of new legal technologies. He also teaches legal ethics, civil procedure, and legal theory on the Melbourne JD.

Part I
Introduction

1 Legal education research *as* an imperative

*Ben Golder, Marina Nehme, Alex Steel and Prue Vines**

I Understanding the 'project' of legal education research

Understanding how we teach and how we learn has long been recognised as profoundly important to education. In this chapter we argue that legal education research is an imperative in itself. The study of teaching and learning, or education more generally, is a long established and respected academic discipline.[1] Most universities contain schools or faculties of education. For many years the focus of these schools and faculties was on primary and high school education (both in terms of graduating qualified teachers to work in schools and, in a scholarly sense, reflecting on the practice of school-level education from a sociological, historical or philosophical perspective, for example). However, as university education has extended to larger sections of the community, and as the notion of 'lifelong learning' becomes more prominent,[2] so too has the increasing focus on professional and evidence-based approaches to tertiary level teaching and learning.

For many disciplines, this initial focus on school learning moved naturally onto tertiary learning, and insights gained into teaching those disciplines at school level could be translated to the tertiary context. Consequently, many tertiary disciplines have well-established fields of research into their students' learning and, relatedly, their colleagues' teaching.[3] Without wishing to disparage the significant efforts of individuals over the years, it is probably fair to say that law as a discipline has been relatively late to this field and tardy in recognising its centrality.[4] Yet it is clear that research into legal education is vitally important. This is not only because of the inherent need to enhance our students' learning, but also to be able to be responsive and informed when dealing with the necessary changes to legal education occasioned by globalisation, digital technologies and the changing nature of the legal profession,[5] points made strongly by authors of chapters in this book.

For many legal academics, legal education research amounts to an informal version of action research. A new approach is tried in class, and if it appears to work, it is repeated. At times, it might be shared with colleagues. But that legal academic might not have any real empirical evidence for the effectiveness of the technique, or indeed any theoretical, philosophical or political justification or rationale for the innovation. The extent of dissemination of the technique may be nil or limited to a few colleagues.[6] Clearly, this 'cottage industry' approach is ill-matched to the worldwide reach of modern legal education. This approach has also created an unfortunately lukewarm acceptance, or indeed a complete rejection, of legal education research in some scholarly quarters. We seek to reverse this perception: in the same way that law in the common law world became a university discipline in the 20th century,[7] its teaching must develop from a university research discipline.

Law is now taught in many universities and beyond – Australia, for example, has more providers of legal qualifications than it has universities.[8] Law is taught not only across many jurisdictions and legal traditions but to widely ranging demographics.[9] Legal education is thus a profoundly important (global) project, and research into legal education is therefore also of crucial importance. What, in our view, is urgently needed is a formalisation of legal education research as its own distinct research field, with its own taxonomy, alongside traditional doctrinal and socio-legal fields.[10] For example historical, psychological and other forms of research may inform and become part of legal education research. However, achieving this requires the field to establish its own academic standards and scope of ambition and to have these recognised.

II The aims of this book

This book began life as a collection of papers from a legal education research conference held at the University of New South Wales (UNSW) Law School in December of 2017. Our aim in convening that conference was to highlight the importance of legal education research as a disciplinary endeavour, to spur reflection on what amounted to research into legal education, and to encourage excellence in that research. Through that conference we hoped to promote a sense, at least in Australia, of a field of research coming into its maturity. Through the papers, and the efforts of presenters and commentators, we hoped to implicitly see the setting of minimum academic standards. The book you are now reading represents a set of those papers which, each in its own particular way, speaks to that ambition and sets out an agenda for further research. Our intention in the conference was not, and in the present work is not, to try to legislate and to delimit or set boundaries around what is and what is not an appropriate object of disciplinary reflection. To the contrary, it represents an attempt on our part to generate scholarly discussion amongst those engaged in the field to pause and take stock, and to think about future lines of inquiry and nascent research agendas.

Legal education research is a relatively new field of scholarly endeavour. In order to engage in it properly, it is vital to understand the past and current landscape within which it is operating. This means that an understanding of what legal education has been doing in the past and how it is operating now is required. It is also important to recognise that rather than a general social science lens, we need to use a law lens to evaluate excellence in such research. It is appropriate therefore to consider what we might use as criteria to evaluate the research about legal education.

What do we mean by excellence in legal education research? First, it is important to emphasise that legal education research can take different forms and that each of those forms may have its own forms of excellence. For instance, it may be excellent empirically, in that its conclusions validly follow from the data which has been chosen in a way which is most likely to create valid results because they are testable. It may also be excellent theoretically in that the discourse is sound, that its assumptions are tested and valid, and that it illuminates practice in a way which is useful or generative; it may further demonstrate excellence as a literature review or a meta-review of the area. In that case, the research will be excellent when it is both broad and of sufficient depth to be able to lead to meaningful, coherent and valid conclusions. Consequently, legal education research should be an area where a range of approaches to research may be used. That range of approaches is evident in this collection, where we find consideration of the political and regulatory landscape of legal education as well as historical, taxonomic, and empirical approaches in this field (not to mention the diversity of programs of study to which these approaches are applied – from qualifying law degrees and research higher degrees to clinical and practical legal education). This literature not only asks how we teach but why we teach what we do and how we know when we have done either of those things well.

It is also important to remember that legal education research does not stand on its own. As discussed above, research into this field should consider, draw from and utilise general education research. At times, general education research may not be particularly useful for the legal academy, but where general education research has adequately traversed some concept or field there is no need for the legal academy to seek to replicate it. As with all other research, some areas of legal research will inform and strengthen others. In the same way that doctrinal research may be a vital basis for some socio-legal research, so sound general education research is fundamental to legal education research. Furthermore, it is imperative to draw upon the strength of that research and then take pains to ensure that applications to law teaching and the legal system do not ignore the differences between some other types of education and *legal* education. It is also important not to ignore other key distinctions, such as the distinction between scholarship of pedagogy and research into learning and teaching, as emphasised by Cownie in Chapter 2. Again, legal education research needs its own lens, emphasising that it is a developing field rather than a developed one, and seeking to develop this into a body of knowledge that is rich, valid and useful. The task then requires legal academics to recognise the value of using a rigorous body of legal education research in order to create the research-based teaching of which many of our universities boast. That research-based, or research-led, teaching draws upon both the legal research of the teacher (in terms of their substantive subject matter) and on the legal education research of the teacher in terms of broad methodology and aspiration.

III Mapping some of the issues in legal education research

This book is divided into three parts: (1) Introduction, (2) Current Landscapes and (3) Calls for Action. The parts reflect some of the issues we have just discussed. Part I includes this chapter and a chapter by Fiona Cownie, which reflects on the reception of legal education within the academy. Part II includes chapters which attempt to map out what has been the concern of legal education research and why. It thus includes chapters considering those questions at both a higher, political or theoretical level, and in the empirical research landscape, and finishes with a possible taxonomy of legal education research. Part III includes chapters which critique the current regulatory frameworks and trends in legal education reform as they have been considered in Australia, the United Kingdom and the United States in a way which aims to energise legal education research into the future. We now turn to introduce the chapters in a little more detail.

IV The significance of research into legal education

Fiona Cownie starts by discussing the significance of research into legal education. She observes that legal education research mirrors the different categories of research found within the higher education literature. She further highlights the history and possible reasons behind the lukewarm reception of legal education research in the UK. Cownie then notes that, for legal education research to be taken seriously, it should face the same rigour and scrutiny that research into substantive legal topics faces. To reflect this, the chapter refers to a comment made by the Law Research Exercise Framework (REF) Sub-Panel in its Report on REF 2014: 'The sub-panel was pleased to receive submissions relating to legal education, but the methodological rigour and significance exhibited by some of these outputs was uneven'.[11] Additionally, using Boyer's scholarship's framework,[12] Cownie discusses the conflation between the 'scholarship of teaching' and 'research in learning and teaching', the differences between Boyer's classification of scholarships and how a poor understanding of this classification has negatively impacted on the academy's perception of legal education research. The chapter concludes by noting that the reception of legal education research may be enhanced when there is a greater understanding by researchers and evaluators of the differences between legal education research and legal education pedagogic scholarship.

V Current landscape

Part II is titled 'Current Landscapes' – that is, both the current landscape of legal education approaches and the landscape of the research into it. These are distinct but linked literatures which need to speak to each other. The five chapters demonstrate the varied approaches to legal research excellence discussed above and exemplify the ecumenical approach towards thinking about research into legal education that we commend in this book. Burdon and Dixon take a qualitative and historical look at what has, and what has not, been the concern of legal education research. For both authors, even though their concerns and political instincts are somewhat different (and in some instances opposed), their questions are quite similar – what constitutes the limits of the field of legal education research and how does it think about (and hence reconstitute) its object? In his chapter, Peter Burdon analyses, as he puts it, 'the extent to which the literature on legal education addresses neoliberalism and engages the political and economic circumstances that influence our teaching environments and practices'.[13]

Burdon's concern is, broadly, that the field of legal education research has focused far too narrowly on *how* questions and not on *why* questions. In an era which he defines as neoliberal (something those of us working in the higher education sector are familiar with through the dictates and practices of new public management, and a quantitative obsession with metrics, league tables and rankings) Burdon suggests that those scholars writing in journals such as the *Journal of Legal Education* and the *Legal Education Review* have been concerned primarily with *how* to teach law within the context of rising class sizes, or online, or with fewer resources, or in less time, rather than with asking *why* it is the case (historically, politically, economically) that we have to teach in this way or are grappling with these particular challenges in our workplaces and our classrooms. Burdon's chapter presents an incisive critique of the politics of (a certain) legal education research that, in failing to attend to the background politics, context and root causes of contemporary legal education's current malaise, risks reinforcing (through inattention to) the factors that continue to produce the status quo. 'Legal education is not something that takes place in a vacuum', he counsels, and consequently 'everything from class sizes to technology and the content of the curriculum is influenced by politics and economics'.[14] Of course, Burdon's suggestion is that the project of legal education is not politically irredeemable, and suggests promising ways in which the research agenda of legal education might be reoriented towards values of publicity and the public sphere (as central to university knowledge production and dissemination).

David Dixon's chapter, written from the perspective of a former dean of law at UNSW, is titled 'The Poverty of Pessimism'. Dixon takes issue with what he calls a style of 'left pessimism' in 'academic critiques of legal education which present excessively pessimistic, inaccurate accounts, ignoring achievements and marginalising difference and resistance'.[15] Left pessimistic accounts of contemporary legal education, on Dixon's account, characterise the present moment as one of despair and decline, and are suffused with a sense of nostalgia. As Dixon makes clear, his 'is not a critique from the right',[16] and he is far from maintaining that contemporary legal education is free of problems let alone endorsing the values of neoliberalism. (As current colleagues of the author, all of whom worked under him as dean, the authors of the present chapter can attest to his trenchant and often very funny decanal attacks on the latest instance of university hyper-managerialism.) Rather, his response to the work of a diverse set of writers that includes Margaret Thornton, Frank Carrigan and Nick James (in an Australian context) is that their account of contemporary legal education is not simply inaccurate but that, in eliding contrary trends and dissident possibilities, they actually contribute to the problem facing contemporary tertiary legal educators. In a way, then, even though Burdon and Dixon are engaging different literatures (the authors in mainstream legal education journals who disavow politics, and the political critics of mainstream legal education who disavow possibility) and approaching it from different perspectives and with divergent instincts (a suspicion of neoliberalism, and a suspicion that neoliberalism does not explain everything) they are engaged in answering the same question – how is it that certain legal education scholarship constitutes its object of study, and with what practical political effects?

In Chapter 5, Steel reflects on the empirical legal education research that has taken place between 2000 to 2016 and creates a database of such research. As with the Galloway, Castan and Steel chapter which follows later on in this section, this chapter illustrates the diversity of the research topics conducted in the field. Further, the chapter is a reference point for the legal academy as it can provide them with a better understanding of the legal education research that has been conducted in the past. It may also help researchers become familiar with the literature that is already in existence to build, develop, expand, and challenge pre-existing findings.

Whereas Steel's analysis focuses on Australian empirical work, Kristoffer Greaves' chapter provides a detailed analysis of empirically based studies into (post-degree) pre-admission practice-based legal education internationally. Methodologically, Greaves uses computerised data mining of article abstracts to identify 78 articles from 2011 to 2015. He identifies problems with the ranking, or lack of any ranking, of most of these articles in metrics that are relied on by universities for measures of prestige. Greaves also reports on characteristics of the articles in his database that he finds troubling. Few articles expressly described or problematised their methodology, nor were there broad literature reviews. Most were policy-based arguments in favour of a teaching methodology or program design. He also identifies a general lack of linkage between higher level social justice aspirations and detailed analysis of pedagogical practices employed. Most were uncritical of the curriculum framework within which they operated. Greaves argues that if authors more carefully took account of these issues, the outlets for publication and their rankings might increase and thus the respect that publishing in the field commands.

Galloway, Castan and Steel's chapter starts by detailing the early stages of a project designed to set up the scholarship of legal education as a domain of legal research in its own right. Consequently, the chapter focuses on sharing the findings of the first part of their project. The authors develop a taxonomy prototype of legal education research that aims to recognise the diversity of the scholarship of legal education research. Delving into a contested field, the chapter defines legal research and highlights that this concept retains a discipline orientation but can also be interdisciplinary. For instance, legal education scholarship adopts empirical and even scientific methods. The taxonomy prototype developed is based on three dimensions: perspective, research method and legal education. These dimensions allow the authors to then discuss legal education research with the aim of establishing a research framework that supports the scholarship of legal education in the academy.

VI Calls for action

Part III, titled 'Calls for Action', contains a number of lively chapters both critiquing current approaches and providing inspiration for future directions. It considers both the regulatory framework in which legal education operates and various trends in legal education and legal education reform. Anthony Bradney begins with 'Who Controls University Legal Education? The Case of England and Wales'. This chapter is an example of legal education research which focuses on regulatory authority rather than empirical approach. Bradney emphasises the significance of who controls university legal education and how this has changed. Modern British universities are officially autonomous, and academics officially have academic freedom not only as employees but as members of an autonomous body. But the literature Bradney considers clearly shows the burgeoning regulatory regimes are making massive inroads into that autonomy. He discusses a number of regulatory authorities, including, for example the Quality Assurance Accreditation agency, which has established benchmarks for each discipline including law, for some of which the 'justification[s] . . . were not always readily apparent'.[17] Bradney's chapter raises questions about the role of the university and the resistance of academics to that control. He ends by noting that 'Academic freedom is more properly an obligation than a right'.[18]

Sally Kift's Chapter 9 provides both an overview and a critique of the structuring of legal education in Australia. She reviews regulatory developments since 2000 and how calls for change from the profession and others have been received and implemented. Kift finds that as a result of this constant debate and improvement Australian legal education is well placed to respond to the coming changes to the workplace and role of lawyers. In large part she sees this preparedness to be a result of a rich history of legal education research, and specifically a result of a period in which there was government funding of education research – the apotheosis of which was the development of law's threshold learning outcomes. These she sees as balancing the potentially negative effects of professional accreditation, a fear echoed by Bradney. The key for the future is for law schools to remain 'agentic' in the regulatory process.

Chapter 10, 'Galloping Off Madly in One Direction: Legal Education Reform, the (Im?)possibility of Evidence-Based Policy-Making and a Plea for Better Design Thinking', by Julian Webb, considers the unprecedented level of reform in legal education in the last 30 years. This level of reform has had a problematic relationship to legal education research. Legal education reform has often been treated as requiring no research evidence at all, springing whole from the intuition of the reformers. Webb uses the current drive for a return to centralised assessment (such as the New York Bar Exam) to discuss some fundamental flaws in legal education research and policy-making. The chapter is wide-ranging, covering most of the common law jurisdictions and some aspects of European ones. He shows that the problem is widespread and that the need for an evidence-based, that is, research-led, approach to legal education policy-making is imperative.

'Thinking or Acting Like a Lawyer? What We Don't Know about Legal Education and Are Afraid to Ask' is Carrie Menkel-Meadow's chapter. It sets the scene of the development of American legal education from Langdell's introduction of the Socratic method through the American realists, the critical legal scholars, experiential learning, responsibility and ethics up to the impact of legal technology. Many of these movements were taken up elsewhere in the world. Menkel-Meadow takes us through some of the 'big bang' moments. The underlying premise here is the link between legal education research and legal research generally so that the chapter concludes, fittingly, with a call for as much legal education research as possible.

Tania Leiman's chapter then considers a range of factors that may be affecting and changing the legal education landscape. The chapter begins with a review of the disruption taking place in the legal sector. Using a case study, Leiman further explores the changing face of the ethical obligations that lawyers face. The issues raised by this chapter illustrate that there is a question surrounding whether the current legal curriculum is fit to deal with the challenges of the 21st century. Leiman then considers how new opportunities may allow the academy to re-envision legal education in a bid to empower law graduates and equip them with the necessary skills to face the unknown challenges that they may come across in the future.

In the concluding contribution to the book, Paul Maharg argues that legal education is a synthetic discipline, containing at least the distinct disciplines of law and education. He sees this synthesis as having led to infrastructural problems in the organisation of the field. He sees a paucity of overall meta-studies, a lack of coordination between the efforts of researchers and regulators, and a thin understanding of history in much research. He argues for a broader vision of legal education that examines the relationships between legal education, society and law schools across time, space, theory and history. But in order to do that, Maharg argues, we need collective spaces where this information and insight is easily accessible. Maharg discusses the often unreflexive introduction of technologies in the classroom, or instead of the classroom, as an example. He highlights how recorded lectures can change the way students learn and support a corporatisation of knowledge, largely without academic comment, and in ignorance of similar profound changes in history. Drawing on the example of medical education, Maharg argues for a mapping of the field of legal education and a collation of research in an easily accessible format – the method of research review. Such reviews can map not only practice and empirical findings, but also underpin the formulation of theory.

VII Conclusion

The chapters in the book offer both examples of excellence in legal education research and challenges to those who wish to enter into such research to take it seriously. Our view is that the importance of this research cannot be contested and that recognition of the need for and methodology of legal education research as a general field can no longer be treated with the slightly negative nonchalance it has sometimes received in the past. Our hope is that the volume whose substantive chapters you are about to read represents collective provocation to further thought, reflection and research into legal education.

Notes

* Associate Professor, Senior Lecturer and Professors, respectively, UNSW Law.

1 David Labaree, 'An Uneasy Relationship: The History of Teacher Education in the University' in Julie Gorlewski and Eve Tuck (eds), *Who Decides Who Becomes a Teacher?* (Routledge, London 2018).

2 Des Butler and others, 'Embodying Life-Long Learning: Transition and Capstone Experiences' (2017) *Oxford Review of Education* 1.

3 For example, from a US perspective see the list of discipline based journals at <www.fctl.ucf.edu/researchandscholarship/sotl/journals/>.

4 See, e.g., David Barker, *A History of Australian Legal Education* (Federation Press, Sydney 2017).

5 These trends are popularly condensed in Richard Susskind, *Tomorrow's Lawyers: An Introduction to Your Future* (2nd edn, Oxford University Press 2017).

6 For a best practice model of dissemination of teaching innovation see Tilly Hinton and others, 'The D-Cubed Guide: Planning for Effective Dissemination' (Australian Learning and Teaching Council 2011).

7 Joshua Krook, 'A Brief History of Legal Education: A Battle between Law as Science and Law as a Liberal Art' (2017) 17(2) *Legal History* 30.

8 See <https://en.wikipedia.org/wiki/List_of_law_schools_in_Australia>.

9 See, e.g., Carel Stolker, *Rethinking the Law School: Education, Research, Outreach and Governance* (Cambridge University Press 2015); David Sugarman and Avrom Sherr, 'Globalisation and Legal Education' (2001) 8 *International Journal of the Legal Profession* 5; Colin B. Picker and others, 'Comparative Perspectives on Teaching Foreign Students in Law: Pedagogical, Substantive, Logistical and Conceptual Challenges' [2015] *Legal Education Review* (26 February 2015) <http://papers.ssrn.com/sol3/papers.cfm?abstract_id=2571059>, accessed 12 April 2015.

10 Similar efforts are being undertaken at a macro level. See Malcolm Tight, *Higher Education Research: The Developing Field* (Bloomsbury Publishing, London 2018).

11 At p 14.

12 Ernest L. Boyer, *Scholarship Reconsidered: Priorities of the Professoriate* (Carnegie Foundation, New York 1990).

13 At p 31.

14 At p 40.

15 p 49.

16 p 49.

17 p 146.

18 p 152.

2 The reception of legal education research in the (legal) academy

*Fiona Cownie**

I Introduction

The quality of research into legal education is a question that (outside this current publication) rarely receives much serious attention from the majority of legal academics. There is a general assumption that

> such work is of little intellectual value beyond the improvement of an individual's practice in a localised context. This, of course, only applies to some pedagogic research but everything labelled as 'learning and teaching research' tends to be tarred with the same brush.[1]

It is this tendency to conflate 'scholarship' and 'research' when talking about and evaluating legal education research that lies at the heart of this chapter. Using the United Kingdom as a case study, this chapter utilises the framework of scholarship first developed by Ernest Boyer in his seminal work *Scholarship Reconsidered: Priorities of the Professoriate* to analyse the key issues surrounding the reception of legal education research.[2] Boyer's classification of research provides a clear theoretical framework, systematically applied here for the first time to legal education research, to enable a better understanding of the reception of legal education research by the legal academy in general.

II The significance of research into legal education

It is surely a truism that education is one of the most important tasks facing any society. It is therefore unsurprising that legal education, alongside research, is one of the primary tasks of university law schools and the legal academics who work in them. With the contemporary emphasis on evidence-based practice and the use of metrics to inform policy decisions, it follows that research which identifies best practice analyses potential changes in legal education and considers 'what law schools are for' could be used routinely to shape the law schools of the future and the legal education they deliver.[3] Indeed, a recent joint report by the Royal Society and British Academy, *Harnessing Educational Research* notes the growing recognition that teaching at all levels of the educational system needs to be a 'research-literate profession'.[4] This is as true of university legal education as it is of any other aspect of the educational system. However, despite its significance, the reality facing legal education research is very different. Anecdotally, it appears that research focusing on legal education has often not been well-regarded by legal academics outside the specialism, and consequently such work has had much less impact on the policy and practice of legal education than might be expected, given the importance of the subject matter.

The way in which research into legal education is regarded within the academy is a matter of importance, not just for legal education specialists but for all members of the legal academy. This is particularly true when, in the UK as in other jurisdictions, there are considerable uncertainties surrounding the future of legal education due to changes made or proposed by the regulators of the legal profession which may have wide-ranging consequences.[5] These potentially fundamental changes increase the importance of all legal academics being able to identify high-quality legal education research, which can assist them in developing a sophisticated understanding of the debates surrounding contemporary legal education.

If research into legal education is going to be taken seriously by the legal academy as a whole, it must be able to satisfy the same standards of scrutiny that are applied to research into substantive legal topics. In the context of the UK, using the criteria applied by the periodic national-level reviews of research (currently termed the 'Research Excellence Framework', or REF) would appear to be a reasonable proxy for generally accepted standards of 'good research'.

It is important to acknowledge that there has been sustained criticism of the effectiveness of the various iterations of research evaluation exercises which have taken place in the UK since 1985–1986. Much criticism has focused, for example, on the pressures such exercises place on individuals due to the high level of contestation they generate, with many academics feeling compelled to comply with the processes involved, despite having reservations about them, seeing such compliance as 'the only way to continue to do the research they love, and to remain in employment'.[6] Particular attention has been drawn to the gendered consequences of such exercises; Harley notes that many of the respondents (both men and women) to her survey of over 1,000 academics (to which she received over 800 responses) believed that the result of such exercises was that

> the collegiality of traditional academe had been subverted by a new and aggressive individualism, what Collinson and Hearn (1994) have described as a combination of entrepreneurial and careerist masculinities, reinforced by the bureaucratic bullying of a managerialist rather than intellectual elite. This new culture has strong elements of the 'smart macho' gender regime described by Maddock and Parkin (1993) in their study of different public sector sites, where women are included as long as they compete on equal terms with men and are 'needy and greedy' enough to win.[7]

As an audit/management exercise, the REF remains controversial for these and other reasons, including in particular the emphasis upon the 'impact' of research, seen by many as an indication of the increasing marketisation of higher education (although others see it as reasonable accountability).[8] However, the actual criteria used to judge the quality of individual 'research outputs' appear to be much less contentious.[9] Consequently, considering research in legal education in the context of an analysis based on the REF criteria is a useful exercise for the purposes of this chapter.

The criteria used in the 2014 REF (the last completed iteration of the exercise) were as follows:

> Four Star: Quality that is world-leading in terms of originality, significance and rigour.
> Three Star: Quality that is internationally excellent in terms of originality, significance and rigour but which falls short of the highest standards of excellence.
> Two Star: Quality that is recognised internationally in terms of originality, significance and rigour.
> One Star: Quality that is recognised nationally in terms of originality, significance and rigour.
> Unclassified: Quality that falls below the standard of nationally recognised work. Or work which does not meet the published definition of research for the purposes of this assessment.[10]

From this it can be seen that 'originality', 'significance' and 'rigour' are the key concepts used to judge the quality of research. However, comments made by the expert assessors for law after REF 2014 suggest that research on legal education submitted for assessment did not consistently meet these criteria: 'the sub-panel was pleased to receive submissions relating to legal education, but the methodological rigour and significance exhibited by some of these outputs was uneven'.[11]

So, while *some* legal education research was judged to be rigorous and so on, there is clear concern that other submissions very definitely did not reach those standards. The lack of 'significance' and 'methodological rigour' identified by the law sub-panel as hallmarks of some legal education research submitted to the 2014 REF exercise represent serious criticisms of the work. Essentially, what is implied is that the focus of the research is narrow and rather trivial, and that the methods used to provide evidence to substantiate what is said are unsatisfactory. Such research would not meet the REF criteria at the highly desired standards of 'world-leading' or internationally excellent', or even the less desirable 'recognised internationally' or 'recognised nationally'.[12] More importantly, research which is narrow in focus and poorly evidenced does not add much, if anything, to the sum of human knowledge, and on those grounds alone would be unlikely to influence policy-making in university law schools, or to contribute anything significant to the development of law as a discipline. Neither is it likely to be of much, if any, assistance to legal academics outside the specialism who wish to develop their understanding of the key contemporary debates about legal education.

It appears that concerns about the quality of research into higher education are not restricted to the discipline of law, but permeate the academy in general. In the consultation document on the draft criteria and working methods for the next iteration of the REF, scheduled to take place in 2021, it was felt necessary to include, alongside other potentially contentious issues around submissions, such as 'interdisciplinary research' and 'work on the boundaries between Units of Assessment', a specific section on 'pedagogic research', in order to clarify how it would be treated in each discipline, whether by being submitted to the discipline panel or to the education panel, suggesting that in some disciplines, research into what the REF terms 'pedagogy' is not really regarded as part of the discipline, but as sufficiently 'other' to be judged by experts from another discipline.[13] Even within the discipline of education itself, reservations were expressed after the 2014 exercise about the quality of higher education research (along with research into all the other levels of the education system). What is particularly interesting in the context of the current discussion are the qualities which were highlighted by the education sub-panel as being characteristic of excellent and weaker research respectively. The four-star, world-leading research 'was characterised by close theoretical engagement, a focus on contemporary social issues, and the ability to engage in comparative and international studies'. However, 'weaker work tended to be focused on provision or student experience in particular universities and to lack analytical rigour'.[14] The reservations are clear; the interesting question, to which we now turn, is whether such reservations are justified.

III What do we mean by legal education research?

Understanding the reception of legal education research can best be understood by first considering the range of work which makes up the body of contemporary research on legal education. Once that is established it is possible to consider the extent to which it fulfils the criteria of originality, significance and rigour. Overall, as a field of knowledge, I would argue that research on legal education mirrors the different categories of research which have been identified as forming the subject matter of the sub-discipline of higher education studies. In his extended examination of the principal areas of research into higher education, Tight identified eight key themes addressed by the sub-discipline:

- Teaching and learning: including student learning and the 'how-to' genre;
- Course design: including the curriculum and technologies for learning;
- The student experience: including accessing higher education and the on-course experience;
- Quality: including course evaluation, grading and outcomes;
- System policy: including national policies and comparative policy studies;
- Institutional management: including institutional leadership and governance;
- Academic work: including academic roles and careers, and women academics;
- Knowledge: including the nature of research and the nature of the university.[15]

Readers familiar with contemporary research into legal education (or those who peruse the contents pages of *The Law Teacher*, the *Legal Education Review* or other specialist journals) will recognise the way in which these themes are reflected within such research. The contents of the 2017 volume of *The Law Teacher*, the leading UK specialist journal on legal education, serve to illustrate this point. The majority of the 28 articles fall into the 'Teaching and Learning' category: for example, 'The Impact of Student-Generated Flashcards on Student Learning of Constitutional Law' (Issue 1); 'Teaching Collaborative Problem-Solving Skills to Law Students' (Issue 2); 'Use of Reading Quizzes to Foster Learning: Evidence from Teaching Company Law in Business Programmes' (Issue 3); 'Authentic Assessment in Contract Law: Legal Drafting' (Issue 4). However, other themes are also represented: for example, 'Course Design' in Issue 4: ('Rethinking Property Law Modules: Putting Theory into Practice') and 'The Student Experience' in Issue 2: ('Law's Not Hard, It's Just Hard to Get Into: A Study of Alternative Entry Methods to Law School'). So when we are talking about legal education research, we could be talking about a wide variety of different topics, but it is clear that overall, such work falls squarely within Tight's thematic analysis of higher education research.

Tight went on to identify eight methods/methodologies commonly used in higher education research:

- Documentary analysis: including literature reviews and policy analyses;
- Comparative analysis: international studies comparing two or more national systems;
- Interviews: including focus groups;
- Surveys and multivariate analyses: including questionnaires and analysis of large databases;
- Conceptual analysis: including more theorised and philosophical studies;
- Phenomenography: and related approaches such as phenomenology;
- Critical/feminist approaches: including studies that critique established positions;
- Auto/biographical and observational studies: including accounts based largely on personal experience.[16]

Interestingly, Tight comments that he did not separately identify 'case study' as a method, despite initially identifying this as a method, because 'most pieces of research can be described as being, in some sense, case studies' and was not therefore a very useful category for Tight to use.[17] Looking at the research methods used in the 2017 volume of *The Law Teacher*, apart from those articles which are clearly based on library research, all the other articles could accurately be described as 'case studies', using experience from one module, or one law school, to illustrate a teaching method or approach, which can be adapted for use by other law teachers.[18] However, on closer examination, examples of several of Tight's categories of research methods can be found – documentary analysis, interviews (in the form of focus groups), surveys, conceptual analysis and critical approaches. Again, research into legal education appears to closely reflect research into higher education in general.

Tight's analysis of research into higher education is particularly useful in the current context, because it provides a framework for discussion of a sub-discipline where otherwise, as Tight himself comments, such a field may appear as 'relatively disorganized'.[19] He adds that without creating some order, in the form of organising ideas such as those he puts forward, such research may also be 'little understood or appreciated'; I would argue that the same is true of legal education research. The identification of themes and methods which can be used as a basis for consideration of this work helps those outside the field to focus on the different purposes of research outputs and the methods used to provide evidence for the arguments they contain. I would argue that combining Tight's categories with the framework provided by Ernest Boyer, in his seminal work *Scholarship Reconsidered*, will enable us to move to a much clearer understanding of the reception of legal education research.[20]

IV Using Boyer's framework to understand the criticism of research into legal education

Now that the field of legal education research has been outlined in broad terms, it is possible to move on to the central question with which this chapter is concerned. Is the general criticism of legal education research justified? It is important to remember at this point that while this chapter is using the UK's REF criteria as one means of answering that question, it is not a chapter about the efficacy of the REF exercise itself. The question here is whether, judged as objectively as possible, and using the same criteria that are used to judge research into substantive areas of law, the somewhat lukewarm reception of legal education research is justified or not.

It is at this stage that it is useful to consider the four types of scholarship put forward by Ernest Boyer in *Scholarship Reconsidered*, published in 1990. Boyer was at that time the President of the Carnegie Foundation for the Advancement of Teaching, and had been, among other things, US Commissioner of Education during the Carter administration (1977–1979), so he had extensive experience of the education system at all levels to bring to the debate.[21] His primary concern was that the culture of higher education in America had moved away from an emphasis on undergraduate education and teaching to one in which research was not only the most prestigious endeavour, but the only one that was truly valued by institutions, with promotion and tenure depending solely on success in research and publication.[22] Furthermore, Boyer argued that certain kinds of research, as well as teaching and service/collegiality, were not valued by institutions of higher education. He wanted a much more diverse higher education sector: 'we need especially to ask how institutional diversity can be strengthened and how the rich array of faculty talent in our colleges and universities might be more effectively used and continuously renewed'.[23]

In order to achieve such a diversity of institutions, he argued that the meaning of scholarship had to be 'creatively considered' and that the rigid categories of teaching, research and service should be more flexibly defined.[24] This led him to suggest that the work of academics should be thought of as having four separate, but overlapping functions:

- The scholarship of discovery;
- The scholarship of integration;
- The scholarship of application;
- The scholarship of teaching.[25]

Having undertaken extensive empirical research across the higher education sector with a colleague from the Carnegie Foundation during 1989, Boyer was also able to base his arguments on the results of this survey.[26] Boyer's classifications are particularly useful in the context of this discussion of research into legal education, because they can help us to understand why certain types of legal education research are well received and others less so (or not at all).

Boyer regards the 'scholarship of discovery' as the most familiar element in his model, and that which is highly valued:[27] 'no tenets in the academy are held in higher regard than the commitment to knowledge for its own sake, to freedom of inquiry and to following, in a disciplined fashion, an investigation wherever it may lead'.[28]

In other words, the scholarship of discovery covers the type of endeavour that we generally think of when we talk of academic research, closely aligned, as Glynis Cousin has noted, with a traditional view of the purpose of a university.[29] Talking about his model to the American Accounting Association in Nashville in August 1991, Boyer commented that 'research is a central ingredient of the academic life, and sustaining this creative process within the academy itself is absolutely crucial if scholarship is to be vigorously advanced'.[30]

'The scholarship of integration' is closely related to the scholarship of discovery, but specifically covers research which makes connections across disciplines, moving beyond traditional disciplinary boundaries. Boyer argues that scholars need to 'communicate with colleagues in other fields, and discover patterns that connect.[31]

'The scholarship of application' is about applying scholarly knowledge to important problems faced by society. Boyer questions: 'How can knowledge be responsibly applied to consequential problems?' 'How can it be helpful to individuals, as well as institutions?' And further, 'Can social problems *themselves* define an agenda for scholarly investigation?'[32]

Boyer characterises this kind of research as 'service', but is careful to distinguish it from 'citizenship'. Citizenship covers all the day-to-day activities involved in engagement with the institution – sitting on committees, advising students, generally 'performing departmental chores'.[33] As Boyer says:

> All too frequently, service means not doing scholarship, but doing good. To be considered *scholarship*, service activities must be tied directly to one's

> special field of knowledge and relate to, and flow directly out of, this professional activity. Such service is serious, demanding work, requiring the rigor – and the accountability – traditionally associated with research activities.[34]

And Boyer is careful to emphasise that the scholarship of application is not merely a variant of the scholarship of discovery. It is not the case that knowledge is first 'discovered' and then 'applied', he says; the process is much more dynamic, since

> new intellectual understandings can arise out of the very act of application – whether in medical diagnosis . . . shaping public policy, creating an architectural design or working with public schools. In activities such as these, theory and practice vitally interact, and one renews the other.[35]

Finally, he turns to the scholarship of teaching. In order for teaching to be a scholarly enterprise, teachers must be 'steeped in the knowledge of their fields', 'widely read' and 'intellectually engaged'.[36] And in order to be effective, this knowledge must be underpinned by 'pedagogical procedures' which are 'meticulously planned, continuously examined, and relate directly to the subject taught'.[37] What Boyer was trying to communicate in this part of his model were the intellectual aspects of teaching.[38] Excellent teaching requires a real understanding of, amongst other things, learning theory, pedagogical techniques, curriculum design and so on.[39]

Boyer's views on scholarship have generally been well received, although some commentators have been critical of the lack of specificity in his framework, which they find confusing.[40] Attempts to clarify Boyer's framework have continued, but despite its drawbacks, Moser notes that 'the volume of citations in educational literature speaks to Ernest Boyer's continuing influence'.[41] I am not arguing for the uncritical reception of Boyer's framework; my own views on research differ markedly from those of Boyer. However, in my view, that does not detract from the utility of his framework as a way to explain the reception of legal education research in the academy.

A noticeable feature of Boyer's views on research is the emphasis he placed on community; for him, 'scholarship was a highly communal act' and he placed great store on the ability of scholarship to be of immediate utility to society.[42] As we saw in the outline of his ideas above, he was not someone who defended the idea of research being a valuable endeavour in itself.

> A vibrant community of scholarship, according to Boyer, is one that reaches beyond the campus to address the world's deepest needs. Boyer believed scholarship for scholarship's sake was wasteful. Scholarship's full potential would be realized when it served the public. This service-orientation to scholarship led him to introduce a new term to his scholarship lexicon: engagement. Boyer championed engagement as the key to restoring the

> country's faith in its educational system. He lobbied for colleges to focus their educational and scholarly efforts on addressing the society's pressing problems.[43]

The UK's REF exercises reflect a very similar view of research, in that they too value the effect that research has on society (termed 'impact'). Impact was introduced to the REF in the 2014 exercise.[44] In the REF, impact is defined as an effect on, change or benefit to the economy, society, culture, public policy or services, health, the environment or quality of life, beyond academia.[45] Impact will be worth 25 per cent of the REF2021 assessment.[46] But despite the growing influence of impact, as will be highlighted below, it is Boyer's scholarship of discovery and his scholarship of integration which remain the primary focus of the REF exercises, and I would argue that the reception of legal education research is dependent upon its ability to fall into one or both of those categories.

V The 'research' debate

If we understand that to be generally accepted as 'research', legal education research must fall into Boyer's 'scholarship of discovery' or 'scholarship of integration', then it becomes clear that work which falls within Boyer's other two categories, 'the scholarship of application' and 'the scholarship of teaching', is simply not regarded as 'research'. This does not mean that work falling into the latter two categories has no value. Work which showcases a very effective method of teaching or assessment is a valuable endeavour – it can stimulate others to engage in similarly effective teaching or assessing and be of great potential benefit to students. However, it is not 'research' in the sense that it does not add to the sense of human knowledge, because what it is doing is applying existing knowledge to a particular teaching 'problem' (How do we best teach law to business students? How do we get students to read statutes?). And this remains the case, however firmly grounded that teaching or assessment method is in the relevant literature. Such work, at its best, fulfils Ernest Boyer's concept of the scholarship of teaching; he wanted teaching as scholarship to 'stimulate active, not passive, learning and encourage students to be critical, creative thinkers, with the capacity to go on learning after their college days are over'.[47]

However, Boyer himself realised that this category of scholarship was very different from the scholarship of discovery. His point was that he wanted the academy to value both. However, it is clear that the REF (and similar exercises in other jurisdictions) does not do this. In looking for 'significance, originality and rigour', what is valued is the scholarship of discovery or of integration. It is only legal education research which is 'research' in this sense that will be valued in the same way as research into substantive legal topics.

Comments made by the 2014 sub-panels serve as an illustration of what the academy is looking for in research which will be valued and reinforce the view that what the academy values most is work which falls within Boyer's scholarship of 'discovery' or 'integration'. We can see this played out in the context of the academy when we consider the qualities that the Education sub-panel saw in the best research into higher education. That work was 'characterised by close theoretical engagement, a focus on contemporary social issues, and the ability to engage in comparative and international studies'.[48] Those comments sit squarely with comments made by the Law Sub-Panel in their Overview Report:

> We were particularly impressed by those monographs derived from doctoral theses which were innovative and exciting and displayed strong significance and rigour. However, fragmentation and increasingly narrow specialisation sometimes produced outputs which suffered from failing to situate their analyses within the wider legal or contextual frame of reference.[49]

Work which is valued, therefore, will display characteristics which have traditionally been valued by the academy – originality, seen as the extent to which an output makes an important and innovative contribution to understanding and knowledge in the field; significance, seen in terms of the contribution made to the intellectual development of the field, and rigour, understood as the extent to which the work demonstrates intellectual coherence and integrity, and adopts robust and appropriate concepts, analyses, theories and methodologies.[50]

Looking back to Tight's eight categories of education research (which are particularly useful in clarifying the extent of the field for non-specialists) it is apparent that whatever type of legal education research is carried out, from course design and debates about the quality of learning and teaching to policy analyses of the system as a whole, in order to be accepted as 'research' it must satisfy the criteria of originality, significance and rigour. Once this is understood, it becomes clear why much legal education research fails to be accepted by the academy as 'research'. Work which focuses on incremental improvements to teaching methods will not be sufficiently significant; work which relies on data drawn from very small case studies will arguably fail to satisfy the criterion of rigour. However, since legal education research which focuses on the improvement of practice performs a valuable function, there is often considerable resistance on the part of (legal) education researchers to reach such judgements about this work.

VI Looking to the future

Legal education research is not alone in facing these issues. They are frequently discussed in the context of the academy as a whole. Cotton and others, in a recent article in *Studies in Higher Education*, arguably the leading UK higher education journal, report the findings of a small-scale exploratory empirical research project which gathered views about the standing of pedagogical research from 'selected stakeholders having interest and expertise in pedagogic research' ranging from academic researchers through REF co-ordinators at Departmental and institutional levels, to Heads of Educational Development and institutional-level REF impact co-ordinators taken from 13 institutions.[51] The findings were thus obtained from a small but strategically important set of respondents, and provide interesting insights into some of the key issues surrounding pedagogic research. Cotton et al. found evidence that while it was acknowledged that at least some pedagogic research was reaching standards of the highest quality, there were nevertheless structural and political factors within institutions which not only resulted in such research being under-valued by those making decisions about the REF, but also led to it being less valued in wider decision-making about funding of research and the career development of individuals.[52] Their data threw up three main reasons for what I have termed the 'lukewarm reception' of legal education research. These were issues of quality in the research itself; a lack of expertise on the part of those judging the research; and political issues. To these I would add the issue of terminology – the fact that anything designated as 'pedagogic research' is assumed to be an example of Boyer's 'scholarship of teaching' whether that is actually the case or not. It is these four factors which need to be confronted in the context of the reception of legal education research.

In relation to the first issue, that of quality, the concerns expressed to Cotton et al. by REF coordinators (those responsible for the process of assessment within institutions) were about issues of method, such as small sample sizes, as well as limited use of or contribution to theory. As one respondent said: 'the typical paper was "I tried this new teaching methodology with my class and they liked it" which was essentially what the papers were which was a good thing but you know we felt it wasn't REF-able'.[53]

These views about empirical research in education are very similar to the narrow approach identified by the 2014 REF law sub-panel in some legal education research. Good legal education research must reflect expertise in terms of method and use of theory in the same way as any socio-legal empirical research. Very small samples and the lack of a clear theoretical framework are likely to be hallmarks of poor research, lacking in particular the hallmarks of significance and rigour (although such work *may* have a contribution to make in terms of the scholarship of teaching and learning).

The next issue raised by Cotton et al.'s respondents was the clear perception that the people judging pedagogic research did not necessarily possess the relevant expertise.[54] Sometimes concerns were about judgements made locally, but questions were also raised at the national level. Similar concerns could be expressed in relation to legal education research. Looking at the composition of the 2014 REF law sub-panel, only one of its 18 members claimed any expertise in legal education, and then not as a primary area of publication.[55] Although there was provision for sub-panels to appoint additional assessors to assist with particular areas of expertise, and eight such assessors were appointed to the law sub-panel, none of them claimed any expertise in legal education either. It is hard not to draw the conclusion that legal education research was 'something that anyone who has taught can understand', which ignores the fact that just as with substantive areas of law, evaluating the quality of research into legal education requires extensive expertise, including in this case knowledge of a research literature drawn from higher education studies, a completely different discipline.

The final issue that Cotton et al. unearthed was a range of claims about the ways in which 'institutional politics' might affect pedagogic researchers. Although many of these appeared to be general issues with the process, rather than specifically affecting the treatment of pedagogic research, reports of staff being discouraged by heads of department from pursuing pedagogic research because it was of 'lower status' reflects the attitudes towards legal education research discussed at the beginning of this chapter.[56] As Macfarlane comments, such attitudes are prevalent within the academy:

> Apparently, unlike subject-based research, 'pedagogic' research is not 'proper' research. It is not, therefore, any good for the purposes of research assessment. Or so we are told by those charged with responsibility for getting universities the most money from this exercise. Here, the operating assumption is that such work is of little intellectual value beyond the improvement of an individual's practice in a localised context. This, of course, only applies to some pedagogic research but everything labelled as 'learning and teaching research' tends to be tarred with the same brush.[57]

It is clear that attitudes towards 'pedagogic research' are very unhelpful to the development of high-quality research in the area, and there is no reason to think that attitudes within Law Schools differ significantly from those found elsewhere in the academy. In an increasingly competitive environment, it is arguable that for some scholars at least, such attitudes will have a 'chilling' effect, leading them to turn away from pedagogic research to other work which more easily finds acceptance.

In order for their research to be judged on equal terms with research into substantive legal topics, it is important for legal education researchers to be able to signal clearly what kind of research they are publishing, not only for the purposes of the REF audit, but in order that it should reach the correct audience and thus be most effective in communicating its ideas. If they are engaged in Boyer's scholarship of discovery or integration, they need to be able to communicate this, and distinguish their work from the scholarship of application or teaching. Consequently, I would argue that there is another, and in many ways more fundamental, issue with which legal education researchers need to engage if they are to make progress in securing a more knowledgeable assessment of their research. That issue is terminology.

Changing the way in which others in the academy refer to legal education research is, I would argue, fundamental to improving the understanding of such research, and in turn to its reception by non-specialists. One of the main problems in analysing the reception of legal education research is the loose use of the terminology involved. 'Pedagogic research' tends to be used as a generic term for all the different types of higher education research which Tight identified. This conflates Boyer's 'scholarship of discovery/integration' with his 'scholarship of application/learning and teaching'. This conflation of Boyer's different types of scholarship leads to a widespread attitude that anything labelled 'pedagogic research' is second rate. This does not pay sufficient attention to the type of endeavour involved, and misses the point that, just as with any other type of research, the real distinctions that need to be made are those between good research and bad research.[58] It is for this reason that I would argue that the nomenclature used in the context of legal education research is so important. Research in the sub-discipline must be viewed as a *research* endeavour, rather than as 'scholarship'. 'Scholarship' is traditionally regarded as a process of reading research in order to keep up to date in one's subject; it is not primary research in the way that the best legal education research is. Similarly, a distinction must be drawn between research and on the improvement of an aspect of learning and teaching. One of the main strategies for improvement in the reception of legal education research, therefore, could be to use the term 'research into legal education' or 'research into higher education' for Boyer's scholarship of discovery and integration, and 'pedagogic scholarship' for Boyer's scholarships of practice and teaching. Conflating the four categories masks the fact that the former types can stand comparison with discipline-based research, on an equal basis, while the other two types should be acknowledged as valuable, but different.

VII Conclusion

A number of commentators have attempted to use Boyer's framework to 'equalize' the treatment of the four different types of research he outlined, and in particular, to argue that the scholarship of teaching and learning should be treated in the same way as the scholarship of discovery.[59] However, like Macfarlane, I would argue that this strategy is counter-productive, and only serves to further devalue legal education research, by ignoring the fact that Boyer's four types of scholarship are hierarchical; essentially the scholarship of discovery and of integration are 'research' in the traditional sense; the scholarship of application and the scholarship teaching describe scholarship which is not of the same nature and which cannot be valued in identical ways.[60] Failing to acknowledge this merely plays into the hands of those who dismiss all legal education research as applied scholarship. For example, it is important here not to over-generalise. It is not the case that research which investigates practice can never be scholarship of discovery. It is not the subject matter but the way in which it is analysed which makes the difference. As Cousin argues, there is a danger that 'misunderstandings about practice-based or applied research have produced a vicious circle, in which poor examples become the basis on which it is judged'.[61] It is crucial that legal education researchers should communicate these ideas to all those who are judging their research.

In the short term, in the UK at least, the introduction of the national Teaching Excellence Framework (TEF) may provide an alternative source of recognition for work in legal education which falls into Boyer's categories of application and teaching. One of the original purposes of the TEF was to achieve parity of esteem within the academy between research and teaching. The Green Paper which presented the first iteration of the exercise stated that 'some rebalancing of the pull between teaching and research is undoubtedly required: this should not be at the expense of research, but through additional incentives to drive up teaching quality'.[62]

Once the shape of the exercise was finalised, 'recognising and rewarding excellent teaching' became one of the four main aims of the process.[63] In the criteria used to assess teaching excellence, there were some specific references to pedagogic research, for example 'the impact and effectiveness of innovative approaches, new technology or educational research' was given as an example of evidence of teaching quality, and in a discussion of the learning environment reference is made to 'the extent to which the learning environment is enriched by student exposure to teaching innovation and processes at the forefront of scholarship, research and/or professional practice'.[64] As the TEF develops, it is arguable that institutions will increasingly realise the benefits of supporting pedagogic scholars, if not for any other reason than the pragmatic one that their work can contribute to a successful TEF award.

Recent developments in relation to the REF, may also offer the potential for the work of pedagogic researchers to gain more recognition. In July 2016, Lord Stern's review of the REF recommended that 'better to align the REF with the TEF, we also recommend that research leading to major impacts on curricula and/or pedagogy within or across disciplines should be included'.[65] This recommendation, if implemented, would open up another possibility for the increased valuing of legal education scholarship by permitting it to form the subject of an 'impact case study' in a way which was not possible in the previous iteration of the REF. Again, this is most likely to assist those engaging in pedagogic scholarship, but legal education researchers may also be able to take advantage of this development.

Overall, the reception of legal education research and pedagogic scholarship is likely to remain 'lukewarm' until there is greater understanding of the differences between legal education research and legal education pedagogic scholarship, both by those who undertake these activities and those who evaluate them. As teaching excellence takes on a more prominent role due to the TEF, in the UK at least the academy as a whole may gain greater understanding of the different types of research and scholarship involved, so that both can achieve the respect they deserve.

Notes

* Professor of Law, Keele University, and Senior Associate Research Fellow, Institute of Advanced Legal Studies, University of London. The author would like to

thank Dr Liz Carter and Professor Anthony Bradney (Keele University) and Emeritus Professor David Sugarman (Lancaster University) for their comments on this chapter.

1 Bruce MacFarlane, 'Prizes, Pedagogic Research and Teaching Professors: Lowering the Status of Teaching and Learning through Bifurcation' (2011) 16 *Teaching in Higher Education* 127.

2 Ernest Boyer, *Scholarship Reconsidered: Priorities of the Professoriate* (Berkeley, CA, The Carnegie Foundation for the Advancement of Teaching 1990).

3 For the ubiquity of 'evidence-based policy', see Ray Pawson, *Evidence-Based Policy: A Realist Perspective* (London, Sage 2006).

4 The Royal Society and British Academy, 'Harnessing Educational Research' (*The British Academy* 2018) 51 <www.thebritishacademy.ac.uk/projects/harnessing-educational-research>, accessed 16 October 2018.

5 Proposed changes by the Solicitors' Regulation Authority in the UK can be found at: <www.sra.org.uk/sra/policy/sqe.page>, accessed 6 August 2018. Changes in Canadian legal education as a result of action by law societies is discussed in www.canadianlawyermag.com/article/the-evolution-of-legal-education-2383/>, accessed 6 August 2018. In Australia, the Law Admissions Consultative Committee has tasked a small group with considering the re-casting of the 'prescribed areas of academic knowledge' as learning outcomes (private correspondence from Professor Sally Kift on file with the author).

6 Carole Leathwood and Barbara Read, 'Research Policy and Academic Performativity: Compliance, Contestation and Complicity' (2013) 38 *Studies in Higher Education* 1162, 1172. On the introduction of research assessment in the UK see Maurice Kogan and others, *Transforming Higher Education: A Comparative Study* (Jessica Kingsley Publishers 2000) 58.

7 Sandra Harley, 'Research Selectivity and Female Academics in U.K. Universities: From Gentleman's Club and Barrack Yard to Smart Macho?' (2003) 15 *Gender and Education* 377, 387; David Collinson and Jeff Hearn, 'Naming Men as Men: Implications for Work, Organization and Management' (1994) 1 *Gender, Work and Organization* 2; Su Maddock and Di Parkin, 'Gender Cultures: Women's Choices and Strategies at Work' (1993) 8 *Women in Management Review* 3.

8 For various views on the 'impact agenda' see Richard Watermeyer, 'Issues in the Articulation of "Impact": The Responses of UK Academics to "Impact" as a New Measure of Research Assessment' (2014) 39 *Studies in Higher Education* 359.

9 Published research is invariably referred to as an 'output' in REF documents. See, e.g., the Draft Guidance on Submissions REF 2018/01 July 2018 <www.ref.ac.uk/publications/2018/draftguidanceonsubmissions201801.html>, accessed 14 September 2018.

10 See <www.ref.ac.uk/2014/media/ref/content/pub/assessmentframeworkand guidanceonsubmissions/GOS%20including%20addendum.pdf>, accessed 3 November 2018.

11 Research Excellence Framework, 'Research Excellence Framework 2014 Overview Report by Main Panel C and Sub-Panels 16 to 26' (Report, January 2015) 71, [6] <www.ref.ac.uk/2014/media/ref/content/expanel/member/Main%20 Panel%20C%20overview%20report.pdf>, accessed 15 July 2018.

12 For more information on the REF criteria, see <www.ref.ac.uk/2014/panels/ assessmentcriteriaandleveldefinitions/>, accessed 22 July 2018.

13 Research Excellence Framework, 'REF 2021: Consultation on the Draft Panel Criteria and Working Methods' (Report, July 2018), [178–183]. <www.ref.ac.uk/media/ref,2021/downloads/Consultation%20on%20the%20draft%20

panel%20criteria%20and%20working%20methods%20REF%202018_02.pdf>, accessed 6 August 2018. In law, it is proposed that, as with all previous exercises, pedagogical research will be considered by the law sub-panel.
14 Research Excellence Framework (n. 11) 105, accessed 12 September 2018.
15 Malcolm Tight, *Researching Higher Education* (Maidenhead, SRHE & Open University Press 2003) 7.
16 Ibid., 8–9.
17 Ibid., 9.
18 For discussion of the case study as a research method, see Sharon B. Merriam, *Qualitative Research: A Guide to Design and Implementation* (Jossey-Bass, San Francisco, CA 2009) 39–54.
19 Tight (n. 15) 3.
20 Boyer (n. 2).
21 Drew Moser, 'To Lift the Leaden-Eyed: The Historical Roots of Ernest Boyer's *Scholarship Reconsidered*' (2014) 41 *American Educational History Journal* 337, 338.
22 Boyer (n. 2) 2.
23 Ibid., 13.
24 Ibid., 13, 14.
25 Ibid., 16.
26 Moser (n. 21) 339.
27 Ibid., 17.
28 Ibid.
29 Glynis Cousin, 'Reconsidering Scholarship Reconsidered' in Rowena Murray (Ed.) *The Scholarship of Learning and Teaching in Higher Education* (Maidenhead, Open University Press; London, Society for Research into Higher Education 2008) 91.
30 Ernest Boyer, 'Scholarship Reconsidered: Priorities of the Professoriate' (1992) 7(1) *Issues in Accounting Education* 87.
31 Boyer (n. 2) 20.
32 Ibid., 21 (emphasis in original).
33 Ibid., 22.
34 Ibid. (emphasis in original).
35 Ibid., 23.
36 Ibid.
37 Ibid. 24.
38 Marian McCarthy, 'The Scholarship of Teaching and Learning in Higher Education: An Overview' in Rowena Murray (ed) *The Scholarship of Learning and Teaching in Higher Education* (Maidenhead, Open University Press; London, Society for Research into Higher Education 2008) 11.
39 On the importance of theory in legal education, see F. Cownie, 'Searching for Theory in Teaching Law' in F. Cownie (ed) *The Law School – Global Issues, Local Questions* (Aldershot, Ashgate/Dartmouth 1999).
40 See, e.g., Alexander McNeil, 'Reflections on Scholarship Reconsidered' 48 *Quest* (1996) 140, 143; Alan Rubin, 'Is Boyer Misguided or Misused? The Scholarship of Confusion' 29 *Journal of the Association for Communication Administration* (2000) 260, 263.
41 Moser (n. 21) 352.
42 Ibid., 351.
43 Ibid., 344–5.
44 Research Excellence Framework, 'Assessment Framework and Guidance on Submissions' (Publication REF 02.2011, July 2011) [146] <www.ref.ac.uk/2014/pubs/2011-02/>, accessed 23 September 2018.

45 Ibid.
46 Higher Education Finding Council for England (HEFCE), 'Initial Decisions on REF 2021' (Circular Letter 33, 2017) [8].
47 Boyer (n. 2).
48 Research Excellence Framework (n. 11) 105, accessed 12 September 2018.
49 Ibid., 72.
50 Research Excellence Framework, 'Consultation on the Draft Panel Criteria and Working Methods' (Report REF 2018/02, July 2018) 142–3.
51 Debby Cotton and others, 'The Cinderella of Academia: Is Higher Education Pedagogic Research Undervalued in U.K. Research Assessment?' 43 *Studies in Higher Education* (2018) 1625.
52 Ibid., 1635.
53 Ibid., 1629.
54 Ibid., 1630.
55 The institutional web pages for all members of the panel list their research expertise. In only one case (Professor Rosemary Auchmuty, Reading) is legal education mentioned as an interest, and then in the context of work on gender, careers and the legal academy.
56 Cotton and others (n. 51) 1631.
57 Macfarlane (n. 1) 127.
58 Ibid., 128.
59 See, e.g., C. Glassick, M. Huber and G. Maeroff, *Scholarship Assessed: Evaluation of the Professoriate* (San Francisco, Jossey-Bass 1997) 25.
60 Ibid., 128.
61 Cousin (n. 29) 96.
62 Department for Business Innovation & Skills, 'Fulfilling our Potential: Teaching Excellence, Social Mobility and Student Choice' (Publication Cm 914, November 2015) [20].
63 Department for Education, 'Teaching Excellence and Student Outcomes Framework Specification' (Publication, October 2017) [1.3].
64 Ibid., 21, 38.
65 Nicholas Stern, 'Building on Success and Learning from Experience: An Independent Review of the Research Excellence Framework' (July 2016) <https://www.gov.uk/government/publications/research-excellence-framework-review>, accessed 29 June 2019 [83].

Part II

Current landscapes

3 Neoliberalism in legal education research

*Peter D. Burdon**

This chapter examines the extent to which the literature on legal education addresses neoliberalism and engages the political and economic circumstances that influence our teaching environments and practices. To peruse this question, I begin by introducing neoliberalism and consider the ways it has influenced the development of higher education in Australia. While there is a burgeoning literature on the corporatization of universities, the explicit consideration of neoliberalism remains a marginal discourse in legal education scholarship. To substantiate this point, I reviewed two specialist legal education journals between 2007–2017. The journals in question are the *Legal Education Review* and the *Journal of Legal Education*. Consistent with previous arguments, I found that the literature on legal education is largely apolitical and focused on teaching materials, techniques and skills. Thus, it is not unusual to see papers with helpful advice on how to teach large classes but without any reflection on why student/teacher ratios have increased or what is underlying the demand to increase efficiency.

Several explanations have been offered for the lack of political and economic analysis in legal education research. For example, it has been suggested that legal academics lack the time and energy to undertake a substantive critique of higher education and feel that their limited time is better spent thinking about best practice and adaptation.[1] Others argue that neoliberalism has muted critical voices through managerialism, overwork and self-policing.[2] Further to these arguments, I draw on Wendy Brown's description of neoliberal rationality to make a subtler argument.[3] According to Brown, neoliberalism is primarily a mode of reason that economizes all things and moulds human conduct to the model of the market. Understood in this way, neoliberalism has us tending to our own immediate needs and encourages scholars to develop entrepreneurial research identities which are often in conflict with the practice of critique.

However, rather than thinking about neoliberal rationality in a totalising way, in the final part of the chapter I consider what spaces and ideas are available in public universities that might support legal education researchers to think more broadly outside of the logic of economization. This discussion draws on Bonnie

Honig's notion of 'public things'[4] and her provocation that material objects might provide a 'holding environment' from which we identify neoliberalism and articulate alternative values that are consistent with the public good.

I Neoliberalism and higher education

> The words are stretched across the side of the red-brick northern extension of RMIT University in Melbourne, a huge banner that could not be more succinctly self-parodic if it tried: 'Don't study problems, solve them'. The advertisement is for the institution's engineering courses, an obvious punk move – one whole side of a [university] dissing the very idea of reflection, analysis, contemplation.[5]

Over the last decade there has been a rapid growth in generalist books critiquing the corporatization of higher education and the gradual death of humanities. Titles like 'The Last Professors', 'Educations End', 'The Fall of the Faculty', 'Speaking of Universities',[6] 'University, Inc.' and 'The Lost Soul of Higher Education' adorn many of our bookshelves. While this genre has a propensity toward nostalgia it also puts forward a broadly consistent critique of higher education and its relationship to neoliberalism. Neoliberalism is one of the most overused terms in academic literature and it is subject to diverse interpretations. As Elizabeth Humphrys notes, neoliberalism can be used to describe

> (1) a doctrine, set of ideas and/or ideology; (2) a set of economic policies, an entire economic regime and/or a distinct phase of capitalism; (3) a political project, form of political rule and/or type of state; (4) a category of denunciation or criticism; and (5) a complex mix of some or all of these elements.[7]

It is the first two interpretations that are most relevant to developments in higher education. While the dominant history of neoliberalism stresses the role of new-right governments[8] and conservative think tanks[9] in Australia, the shift was ushered in by the Labor Party and the Dawkins reforms which started in 1987.[10] While not every aspect of these reforms was neoliberal,[11] it was during this period that fields of study were expanded in areas considered vital for economic growth and the cost burden began to shift from the state to individual students (a trend that continues today[12]). Moreover, if more students were to gain access to higher education, it became important for courses to become more practical and less theoretical or abstract – a consideration that might have given the minister pause before amalgamating smaller technical institutions into the UN System of Higher Education.

Changes in funding, combined with the dominance of free market liberalism in public policy, economized the idea of higher education and allowed it be described in terms of 'individuals exchanging goods and services at prices set by the laws of supply and demand, these prices providing the signals that allowed factors of production to be allocated with maximum efficiency'.[13] In practical terms this rendered higher education as a 'service to the consumer that should be bought and sold like any other commodity'[14] rather than something that could be framed in non-instrumental terms or through alternative values such educating citizens for robust participation in a democracy.[15]

In Australia, Margaret Thornton's book *Privatising the Public University*[16] remains the most sustained and detailed analysis of how neoliberalism has impacted Australian law schools.[17] Thornton theorizes neoliberalism primarily as a political theory that promotes the marketization of public goods and the erosion of state responsibility for producing an 'educated and culturally aware citizenry'.[18] Marketization, according to Thornton, is a process rather than something that has been fully accomplished. Thus, she argues that while 'there has been a notable shift away from public to private responsibility', we currently operate in a hybrid public/private system.[19]

To substantiate her argument, Thornton considers four aspects of the contemporary university which can loosely be categorized as relating to administration, teaching, research, and academic workloads. Under these headings, Thornton provides a detailed (and I think mostly convincing) analysis of how neoliberalism has impacted the curriculum and teaching practices of law schools;[20] led to the jettisoning of theoretical and critical perspectives in favour of skills and instrumental knowledge;[21] the expansion of managerial governance, top-down decision making, the rise of precarious workers and quantitative performance measures;[22] and the shift toward entrepreneurial research identities, which is beholden to the logic of competition and relentless performance.[23] This is a familiar list for anybody versed in the critical literature on higher education, and Jeffrey Goldsworthy noted that they will be 'familiar to all of us who suffer from them'.[24]

Thornton's analysis has been critiqued on the basis that it presents an overly bleak picture of the university[25] and because her interviewees tend to share her critique of neoliberalism and the direction of higher education.[26] Of greater substance are critiques related to causation and the extent to which the changes Thornton describes can be isolated and attributed to neoliberalism. For example, in response to Thornton's argument that the profession has too much influence over the curriculum of law schools one might argue that this predates the 1980s. Goldsworthy, for example, states 'law schools have long been deferential to the legal profession, wanting to be noticed and appreciated, especially by the judiciary'.[27]

Moreover, while Thornton connects 'massification' to the desire to 'augment the supply of new knowledge workers with the aim of ensuring that nation states are competitive within the global economy',[28] it might also be interpreted in terms of increasing upward mobility and broadening opportunity.[29] Further, if neoliberalism was the rationale for expanding admission levels then one might wonder why the government did not further and completely deregulate the sector?[30] Finally, moves to combine universities and centralize departments do not naturally align with neoliberal theory. Neither does the shift to audit culture and accountability to a designated federal minister. Arguably, better explanations can be found in the desire to make universities more productive and efficient[31] and competitive in the international student market.[32] These objectives are heightened under neoliberalism but they did not originate from that source and were not progressed through pure market mechanism or by a withdrawal of public support. However, as Thornton argues,[33] we are seeing a steady redistribution of financial responsibility from the federal government to the private sector and individual students.[34]

Thus, in Australia neoliberalism has given rise to a hybrid system of higher education. It has exacerbated some existing impulses while giving rise to new and sometimes unnerving outcomes such as the economisation of how universities view their relationship to students (or 'customers'). While neoliberalism is not solely responsible for these changes one might expect legal academics to have engaged robustly in debates about the political economy of higher education and sought to understand the underlying factors that are shaping our workplace. As Gina Anderson has suggested, legal academics are trained in analytical thinking and critique and so are 'unlikely to passively accept changes they regard as detrimental'.[35] In section II of this chapter I problematize this reasoning by considering the extent to which neoliberalism has been engaged by legal scholars in specialist legal education journals.

II Neoliberalism in legal education research

In Australia, neoliberal reform has proceeded with little overt analysis or resistance from legal academics.[36] Moreover, Thornton contends the 'critical space within the academy has contracted'[37] and scholars have not provided a thoroughgoing understanding or critique of neoliberalism. With respect to legal education research she argues that 'there is an extensive legal education literature but, for the most part, it is directed towards improving the quality of pedagogical practices without regard to their political context which has rendered those practices more difficult'.[38]

This point is not substantiated in the book and appears to be based on Thornton's own survey of the literature. Moreover, it should be noted that legal education research is only one way to gauge the extent to which academics comprehend the impact of neoliberalism on higher education. Other literatures describe resistance to neoliberalism through a range of tactics such as forgetting and non-compliance[39] and advocacy against government policy through academic associations.[40] To this we should also note analysis that has emerged from students regarding how law schools might respond to neoliberalism.[41]

Returning to the literature, one factor that is immediately apparent in legal education research is the almost complete lack of synthesis as a scholarly endeavour.[42] There is self-reflection and scholars continually build on the work of others, but this is rarely done in a way that provides a reader with a sense of field or an understanding of the dominant positions that are advanced and contested. This same critique could be made of legal research more generally, although that is starting to shift in some areas.[43] In part this is because of the relative infancy of legal scholarship,[44] the lack of training lawyers receive in research methods[45] and a long-standing bias toward doctrinal research.[46]

To gauge the extent to which academics have engaged with neoliberalism in legal education I undertook an observational meta-analysis to identify dominant themes in the literature.[47] My study was partial in that it did not investigate every article written on legal education. Following Jeremy Blumenthal, I hoped that this method would allow me to 'summarize' a specific aspect of the literature in legal education and give 'practitioners, academics, researchers, and policy makers the best view of the state of a literature'.[48] A meta-analysis can also help 'explain why [a] literature' has developed in a particular way and develop ideas for further research in an area.[49] With this in mind I read deeply into two specialist legal education journals – *The Journal of Legal Education* (US) and the *Legal Education Review* (AUS) – between the years 2007–2017.[50] This date range was chosen for two reasons; first it coincides with a growth in books specifically addressing the corporatisation of universities and[51] because ten years is a sufficiently long period of time to make some preliminary comments about trends in a literature.[52]

The two journals were chosen because of their specific focus on legal education and because of their prominence as an outlet for specialist legal education researchers in Australia.[53] Moreover, while both journals have a reputation for focusing on practical aspects of teaching they each have a broader mandate. The *Journal of Legal Education* seeks to 'foster [an] . . . interchange of ideas and information about legal education . . . including but not limited to the legal profession, legal theory, and legal scholarship'.[54] Similarly, the *Legal Education Review* aims to 'encourage and disseminate . . . high quality research into legal education; and inform and stimulate discussion, debate and experimentation on topics related to legal education'.[55] Clearly there is a lot of flexibility within both journals for reflective and critical scholarship. By critical here I do not mean trashing or rejecting something. Rather, critique is a practice which can be used to evaluate the premises, preconditions and implications of something that may not be obvious or reveal itself in everyday self-description.[56]

Normally a meta-analysis would then code for identified categories (i.e. sample size, equation structure or type) and analyse their prevalence in the literature and any variables that might impact the data.[57] However, because I conducted an observational study and the literature was entirely doctrinal there was little that could be learned from such comparisons. Instead, I constructed broad themes and characterised the articles under the following headings:[58]

1 Political economy and neoliberalism;
2 Teaching materials, content and curriculum;
3 Legal history;
4 Teaching method and skills;
5 Technology;
6 Critical theory and thinking;
7 Society and social justice;

8 Grading and assessment;
9 Vocationalism and professionalization;
10 Institutional issues (staffing, governance, school culture);
11 Curriculum design;
12 Legal education research.

These categories were interpreted broadly, and in almost every case I applied multiple categories to an article. For example, articles about teaching skills frequently overlapped with technology and teaching materials/content.[59] Similarly, articles about student wellbeing often overlapped with analysis of law school culture and the breadth of topics available in curriculum.[60] Rather than just noting overlap, for each article I assigned a major category to represent the dominant theme and subcategories to indicate where a paper had addressed a topic in a substantive way. If a paper simply mentioned a category without attempting to make it relevant to the dominant theme, it was not recorded.

With this noted, my preliminary findings largely supported Thornton's assertion that legal education research is weighted toward skills over critique and has little to say about the political or economic context of our work.[61] For example, between 2007–2017 the *Journal of Legal Education* published 343 scholarly articles (excluding book reviews). Of these articles only 1.5 per cent said anything substantial about neoliberalism or connected teaching practices to broader political/economic trends. By contrast 13 per cent of articles focused on teaching materials and 23 per cent of articles focused on teaching method. A further 19 per cent of articles focused on vocationalism and on the professionalization of the student body. These are the major trends in the literature, and it should also be noted that since 2010 there has been an increase in articles focusing on student wellbeing (5 per cent) and ideas for incorporating critical thinking and identity based injustice (12 per cent) into the curriculum. However, while these topics provide an opening to connect legal education to broader political/economic trends, the clear majority of articles did not.

For example, in 2012 the journal published a series of articles on student wellbeing. Contributions focused primarily on student experience[62] but also included perspectives from members of the profession.[63] The major idea articulated in this edition was that students are increasingly feeling anxious and detached from their schools and classmates. These feelings do not always dissipate upon graduation and data from within the profession reports high rates of depression and lack of job satisfaction.[64] To combat this, articles such as 'Toward Lawyering as Peacemaking' advocate a range of practices such as mindfulness and meditation.[65] These are the most common recommendations, but what is most striking is the fact that every wellbeing article sought to understand the problem and ground potential solutions in purely individualistic terms and without any political analysis. An alternative position which seeks to problematize the discourse around wellbeing is articulated here by Zoë Krupka:

> No amount of multivitamins, yoga, meditation, sweaty exercise, superfoods or extreme time management, as brilliant as all these things can be, is going

> to save us from the effects of too much work. This is not something we can adapt to. Not something we need to adjust the rest of our lives around. It is not possible and it's unethical to pretend otherwise. Like a low-flying plane, the insidious culture of overwork is deafening and the only way we can really feel better is if we can find a way to make it stop.[66]

The *Legal Education Review* has been slightly more willing to engage in broader political and economic analysis. Of the 117 articles published during the period studied, 7 per cent connected teaching practices to neoliberalism.[67] More generally, 20 per cent of articles were on teaching materials, 26 per cent on teaching method and 17 per cent on vocationalism. Articles addressing student wellbeing (10 per cent) and embedding critical thinking and social justice (8 per cent) have also gained momentum in recent years, but once again none of these articles connects their topic back to anything systematic or overtly political. Noteworthy here is the literature on critical thinking and social justice – both of which deal with overtly political themes. For example, critical thinking is now part of the graduate attributes of all Australian law schools and it is defended as integral to training lawyers and democratic citizens. However, articles such as 'How to Develop Law Students' Critical Awareness'[68] say nothing about the dominance of instrumental rationality[69] or the way it is reflected in curriculum design and student expectations, for example comments such as 'is this going to be in the exam?'[70] Moreover, while articles like 'Putting Justice Back into Legal Education' make a strong case for strategically incorporating social justice content across the degree, this is justified on instrumental grounds and no attempt is made to understand those forces which have led either to the jettisoning of critical material or to resisting their inclusion in the first place. This is a significant gap because without engaging those pressures there is little hope that advocacy for future inclusion will be successful.

III Neoliberal rationality

The picture that emerges from reading the literature on legal education is largely apolitical, strives to be neutral and prioritises skills, technology and practice over critical analysis. Scholars have offered several explanations for this state of affairs. James focuses on the 'weight of tradition', the fact that most legal academics in Australia have a narrow intellectual background and institutional pressures related to research and service.[71] To these concerns, Thornton adds that 'new forms of managerialism, in conjunction with the massive increase in student's numbers, have effectively muted dissentient voices in favour of bland orthodoxy that legitimates the market message'.[72] This is supported by other literature that suggests that academics lack a sense of agency to challenge undesirable reforms. For example, Suzanne Ryan describes the effort to survive inside the contemporary university as resulting in 'zombification',[73] and Bronwyn Davies and Peter Bansel's research describes 'disillusioned and distressed individuals' rather than 'collective academic critique and resistance'.[74]

To these accounts, we should also note that many colleagues do not agree with the neoliberal critique of higher education or, if they agree with aspects of the argument, do not feel that it has the explanatory power that scholars suggest.[75] Others note that the legal academy tends to be conservative, focused on black-letter law and is sceptical or perhaps uncomfortable with the role of theory in legal scholarship.[76] And finally we might consider the possibility that editors and reviewers act as gatekeepers by defining what counts as legal education research.[77] While I do not have the space to develop this argument, it ought to be remembered that overtly political analysis of legal education was attacked during the education wars of the 1970s and '80s.[78] Most prominent here was the Critical Legal Studies (CLS) movement in the United States, which addressed itself specifically to the way legal education reproduces hierarchal power relationships[79] and how knowledge is produced in law schools.[80] Today it is commonly said that CLS is 'dead' as a political movement,[81] but it could equally be argued that it has been supressed as legal research became more professionalised and journals exercised greater control in defining the parameters of their discipline.[82]

Further to these perspectives, I want to introduce a different explanation for the lack of engagement with neoliberalism in legal education research. This explanation theorises neoliberalism in a different way to Thornton and others who describe it primarily as an economic policy or political project. Drawing on Michel Foucault[83] and Wendy Brown,[84] I want to think about neoliberalism as a mode of reason that economizes everything and 'configures all aspects of existence in economic terms'.[85] According to this perspective human beings are shaped as market actors and every field of activity is construed on the model of the firm.[86]

Brown's argument is not merely that neoliberalism is corrupting or degrading public things such as democratic institutions and universities. Rather, her argument is that *economization* has become 'common sense, a reality principle, which remakes institutions and human beings wherever it settles'.[87] One key difference between Brown and Thornton's account of neoliberalism is that Brown does not claim that neoliberalism monetizes every sphere of our work – rather she suggests that 'neoliberal rationality disseminates the model of the market to all domains and activities – *even where money is not at issue*'.[88]

Some examples will help us understand the difference between economization and marketization. Consider, for example, the way governments frame immigration[89] in terms of economic growth or efforts to address climate change in terms of national competitiveness.[90] Even dating services speak to their clientele in terms of a 'return on investment'.[91] Money is not the direct object in any of these examples and yet citizens are encouraged to interact with the issue or service as an investor.[92]

A similar thing is happening when law students take unpaid internships just so they will be more attractive to prospective employers or when academics feel guilty for not 'networking' enough during a conference. Further to these examples, it is also important to recognise that neoliberalism gained ascendency alongside financial capitalism and so the process of economization does not necessarily concern material products or the exchange of commodities. Today market actors such as universities are increasingly concerned with their 'speculatively determined value',[93] which can be expressed in terms of their ratings and rankings. This is 'financialized market conduct', and it is not captured by the usual descriptions of neoliberalism which focus on material structures and the redistribution of wealth.[94]

Brown dedicates a chapter in *Undoing the Demos* to the impact of neoliberal rationality to higher education in the United States.[95] It is not necessary for me to cover this analysis in detail and I think that most academics would recognize the prevalence of this logic in their workplace. However, if you are reading this and thinking 'I don't *buy* that argument', you might just be proving my point. When something becomes 'common sense' or a 'reality principle', it can be hard to think outside of its parameters or imagine spaces of differences. Regimes of truth invade our private thoughts and inhibit the freedom of our thought and communication.

What impact might neoliberal rationality and economization have on academic research? According to Brown, neoliberalism shapes people as 'human capital' who must 'comport' themselves in 'ways that maximise [our] capital value in the present and enhance [our] future value through practices of entrepreneurialism, self-investment and/or attracting investors'.[96] It is not too difficult to point to concrete examples of this economization – for example, academic performance is increasingly measured with respect to our h-index, citations or the money we can bring into an institution. Academics also increasingly invest in self-promotion through networking sites, such as ResearchGate and Academia, or even sticking our latest publications to our office doors.

Participating in at least some of these practices is the 'price of admission' for many academics. Institutional pressures, competition and the propensity to personalize rather than politicize issues[97] have us tending predominately to our own immediate needs such as teaching materials and skills of teaching larger classrooms. Moreover, the shift toward entrepreneurial research identities has encouraged a degree of self-discipline[98] in the kinds of topics that scholars address.[99] One the one hand, the metrics that judge our performance and the speculative value of our institutions allow degree of freedom. In Australia, so long as research can count in the Excellence in Research Australia, it is entirely possible for a scholar to produce voluminous critiques of the relationship between higher education and neoliberalism. Critique can become economized and scholars might find themselves in the curious position of having their intellectual efforts simultaneously reproduce the system they are challenging. Whether this situation could exist if the critiques seriously challenged the hegemony of neoliberalism, is I think, an open question.

However, a much more common outcome is that perspectives that try to connect legal education to broader political/economic trends are rarely being made.[100] While further study is required, that conclusion is supported by my investigation into the two specialist legal education journals which I discussed previously.

The metrics shaping our work make it increasingly difficult to talk about universities as a public good and to advocate non-instrumental reasons as to why they should be adequately provisioned. These arguments do not speak to politicians and may even fail to gain traction at a faculty or school meeting. Further, because neoliberal rationality configures our students as customers or 'self-investing human capital',[101] it is difficult to talk legibly about non-instrumental learning or the value of acquiring the 'knowledge and experience needed for intelligent democratic citizenship'.[102]

This is perhaps the most challenging aspect of Brown's description of neoliberalism. If economization is eroding the lexicon scholars might use to describe alternative educational values, then from what basis might a more 'ambitious democratic [project] be launched?'[103] Where might those of us seeking to highlight alternative values and practices find conversation partners? To address these questions, I turn to consider the potential of a discourse grounded in 'public things' to challenge neoliberal rationality and provide spaces to bind collective identify.

IV Concluding comment: in defence of public things

> What democracy has always been about is fighting over the public thing.[104]

Legal education is not something that takes place in a vacuum. Everything from class sizes to technology and the content of the curriculum is influenced by politics and economics. To take a simple example – my own teaching in property law has been impacted by larger seminar classes, requirements to record lectures and expectations that teaching materials will be orientated toward practice rather than history or theory. And yet research that seeks to understand or critique the impact of economics and politics on legal education is overshadowed by an overriding concern with skills, technology and vocationalism. Authors have advanced several explanations for this fact, and in the last section I considered how neoliberal rationality economizes higher education and makes 'unintelligible the idea and practice of education as a democratic public good'.[105] Put another way, neoliberalism undermines the very idea of the public and seeks to replace it with an image of the world that reflects Margaret Thatcher's suggestion that 'there is no such thing as society . . . [only] individual men and women'.[106]

As described by Brown, neoliberal rationality is an almost totalizing discourse, and one could read her as suggesting that the contemporary process of subject formation has rendered scholars unfree in novel ways. And yet Brown leaves open the possibility of identifying and countering neoliberalism and suggests that such work is necessary to 'afford the slightest hope for a just, sustainable and habitable future'.[107] Further to this, it is also clear that academics can and do provide political and economic accounts and critiques of legal education. It is a marginalized discourse, but it does exist.

One strategy for making such work more visible would be to try and ground future research projects in notions and objects that resist individualism and competition and which bind collective identity even if they are also impure and sites of contestation. Responding directly to Brown, Bonnie Honig suggest that 'public things' might serve this function.[108] While Honig does not define this term, it is clear from the examples that she provides that she is talking about material objects such as public lands, parks, infrastructure and memorials. While 'things' have been sidelined in political theory, Honig argues that they are central to the creation of a public and their finitude gives rise to a friction which is the 'electricity of political life, or one source of its charge'.[109] Drawing on the English psychoanalyst D. W. Winnicott, Honig describes 'public things' as a 'holding environment' that 'constitute us, complement us, limit us, thwart us, and interpellate us into democratic citizenship'.[110]

Might there be something the public nature of most Australian law schools[111] that might act as a catalyst for scholars who agree on the importance of public things? Such values are under attack[112] and law schools are sites of contestation. And yet, law schools are fundamentally engaged with the public either through the subjects we teach, our research and advocacy or our commitment to produce graduates who can think critically and participate in democratic life. While there are clear differences in our analysis, it is at this juncture that I agree with David Dixon, who notes that law schools ought to resist being 'soaked up by business schools'[113] whose interests are primarily private. Moreover, in differing from David's characterisation of 'left pessimism', I contend that rather than reacting to the 'prominent offensiveness that is neoliberal privatisation' we might try and think about how the public nature of law schools might provide a basis for research and advocacy that is a 'proactive and public-things oriented mode of emergent politics'.[114]

This has been attempted in the past[115] and there are strong similarities with the modest 'slow professor' movement.[116] Drawing on these sources, future research in this direction might explicitly enumerate the distinctive attributes of public universities such as government support, public property, the provision of education as a public good and responsibilities to produce research that benefits society – from law reform recommendation to vaccines. They might also find ways of using the space to obtain a visceral sense of our collective identity. Here it should be emphasized that public universities provide multiple sites of contestation including libraries, radio stations, governance structures with public representation, preserved wilderness spaces, public pools, and exercise equipment. Further to this list, one of the most visible struggles on university campuses in recent memory has concerned demands to divest university money from the fossil fuel industry. Here again we can see academics, students and members of the public come together to uphold the public good over the logic of economization and short-term profit.[117]

Some readers may find it odd to place emphasis on public things as a method to influence future scholarship in legal education. And yet, Honig suggests, it is at this juncture that we need to return to public things and revitalize their ability to constitute us collectively and articulate values outside of neoliberal rationality. As Honig argues:

> perhaps it is useful to think about public things now precisely because it is not quite too late to defend those we still have, to render them more fully accessible and egalitarian, and to generate or promote new ones if we can appreciate their constitutive necessity to democratic life and act in concert to secure them.[118]

Notes

* Adelaide Law School, University of Adelaide.

1 Suzanne Ryan, 'Academic Zombies: A Failure of Resistance or a Means of Survival?' (2012) 54(2) *Australian Universities Review* 3. See also Eva Bendix Peterson, 'Staying or Going? Australian Early Career Researchers' Narratives of Academic Work, Exit Options and Coping Strategies' (2011) 53(2) *Australian Universities Review* 34.

2 For a review of this literature, see Mary Heath and Peter Burdon, 'Academic Resistance to the Neoliberal University' (2013) 23(2) *LER* 379. Note also David Dixon's comments on managerialism in this volume.

3 Wendy Brown, *Undoing the Demos: Neoliberalism's Stealth Revolution* (Zone Books, Massachusetts 2017).

4 Bonnie Honig, *Public Things: Democracy in Despair* (Fordham University Press, New York 2017). I am grateful to Ben Golder for this suggestion.

5 Guy Rundle, 'The Bonfire of the Humanities' (*The Saturday Paper* 2018) <www.thesaturdaypaper.com.au/opinion/topic/2018/05/19/the-bonfire-the-humanities/15266520006253>, accessed 19 May 2018.

6 Frank Donoghue, *The Last Professors: The Corporate University and the Fate of the Humanities* (Fordham University Press, New York 2018); Anthony T. Kronman, *Education's End: Why Our Colleges and Universities Have Given Up on the Meaning of Life* (Yale University Press 2008); Benjamin Ginsberg, *The Fall of the Faculty* (Oxford University Press 2013); Stefan Collini, *Speaking of Universities* (Verso, New York 2018); Jennifer Washburn, *University, Inc.: The Corporate Corruption of Higher Education* (Basic Books, New York 2006); Ellen Schrecker, *The Lost Soul of Higher Education: Corporatization, the Assault on Academic Freedom, and the End of the American University* (The New Press, New York 2010).

7 Elizabeth Humphrys, *The Corporatist Origins of Neoliberalism: Australia's Accord, the Labour Movement and the Neoliberal Project* (PhD Thesis, University of Sydney 2015) 70–71.

8 On the Thatcher and Reagan governments see David Harvey, *A Brief History of Neoliberalism* (Oxford University Press 2007) 39–63. Neoliberalism was also enforced through military force: see Marcus Taylor, *From Pinochet to the 'Third Way': Neoliberalism and Social Transformation in Chile* (Pluto Press, London 2006).

9 Philip Mirowski and Dieter Plehwe (eds), *The Road from Mont Pèlerin: The Making of the Neoliberal Thought Collective* (Harvard University Press 2015).

10 Elizabeth Humphrys and Damien Cahill, 'How Labour Made Neoliberalism' (2016) 43(4–5) *Critical Sociology* 669. See also Elizabeth Humphrys, 'Is the Term Neoliberalism Useful?' (*An Integral State* 12 November 2006) https://anintegralstate.net/2016/11/12/476/, accessed 19 February 2018. Here Humphrys argues, 'we argue that the labour movement was not simply an object or victim of neoliberal change but an active constructor of it'.

11 For example, a critical aspect of the Dawkins reforms involved linking funding to a set of national objectives for the economy, society and culture. This goes against the logic of a purely free market as articulated by Milton Friedman. See Milton Friedman, 'The Social Responsibility of Business Is to Increase Its Profits' (*New York Times Magazine* 13 September 1970). Against this reading scholars have pointed to the role of the state in securing the conditions for capital accumulation. See, e.g., Noam Chomsky, *Profit over People: Neoliberalism & Global Order* (Seven Stories Press, New York 1999) 65.

12 Paul Karp, 'Universities Australia Attacks Coalition's $2.2bn Funding Cut Revealed in Myefo' (*Guardian*, Sydney, 18 December 2017) <www.theguardian.com/australia-news/2017/dec/18/coalitions-22bn-cut-from-universities>, accessed 20 December 2017.

13 Stuart Macintyre, Andre Brett and Gwilym Croucher, *No End of a Lesson: Australia's Unified National System of Higher Education* (Melbourne University Press 2017) 37.

14 Ibid.

15 Brown (n. 3).

16 Margaret Thornton, *Privatising the Public University: The Case of Law* (Routledge 2012). This book builds on early work such as Margaret Thornton, 'The Demise of Diversity in Legal Education: Globalisation and the New Knowledge Economy' (2001) 8 *IJLP* 37; Margaret Thornton, 'Among the Ruins: Law in the Neoliberal Academy' (2001) 20 *WYAJ* 3; Margaret Thornton, 'Technocentrism and the Law School' (1998) 36 *Osgoode Hall Law Journal* 369; Margaret Thornton, 'Gothic Horror in the Legal Academy' (2005) 14 *Social and Legal Studies* 267. More broadly, see Michael Chesterman and David Weisbrot, 'Legal Scholarship in Australia' (1987) 50 *MLR* 709; Jane Kelsey, 'Privatizing the Universities' (1998) 25 *JLS* 51; Jan Currie and others, *Gendered Universities in Globalized Economies: Power, Careers, and Sacrifices* (Lexington Books 2003) and Nickolas James, 'Power-Knowledge in Australian Legal Education: Corporatism's Reign' (2004) 26(4) *SLR* 587.

17 See also a special edition of the LER (2013) 23(2). For an earlier summary of this topic, see volume 5 of the AJLS (1988–89).

18 Thornton, *Privatising the Public University* (n 16) 1. At p. xiv, Thornton captures this shift with reference to a government report which stated: 'The term "public" university now refers more to the historical circumstances at the time of foundation rather than the nature of institutional financing'. See also Department of Education, Employment and Workplace Relations, 'Review of Australian Higher Education, Working Paper, Department of Education, Employment and Workplace Relations' (Canberra, June 2008) 10.

19 Thornton, *Privatising the Public University* (n. 16) 1.

20 Ibid., 27–58.

21 Ibid., 59–109. See also Nickolas James, 'A Brief History of Critique in Australian Legal Education' (2000) 24(3) *MULR* 965; Nickolas James, 'Australian Legal Education and the Instability of Critique' (2004) 28(2) *MULR* 375; Nickolas James, 'Expertise as Privilege: Australian Legal Education and the Persistent Emphasis Upon Doctrine' (2004) (8) *Western Sydney Law Review* 1 and Nickolas James, 'The Marginalisation of Radical Discourses in Australian Legal Education' (2006) 16(1/2) *LER* 55–74.

22 Thornton, *Privatising the Public University* (n. 16) 110–164.

23 Ibid., 165–206.

24 Jeffrey Goldsworthy, 'The Law and the Profits' (2013) 55(1) *Australian Universities Review* 92, 93. There are also several thoughtful critiques of Thornton's books. See, e.g., Goldsworthy from p. 94.

25 Goldsworthy (n. 24) 93. See also Huw Morris, 'A Matter of Quid Pro Quo, M'lud' (2012) *Times Higher Education* 52. A similar argument is made in

Fiona Cownie and Anthony Bradney, 'Gothic Horror? A Response to Margaret Thornton' (2005) 14(2) *Social and Legal Studies* 277. For an alternative reading, see Robert Van Krieken, 'Privatising the Public University: The Case of Law' (2014) 43(4) *Contemporary Sociology: A Journal of Reviews* 581, 582: 'it should not be read as a pessimistic account of the evils of neoliberalism in university life, but as a resource for understanding how the structure and dynamics of higher education have changed, possibly in order to inform strategies that might push those changes in directions that better retain what has been valuable and useful about universities'.

26 Richard Joseph, 'Privatising the Public University: The Case of Law' (2012) 30(3) *Prometheus* 329, 332.

27 Ibid., 97.

28 Thornton, *Privatising the Public University* (n. 16) 13.

29 Macintyre (n. 13) 11.

30 Goldsworthy (n. 24) 57.

31 W. Max Corden, 'Australian Universities: Moscow on the Molongo' (2005) 11 *Quadrant* 7–20.

32 Macintyre (n. 13) 154–7.

33 Thornton, *Privatising the Public University* (n. 16) 9–13.

34 On the relationship between neoliberalism and individual responsibility, see Grahame Thompson, 'Responsibility and Neo-Liberalism' (*Open Democracy*, 31 July 2007) <www.opendemocracy.net/article/responsibility_and_neo_liberalism>, accessed 25 February 2017. With respect to higher education a recent paper from University Australia found that 'universities and their students have contributed $3.9 billion to Budget repair since 2011/12'. See further Universities Australia, 'The Facts on University Funding' (2017) <www.universitiesaustralia.edu.au/Media-and-Events/submissions-and-reports/The-facts-on-university-funding>, accessed 1 February 2017. On cuts during the Howard Government see Macintyre (n. 13) 246–8.

35 Gina Anderson, 'Mapping Academic Resistance in the Managerial University' (2008) 15 *Organization* 251, 252. See also Paul Trowler, *Academics Responding to Change – New Higher Education Frameworks and Academic Cultures* (Open University Press, Maidenhead 1998) 13.

36 Heath and Burdon (n. 2).

37 Thornton, *Privatising the Public University* (n. 16), p. xv.

38 Ibid.

39 Anderson (n. 35). Anderson draws on James C. Scott, *Weapons of the Weak: Everyday Forms of Peasant Resistance* (Yale University Press 1985).

40 Cownie and Bradney (n. 25). At p. 278 the authors argue that 'resistance (sometimes overt, more often hidden), rather than being an occasional and diminishing feature of the law school, characterizes the work of many academics in British university law schools'. This is particularly true of professional associations such as the Socio-Legal Studies Association. See further Peter Birks, 'The Academic and the Practitioner' (1998) 18 *Legal Studies* 397 and Fiona Cownie, *Legal Academics: Culture and Identities* (Hart, Oxford 2004) 205–6.

41 Law School Reform, 'Breaking the Frozen Sea: The Case for Reforming Legal Education at the Australian National University' (2010) <www.anulss.com/wp-content/uploads/2016/05/Breaking-the-Frozen-Sea-Report.pdf>, accessed 13 February 2010.

42 Harsh Suri and John Hattie, 'Meta-Analysis and Research Synthesis in Education' (2017) <www.oxfordbibliographies.com/view/document/obo-9780199756810/obo-9780199756810-0091.xml>, accessed 3 March 2017.

43 William Baude, Adam Chilton and Anup Malani, 'Making Doctrinal Work More Rigorous: Lessons from Systematic Reviews' (2016) <https://chicagounbound.uchicago.edu/cgi/viewcontent.cgi?article=2439&context=law_and_economics>, accessed 4 October 2018.

44 Terry Hutchinson, *Researching and Writing in Law* (Thomson Reuters, Sydney 2018) 12.

45 Jeremy A. Blumenthal, 'Meta-Analysis: A Primer for Legal Scholars' (2007) 80 *Temple Law Review* 201, 203 and Terry Hutchinson, 'Developing Legal Research Skills: Expanding the Paradigm' (2008) 32 *Melbourne University Law Review* 1065, 1067–73.

46 For a strident defence see Richard Posner, 'The Present Situation in Legal Scholarship' (1980) 90 *Yale Law Journal* 1113.

47 For an excellent introduction to meta-analysis in law, see David B. Wilson, 'Meta-Analytic Methods for Criminology' (2001) 578 *The Annals of the American Academy of Political and Social Science* 71, 72: 'averaging across studies is analogous to averaging across individuals within a single study'.

48 Blumenthal (n. 45) 202.

49 Ibid.

50 While my research was limited to published research, Blumenthal (n. 45) argues at p. 220 that researchers 'should make the effort to obtain data not formally published as well-for instance, research reported at conference or symposium proceedings, in working papers, or in other works in progress, as well as those reporting null findings'.

51 See endnote 6.

52 There is a diverse literature on how many papers ought to be analysed for spastically relevant results. See, e.g., Jeffrey C. Valentine, Therese D. Pigott and Hannah R. Rothstein, 'How Many Studies Do You Need? A Primer on Statistical Power for Meta-Analysis' (2010) 35(2) *Journal of Educational and Behavioral Statistics* 215. In this chapter I am not claiming to have conducted a formal meta-analysis. However, reading papers like this gave me confidence that my sample was sufficiently large to draw some preliminary conclusions.

53 I acknowledge that legal education specialists also publish in journals such as the *Journal of Commonwealth Law and Legal Education*, the *Journal of Legal Studies Education*, the *International Journal of Law & Education* and the *Australasian Law Teachers Association*. Others publish in generalist law reviews and socio-legal journals such as the *Griffith Law Review* and the *Social and Legal Studies*. My survey makes no pretence to being comprehensive but merely indicative of the leading journals where Australian researchers publish their work.

54 See further <www.northeastern.edu/law/academics/journals/journal-legal-ed/index.html>, accessed 14 April 2017.

55 See further <https://epublications.bond.edu.au/ler/>, accessed 14 April 2017.

56 For more on this point see Mary Heath, 'On Critical Thinking' (2012) 4 *The International Journal of Narrative Therapy and Community Work* 11–18, Stephen Brookfield, *Teaching for Critical Thinking: Tools and Techniques to Help Students Question Their Assumptions* (Jossey-Bass, New York 2012) and bell hooks, *Teaching Critical Thinking: Practical Wisdom* (Routledge, London 2010).

57 Blumenthal (n. 45) 205, 221–2.

58 In putting together this list I have extrapolated from those proposed by James, 'The Marginalisation of Radical Discourses in Australian Legal Education' (n. 21). James proposes the following discourses: doctrinal, vocational,

corporatist and radical. Engagement with neoliberalism might fit within James's definition of radical discourses but there are also important differences – most notably engagement with neoliberalism need not be oppositional. In other words, it is entirely possible to recognise the impact that neoliberalism has had on higher education and write in support of that influence.

59 See Liesel Spencer and Elen Seymour, 'Reading Law: Motivating Digital Natives to "Do the Reading"' (2013) 23(1) *Legal Education Review* 177.

60 See Molly Townes O'Brien, Stephen Tang and Kath Hall, 'Changing Our Thinking: Empirical Research on Law Student Wellbeing, Thinking Styles and the Law Curriculum Law Student' (2011) 21(1–2) *Legal Education Review* 149.

61 Thornton, *Privatising the Public University* (n. 16) p. xv.

62 Katherine Larkin-Wong, 'A Newbie's Impression: One Student's Mindfulness Lessons' (2012) 61(4) *Journal of Legal Education* 665.

63 Charles Halpern, 'The Mindful Lawyer: Why Contemporary Lawyers are Practicing Meditation' (2012) 61(4) *Journal of Legal Education* 641.

64 In Australia, see Jerome Doraisamy, *The Wellness Doctrines: For Law Students & Young Lawyers* (Brio Books, Sydney 2015).

65 Angela P. Harris, 'Toward Lawyering as Peacemaking: A Seminar on Mindfulness, Morality, and Professional Identity' (2012) 61(4) *Journal of Legal Education* 647.

66 Zoë Krupka, 'No, It's Not You: Why "Wellness" Isn't the Answer to Overwork' (*The Conversation* 22 May 2015), <https://theconversation.com/no-its-not-you-why-wellness-isnt-the-answer-to-overwork-42124>.

67 Part of this increase can be accounted for by a special edition that I co-edited with Mary Heath in response to Thornton, *Privatising the Public University* (n. 16).

68 Lucy Maxwell, 'How to Develop Law Students' Critical Awareness – Change the Language of Legal Education' (2012) 22(1–2) *Legal Education Review* 99.

69 Max Weber, *Economy and Society: An Outline of Interpretive Sociology* (University of California Press 1978) 24. This idea is developed further in Wendy Brown's discussion of economization in the next section.

70 Tamara Walsh, 'Putting Justice Back into Legal Education' (2007) 17(1/2) *Legal Education Review* 119.

71 James, 'The Marginalisation of Radical Discourses in Australian Legal Education' (n. 21) 63–64.

72 Thornton, *Privatising the Public University* (n. 16) p. xv. Despite disagreeing on the cause, both Thornton and David Dixon share some common concerns regarding the rise of managerialism.

73 Ryan (n. 1) 4.

74 Bronwyn Davies and Peter Bansel, 'The Time of Their Lives? Academic Workers in Neoliberal Times' (2005) 14 *Health Sociology Review* 47.

75 See, e.g., David Dixon's chapter in this collection.

76 James, 'The Marginalisation of Radical Discourses in Australian Legal Education' (n. 21) 58, 60. See also Mark Van Hoecke, *Methodologies of Legal Research: Which Kind of Method for What Kind of Discipline?* (Hart Publishing, Oxford 2013) 4–10.

77 There is a well-developed literature on this topic in the sciences. See, e.g., Michael N. Dawson, Richard Field and Joaquín Hortal, 'Guides, not Gatekeepers' (2014) 6(3) *Frontiers of Biogeography* 108.

78 Margaret Davies, *Asking the Law Question* (Law Book Co., Sydney 1994) 144. See also Michael Fischl, 'The Question that Killed Critical Legal Studies' (1992) *Faculty Articles and Papers* 76.

79 Duncan Kennedy, *Legal Education and the Reproduction of Hierarchy: A Polemic Against the System* (NYU Press 2007).
80 See, e.g., Duncan Kennedy, 'Legal Formality' (1973) 2 *Journal of Legal Studies* 351.
81 Duncan Kennedy, 'Two Globalizations of Law & Legal Thought: 1850–1968' (2003) 3 (XXXVI) *Suffolk University Law Review* 631: 'although critical legal studies as a political movement has been dead for a number of years, critical legal studies as a legal academic school of thought is very much alive, and has an analysis to contribute, not to peripheral countries generically, but to the part of the intelligentsia of peripheral countries that is interested in left/modernist/post-modernist critiques of the current world system'.
82 I am grateful to Ben Golder for this point.
83 Michel Foucault, *The Birth of Biopolitics: Lectures at the Collège de France, 1978–79* (Graham Burchell tr, Picador, London 2004). In drawing this distinction, I also recognise that Thornton does 'think' with Foucault in her analysis of social change, managerialism and governmentality. See Thornton, *Privatising the Public University* (n. 16) pp. xv, 20, 107, 112, 114, 230.
84 Brown (n. 3). See also Michel Feher, *Rated Agencies: Political Engagements with Our Invested Selves* (Zone Books, New York, forthcoming) and Michel Feher, 'Self-Appreciation; or, the Aspirations of Human Capital' (2008) 21(1) *Public Culture* 21–41.
85 Ibid., 17.
86 Ibid., 35.
87 Ibid. The notion of a 'common sense' or 'reality principle' derives from Michel Foucault, *Discipline and Punish: The Birth of the Prison* (lan Sheridan tr, Vintage Books, New York 1995) 23 and Michel Foucault, *Society Must Be Defended. Lectures at the Collège de France 1975–1976* (David Macey tr, Picador, London 2003) 164.
88 Brown (n. 3) 31.
89 Daniel Moss, 'A Turn Against Immigration Would Devastate Australia' (*Bloomberg*, 16 March 2018) <www.bloomberg.com/view/articles/2018-03-15/australia-needs-to-sustain-immigration-to-sustain-economic-growth>, accessed 14 May 2018.
90 Dana Nuccitelli, 'Global Warming Will Depress Economic Growth in Trump Country' (*Guardian*, 7 May 2018) <www.theguardian.com/environment/climate-consensus-97-per-cent/2018/may/07/global-warming-will-depress-economic-growth-in-trump-country> accessed 10 May 2018. See also Brown (n. 3) 26–27.
91 Brown (n. 3) 31.
92 Ibid.
93 Wendy Brown, 'What Exactly Is Neoliberalism?' (*Dissent Magazine*, 2 April 2015) <www.dissentmagazine.org/blog/booked-3-what-exactly-is-neoliberalism-wendy-brown-undoing-the-demos>, accessed 17 February 2018.
94 Ibid. See further Francisco Marmolejo, 'Are We Obsessed with University Rankings?' (*The World Bank*, 15 December 2015) <https://blogs.worldbank.org/education/are-we-obsessed-university-rankings>, accessed 17 February 2018.
95 Brown (n. 3) 175–200.
96 Ibid., 22.
97 See Mark Fisher, 'Good for Nothing' (*The Occupied Times*, 19 March 2014) <https://theoccupiedtimes.org/?p=12841>, accessed 12 March 2018. Fisher's elaboration of 'magical voluntarism' is drawn from David Smail, *The Origins of Unhappiness: A New Understanding of Personal Distress* (Routledge, London 2015).

98 Thornton, *Privatising the Public University* (n. 16) 112 and James (n. 16) on Foucault and disciplinary power.
99 See further James, 'The Marginalisation of Radical Discourses in Australian Legal Education' (n. 21). James also cites Jennifer Gore in support of the marginalisation of radical critiques in higher education research. See further Jennifer Gore, *The Struggle for Pedagogies: Critical and Feminist Discourses as Regimes of Truth* (Routledge, London 1992).
100 See further James, 'The Marginalisation of Radical Discourses in Australian Legal Education' (n. 21).
101 Brown (n. 3) 177.
102 Ibid.
103 Ibid., 18.
104 Nick Pearce and Bonnie Honig, 'Juncture Interview: Bonnie Honig' (2013) 19(4) *PPR* 226, 229.
105 Wendy Brown, 'Neoliberalism's Frankenstein: Authoritarian Freedom in Twenty-First Century "Democracies"' (2018) 1(1) *Critical Times* 60, 62.
106 Margaret Thatcher interview by Douglas Keay, 23 September 1987, published as 'AIDs, Education and the Year 2000!' (*Woman's Own*, 31 October 1987) 8–10.
107 Brown (n. 3) 222.
108 Honig (n. 4).
109 Pearce and Honig (n. 104) 229.
110 Honig (n. 4) 5.
111 Bond University is currently the only private university in Australia.
112 Wendy Brown, 'Neoliberalized Knowledge' (2011) 1(1) *History of the Present* 113, 118–19.
113 See the contribution by David Dixon in this volume.
114 Pearce and Honig (n. 104) 229.
115 Mary Heath and Peter Burdon, 'Academic Resistance: Landscape of Hope and Despair' in A. Nocella II, and E. Juergensmeyer (eds), *Fighting Academic Repression and Neoliberal Education: Resistance, Reclaiming, Organizing, and Black Lives Matter in Education* (Peter Lang Publishing, Bern 2017) 33–45.
116 Maggie Berg and Barbara K. Seeber, *The Slow Professor: Challenging the Culture of Speed in the Academy* (University of Toronto Press 2017).
117 For information see 'University Fossil Fuel Divestment Total Tips £80 Billion Globally' (*Times Higher Education*, 17 August 2017) <www.timeshighereducation.com/news/university-fossil-fuel-divestment-total-tips-ps80-billion-globally>, accessed 17 April 2018.
118 Honig (n. 109) 15.

4 The poverty of pessimism*

David Dixon

I Introduction

Analysing the concept of 'left pessimism' may assist in understanding a kind of masochism which characterises some critical work on Australian legal education, notably by Margaret Thornton, Frank Carrigan and Nick James (who are academics at ANU, Macquarie and Bond, respectively). Thornton's book, *Privatising the Public University: The Case of Law*,[1] is significant and has been influential. Carrigan's is a cruder approach, to which I take particular objection for his depiction of UNSW Law.[2] I was dean of that school for ten years, an experience on the managerial dark side which naturally colours my perspective, provides most of my examples, and explains the tone of what follows. James echoes themes from Thornton and Carrigan in the kind of rhetoric for which Foucault has much to answer.[3] The politics of their writing ranges from Carrigan's reductionism through Thornton's theorising to James' affectation of political distance. Despite these differences, they can be grouped together as academic critics of legal education who present excessively pessimistic, inaccurate accounts, ignoring achievements and marginalising difference and resistance. To anticipate the question about *my* politics, this is not a critique from the right: my disagreement with left pessimists stems from conviction that there is nothing authentically progressive about inaccurate accounting and hopeless negativity.

When reading their work, I realised that it reminded me of something. Unlikely as the comparison is, there are distinct similarities to a body of work on English policing, most notably McConville, Sanders and Leng's much-cited *The Case for the Prosecution*,[4] which I characterised as 'left-pessimist'.[5]

Central elements of pessimistic accounts are:

1 *The good old days* – nostalgia and a rosy view of the past. In policing, this meant summoning a mythical past in which the common law effectively regulated police practice and police were part of the 'community'. There was wilful blindness to problems in that past which required and invited action, for example ignoring the consequences for suspects of the reality of unregulated search, detention and questioning.

2 *A glass half-empty* – simplifying complex processes by emphasising problems and identifying intent, often expressed through writing in a passive voice which does not specify the source of the intention. The failings, but never the achievements, of police reform are identified.
3 *Good is bad* – contrariness in either ignoring evidence running contrary to their thesis or claiming that it is merely the exception that proves the rule. McConville et al.'s crude, circular functionalism insisted that any effective regulation simply legitimates police power: 'For the state, existing modes of law enforcement *work*. And this is even when they sometimes fail . . . indeed occasional failure . . . is a *requirement* for an effective *legal* system'.[6]
4 *Hate the one you're with* – antagonism towards the object of study, for example assuming that policing is 'a bad thing', despite apparent need for any complex society to have organised policing of some kind.
5 *We're doomed* – pessimism about the possibility of change. McConville and others reject reform of policing as 'the false promises of liberal legalism', concluding that 'it is obvious that there is no constituency of any note for reform which involves real protections for vulnerable citizens or substantive changes to existing modes of policing'.[7]

II Pessimism and Australian law schools

Left-pessimism applied to Australian law schools looks like the following.

A *The good old days*

To the Australian Left, the good old days inevitably invoke the 'social liberalism of the Whitlam era (which) succeeded in bringing about a degree of modernisation to the curriculum',[8] characterised by 'critical interdisciplinary perspectives'.[9] Legal professional conservatism and 'the gendered and classed elitism of the past' ensured that this was no golden age,[10] but Thornton claims that 'there was a mood of optimism that acknowledged the legitimacy of social justice and law reform'.[11]

It couldn't last: 'the inclusion of critical perspectives on law occupied a prominent place for only a brief moment before there was a resiling induced by the neoliberal turn',[12] so 'the liberal law degree has been a short-lived aberration'.[13] This decline is presented in apocalyptic terms: 'Just when it appeared that legal education was becoming more critical, more humane and more diverse . . ., [t]he earth opened up and the positive developments of two decades or more began to slip and slide inexorably towards a gaping abyss'.[14] Curricula were purged: the 'neoliberal agenda offered the perfect opportunity to blanch the curriculum of *all vestiges* of discomfiting aspects of the social'.[15] Law schools reverted to 'the automatic transmission of doctrine'.[16] For Carrigan, '[t]he closing of the mind in a dark age of orthodoxy is the present keynote of legal education in Australia,[17] while for Thornton, '[t]he market narrative has effectively entered the social psyche and muted public resistance'.[18] I will suggest below that these are distorting exaggerations of (and capitulation to) real tendencies.

According to Carrigan, 'the modern university has become a travesty of its ideal image. It has been reduced to an appendage of the state and an adjunct of a corporate market society'.[19] Carrigan's principal concern is Macquarie Law School, the site of a bitter ideological schism in the 1980s. After prolonged controversy, the leaders of a critical faction, Gill Boehringer and Andrew Fraser, were shifted out of the law school. Carrigan tells us: 'The defeat of the Boehringer and Fraser group . . . symbolised the death of the ancient ideal of universities'.[20]

A corollary of nostalgia is the belief that there was little which needed to be fixed in the legal academy (except, of course, sex and class bias). The harsh reality is that the 'traditional', pre-neoliberal university had weaknesses, and the failure to address them invited hostile interventions. The solutions may not be desirable, but the gates to them were opened by wilful blindness about some academic working practices.

Managerialist shifts to assessing performance in the clumsy processes that academics now endure would have made much harder progress if the working practices of some had not left so much to be desired. When I became dean of UNSW Law, one-third of my colleagues (who were on a 40/40/20 contractual division of research/teaching/service) were unable to meet a minimal expectation of writing for publication. Asking what people did on two of the five days for which they were paid would be unexceptionable in any occupation other than the academic. Thornton complains that 'legal academics are no longer free to be dilettantes, dabbling in research over the summer as the mood takes them'.[21] Furthermore, 'It is no longer possible for academics to cruise along attending to their teaching and pursuing research interests in a desultory and uncoordinated fashion'.[22] Should they be? Would Thornton like her dentist or her plumber to be a dilettante who works in a desultory and uncoordinated fashion?

Thornton objects that academics 'are increasingly treated like any other body of employees whose labour needs to be coordinated and managed. . . . Academics in the neoliberal academy are struggling to retain their status, which was formerly closer to that of independent contractors than employees'.[23] This is unintentionally revealing in identifying a real problem – academics who think they should be able to decide unilaterally if, when and how much they work. If a magic wand could deliver common, coordinated, equal contributions, such an arrangement might be feasible. Unfortunately, against the mythical image of the independent don was the reality of a manifestly unfair division of labour in which, all too often, an autocratic head of school determined promotions and allocated work, women and junior colleagues taught, researched and ran the law school, and some senior colleagues 'worked from home'. Academic independence in what is researched and taught is essential, but it is not inconsistent with being treated 'like other employees'. Professional and technical staff often resent the claims of academics to protected status. It is an indication of the unworldliness of some academics that they think it strange that their employer might want to know what they spend their time doing. Such an exercise need not be metric-bashing performance management: it can be a welcome opportunity for constructive discussion about work and career planning. This is how UNSW Law shaped a university requirement for annual reviews.

As for students, the good old days were apparently when one of Thornton's informants was able to regard them as 'an interruption to our work'.[24] She complains that moving from six to eight hours teaching per week 'affects one's capacity to do research'.[25] Eight is only 21 per cent of a notional 38-hour week, and then only for teaching periods which take up less than half the year. It is hardly the salt mines. Then there are higher degree candidates. In the 'good old days', thesis completion rates were below 50 per cent, leading to so many people's frustration and disillusionment. Much of the responsibility for this was pathetically inadequate supervision. When we introduced annual progress reviews for research students, an old-guard colleague accused me indignantly of 'gestapo tactics'.

James defines corporatism as emphasising and prioritising 'the accountability of teachers and students, the efficiency of the teaching process, and the marketability of the law school'.[26] Legal academics often demand that others should be accountable, so it is a little odd to see this objection to accountability.[27] He provides a long, familiar list of 'law school policies'.[28] Some of these are tiresomely bureaucratic, but others simply express good practice. Some are both: usually, it depends how they are done. As for efficiency, James quotes the Commonwealth Tertiary Education Commission's (CTEC) view that

> the justification of appropriate levels of public funding for higher education carries with it an obligation on higher education institutions to demonstrate that their teaching and research is being carried out at suitable standards, avoiding waste and unnecessary duplication and in a manner that is responsive to community needs.[29]

'Efficiency' may be a dirty managerialist word, but what the CTEC said seems merely good sense – and good politics, given that public funding flows from a regressive taxation system.

Of course, it depends what you mean by accountability. As Collini points out, 'The entirely legitimate demand that universities be accountable to society has . . . resulted in the growth of a particular kind of audit culture that is having very damaging unintended consequences'.[30] But Thornton dismisses *any* attempts to assess performance. As regards publications, she claims that 'attempts to define quality are doomed from the outset. Not only is any definition circular, peer review is all too often an exercise in gamesmanship, '"clubbiness" and elitism'.[31] This kind of pessimistic abstention from the hard work of identifying and explaining judgement of quality and significance on our terms just leaves the field open to the imposition of inappropriate STEM metrics.[32] Reducing quality assessment to numbers is a basic error which no university should make, but dismissing peer review as equally pernicious is hopelessly defeatist.

B A glass half-empty

In Thornton's account, half-empty glasses are more common than at a house party, notably in her tendency to find fault and to assume the worst. An example is an article on law school 'branding'. Efforts at self-publicity and advertisement are always soft targets, so she enjoys mocking law school marketing.

> Attractiveness and desirability are construed in terms of consumerism with advertising often redolent of a tourist brochure. The student who undertakes a law degree is promised employability, prestige and wealth; he or she is also assured of a glamorous and fun-filled career. As a result, the serious and difficult aspects associated with the study of law are sloughed off, as well as the centrality of justice and critique.[33]

As it happens, I am very proud of the work done by smart, skilful and committed marketing professionals at UNSW Law who are insulted by the belittling claim that 'rather than aiming to produce critical thinkers who can contribute constructively to the public debate on the pressing issues of our time, law school marketing encourages consumerism and the ultimate telos of the good life'.[34]

Working with a talented marketing team was helpful in making UNSW Law clarify to ourselves what we value, and then to communicate it, not just to potential future students ('selling the dream') but also to ourselves, to our colleagues in the university, and to our alumni and other external audiences. We attempted to articulate for a new generation the founding vision of UNSW Law in which commitments to a distinctive combination of legal professionalism and social justice are fundamental. So, yes, we have large banners with smiling students on the outside of the law school, with their own words expressing commitment to being where students will study the 'law in action' and 'where law meets justice'. Far from apologising for this, I am proud of it as an effective way of building our culture and communicating our identity.

A common stylistic feature of 'half-empty' claims is over-statement and writing in the passive. Thornton claims 'any semblance of the idea' of 'the university as a community of scholars engaged in the dispassionate pursuit of truth . . . seems to have gone forever as . . . governments seek to deploy universities for instrumental ends'.[35] *Any* semblance? Empirically, this does not describe the world in which I work; ideologically, it drives a fake wedge between truly academic and merely applied work; and politically, it simply overstates the significance of universities to government. There is also the irony that Thornton writes in a book funded by a government research council grant.

Intent can always be asserted rather than proved by writing in passive style: so for example, James claims that

> Liberalism is an insidious and effective constraint upon radical legal education discourses. The liberal ideology, and its veneration of ideas like equality and liberty, encourages such efforts with the intent not of destabilising dominance but of stabilising it by reconciling all alternative perspectives with the liberal worldview.[36]

How an ideology acts with intent is not clear. While Carrigan's marxisant prose clanks like tanks in a Red Square parade, making his meaning all too apparent, Thornton's prose drifts into sub-Foucaultian affectation when issues become complex: 'the liberal carapace of the academy occludes these tensions'.[37] She repeatedly uses pretentious terms and phrases, including 'resiling from', 'carapace', 'sloughed off', 'performative' and 'affect'. She consistently writes passively, an effective way of obscuring meaning and responsibility: 'There has been a resiling from small-group teaching and interactive learning'.[38] Apparently, 'thinking . . . is deemed to be unproductive in a performative environment'.[39] Inevitably perhaps, I point to Orwell as a corrective: expression is political and such writing is politically corrosive.[40]

Ever since E. P. Thompson's critique of Warwick University,[41] 'the business university' has been a half-empty glass. If left-pessimist criminologists expressed surprised outrage at the discovery that police are agents of social control (who would have guessed?), left-pessimist commentators on Australian universities are similarly outraged that they 'began to be corporatised, which involved the application of business practices to the way they were run'.[42] It is an indication of the problems of market societies that 'acting like a business' is an insult: Thornton is able to assume that this means 'top-down managerialism' and 'weakened democratic norms and collegial bonds' and commitment to 'maximise profitability'.[43] Public universities may answer that they do not make profits for share-holders: any surplus goes to meeting the modern vice chancellor's crucial key performance indicator (KPI) – the number of cranes on his or her campus. However, it is true that universities have been sucked into justifying their existence in economic terms. While it is quite justifiable to show higher education's contribution as an 'export industry', this has become an end in itself, leading to ever-increasing dependence on international students. Welcome as they are, they are not the raison d'être of the university, any more than scientific research which translates directly into industrial production provides the only kind of value.

Looking beyond easy jibes about overpaid men in suits bustling self-importantly around chancelleries, I suggest that 'running like a business' is not self-evidently bad – it depends what kind of business. More is involved in running a university than organising tea money in the senior common room. A university is a large, complex institution which employs thousands of people, administers a budget of many millions (much of which, despite privatisation, comes from taxpayers), and has responsibilities to students, employees and the community. In a university context, 'acting like a business' might also mean using public funds properly and efficiently, acting ethically and treating workers decently – it depends what kind of business, and it depends what kind of efficiency. 'Acting like a corporation' could mean acting like a socially progressive and responsible corporation. The glass might be half-full.

C *Good is bad*

Contrariness is expressed in that inexorable functionalism which so often discredits what claims to be marxist analysis. One of Carrigan's key sources informs us:

> It is important to understand that . . . the Law Faculties serve capitalism, their most important function. For when the structures of capitalism required a new, more creative reform-oriented legal education than could be offered by the entrenched conservatives of the conventional universities . . . it was certain that the 'logic' of capitalism would produce a UNSW Faculty with its almost self-conscious zeal for reform.[44]

The historical function of UNSW (and other progressive schools) was

> developing the legal cadres which would lend legal technical support to the restructuring of Australia's political economy and the reformation of the socially permitted norms of behaviour necessary for the creation of a fully modern capitalist society based on mass consumption.

So the exception proves the rule because the logic of capitalism requires it to do so.

The contribution of significant public figures such as ex-UNSW Law deans Hal Wootten, Garth Nettheim and Ronald Sackville is lazily brushed off: the 'task of liberal law schools such as UNSW was to provide ideological cover and technical solutions e.g. Sackville and poverty'.[45] With a dismissive backhand, Ronald Sackville's Commission of Inquiry could be dismissed as ideological camouflage.[46] This was stretching it a bit, so the logic of change is introduced: 'to the extent that the reforming liberals at UNSW Law School threatened the ruling class' ideological hegemony, they had to be isolated and the faculty tamed'.[47] One might wonder how marxists could ever have been appointed to law schools in the first place. The answer is simple: 'the composition of (the modern law school's) staff mirrors the contradictions of capitalism'.[48] Anything can be explained with this kind of empty rhetoric.

Useful as misuse of Marx is, the best excuse for having it all ways at once is to refer to Foucault, a citation to whom allows any statement of the crassly obvious to be tarted up into something portentous such as 'While social change never progresses evenly or linearly' . . . [49] I stress that this is not an anti-intellectual dismissal of Foucault: as in the case of Marx, my objection is to misuse, not use. Referring to Foucault like this is little more than an excuse for having it both ways: '[r]esistance, of course, is an inevitable by-product of the operation of power, which is another valuable insight of Foucault'.[50] So we are told that academics' compliance under corporate surveillance and control is not absolute: '[i]t goes without saying, of course, that legal education can never be an entirely closed system and there will always be some who resist deference to the market',[51] and indeed

> the vestiges of the old-fashioned liberal values of diversity and tolerance are still to be found in pockets everywhere. It is just that they can no longer be said to be part of the mainstream, where they have been supplanted by corporatism and vocationalism.[52]

Of course: black is black except when it is white.

Legal positivism's critics could never succeed: '[t]he upshot of the contest of ideas in law is preordained. In the absence of large-scale changes in the wider polity, the progressive forces will eventually experience a rollback', so UNSW Law's was 'a doomed struggle'.[53] Similarly, Thornton tells us that 'while critique is permissible, the freedom to do so is circumscribed, for it must not challenge the fundamental presuppositions of market orthodoxy'.[54] Why, one wonders, did anyone bother, if failure was 'pre-ordained'?

Doing anything for the better is said to have ulterior motives. So, actions such as appointing 'the occasional dissentient feminist law teacher' or introducing 'a feminist legal theory course' simply 'serve to mask the nature of male dominance'.[55] The same is apparently the case if you take action to have women as more than half your professors:[56] 'the proportion of female law teachers is increased not with the intent of challenging patriarchy and feminising the curriculum but with the intent of warding off criticism and ultimately maintaining the masculine status quo'.[57] Appointing Aboriginal academics and supporting Aboriginal students and institutions[58] are probably even more despicably self-serving. After all, 'Law school and university administrators, legal practitioners and senior law teachers' will not go beyond 'the occasional liberal platitude'.[59]

In general, this kind of determinism is merely unconvincing and tiresome, but when it becomes more specific, the cynicism becomes objectionable. For example, Thornton sneers at social justice activity by law schools as 'a salve to their consciences'.[60] Similarly, she denigrates the shift to experiential learning: 'law schools market experiential learning not so much because it will result in better lawyers but because it accords with the market's demand for graduates with "job ready" skills'.[61] Apart from the strange counter-position of being a good lawyer and being 'job ready', this simply displays ignorance of experiential education (which is a better way to learn, not trade school) and of the radicalism of the clinical legal education movement, in which UNSW Law's Kingsford Legal Centre is a leader.[62]

On international experiential learning opportunities, Thornton claims that '"branding" is about distinctiveness, not quality' and that 'more attention is likely to be paid to marketing the product than to the educational product being marketed'.[63] Comments quoted in law schools' publicity material about students' experiences overseas are twisted to make it seem that they had gone on a belated 'gap yah',[64] seeking 'fun, adventure and new experiences. . . . Such texts evoke images of globetrotting careers pursued for pleasure'.[65]

Thornton and Shannon smugly claim that

> [t]here is no acknowledgement that these roles, particularly those involving the examination or prosecution of human rights abuses, are premised on the suffering of the world's most vulnerable people. In order to set up these idealised visions of future employment, the routine and disturbing aspects of international opportunities and perspectives are excised.[66]

They seize on the profile of a UNSW graduate working at the Rwandan Criminal Tribunal. It is true that this does not detail the suffering of victims, but it certainly does not glamorise the mundane nature of her work: Thornton and Shannon quote selectively, omitting the student's explanation that it involves prosaic research, writing and administrative tasks.[67] I happen to know the UNSW Law students whom Thornton and Shannon suggest are self-centred millennials in 'globetrotting careers pursued for pleasure'.[68] All three alumnae now work in international human rights – their international university experience was not a dalliance before corporate law. They credit UNSW Law in helping them to get to do this, and I hope their stories inspire students to follow their example.

Even if you believe the glass really is half-empty rather than half-full, you need to treat what is in the glass more than just negatively. This point was made very well in a review of Thornton's book:

> Unfortunately, the common thread of state-led and market-mediated privatisation that Thornton focuses on is described with a slew of shibboleths – Americanisation, casualisation, commodification, corporatisation, massification and McDonaldisation – that share the same suffix but do not always extend our understanding of how these changes have altered the balance of public and private goods and bads for all involved in legal education, not just the academics who were interviewed. So while these trends may be evident, these terms have not themselves been critically reviewed. As a consequence of these silences, these epithets foreground the negative and draw attention away from the beneficial changes that have also taken place.[69]

Carrigan presents his analysis as 'a march towards facts'.[70] Unfortunately, he doesn't get far. For his account of UNSW Law, he relies on one brief paper by Brian Kelsey from a student magazine published in 1975 and a commentary on a subsequent reprint of it.[71] Despite having apparently done no further research on his subject, Carrigan feels able to claim that

> The dream of a community of academics at UNSW pursuing a progressive legal program was terminated by the mid-1970s. The UNSW Law School

> retreated into being a positivistic carbon copy of Sydney University. A few maverick thinkers survived at UNSW, but lacking an institutional framework to promote their cause they were reduced to token rebels. The battle over legal pedagogy shifted elsewhere as the UNSW experiment collapsed.[72]

I am somewhat surprised to hear that I was, for a decade, dean of 'a desert'.[73] There is no space here for a full rebuttal, so a few examples from the reality of UNSW Law must suffice: thematically structured curricula[74] delivered through interactive teaching; public engagement through leading contributions to the Uluru Statement; housing two refugee centres, one on international law, one providing legal advice and representation; a community legal centre which is an international exemplar for clinical legal education and law reform; and a 'community of scholars' with a very healthy intellectual culture sustained by a torrent of workshops, seminars, and conferences. While insisting that it is ludicrous to describe this as a desert, I must emphasise that I am not complacently presenting UNSW Law as perfect, or as unique: there are excellent law schools elsewhere. On the contrary, we have major problems caused by underfunding, STEM prejudice and managerialism. But the question to be asked is: compared to what?

Carrigan's lengthy, turgid and selective history of Macquarie Law School is useful in making clear his answer to the 'Compared to what?' question. If your idea of an oasis is Drew Fraser's,[75] then I will happily stick to the desert. Carrigan states that it 'would be wrong to cast Boehringer and Fraser in a hagiographic light',[76] then proceeds to do so. There was infamy at Macquarie, according to Boehringer.[77] Well, they certainly (as Kenneth Williams would have said) had it in for him[78] and Fraser, and who can blame them?

D Hate the one you're with

Left-pessimists are antagonistic towards and dismissive of many of the figures in their landscape. My experience of each has been rather different.

1 Corporate law firms and the profession

According to Thornton, 'Members of the profession believe they are endowed with almost divine authority to prescribe the curricular content'.[79] She claims that corporate law firms are directive and overbearing:

> Those who encourage critical skills with the aim of producing responsible citizens, not merely competent legal practitioners, speak a language that corporatist interests have little interest in hearing. . . . If the legal literature moves too far away from the practical concerns of the legal profession, academics are quickly taken to task.[80]

With one exception, my consistent experience was of dealing with leaders of corporate firms who were enthusiastic about our plans to introduce more international and experiential opportunities, supported social justice activities, and who were respectful, even deferential, rather than directing. They appreciated being consulted, but valued the independence and expertise of academics.

2 *Donors*

Universities increasingly seek philanthropic support. Thornton sees this in bleakly negative terms: 'Courting the profession, particularly the wealthy corporate firms as a source of funding serves only to entrench the subordinate role of law schools'.[81] She warns that

> [B]estowing naming rights on a donor undoubtedly suggests deference and raises questions about the extent of independence and critique that is permissible. . . . A patronal relationship undoubtedly enables the profession to influence subtly the direction and substance of school policies and curriculum so that students are groomed for employment in their firms. . . . If a law firm donates to a law school, it wants to support the areas in which it practices in order to profile its brand name and ensure the conveyor belt is working for the school's top students.[82]

In a final flourish, she writes:

> [i]n deference to the great god Mammon, academic freedom and the aspirations of the liberal law school are liable to be cast to the winds in the desperate search for donors. Fund-raising . . . is therefore bound to reify the dominant values of neoliberalism.[83]

'Bound to'? In my experience, corporate donors are not directive and demanding: they have better things to do with their time. Nor does philanthropy only go to commercial initiatives. It's strange but sad that universities underestimate the extent to which the public (including the profession) views them as a public good worth supporting.[84] For example, Gilbert + Tobin may well get some reputational benefit from its association with UNSW's Centre of Public Law, but it would be merely cynical to say that that is the firm's main motive. Fund-raising can also allow, as at UNSW, the establishment of a refugee law centre[85] and a scholarship for socially disadvantaged young people from South West Sydney.[86] From my biased perspective, this was doing a bit more than reifying neoliberalism (and, of course, salving my conscience).

3 *Curriculum*

Having approvingly quoted Jonathan Sumption's jibe that studying law at university 'narrows the mind and blunts curiosity',[87] Carrigan explains:

> In brief, the rule-based fetishism of law eliminates much of what constitutes intellectual life. . . . Time in the legal classroom is . . . mind-numbing

> work: desiccated, insular, narrow. . . . Students who have to endure law tutorials might fairly say, with T. S. Eliot, 'I have measured out my life with coffee spoons'.[88]

Carrigan's piece was titled 'Law Schools Sell Graduates Down the River', an interesting claim for a law school employee to make.[89]

Thornton insists on a rigid division between 'the teaching of skills and practice-oriented knowledge' and 'critical knowledge. . . . [T]he law degree should concentrate on scholarly academic aims and leave practical skills to dedicated others'. She argues that we should not 'expect a law graduate to emerge from a law school fully trained for whatever area of specialisation they might be employed in'.[90] Does *anyone* expect this? In dismissing anything other than 'critical knowledge' as knowing how to fill in forms, Thornton sounds disconcertingly like the lecturers who long ago sneered at my naïve undergraduate interest in how the law worked in practice (because, of course, they didn't know). Swap doctrinal purity and philosophical abstraction for critical knowledge, and Thornton would fit well into the Cambridge faculty of half a century ago. A fine response was given by my colleague Cathy Sherry: 'there can be no real critiquing of law and no academic rigour unless students genuinely understand the law, and they will never do that if they are not taught how it operates in practice'.[91] Understanding law is what experiential and contextual learning is about, not form-filling skills.

According to Thornton, 'the curriculum is shaped by the supply and demand vectors of the market, rather than intellectual worth or pedagogical practice'.[92] In 2013–14, UNSW undertook a fundamental review of our LLB and JD curricula.[93] We certainly took account of 'the market', if this means being aware of changes in the world of work (within and without the legal profession), not least technological change. We talked to alumni and employers about their perspectives and needs: as noted above, their answers were very different from the crass commercialism expected by Thornton. This contributed significantly to our review, alongside our search for intellectual coherence, integrity, critical perspectives and pedagogical best practice.[94]

4 *Students*

Students, it seems, have gone to the dogs: they 'do not seem to be tantalised by ideas in the way they once were'.[95] Law schools apparently produce 'a swathe of workers who have received a very narrow and technical form of education that quickly becomes superfluous'.[96] Thornton opines that

> fewer students each year speak up about injustices. . . . They are being prepared for life in corporate law firms where, perforce, they are going to be on the side of the powerful. . . . While there is always a committed group of students who are passionate about social justice, this group is shrinking year by year.[97]

Young people today. As Collini suggests, 'commentators in every generation have thought that it was all going to the dogs, but in that case the dogs must live further away than anyone ever realized'.[98] Typically, Thornton gives no evidence for her claim, which certainly does not reflect my experience: social justice activism expanded significantly at UNSW in the last decade, particularly around gender, refugees and Aboriginal rights. The first year class which I have just taught reacted angrily when I quoted Thornton's criticisms to them. Such alienation from students presumably contributed to the dissatisfaction of some students at Thornton's law school.[99]

On student law societies, Carrigan is harsh: 'The students who enrol in such a body are renowned for their ultra-conservative conception of law. . . . Giving credit to the viewpoint of a student body of this type regarding the destiny of an innovative law school is baffling'.[100] Again, my experience was rather different, dealing with an annual succession of UNSW Law Society leaders who were fully engaged in the law school's social justice commitments as well as in initiatives of their own.[101]

5 *Deans*

Deans are apparently part of the increasingly powerful 'managerial class' whose inaccessibility 'serves to depersonalise their relationships with the rank and file, in order to make it easier to admonish recalcitrants and administer disciplinary proceeding, as well as to marginalise or declare redundant those who get in the way of restructuring and cost-cutting plans'.[102] They wield great power: 'Areas of specialisation that are disfavoured can be subject to redundancies at the whim of a dean'.[103] Such 'line managers' may 'even dismiss those who are critical of their activities'.[104] Not surprisingly, no examples are cited for any of these claims. I suspect that the response from any dean who reads this would be 'I wish'.

While deans may be powerful, Thornton tells us that they are essentially 'subalterns'.[105] Of course they are – they are academic leaders, but also middle managers in an organisation. However, Thornton sees a dark side: 'Top-down managerialism encourages the appointment of "yes-men" who are prepared to do the bidding of management'.[106] My appointment might be thought an aberration by Fred Hilmer, until you look at the quality of my peers at other leading law schools. Yes-men (or even yes-women)? I don't think so. In my experience, she is wrong to present the relationship in purely negative terms. Deans have to be shock absorbers between chancellery and faculty. A dean who is merely the messenger from the chancellery will not be respected by his or her colleagues. Equally, a dean who tells the chancellery that his or her faculty is a protected species will be ineffective. A successful dean has to negotiate with integrity and win the respect of both sides. This can be done positively, and doing so involves more than abstractly 'managing contradictions'.

A dean's job is not micromanagement. It is employing and retaining the best staff you can, creating and defending conditions for them to do their work, and building 'morale, commitment, cooperation and a sense of solidarity'.[107]

Despite the cockiness with which university managers stride around claiming credit for everything, it is the academics who count: 'the most lavishly funded and most efficiently run university which has fourth-rate academics will remain a fourth-rate university'.[108]

If deans individually are problematic, collectively they are a menace. Carrigan spies conspiracy when he describes the Council of Australian Law Deans (CALD) as 'an activist organisation that operates beyond the purview of the Deans' fellow academics'.[109] Elsewhere he calls CALD a 'cloistered company' and a 'cosy cartel'.[110] Perhaps only the sorry souls who have endured a CALD meeting will appreciate how ludicrous this is.

6 *Law schools*

Thornton uses exaggeration rhetorically: 'Like breakfast foods, McDonaldisation decrees that the educational "product" sold be basically the same, but with a minor variation in taste or appearance that can be stressed in order to secure a market edge'.[111] She warns that 'Law schools are in danger of becoming pale carbon copies of each other as they slough off any academic distinctiveness they might have developed'.[112] Are Australian law schools really all the same? At one level, of course they are, but only in the sense that all football teams have 11 players and try to kick the ball into the opponents' net more often that the opponents kick it into theirs. At anything than a superficial level, the differences are significant. One of the reasons that it is laughable to portray CALD as a sophisticated cartel is that, for example, Charles Darwin, Melbourne, Sunshine Coast and UTS Law Schools have so little in common.

Thornton and Carrigan are similar in presenting a picture of Australian legal academics as passive victims of their 'neo-liberal' fate. James provides some Foucaultian excess (without, of course, suggesting that he disapproves of what he describes): 'Panoptic power achieves . . . the transformation of members of the law school into self-regulating, self-disciplining and self-motivating docile bodies'.[113] Many adjectives could be used to describe my colleagues at UNSW, but 'docile' is not one of them. To object by saying that academics have agency is true, but the academic term undersells their vitality and commitment, as well as 'the possibilities of individual and collective *resistance*'.[114] My colleagues are people who are passionate about their work, progressive, and highly resistant to poor management. Thornton's claims that 'the communal life of the law school has withered'[115] and that '[r]espect for learning and the pursuit of knowledge for its own sake have disappeared'[116] do not match my experience. She mistakes the sizzle for the sausage or, as Cownie and Bradney put it more gracefully, she treats 'corporatizing tendencies . . . as achieved aims'.[117]

Second, there is much to admire and to be proud about in Australian law schools. There are distinctive Australian approaches: as Phillips argued against the cultural cringe which so often affects Australia, we need more 'progress in the art of being unselfconsciously ourselves'.[118] Notable features of Australian legal education include the quality of students and of academic and professional staff; teaching methods; combined degrees; clinical legal education; interdisciplinary research; experiential learning; international awareness; and engagement in reform. Ironically, the articles by Carrigan and by Thornton and Shannon which were criticised above are published in a volume of the *Legal Education Review* which showcases a range of interesting, innovative, challenging work, including articles on teaching ethics in a developing country, on restructuring criminal law teaching around Indigenous perspectives, on e-learning and on critical thinking in legal education. There is real strength in depth: there are some excellent law schools outside the Group of Eight. Collier's comment on the reality of United Kingdom law schools can also apply to those in Australia:

> [F]ar from being marginalized, socio-legal research has become embedded and well-established within legal research and teaching . . . (if not, indeed, the new orthodoxy itself). Far from seeing a re-visioning of commitments and aspirations of legal academics as aligned to the imperatives of the new economy, what the majority university law students . . . study in, and what legal scholars teach and research in is a 'liberal law school'; an organization marked by methodological and epistemological diversity; a commitment to a distinctive academic (as opposed to vocational) stage of legal education; a less deferential relation to the legal profession and legal hierarchy compared to the past; and . . . by an institutional acceptance of original, often interdisciplinary, legal research. Further, contextual, socio-legal, critical 'essentially academic' subjects abound (and moreover prove popular with students.[119]

UNSW is one example of quality and diversity in Australian legal education. Crucial to the vision of Hal Wootten and the others who built UNSW Law was the idea of the lawyer as a professional dedicated not primarily to the accumulation of personal wealth but to service to the community.[120] Such legal service should be structured around commitments to basic principles of justice and the rule of law. The direct and strong implication of this is that lawyers should serve all sections of the community (and that law students should be taught how to do so). This involved no downgrading of lawyers' traditional commitment to serving business, corporations and government. It does mean that such commitment (a) includes high ethical, professional standards and (b) should be extended to serving the rest of society: those excluded from using the law and those who usually have the law used against them. In the entrance hall of the UNSW Law Building, a banner carries Hal Wootten's words: 'A Law School should have and communicate to its students a keen concern for those on whom the law bears harshly'. These are people who, in Brown's words, 'experienced law not as a guarantor of freedom but as an engine of dispossession, a source of bewilderment and a bearer of tribulation'.[121]

E We're doomed[122]

So what do the pessimists recommend? Having argued that reform serves to entrench the status quo, their options are limited. Logically, one might expect them to resign from these appalling institutions and go off to do something more useful. Why don't they

> slough off the constraints of the corporatized academy altogether by reinventing themselves as independent legal scholars, rather than be made anaemic by an involuntary transfusion of their intellectual energy by a line manager desperately seeking to prop up the university's latest marketing venture?[123]

But of course that would mean giving up a tenured position and a comfortable salary, so Thornton's book ends with a call to keep on fighting, which brings to mind Monty Python's Black Knight.[124]

She tells us that 'the revolution in the university . . . has swept the ground from beneath our feet' and 'it is not easy to see a way out of the abyss'. Nonetheless, 'we must not languish in apathy and despair': it is 'essential that we do not give up . . . we must cling valiantly to the idea of a university legal education as a public good . . . as a few radical thinkers have sought to do'. So, what do we do? Apparently, it is 'too late' for 'taking to the streets'. What then? 'We owe it to our students and the next generation to do what we can by at least having a conversation about what has become ineffable'.[125] I do not know how one has a conversation about something that is 'too great or extreme to be expressed or described in words', but then neither, I think, does Margaret Thornton.

Can we do better? Are there some reasons to be cheerful or does the slough of despond really beckon?

III Reasons to be cheerful[126]

I am not one of those pragmatists in a suit, telling academics to cowboy up and face 'the real world', whom Collini satirises so well.[127] On the contrary, many trends in universities appal me and it would be foolish to understate the constraints on Australian law schools. Some of these are identified by the pessimists: it is their analysis and diagnosis which is deficient. The policing scholars who decried 'the false promises of liberal legalism' painted themselves into a corner of negativity. Similarly, Thornton, Carrigan and James offer nothing but critique and resignation to what Gough Whitlam dismissed as 'a philosophy of failure which finds in defeat a form of justification and a proof of the purity of our principles. Certainly, the impotent are pure'. Those who stand back and sneer enjoy the 'luxury of irresponsibles'.[128] Alternatives are available and inaction is not necessary. For example, as suggested above, over the last decade, UNSW Law has progressed in unlikely circumstances – a commercially focused university leadership, STEM hegemony and financial constraints. Despite all this, we achieved what we did because of the commitment of academics, professional staff and students to contest and to innovate, not to wring hands and declare that we are doomed.

A guide to a positive response has three elements. First, we can again take lessons from criminal justice on the limits of pessimism and of opposition to 'reformism'. In any commitment to reform, we have to be aware of the dangers of deflection, co-optation and legitimization, but equally we should not consider the success/failure of specific reforms in isolation:

> [t]he point is that such developments have a multitude of effects . . . And further that these effects are not fixed once and for all but are the subject of continuing struggles which seek to overturn, subvert or bypass a particular balance of forces . . . which in turn generate fresh struggles.

This means accepting 'a conception of reform as partial, limited, continual struggle'.[129]

Second, we need to articulate and defend the ideas of a university as committed to knowledge through research and teaching and of a law school's place in such a university. While universities have changed and will continue to do so, they have an essence, which is to be 'organizations for the maintenance, extension and transmission of intellectual inquiry'.[130] Creating other social impacts and economic benefits are secondary outcomes of the distinctive nature of the university as an institution: 'Universities have to be partly-protected spaces in which the extension and deepening of human understanding has priority over any more practical purpose, no matter how politically or economically desirable such practical purposes might be'.[131] Here I repeat that experiential learning is not crass instrumentalism: it is about *understanding* law in a way that exclusively doctrinal or theoretical inquiry cannot. As for law schools, I have argued above against their under-estimation. We need to be more confident in addressing not only our managers but also external stakeholders. As noted above, it is simply wrong to assume that the profession is uniformly antagonistic towards progressive law schools.

Third, we need to specify threats and avoid unhelpful slogans which accumulate problems so that they seem unsurmountable. In policing in the 1980s, a reference to 'Thatcherism' was self-explanatory condemnation which elided inconsistencies and contradictions in law and policy.[132] In the university context, the equivalent is use of the term 'neo-liberalism': its universal applicability is indicated by its appearance 80 times in Thornton's index. As Frew shows, neo-liberalism's explanatory power is largely illusory because of indiscriminate overuse: 'neo-liberalism' encompasses several different strategies and dispositions.[133] I would suggest that what is packaged as 'neo-liberalism' in the university context needs to be broken down into three elements: market commercialism; managerialism and inappropriate regulation; and STEM hegemony. Only the first of these has much connection with the economic core of 'neo-liberalism'. Market economics and managerialism do not necessarily go together, as is illustrated by the fact that UNSW's previous Vice Chancellor, Fred Hilmer, whose name is associated with competition policy, led the successful campaign against the worst excesses of Tertiary Education Quality and Standards Agency regulation.[134]

A Market commercialism

Public funding is tight and getting tighter. Australia lacks the tradition of philanthropy which supports leading law schools in the United States. Consequently, we are pushed to take in too many, particularly too many international, students. The international diversity of student cohorts is one of the joys of university life, but taking unlimited numbers in attempts to win favour as an export industry is good neither for them nor the universities. Commercialism is a hard target because it is so entrenched in modern society. However, it can be challenged. A fine example is the lone campaign by Stephen Parker (then Vice Chancellor of the University of Canberra) against deregulation of student fees.[135] This was at considerable personal cost: other vice chancellors derided him. Parker won the argument, providing an example of how public support for funding universities can be mobilised if their public purpose is demonstrated.

B Managerialism and metrics

We carry a heavy burden of performance assessment by metrics, managerialist excess, and university, state professional regulation. As regards metrics, there is room for optimism that the 'logic of punitive quantification'[136] with its 'metric fixation'[137] is a fad which has had its day: there is increasing recognition of its limits, failings and counterproductive effects.[138] As Collini insists, 'what is most distinctive, and perhaps distinctively valuable, about what universities do is precisely what cannot be captured by the metrics societies increasingly use to measure value'.[139] When the problems of metrics are acknowledged, they are defended as 'proxies', but such 'proxies might be glossed as "largely irrelevant indicators"'.[140] Far from helping, 'the all-devouring audit culture . . . has so signally contributed to making universities less efficient places in which to think and teach'.[141] Perhaps the most meaningless metric gets most attention – the international rankings. While vice chancellors continue to be obsessed with them, anyone with half an ounce of sense (including them) knows that these largely worthless, 'vacuous exercises'[142] are 'chiefly a guide to the level of expenditure on big science, not to the quality of the education universities provide, and certainly not to how well they serve the culture of their host country'.[143] The faddish nature of metrics is illustrated by the current shift in emphasis from quantity to quality: vice chancellors who so recently were insisting that we publish more now say we should publish less. . . . The other current obsession is 'impact', definitively satirised by Collini.[144] The only advice which can be given with integrity to a junior colleague is to publish their work where and how they think is most appropriate.

The bureaucratisation of teaching via demands for course learning outcomes, graduate attributes and others is almost beyond parody.[145] At university level, if you can specify in this way what students will learn from your class, it's probably not worth teaching. Good teachers inspire and challenge in ways that a turgid list of Course Learning Outcomes (CLOs) cannot predict: there is a distinction worth maintaining between teaching and putting sausage meat into sausage skins. Not doing so 'represents a failure of nerve. It is an attempt to justify an activity not in its own appropriate terms, but in terms derived from another set of categories altogether'.[146] Shaw's cruel aphorism needs to be rephrased: those who can't, don't teach, they invent course learning outcomes.

Managerialism seeks to centralise power and control: 'We talk of managerialism when procedures, values and interests of those charged with running an institution take priority over the purposes for which it is supposedly being run'.[147] A key tactic is replacing recognised faculties, schools and departments with a combination of mega-faculties and thematic, problem-centred units and initiatives. Here, what should be the welcome encouragement of interdisciplinarity is used as a Trojan horse to challenge the status of academics, schools and faculties.[148] 'The recent mania . . . for abolishing departments . . . is driven by a particular kind of managerialist dogma . . . The result is to break down the ties that bind colleagues to a discipline and a shared professional experience'.[149] Australian law schools face the continuing threat of being soaked up by business schools: only someone who either has not bothered to find out what law schools do or is antagonistic to them (or both) would think this is appropriate. In fighting this battle, we should remind chancelleries that, in the Ivy League universities which they want us to mimic, a distinctive feature is the strength of the academic faculty and the independence of schools.[150]

C *STEM hegemony*

Within universities, legal academics have to constantly defend our academic standing and methods in a context where the biological, physical and medical sciences rule. Knowing your enemy is important here, and it is not STEM colleagues generally. Most leading scientists 'acknowledge the shared character of intellectual inquiry' and know that the quality of research does not depend on how expensive it is to conduct. They appreciate that

> work in the humanities is . . . in many ways not so different from work in the natural and social sciences. The effort to understand and explain that is at the heart of all scholarly and scientific inquiry and is governed by broadly similar canons of accuracy and precision, of rigour in argument and clarity in presentation, of respect for the evidence and openness to criticism, and so on.[151]

The threat usually comes from those who 'feel some kind of cultural insecurity about their identities as scientists or among those who administer science rather than doing it'.[152] In dealing with them, there is no alternative to the repetitive explanation of what we do, why it is valuable and why assessment by STEM criteria is inappropriate. We should however be less defensive: it is time that we pointed out that some of the authorship and grant-claiming practices which are common in some STEM disciplines would be regarded as disreputable in the humanities and social sciences.

These three dragons are obviously related – for example, STEM is able to use metrics to demonstrate economic contribution and to meet KPIs. However it is better to try to kill them one by one (or more realistically train them to play nicely) than to bow down to a massive fictional creature called neo-liberalism.

IV Keep calm and carry on

Perhaps I'm wrong and Private Frazer and the pessimists are right, that we are doomed, or, in a more fashionable reference, that we have all become neoliberal zombies.[153] There are certainly reasons not to be cheerful: universities appear increasingly to be run by consultants, those new masters of the universe who have metamorphosed from accountants to experts on everything, but who seem often to lack knowledge about either academic work or running a business. Zombification is an irrefutable argument: you can't deny being a zombie any more than you can deny being inside the whale or suffering from false consciousness.[154]

I reject these arguments as an intellectual version of Penrose stairs, leading nowhere. Naïve empiricist I may be, but when I look around, I don't see zombies. My first year class has just reported on a project identifying lawyers they admire: their subjects included Shirin Abadi, Nasrin Sotoudeh, Beverley McLachlin, Tang Shuai, Ruth Bader Ginsburg, Menaka Guruswamy, and Haben Girma. No one mentioned Brett Kavanaugh. Later today, I'm going to the launch of a special issue of our students' social justice journal, *Court of Conscience*. It focuses on Redfern, a place with which UNSW Law has renewed connections through our Police Powers Clinic at Redfern Legal Centre. Later this month, I'll attend the graduation of our 100th Indigenous student and the award of the fifth PhD to Palestinian students in a program helping to develop Palestine's law schools. My colleagues are publishing brilliant theoretical, doctrinal and empirical research. The success of neo-liberalism as a hegemonic project is limited: I see no evidence that they have internalised its values. Rather, they (to summon a final English cliché) keep calm and carry on. So while the pessimists identify some real problems, they misdiagnose them, thereby discrediting critical positions and perversely strengthening what they oppose.

Notes

* Many colleagues have generously commented on earlier drafts, including Justine Rogers, Cathy Sherry, Brendan Edgeworth, Andrew Lynch, Martin Krygier

and Ben Golder. Demonstrating my commitment to technologically enriched teaching, the original presentation of this chapter was accompanied by visual material. Links are provided at appropriate points below, giving readers a taste of the experience while disclosing my age and national origin. All sites last visited on 1 April 2018.

1 Margaret Thornton, *Privatising the Public University: The Case of Law* (London, Taylor & Francis 2012). See also Margaret Thornton, 'Gothic Horror in the Legal Academy' (2005) 14 *Social & Legal Studies* 267–76; Margaret Thornton, 'Legal Education in the Corporate University' (2014) 10 *Annual Review of Law & Social Science* 19–35 and other papers noted below.

2 Frank Carrigan, 'They Make a Desert and Call It Peace' (2013) 23 *Legal Education Review* 313–43. I would follow advice from colleagues simply to ignore Carrigan's diatribe if it had not been published in a respectable journal, Australia's *Legal Education Review*, leading it to be cited as if it is reliable in, for example, a sober, revisionist account of Australian legal education: see Susan Bartie, 'Towards a History of Law as an Academic Discipline' (2014) 38 *Melbourne University Law Review* 442–81, 451.

3 Nickolas J. James, 'Power-Knowledge in Australian Legal Education: Corporatism's Reign' (2004) 26 *Sydney Law Review* 587–612; Nickolas J. James, 'The Marginalisation of Radical Discourses in Australian Legal Education' (2006) 16 *Legal Education Review* 55–74.

4 Michael McConville, Andrew Sanders and Roger Leng, *The Case for the Prosecution* (London, Routledge 1991).

5 David Dixon, *Law in Policing: Legal Regulation and Police Practices* (Oxford, Clarendon 1997); David Dixon, 'Legal Regulation and Policing Practice' (1992) 1 *Social & Legal Studies* 515–41.

6 McConville and others (n. 4) 208 (emphasis in original).

7 Ibid., 191.

8 Margaret Thornton and Lucinda Shannon, '"Selling the Dream": Law School Branding and the Illusion of Choice' (2013) 23 *Legal Education Review* 249–71 at 269.

9 Thornton, *Privatising the Public University: The Case of Law* (n. 1) 59.

10 Ibid., 224.

11 Ibid., 62.

12 Thornton and Shannon (n. 8) 269.

13 Thornton, *Privatising the Public University: The Case of Law* (n. 1) 63.

14 Margaret Thornton, 'The Demise of Diversity in Legal Education: Globalisation and the New Knowledge Economy' (2001) 8 *International Journal of the Legal Profession* 37–56, 37.

15 Thornton, *Privatising the Public University: The Case of Law* (n. 1) 63 (emphasis added).

16 Ibid., 72.

17 Carrigan (n. 2) 343.

18 Thornton, *Privatising the Public University: The Case of Law* (n 1) 12.

19 Carrigan (n. 2) 313.

20 See Gill H. Boehringer and others, 'Historical Documents' (1988) 5 *Australian Journal of Law and Society* 51–132; Michael Chesterman and David Weisbrot, 'Legal Scholarship in Australia' (1987) 50 *Modern Law Review* 709–24.

21 Thornton, 'Legal Education in the Corporate University' (n. 1) 26.

22 Thornton, *Privatising the Public University: The Case of Law* (n. 1) 113.

23 Ibid., 17, 135.

24 Ibid., 186.

25 Ibid., 86.

26 James, 'Power-Knowledge in Australian Legal Education' (n. 3) 593.
27 James claims that his account is non-evaluative in James, 'Power-Knowledge in Australian Legal Education' (n. 3) 588, but this is unconvincing, although convenient given that he is currently 'Executive Dean' of a private law school which claims to be 'defining what is best in professional and skills based legal education': <https://bond.edu.au/about-bond/academia/faculty-law>.
28 James, 'Power-Knowledge in Australian Legal Education' (n. 3) 593.
29 Ibid., 597.
30 Stefan Collini, *Speaking of Universities* (London, Verso 2017) 36.
31 Thornton, *Privatising the Public University: The Case of Law* (n. 1) 186.
32 See Stegan Collini, *What Are Universities For?* (London, Penguin 2012) 78–79, 122; Kathy Bowrey, 'Audit Culture: Why Law Journals are Ranked and What Impact This Has on the Discipline of Law Today' (2013) 23 *Legal Education Review* 291–312.
33 Thornton and Shannon (n. 8) 251.
34 Ibid., 270.
35 Thornton, *Privatising the Public University: The Case of Law* (n. 1) 2.
36 James, 'The Marginalisation' (n 3) 66.
37 Ibid., 170.
38 Ibid., 86.
39 Ibid., 113.
40 George Orwell, 'Politics and the English Language' (1946) in Orwell, *Shooting an Elephant and Other Essays* (Harmondsworth: Penguin 2009) 358–75.
41 E. P. Thompson, 'The Business University' (1970) *New Society* reprinted in Thompson, *Writing by Candlelight* (London, Merlin 1980) 13–27.
42 Thornton, *Privatising the Public University: The Case of Law* (n. 1) 16.
43 Ibid., 16, 17; Collini, *What Are Universities For?* (n. 32).
44 Critique of Law Editorial Collective, *Critique of Law: A Marxist Analysis* (UNSW Critique of Law Society 1978), reprinted in Boehringer (n. 20) 85–88. An example from the policing literature: 'Crime control ideology . . . is a product of capitalism's requirement of a strong state': McConville and others (n. 4) 182.
45 Critique of Law Editorial Collective (n. 44) 84–85.
46 For a rather different account of its significance, see Andrea Durbach, Brendan Edgeworth and Victoria Sentas (eds), *Law and Poverty in Australia: 40 Years after the Poverty Commission* (Sydney, Federation 2017).
47 Critique of Law Editorial Collective (n. 44) 85.
48 Carrigan (n. 2) 319.
49 Thornton, *Privatising the Public University: The Case of Law* (n. 1) 107.
50 Ibid., 113–14.
51 Ibid., 72. Note the smug 'of course' here and in the previous quotation.
52 Ibid., 76.
53 Carrigan (n. 2) 320.
54 Thornton, *Privatising the Public University: The Case of Law* (n. 1) 195.
55 Margaret Thornton, 'Women and Legal Hierarchy' (1989) 1 *Legal Education Review* 97–100, 99.
56 See <www.law.unsw.edu.au/staff>.
57 James, 'The Marginalisation' (n. 3) 67.
58 See <www.law.unsw.edu.au/future-students/indigenous-entry>.
59 James, 'The Marginalisation' (n. 3) 67.
60 Thornton, *Privatising the Public University: The Case of Law* (n. 1) 35, also 201.
61 Thornton and Shannon (n. 8) 262.
62 See Frank S. Bloch (ed.), *The Global Clinical Movement Educating Lawyers for Social Justice* (Oxford, Oxford University Press 2010); Adrian Evans and others ed., *Australian Clinical Legal Education* (Canberra, ANU Press 2017).

63 Thornton, *Privatising the Public University: The Case of Law* (n. 1) 34, 35.
64 See Matt Lacey, 'Gap Yah' <www.youtube.com/watch?v=eKFjWR7X5dU>.
65 Thornton and Shannon (n. 8) 266, 268.
66 Ibid., 268.
67 See <www.law.unsw.edu.au/student-profiles/graduate-profile-3>.
68 Thornton and Shannon (n. 8) 268.
69 H. Morris, 'Review of Thornton' (*Times Higher Education Supplement*, 23 February 2012).
70 Carrigan (n. 2) 314.
71 Brian Kelsey, 'What's Wrong with the Law School?' (1978) in Boehringer (n. 20) 81–84.
72 Carrigan (n. 2) 321.
73 Ibid.
74 UNSW Law, *Curriculum Review: Designing an International, Experiential, Research-Focused Curriculum for a C21 Law School* (UNSW Law 2013).
75 See his contemptible performance on *A Current Affair* <www.youtube.com/watch?v=7hZz1-lKuTk> and his books, *The WASP Question* (Budapest, Arktos 2011) and *Dissident Dispatches: An Alt-right Guide to Christian Theology* (Budapest, Arktos 2017).
76 Carrigan (n. 2) 325.
77 Gill Boehringer, 'Infamy at Macquarie: Economic Rationalism and the New McCarthyism' (1999) 24 *Alternative Law Journal* 30, 32.
78 In *Carry on Cleo*: see <www.youtube.com/watch?v=kvs4bOMv5Xw>.
79 Thornton, *Privatising the Public University: The Case of Law* (n. 1), 38.
80 Ibid., 70, 167; see also James, 'Power-Knowledge in Australian Legal Education' (n. 3) 601.
81 Thornton, *Privatising the Public University: The Case of Law* (n. 1) 50.
82 Ibid., 52, 54.
83 Ibid., 55–56.
84 See Collini, *What Are Universities For?* (n. 32) ch. 5.
85 See <www.kaldorcentre.unsw.edu.au/>.
86 See <www.law.unsw.edu.au/alumni-community/ngoc-tram-nguyen-scholarship>.
87 Sumption, who did not read law at university, was referring to England.
88 Frank Carrigan, 'Law Schools Sell Graduates Down the River' (*Australian Financial Review*, 8 August 2016).
89 See Caroline Evans' reply: 'Law School Is Still the Best Bet for a Graduate Job That Pays Well' (*Australian Financial Review*, 11 August 2016).
90 Quoted in ANU Law School Reform Committee, *Breaking the Frozen Sea* (ANU 2010) 11 <https://trove.nla.gov.au/work/180620822?q&versionId=196650922>.
91 Personal communication.
92 Thornton, *Privatising the Public University: The Case of Law* (n. 1) 70.
93 UNSW Law (n. 74).
94 See <www.law.unsw.edu.au/news/2014/10/unsw-law-curriculum-review>.
95 Thornton, *Privatising the Public University: The Case of Law* (n. 1) 100.
96 Carrigan (n. 2) 342.
97 Thornton, *Privatising the Public University: The Case of Law* (n. 1) 42, 67.
98 Collini, *Speaking of Universities* (n. 30) 33.
99 ANU Law School Reform Committee (n. 90).
100 Carrigan (n. 2) 323.
101 See their crowd-funding for the Ngoc Tram Nguyen Scholarship at <www.pozible.com/project/174604> and their documentary, Yindyamarra at <www.youtube.com/watch?v=KvsvigEUkX8> and <https://newsroom.unsw.edu.au/yindyamarra-%E2%80%93-search-respect-wiradjuri-country>.

102 Thornton, *Privatising the Public University: The Case of* Law (n. 1) 17.
103 Ibid., 138.
104 Margaret Thornton, 'Law as Business in the Corporatised University' (2000) 25 *Alternative Law Journal* 269–73, 270.
105 Thornton, *Privatising the Public University: The Case of Law* (n. 1) 124–31.
106 Ibid., 128.
107 Collini, *What Are Universities For?* (n. 32) 161.
108 Collini, *Speaking of Universities* (n. 30) 45.
109 Carrigan (n. 2) 341.
110 Carrigan (n. 88).
111 Thornton, *Privatising the Public University: The Case of Law* (n. 1) 43.
112 Thornton (n. 104) 269. See also Thornton (n. 14).
113 James, 'Power-Knowledge in Australian Legal Education' (n. 3) 608.
114 Richard Collier, 'Privatizing the University and the New Political Economy of Socio-legal Studies' (2013) 40 *Journal of Law and Society* 450–67, 463 (emphasis added).
115 Thornton, *Privatising the Public University: The Case of Law* (n. 1) 214.
116 Thornton, 'Gothic Horror in the Legal Academy' (n. 1) 272.
117 Fiona Cownie and Anthony Bradney, 'Gothic Horror?' (2005) 14 *Social & Legal Studies* 277–85, 278.
118 Arthur Angell Phillips, 'The Cultural Cringe' (1950) in Phillips, *AA Phillips on the Cultural Cringe* (Carlton: Melbourne University Press 2006) 1–9, 9.
119 Collier (n. 114) 463–4.
120 Hal Wootten, 'Living in the Law' (2009) 31 *University of New South Wales Law Journal* 198–212.
121 D. B. Brown, *Address to the 30th Anniversary Dinner* (UNSW Law, unpublished 2011) 5.
122 Private Frazer in *Dad's Army* <www.youtube.com/watch?v=sxqvwkmTNy8>.
123 Thornton, 'Gothic Horror in the Legal Academy' (n. 1) 273.
124 See <www.youtube.com/watch?v=ZmInkxbvlCs>.
125 Thornton, *Privatising the Public University: The Case of Law* (n. 1) 228.
126 Ian Dury, <www.youtube.com/watch?v=9RMQSUBk5kg>. More conventionally, a sustained, empirically based case against pessimism is made by Steven Pinker, *Enlightenment Now: The Case for Reason, Science, Humanism and Progress* (London, Allen Lane 2018).
127 Collini, *What Are Universities For?* (n. 32) 145.
128 Speech to the Victorian Labor Party, June 1967 <http://whitlamdismissal.com/1967/06/09/the-impotent-are-pure-speech.html>; <www.whitlam.org/collection/>.
129 David Brown, 'The Politics of Reform' in George Zdenkowski, Chris Ronalds and Mark Richardson (eds), *The Criminal Injustice System* (Sydney, Pluto 1987) 254–81, 260, 267. See also David Brown, '"Losing my Religion": Reflections on Critical Criminology in Australia' in Russell Hogg and Kerry Carrington (eds), *Critical Criminology: Issues, Debates, Challenges* (Cullompton, Willan 2002) 73–113.
130 Collini, *What Are Universities For?* (n. 32) 147.
131 Collini, *Speaking of Universities* (n. 30) 58–59, see also 156 and Collini, *What Are Universities For?* (n. 32) 87–88.
132 Dixon, *Law in Policing* (n. 5).
133 Terry Flew, 'Six Theories of Neoliberalism' (2014) 122 *Thesis Eleven* 4–71; see also Collini, *Speaking of Universities* (n. 30) 37.
134 See <https://clmr.unsw.edu.au/article//the-regulatory-threat-to-australian-legal-education>.

135 See <https://theconversation.com/stephen-parker-higher-education-changes-a-fraud-on-the-electorate-34909>; see also Collini, *What Are Universities For?* (n. 32) ch. 10.
136 Collini, *Speaking of Universities* (n. 30) 151.
137 Jerry Muller, *The Tyranny of Metrics* (Princeton, Princeton University Press 2018) 17.
138 See Collini, *What Are Universities For?* (n. 32) ch. 6; Muller (n. 137). It's important to note that this is an argument against the *abuse* of quantification, not against quantification per se. Pinker brilliantly demonstrates the need accurately to count what can be counted and the perversity of dismissing all quantification as 'bean-counting': Pinker (n. 126) 139 and *passim.*
139 Collini, *What Are Universities For?* (n. 32) 25.
140 Collini, *Speaking of Universities* (n. 30) 165.
141 Collini, *What Are Universities For?* (n. 32) 33.
142 Ibid., 17.
143 Collini, *Speaking of Universities* (n. 30) 190.
144 Collini, *What Are Universities For?* (n. 32) ch. 9; Collini, *Speaking of Universities* (n. 30) 51.
145 However, for an educationalist on 'pupil teacher learning centres', see Chris Langham and John Morton, *The Head Teacher* <www.dailymotion.com/video/x3bj2bx>.
146 Collini, *What Are Universities For?* (n. 32) 144.
147 Collini, *Speaking of Universities* (n. 30) 46.
148 Ibid., 48.
149 Collini, *Speaking of Universities* (n. 30) 213. As Peter Burdon points out in this volume, there is nothing neoliberal about excessive governance.
150 Collini, *What Are Universities For?* (n. 32) 29; Collini, *Speaking of Universities* (n. 30) 29.
151 Collini, *What Are Universities For?* (n. 32) 62.
152 Ibid., 101.
153 Andrew Whelan, Ruth Walker and Christopher Moore (eds), *Zombies in the Academy: Living Death in Higher Education* (Bristol, Intellect 2013).
154 Or, as Peter Burdon suggests in this volume, think outside 'common sense' or a 'reality principle'.

5 Empirical legal education research in Australia

2000–2016

*Alex Steel**

I Introduction

Over the last two decades there has been a growing understanding in Australia that legal education can be improved and informed by empirical analysis of curriculum design, teaching approaches, student learning strategies and broader contextual factors. However many legal academics who wish to research in the area are unfamiliar with pre-existing studies or the appropriate methodologies.

As a result, it is timely to provide a systematic review of the existing literature. This chapter analyses such a review of 124 peer-reviewed Australian empirical legal research publications from 2000–2016. The aim is to provide a database that is as comprehensive a list as possible of empirically based studies into Australian legal education. In so doing, the project aims to encourage those seeking to innovate curriculum and teaching to begin by a review of previous work; provide an accessible scan of the areas in which research has already been undertaken, for those wishing to build on that research; and produce some understanding of the amount of such research being published; where that research is being published; and what areas are the most common sites for research. This chapter provides an overview of the scope of the publications collected.

II A systematic review?

There are a range of approaches to rigorous literature review: Grant and Booth have identified 14 types[1] ranging from overviews to comprehensive meta-analyses. This project aimed to produce a review of the literature similar to that described as a systematic review. Thus the aim was to capture as comprehensive a collection of publications as possible, using a replicable methodology, clear criteria for inclusion and exclusion, and to provide a basis for quantitative and qualitative analysis.[2] One such review into technology in legal education has been undertaken by Maharg and Nicol,[3] and a review by Greaves is in this collection. However, unlike the approach to reviews common in health sciences[4] this project did not seek to answer a specific research question. Instead the aim was to be descriptive of the research field. Consequently, no analysis of the quality of the research in each publication was attempted. As such the review instead reports on the breadth of researcher interest and publisher acceptance of work in the field.

III Significant omissions

One significant site of empirical research was omitted in this study: national competitively funded research projects. These reports contain significant and foundational research into legal education. However, the complexity of the projects, size of research teams, and scope of data could have distorted the sense of published research in the field. As a result, they are highlighted here at the outset. A full list of projects funded by the Australian government in the period[5] and accessible on the Commonwealth government repository are set out in Appendix 1.

Reports and resources for all these projects can be found on the Learning and Teaching Repository <https://ltr.edu.au/>. They deserve recognition as forming a fundamental basis for legal education research in Australia. It is unfortunate that the removal of government funding, disestablishment of websites, and the consequent relative difficulty of finding the reports via search engines has limited their impact.

One other area of research which is probably underrepresented are research monographs. Although a search was undertaken on both Google Books and Google Scholar, few monographs or essay collections were found. It is likely that there are a range of publications by smaller publishers that have not been captured in this project.

IV Scope of 'empirical legal education research'

For the purposes of creating this project, empirical legal education research was defined following the approach of Herbert Kritzer and Peter Cane as the 'systematic collection of information and its analysis according to some generally accepted method'.[6] Kritzer and Cane emphasise that while data can come from a range of sources, whether generated, observed or collated by the researcher, both the generation and analysis of the data should be systematic. Thus, in the context of generating the definition of empirical legal education publications the need for systematic analysis meant that some publications that might well fall within general definitions of research output were excluded. In particular, four categories of publication were removed.[7]

First, those articles which drew on the empirical research of others to make new contributions fell outside the definition of original empirical research. While their contributions can be significant, they do not add to the quantum of underlying primary data. Second, those papers that merely reported on teaching or assessment innovations in a single course – particularly when not placing the innovation within the larger literature to demonstrate the innovation – were considered not empirical. These case studies, while valuable, did not provide an evidence base with which to critically analyse the findings of the authors. Third, innovations where the only measure of success was an improvement in generic student evaluations were also excluded. Although these were based on an empirical finding, because there are a range of variables that impact on the experience of the student cohort, it was not possible to be certain that the teaching innovation had led to the change in rating.

Finally, an author's personal reflections based on their teaching experience, without objective data, were excluded. Although ultimately not appearing in publications in the time period, auto-ethnography presented an example of a methodology on the cusp of empirical research that might arguably be accepted in the future as an empirical research method.[8]

Publications from the vigorous field of socio-legal analysis of law schools and the modern university[9] were also excluded from this project. Governments and universities clearly have a direct impact on the conditions under which law teachers work, the way they teach and how students are taught. Such studies are critical in explicating the underlying philosophies of teaching and learning, but it was felt they were best seen as a separate field of research given their broader focus on national environments. Some review of this field is contained in the chapter by Burdon in this volume.

As mentioned previously, this analysis did not attempt to set any minimum standards for the rigour of analysis. The rise of the Scholarship of Learning and Teaching[10] movement, and the increasing incidence of teaching-focused roles in academia[11] raises the question of how rigorous an analysis is required for a paper to be properly seen as empirical research. Scholarship of Teaching and Learning (SoTL) emphasises a range of approaches to knowledge that can be broader than traditionally accepted in science-oriented empirical research.[12] One finding of this project was that in the main any analysis of findings in publications was at a descriptive level. The use of statistical models or advanced qualitative methods was rare, as discussed below. However, acceptance of lack of any form of statistical analysis may be in decline and more rigorous explanation of data sources and interpretation is likely to be required in the future. For further discussion see the chapters by Greaves and Galloway et al. in this volume.

V Methods

An initial list of publications was compiled by key word full text searches of academic databases.

Searches were conducted in the following databases using the following terms:

- Austlii – Australian Law Journals – (search: 'law students' AND 'legal education' AND analysis AND findings AND results AND (survey OR interview OR 'focus group')).
- Taylor and Francis online journal database – (search: Australia AND 'law students' AND 'legal education' AND analysis AND findings AND results AND (survey OR interview OR 'focus group')).

- SpringerLink online journal database – (search: Australia AND 'law students' AND 'legal education' AND analysis AND findings AND results AND (survey OR interview OR 'focus group')).
- SSRN – LRN (Social Sciences Research Network – Legal Research Network) Legal Education eJournal (search: Australia AND students)
- Google Scholar – (search: Australia AND 'law students' AND 'legal education' AND analysis AND findings AND results AND (survey OR interview OR 'focus group')).
- Google Books – (search: Australia AND 'law students' AND 'legal education' AND analysis AND findings AND results AND (survey OR interview OR 'focus group').

All databases were searched with a variant of the search terms: Australia AND 'law students' AND 'legal education' AND analysis AND findings AND results AND (survey OR interview OR 'focus group').

A small number of other publications were added on the basis of footnote references or the nominations by others. One limitation was that if the publication was not available for digital download, not all database fields could be completed.

Because an initial pilot of data collection had found few articles using the term 'empirical' or even 'qualitative' or 'quantitative', search terms were used that were proxies for the anticipated main research methods. The use of 'survey', 'interview' and 'focus group' thus created a clear bias in the publications identified. However, it was considered that the bias was mitigated by the likelihood that even if other research methods were used, at some point in the article the terms would be used, often in a literature review. It does, however, remain a limitation of the project.

From these search results a subset of publications that appeared to be based on empirical research were saved into the Zotero bibliographic software platform and further data was added from perusal of the publications. After removal of publications outside of the defined limits of the project, 124 publications remained.

This database was then transferred to Microsoft Excel and IBM SPSS software. The downloaded article data was then again reviewed to ensure consistency in field entries. Entries were assigned keywords corresponding to areas of research and research methods. Sample size, research location, research subjects, authors, year and publication outlet were also captured. These are discussed in detail below.

VI Research areas

All publications were assigned one or more research area keywords, and many were assigned multiple keywords. Keywords were developed in light of the articles reviewed, and then revised as trends emerged. After a period of time had elapsed after the initial coding, the entire process was repeated and keywords further revised.

The keyword areas that emerged from this process are described below. Each heading was captured as separate keyword. Some initial keywords appeared infrequently and so they were subsumed into larger groups, and appear here as subheadings:

- Assessment – discussion of any form of law school assessment, summative or formative.
  - Feedback – any form of giving feedback to students about their learning.
  - Academic Integrity – plagiarism and other forms of student misconduct.
- Clinical Legal Education and Practical Legal Training – clinics, clinical components in doctrinal subjects, internships, professional legal training post degree.
- Curriculum – papers that discuss issues across multiple subjects, or a whole curriculum strategy.
  - Interdisciplinarity – examination of learning across disciplines – both across law doctrines, and across non-law and law areas.
  - Internationalisation – analysis of how curricula deal with international perspectives to law.
- Law Teachers – analysis of the circumstances and attitudes of those teaching law students.
- Student Groups:
  - Graduates – analysis of students at or post-graduation.
  - Indigenous Students – subset of Equity and Diversity, counted separately.
  - International Students – examination of the experience of international students, and efforts to internationalise curriculum to include them.
  - Regional and Rural Students.
  - Equity and Diversity – examination of how different groups of students are impacted by legal education, particularly minority groups, how such groups can be helped.
- Pedagogy – analysis of teaching methods, primarily face-to-face.
- Blended/Online/Technology – analysis of any electronic teaching tool, online element to a course or wholly online course – also including traditional distance education approaches.
- Student Reflection and Soft Skills – analysis of student development of self-reflection and interpersonal skills.
- Student Practical Skills:
  - Collaboration – class participation, group work, collaborative activities.
  - Critical Thinking – papers focusing on development of critical thinking as distinct from research or writing.
  - Professionalism – includes professional attitudes and self-management.
  - Reading Skills/Writing Skills – analysis of development of core lawyer skills and their teaching.

- Legal Practice Skills – skills developed in a law degree that are seen to be practical and oriented to legal practice.
- Student Attitudes/Beliefs – analysis of approaches to learning, beliefs as to profession, student engagement, student voice.
- Student Ethics and Values – professional ethics, social justice values, law in broader contexts.
- Subject Areas – papers that focus on how to improve teaching a particular subject.
- Student Demographics – statistical analysis of student cohorts, where the paper has a descriptive aim, rather than demographics to support other argument (e.g. skills development).
- Student Learning Support – extra curricula assistance, specific interventions, mentoring.
- The First Year Experience (FYE).
- Wellbeing – analysis of student mental health, general wellbeing and emotional barriers to success.

This grouping of topics is not strictly logical, but instead reflects the research reported on. The default approach in the coding was to describe general areas of research despite individual foci within that area. A good example is Student Practical Skills, which contained a range of topics, largely discussed separately but where no one area tended to dominate. However, if a general description did not capture a particularly high concentration of research, that small focus was given its own category. Thus in addition to the general area of Student Learning Support, the particular areas of the First Year Experience and Wellbeing were elevated to their own research areas because of the interest in each.

Figure 5.1 sets out the frequency with which the topics were empirically researched in the period. The figure sets out the numbers for a combined group if individual keywords occurred infrequently.

One significant caveat to this data should be mentioned. This data significantly overcounts the number of articles (there are 246 topics for 124 articles). Some articles contained a large number of topics, and some only one. Significantly, wellbeing articles tended to only be about wellbeing.

Student wellbeing emerges as the most significant area of publication. This is unsurprising as student emotional distress becomes recognised as a significant issue. What is significant is the way in which student wellbeing has emerged as an issue largely due to large-scale empirical work. While some areas of legal education might be seen as 'common sense' or uncontroversial, the issue of student wellbeing has been the subject of sustained critique – including questions over whether international findings are applicable to Australia and whether the Australian studies have been sufficiently rigorous.[13] The sustained empirical work in this area could thus be said to be encouraged and deepened because of the critiques. Mental health is also an area squarely in the health sciences, and so it is also not surprising that health sciences methodologies have crossed into legal research. It is worth contemplating whether the broader field of legal

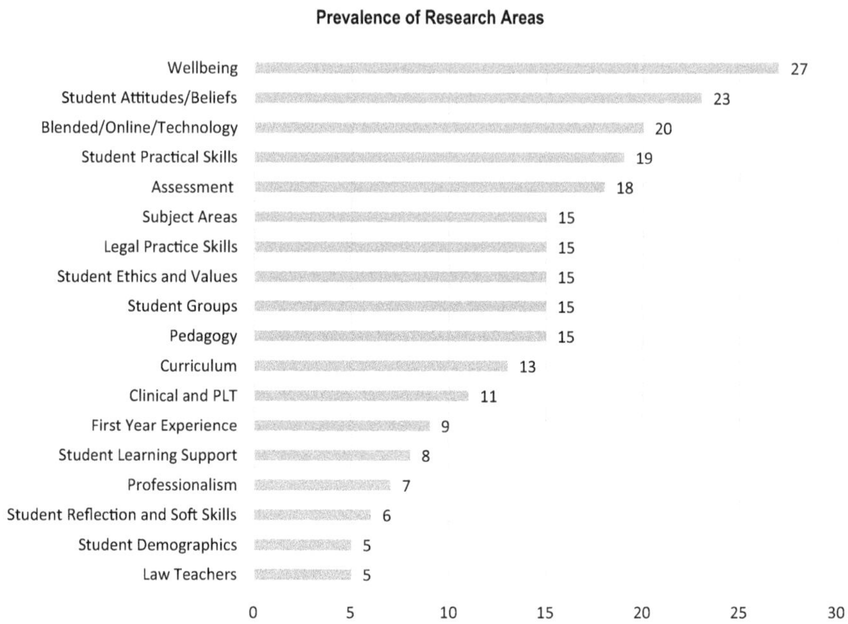

Figure 5.1 Prevalence of research areas

education research could be improved by a similarly critical analysis of the methods and application of findings.

The degree of change to legal education as a result of technological innovation is also reflected in the consistent rate of publications on the topic, as is the consistent interest in how students themselves see the key issues in legal education (for these purposes, beliefs as to wellbeing counted separately). Both of these issues are central to government and university strategic planning and so it is unsurprising that they are seen to be useful sites for empirical research.

All three areas largely emerge in the literature in 2008–2010 at a point that seems to coincide with the rate of empirical publications starting to consistently rise, as discussed below.

One cautionary note that should be sounded about these results is the fact that in a few instances an underlying study gave rise to multiple publications examining different facets of the research findings. One example is the study of law student ethics undertaken by Adrian Evans and others that constitute four of the 12 publications on ethics and values. The size of that longitudinal study (n = 700) lent itself to multiple publications. There is much to be said for well-constructed surveys that provide this depth of data and allow for the data to be used to examine a range of questions.

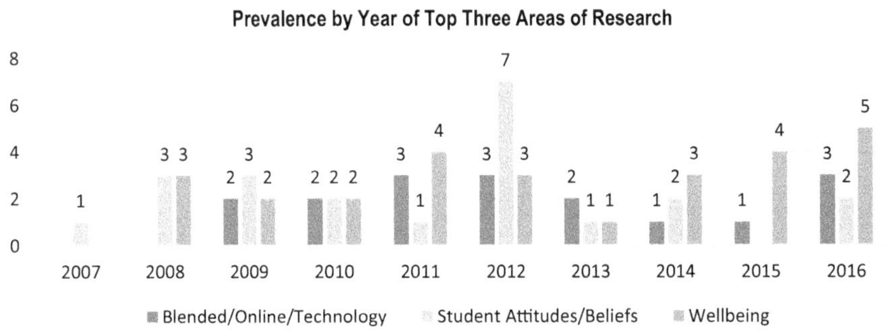

Figure 5.2 Prevalence by year of top three research areas

Note: There are no publications in these areas prior to 2007.

VII Research methods

The publications were also examined to determine the form of empirical research that had been undertaken. There is a potential bias in the data collection for this project in that the search terms 'survey', 'interview' and 'focus group' were used. For this project the research methodologies were coded as follows:

- Surveys – this included both quantitative and qualitative surveys, and combinations of both. It included both paper and online surveys.
- Focus Groups – small groups, sometimes called roundtables, where a qualitative record was taken of facilitated discussions.
- Interviews – records of one-on-one conversations, whether based on structured questions or unstructured. Differentiated from focus groups by their individual nature.
- Case Study – analysis of experiences of individuals or courses not intended to be representative of broader experience. Included when combined with another method.
- Reflective Journals – written accounts of the subject's experiences of an event or course.
- Comparative – use of data from more than one source – often comparison of separate surveys, or qualitative experiences in different jurisdictions.
- Data Analysis – analysis of data not developed for the study, most typically analysis of documentation.
- Emails – analysis based on email correspondence with subjects, often unsolicited.
- Experimental – research where a control group, not part of the innovation is used to establish the innovation's effect.
- Observational – ethnographic research based on passive observation alone.

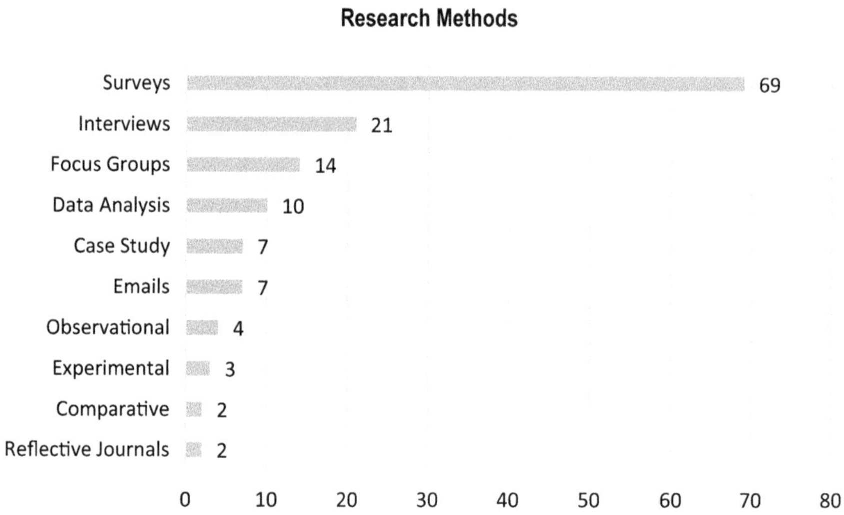

Figure 5.3 Research methods

There was a clear tendency in the publications to examine an issue via a survey, and one that contained both quantitative and qualitative data. This was typically quantitative demographic questions and qualitative questions answered on a Likert scale or via open text. Many publications also triangulated this survey data with analysis of qualitative small focus group discussions. The publications also displayed a wide variety of other empirical methods, though the extent to which those methods were justified and explained varied.

However, few articles analysed the data using statistical models or formulae. In the database only nine articles engaged in an extended use of statistical formulae to verify findings, and a further 33 made some reference to statistical tests.

To some extent this is not surprising. Much survey-based educational research uses samples which represent only small subsections of target populations. It is generally considered that a sample size of 30 is a bare minimum for statistical analysis, but that sample size is needed for each distribution of a variable (e.g. number of female international students in a survey of undergraduate students). As a result the overall number of survey responses often needs to be much larger.[14] As discussed below, many of the sample sizes were smaller than could be usefully analysed using statistical formulae.

In many cases, as in this chapter itself, descriptive statistics were sufficient to provide useable findings. However as the range of variables in the data increases, there is likely to be a need for more statistical analysis.

VIII Sample size

Not all publications recorded the size of their study. However, of the 82 per cent of those that did ($n = 107$), there was a strong preponderance of small sample sizes. In the period the largest groups studied related to wellbeing. The largest were studies of Melbourne University students ($n = 5{,}000$ respondents) and UNSW students ($n = 2{,}528$), but for both of these studies law students were only a small subset ($n = 357$ and $n = 213$, respectively). The Brain and Mind Research Institute's national survey on student and practitioner wellbeing ($n = 2{,}421$) was the largest law only sample followed by a survey of College of Law students ($n = 1{,}216$). Six separate studies were between 500 and 1,000 respondents (five publications reported on one Monash survey). A number of the studies with sample sizes between 100 and 500 also gave rise to multiple publications. This seemed to be due to the complexity of the data gathered and the consequent ability to report on different responses or different implications. Close to half of publications reporting sample size had samples smaller than 100 (47 per cent), and samples of fewer than 30 students were not uncommon (27 per cent).

The chart below demonstrates that range of sample sizes. A number of publications contained more than one set of research subjects. In this case we captured only the largest group of subjects (e.g. if there were ten staff interviewed and 30 students, the result recorded was 30).

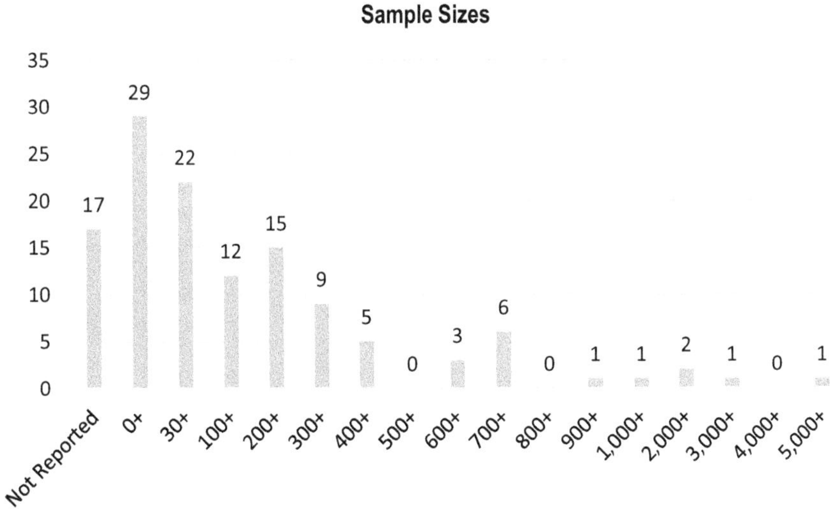

Figure 5.4 Sample sizes

IX Location of study

The project also captured the location of the research in each study. This is significant because the conditions under which students study can vary significantly from one law school to another, and from one city and town to another. Australia has approximately 40 law schools, yet research into legal education is not evenly spread across them. After removing duplicates for multiple publications based on one study, the data demonstrates that over the period studies have taken place in a large number of law schools. Yet there is a very small number of studies that attempted to be national in scope – these are predominantly concerning student wellbeing or interviews with academics.

As Figure 5.5 makes clear, overall more research is being conducted in larger urban law schools (with the notable exception of Newcastle University Law School). These schools attract students with the highest matriculation scores and are often also the wealthiest law schools. They also account for the home institution of many of the multiple site studies. This means that there may be a skew in the findings towards respondents situated in an environment most likely to be one of relative educational and financial privilege and higher levels of student support. Yet the patterns change when one looks at particular topics.

Wellbeing is largely being examined in large law schools and multiple school surveys, perhaps a reflection of the funding needed for the complexity of the studies. Student attitude-related studies have largely been concentrated in three law schools in two cities, and no law school has repeatedly examined the development of student skills. The numbers drop quite significantly when keywords are examined separately, as in that situation each publication is only counted once.

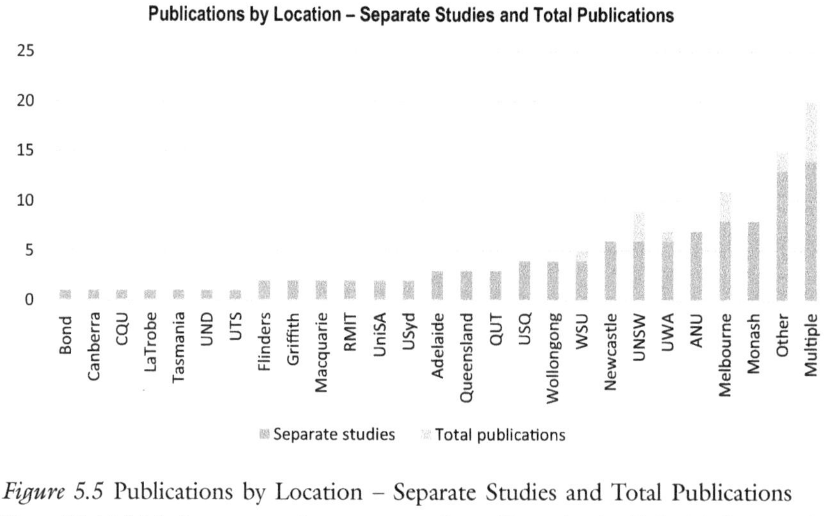

Figure 5.5 Publications by Location – Separate Studies and Total Publications

Note: 'Multiple' indicates research across a number of law schools; 'Other' indicates either that the location is not disclosed or is a non-law school setting.

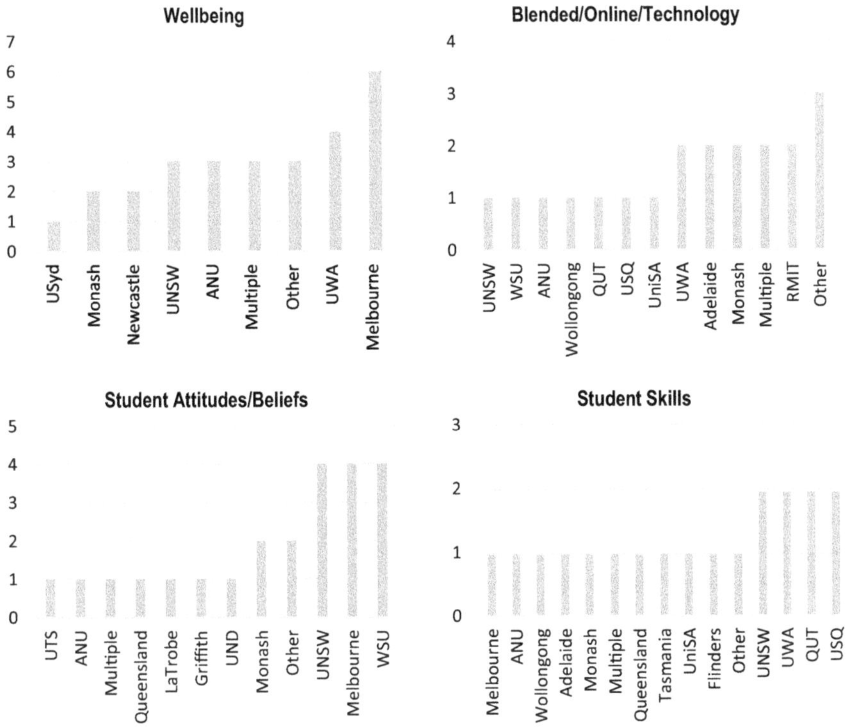

Figure 5.6 Particular topics

The charts demonstrate that a number of law schools did not publish any empirical research into their own students or staff in this 16-year period, and many who did only published one or two.[15] These figures suggest that much more can be done across Australia. One simple approach would be to replicate surveys across multiple law schools. This would both increase sample sizes and also provide triangulation of findings across different environments.

X Focus of study

The publications were also analysed to discover the prevalent subjects of research. Overwhelmingly undergraduate law (LLB) students were the subject of the studies. Graduate Juris Doctor (JD) degrees became popular only in the late 2000s and were only taught in a subset of law schools during the period,[16] so studies of their experiences were less. In Figure 5.7, the relative concentrations are set out.

In coding the publications, a study of both LLB and JD students received two entries. Largely the JD studies recorded here were part of the same study

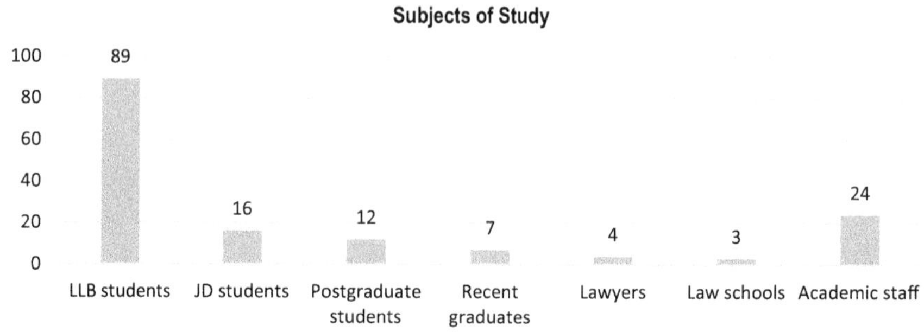

Figure 5.7 Subjects of study

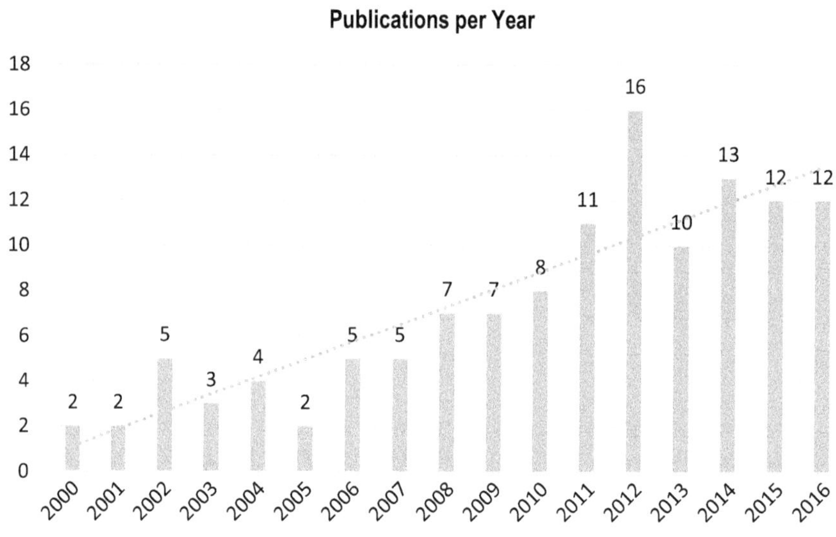

Figure 5.8 Publications per year

of LLB students. Postgraduate students included students studying post degree diplomas of legal practice – and this makes up the bulk of the studies.

The number of studies of individual academic staff is of interest. Increasingly the attitudes of academics are themselves being recognised as having significant influence on how law is taught, and the emotional stress they are under is being recognised. The studies in this database represent the beginning of that focus for research. Additionally there were a small number of studies of law schools themselves, based on document analysis of curricula and publicity materials.

XI Rate of publication

The project also examined the number of publications annually. Unsurprisingly interest in empirical studies into legal education has significantly increased over the period, with a spike in 2012 of 16 publications. As publication dates are impacted by journal reviewing processes and issue availability, it is to be expected that numbers would vary across years. However there is a clear upward trend, and it is not clear if that trend continues or has stabilised. The reasons for that upward trend are beyond the scope of this chapter, but are discussed in other chapters in this book.

The data suggests that at least 10–15 empirically based papers are now being published annually. With time this should lead to a strong evidence base for teaching innovations in Australian legal education.

XII Publication outlets

Overwhelmingly, papers are published in the one specialist legal education journal, the *Legal Education Review*, and a significant number are also published in the UK equivalent, the *Law Teacher*. Generalist law journals do accept empirical research, but the submission/acceptance numbers are much smaller. In the period, empirically based papers were published in 35 journals. Twenty published only one empirically based paper, and five published two papers. Figure 5.9 shows those journals which published three or more papers.

There were eight book chapters, and two refereed conference papers (both of which were for non-law conferences). The small number of refereed conference papers is unsurprising, given the rarity for law conferences to referee or publish presentations. The small number of book chapters is likely to be a combination of the difficulty in finding such publications through the database searching process used, and also a reflection that historically little was published on legal education in book form. There seems to recently have been an increase in interest by publishers in legal education and pedagogy as topics for edited collections. Since 2016 two series now exist that accept Australian research: Emerging Legal

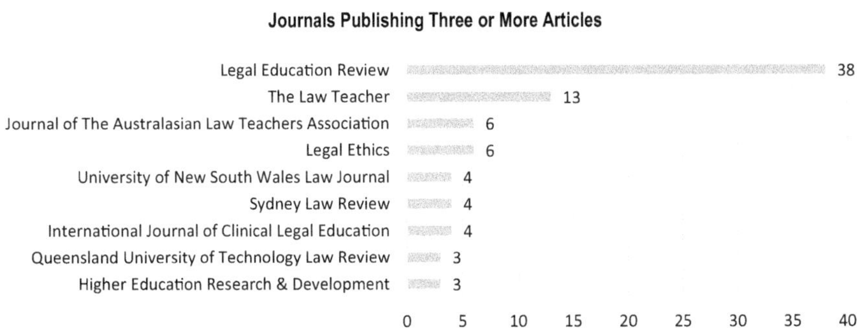

Figure 5.9 Journals Publishing Three or More Articles

Education (in which this book is itself published) and Legal Pedagogy, both published by Routledge. With the rise of e-books and print-on-demand publishing, it may well be that edited collections will become more prevalent.

One significant implication of this data is that other than the *Legal Education Review*, there is no obvious publication outlet for empirical legal research in Australia. Some of the larger studies can find outlets in highly ranked generalist journals, but that is unlikely for smaller scale projects. Another significant implication is that while authors might occasionally find an international journal to publish in, the *Law Teacher* is the only generalist international journal publishing Australian empirical research. Edited books on legal education are also likely to be a significant site of publication given this lack of journal breadth. In the period of this database, book chapters were already the third most popular outlet.

XIII Spread of authors and author gender

The database captured 182 individual authors and 269 separate author attributions. As might be expected with empirical work, many papers had multiple authors.

When the co-authorships are disaggregated, it is possible to determine how often academics publish empirical work on legal education.

What is striking about Table 5.1 is the very large number of academics who publish only once in the field and the small numbers who publish repeatedly.

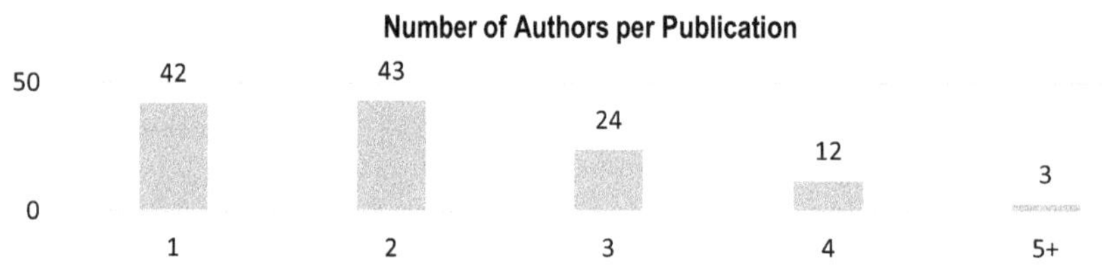

Figure 5.10 Number of Authors per Publication

Table 5.1 Publications per author

Number of articles published	*Total individuals*
1	142
2	27
3	9
4	2
5	4
7	1
8	1

The data is even more striking when it is appreciated that many of the authors engaged in multiple publications are publishing multiple papers arising out of one large study.

Significantly, the most highly published authors are current academics who have continued to publish post-2016. This suggests that empirical analysis of Australian education has not traditionally been a significant publication focus for Australian academics. However, that is changing and some academics are both concentrating on legal education as a research field, and consistently using empirical analysis in their work.

What is also highly significant is the gender balance in publication. On the basis of author first names, there were 131 female authors and only 51 male authors. Given that there have long been more male than female academics[17] this statistic is surprising. The 13:5 ratio requires more examination.

When the top ten authors by quantity of publication are examined, the gender ratio is 6:4 and the top two authors are female. Six are currently in the professoriate with a 3:3 gender ratio. Those figures tell a different story, suggesting that empirical legal education research can be part of a successful research career path and that gender is less of an issue. However, given that the data covers a 16-year period, it seems clear that empirical legal education publishing alone is not yet the basis of an academic career in Australia. All of these authors consistently published in other research areas.

XIV Conclusion

This analysis of empirical legal education research outputs from 2000 to 2016 provides an important overview of the state of play in the field. It demonstrates a growing awareness of the importance of empirical data in analysing legal education with the quantum of such research growing to 10–15 outputs a year. Although government funding for large-scale projects mentioned at the beginning of the chapter has ceased, the degree of research in projects across Australia suggests the field will continue to grow. The ubiquity of online streamlined surveys suggests that the traditionally difficult process of administering surveys is no longer a significant brake on research. Instead, the drafting of quality survey items and the expertise to properly analyse them are the premium needs of researchers.

The range of topics covered in the research is broad and nuanced, and while there are concentrations on wellbeing and technology, there is a wide range of publications on student attitudes, curricula and assessment, student groups and institutional issues. The creation of a bibliography of this research presents an opportunity to more easily bring this research to a wider audience through summaries and citations.

Notes

* University of New South Wales; a.steel@unsw.edu.au. Thanks to Alexandre Fleck for his excellent research work on the database.

1 Maria J. Grant and Andrew Booth, 'A Typology of Reviews: An Analysis of 14 Review Types and Associated Methodologies' (2009) 26(2) *Health Information & Libraries Journal* 91.

2 See, e.g., David Gough, Sandy Oliver and James Thomas, *An Introduction to Systematic Reviews* (Sage, Los Angeles 2017).

3 Paul Maharg, Emma Nicol and others, 'Simulation and Technology in Legal Education: A Systematic Review and Future Research Programme' in *Legal Education: Simulation in Theory and Practice* (Ashgate, London 2014).

4 Debajoyti Pati and Lesa N. Lorusso, 'How to Write a Systematic Review of the Literature' (2018) 11(1) *Health Environments Research & Design Journal* 15.

5 The first law-related report is from 2008.

6 Peter Cane and Herbert Kritzer, *The Oxford Handbook of Empirical Legal Research* (Oxford University Press Oxford 2010) 4.

7 It is worth emphasising that much excellent research falls outside this study. For a leading collection of such research, see Sally Kift and others (eds), *Excellence and Innovation in Legal Education* (Lexis Nexis, Butterworths Chatswood 2011).

8 See, e.g., Carolyn Ellis, Tony E. Adams and Arthur P. Bochner, 'Autoethnography: An Overview' (2011) 36(4) (138) *Historical Social Research/Historische Sozialforschung* 273.

9 A well-known example is Margaret Thornton, *Privatising the Public University: The Case of Law* (Routledge, London 2011).

10 S. Booth and L.C. Woollacott, 'On the Constitution of SoTL: Its Domains and Contexts' (2017) *Higher Education* 1.

11 Dawn Bennett and others, 'What Is Required to Develop Career Pathways for Teaching Academics?' (2017) *Higher Education* 1; Belinda Probert and Judyth Sachs, 'The Rise of Teaching Focused Academics in Universities' (2015) 4(1) *International Journal of Chinese Education* 48.

12 Janice Miller-Young and Michelle Yeo, 'Conceptualizing and Communicating SoTL: A Framework for the Field' (2015) 3(2) *Teaching & Learning Inquiry: The ISSOTL Journal* 37.

13 Much of this critique is canvassed in Christine Parker, 'The "Moral Panic" over Psychological Wellbeing in the Legal Profession: A Personal or Political Ethical Response' (2014) 37 *University of New South Wales Law Journal* 1103.

14 Louis Cohen, Lawrence Manion and Keith Morrison, *Research Methods in Education* (Routledge, London 2018) 203.

15 Data is attributed to 26 law schools in the period. By the end of the period there were 39 law schools in Australia.

16 Margaret Jackson, *Graduate Professional Entry Courses in Accounting and Law: Final Report* (Australian Learning and Teaching Council, Canberra 2012) <https://ltr.edu.au/deeplink.aspx?TN=resources&RF=Full%20Display&AC=QBE_QUERY&XC=%2Fdbtw-wpd%2Fexec%2Fdbtwpub.dll&QY=find%20systemid%20ct%20365412>.

17 Kerry Carrington and Angela Pratt, *How Far Have We Come: Gender Disparities in the Australian Higher Education System* (Information and Research Services, Department of the Parliamentary Library Canberra 2003).

Appendix 1

Projects funded by the Australian Learning and Teaching Council/ Office of Learning and Teaching

Curriculum frameworks

Learning outcomes

Richard Johnstone and Sumitra Vignaendra, (2009) *Highlights of AUTC's learning outcomes and curriculum development in law* https://ltr.edu.au/resources/law-flinders-appendixa-2009.pdf

Sally Kift, Mark Israel, and Rachael Field, (2010) *Bachelor of Laws Learning and Teaching Academic Standards Statement. ALTC Learning and Teaching Academic Standards Project.* https://ltr.edu.au/resources/altc_standards.LAW_.110211_rv2_0.pdf

Clinical legal education

Adrian Evans, Anna Cody, Anna Copeland, Jeff Giddings, Mary Anne Noone, Simon Rice, and Ebony Booth (2013) *Best practices: Australian clinical legal education* https://ltr.edu.au/resources/PP10_1603_Monash_Evans_Report_2013.pdf;

Jeff Giddings (2015) *Reciprocal Professional Development: Enhancing Law Student Supervision in Practice-based Contexts* https://ltr.edu.au/resources/Giddings%2C%20J_NTF_Report_2015.pdf

Internationalising law curricula

Duncan Bentley and Joan Squelch (2012) *Internationalising the Australian law curriculum for enhanced global legal practice* https://ltr.edu.au/resources/PP10_1789_Bentley_Report_2012.pdf

Regional legal education

Amanda Kennedy, Richard Coverdale, Caroline Hart, Claire Macken, Trish Mundy, Jennifer Nielsen and Theresa Smith-Ruig (2015) *Rethinking law curriculum: development strategies to prepare law graduates for practice in rural and regional Australia* https://ltr.edu.au/resources/ID11_2010_Kennedy_Report_2013.pdf

The first year experience

Sally Kift (2009) *Articulating a transition pedagogy to scaffold and to enhance the first year student learning experience in Australian higher education* https://ltr.edu.au/resources/Kift_ALTC_Senior_Fellowship_Report_Sep_09.pdf

Capstone experiences in law

Sally Kift, Des Butler, Rachael Field, Judith McNamara and Cath Brown (2013). *Curriculum renewal in legal education. Office for Learning and Teaching, Australian Government*, Sydney NSW https://ltr.edu.au/resources/PP9-1374_Kift_Report_2013_1.pdf

Graduate professional entry

Margaret Jackson, Joann Cattlin, Lillian Lowe, Glennda Scully, Stacey Porter, Rosalind Mason, Sheryl Jackson and Donna Cooper (2012) *Graduate Professional Entry Courses in Accounting and Law* https://ltr.edu.au/resources/PP9_1386_Jackson_report_2012.pdf

Elements of curricula

Social justice

Susan Banki, Simon Rice, Lisa Hartley, Fiona McGaughey, Paghona Peggy Kerdo, Matthew Stubbs, Phil Orchard, Laurie Berg, Paul Duffill (2016) *Filling the Social Justice Gap: Social Justice Simulations; Social Justice: Case Studies; Social Justice: Exercise Manual.* https://ltr.edu.au/resources/ID13_3093_Banki_report%20 2016.pdf

Reflective practice

Mary Ryan, Michael Ryan, Nan Bahr, Georgina Barton, Louise Bow, Dean Brough, Suzanne Carrington, Tina Cockburn, Christy Collis, Natalie Gamble, Ingrid Larkin, Robyn Nash, Jill Ryan, Melinda Shirley, (2012) *Developing a Systematic, Cross-Faculty Approach to Teaching and Assessing Reflection in Higher Education.*

Academic development

Sessional teaching quality

Kate Galloway (2013) *Building & Consolidating the Law Associate Deans (T&L) Network Final Report* https://ltr.edu.au/resources/SI11-2120%20Law%20AD%20Network%20final%20report.pdf

Kate Galloway, Mary Heath, Anne Hewitt, Mark Israel, Natalie Skead and Alex Steel (2018) *Smart casual: towards excellence in sessional teaching in law* https://ltr.edu.au/resources/ID14-4320_Nettle_Flinders_ReportSmartCasual.pdf

Student learning and wellbeing

Law postgraduate research

Stephen Colbran and Belinda Tynan (2008) *Australian Law Postgraduate network* https://ltr.edu.au/resources/grants_le_project_report_alpn_feb09.pdf

Threshold concepts

Gerlese Åkerlind, Jo McKenzie and Mandy Lupton (2011) *A Threshold Concepts Focus to Curriculum Design: Supporting Student Learning Through Application of Variation Theory.* https://ltr.edu.au/resources/PP8_885_Final_Report_Akerlind_2011.pdf

Law students' mental health and wellbeing

Rachael Field (2014) *Promoting Law Student Well-Being Through the Curriculum* https://ltr.edu.au/resources/Field_R_NTF_report_2014%20.pdf

Teaching innovations

Suzanne Owen and Gary Davis, (2009) *Learning and teaching in the discipline of law: achieving and sustaining excellence in a changed and changing environment* https://ltr.edu.au/resources/altc_LawReport.pdf

Suzanne Owen and Gary Davis (2009), *Some innovations in assessment in legal education* https://ltr.edu.au/resources/law_flinders_appendixb-2009.pdf

Desmond Butler (2011) *Using cost-effective multimedia to create engaging learning experiences in law and other disciplines.* Australian Learning and Teaching Council, Sydney Australia. https://eprints.qut.edu.au/48365/1/Butler_D_QUT_Fellowship_report_2011.pdf

Appendix 2

A full bibliography of articles in database

Table 5.2

Year	*Author*	*Title*	*Citation*
2000	Anker, Kirsten; Dauvergne, Catherine; Findlay, Mark; Millbank, Jenni	Evaluating a Change to Seminar-Style Teaching Note	(2000) 11 *Legal Education Review* 97–144
2000	McNamara, Lawrence	Why Teaching Matters and Technology Doesn't: An Evaluation and Review of Web-Based Lectures	(2000) 11 *Legal Education Review* 175–206
2001	Evans, Adrian	Lawyers' Perceptions of Their Values: An Empirical Assessment of Monash University Graduates in Law, 1980–1998 Part 3: Preliminary Survey Results of the Values of Australian Lawyers	(2001) 12 *Legal Education Review* 209–268
2001	Parker, Christine	What Do They Learn When They Learn Legal Ethics?	(2001) 12 *Legal Education Review* 175
2002	Carroll, Robyn; Wallace, Helen	An Integrated Approach to Information Literacy in Legal Education	(2002) 13 *Legal Education Review* 133–168
2002	Evans, Adrian; Palermo, Josephine	Lawyers' Perceptions of their Values: An Empirical Assessment of Australian Final-Year Undergraduate Law Students—Some Interim Results—2001	(2001) 5 *Legal Ethics* 102–129
2002	Evans, Adrian; Palermo, Josephine	Australian Law Students' Perceptions of Their Values: Interim Results in the First Year—2001—of a Three-Year Empirical Assessment	(2002) 5 *Legal Ethics* 103–129

Year	*Author*	*Title*	*Citation*
2002	Mack, Kathy; Mullins, Gerry; Sidford, Jan; Bamford, David	Developing Student Self-Reflection Skills through Interviewing and Negotiation Exercises in Legal Education	(2002) 13 *Legal Education Review* 221–244
2002	Stifris, Adiva; McNeil, Elspeth	Small Group Learning in Real Property Law Teaching Note	(2002) 13 *Legal Education Review* 189–220
2003	Field, Andrew	The Agency of Innovation: Subject Websites, Their Perceived Value and Student Performance	(2003) 14 *Legal Education Review* 127–152
2003	Hutchinson, Terry	Where to Now – The 2002 Australasian Research Skills Training Survey	(2003) 14 *Legal Education Review* 63–92
2003	Richards, Bernadette	Alice Comes to Law School: The Internet as a Teaching Tool	(2003) 14 *Legal Education Review* 115–138
2004	Hutchinson, Terry; Cuffe, Natalie	Legal Research Project Management: Skills Extension for Upper Level Law Students	(2004) 38 *The Law Teacher* 159–181
2004	Israel, Mark; Handsley, Elizabeth; Davis, Gary	'It's the Vibe': Fostering Student Collaborative Learning in Constitutional Law in Australia	(2004) 38 *The Law Teacher* Jan-26
2004	Sharp, Cassandra	Changing the Channel: What to Do with the Critical Abilities of Law Students as Viewers?	(2004) 13 *Griffith Law Review* 185–199
2004	Tranter, Kieran	'Ethical, Ooh, Yeah Ethical Is Yeah, What's Right Yeah': A Snapshot of First Year Law Students' Conception of Ethics	(2004) 7 *Legal Ethics* 85–109
2005	Evans, Adrian; Palermo, Josephine	Zero Impact: Are Lawyers' Values Affected by Law School?	(2005) 8 *Legal Ethics* 240–264
2005	Peden, Elisabeth; Riley, Joellen	Law Graduates' Skills – A Pilot Study into Employers' Perspectives	(2005) 15 *Legal Education Review* 87
2006	Cantley-Smith, Rowena	Put Down Your Pen: The Role of Oral Assessment in Undergraduate Law Studies	(2006) 13 *James Cook University Law Review* 30–63

(*Continued*)

Table 5.2 (Continued)

Year	*Author*	*Title*	*Citation*
2006	Evans, Adrian; Palermo, Josephine	Preparing Australia's Future Lawyers: An Exposition of Changing Values over Time in the Context of Teaching about Ethical Dilemma	(2006) 11 *Deakin Law Review* 103–130
2006	Finlay-Jones, Jenny; Ross, Nicola	Peer Mentoring for Law Students—Improving the First Year Advocacy Experience	(2006) 40 *The Law Teacher* 23–39
2006	Reid, Anna; Nagarajan, Vijaya; Dortins, Emma	The Experience of Becoming a Legal Professional	(2006) 25 *Higher Education Research & Development* 85–99
2006	Stevens, Elizabeth; Douglas, Heather; Cullen-Mandikos, Bridget; Hunter, Rosemary	Equity, Diversity and Student Engagement in a Law School – A Case Study Approach	(2006) 16 *Legal Education Review* 1–34
2007	Fisher, T.; Gutman, J.; Martens, E.	Why Teach ADR to Law Students? Part 2: An Empirical Survey	(2007) 17 *Legal Education Review* 67
2007	Hewitt, Anne; Castles, Margaret; Goldfinch, Maureen	Using Simulated Practice to Teach Legal Theory – How and Why Skills and Group Work Can Be Incorporated in an Academic Law Curriculum	(2007) 26 *The University of Tasmania Law Review* 120–176
2007	Walsh, Tamara	Putting Justice Back into Legal Education	(2007) 17 *Legal Education Review* 119–142
2007	Welsman, Sandra J.	To Boldly Go! Can Bright Students Realise Their Learning Potential at Universities?	AIC Partnership for World Graduates, Proceedings, RMIT Melbourne, 2007
2007	Welsman, Sandra J.	Double or Nothing! Clever Thinking, Double-Degree Frustration, and Returns to Science	National UniServe Symposium, Science Teaching and Learning Research Proceedings, University of Sydney, 2007
2008	James, Colin	Lawyer Dissatisfaction, Emotional Intelligence and Clinical Education	(2008) 18 *Legal Education Review* 123–138

Year	*Author*	*Title*	*Citation*
2008	James, Colin	Lawyers' Wellbeing and Professional Legal Education	(2008) 42 *The Law Teacher* 85–97
2008	Larcombe, Wendy; Nicholson, Pip; Malkin, Ian	Commencing Law Students' Interests and Expectations: Comparing Undergraduate and Graduate Cohorts	(2008) 1 *Journal of the Australasian Law Teachers Association* 227–238
2008	Larcombe, Wendy; Nicholson, Pip; Malkin, Ian	Performance in Law School: What Matters in the Beginning	(2008) 18 *Legal Education Review* 95–122
2008	Macduff, Anne; Du Moulin, Lynn	New Challenges in Legal Education: Developing an Appropriate Response to the Issue of Student Workload Practice Article	(2008) 18 *Legal Education Review* 179–196
2008	O'Brien, Molly T.; Littrich, John	Using Assessment Practice to Evaluate the Legal Skills Curriculum	(2008) 5 *Journal of University Teaching and Learning Practice* 61–76
2008	Palermo, Josephine; Evans, Adrian	Almost There – Empirical Insights into Clinical Method and Ethics Courses in Climbing the Hill towards Lawyers' Professionalism	(2008) 17 *Griffith Law Review* 252–284
2009	Armstrong, Susan; Campbell, Marnie	Interventions to Enhance the Student Experience of a First Year Law Degree: What They Really Wanted	(2009) 2 *Journal of the Australasian Law Teachers Association* 135–148
2009	Kelk, Norm	Courting the Blues: Attitudes towards Depression in Australian Law Students and Legal Practitioners	Brain & Mind Research Institute, Sydney, 2009
2009	Lansdell, Gaye T.	Have We Pushed the Boat Out Too Far in Providing Online Practical Legal Training: A Guide to Best Practices for Future Programs	(2009) 19 *Legal Education Review* 149–170
2009	Martin, Fiona; Collier, Kate; Carlon, Shirley	Mentoring First-Year Distance Education Students in Taxation Studies	(2009) 19 *Legal Education Review* 217–236
2009	Newlyn, David; Spencer, Liesel	Using Exemplars in an Interdisciplinary Law Unit: Listening to the Students' Voices	(2009) 2 *Journal of the Australasian Law Teachers Association* 121–133
2009	Tani, Massimiliano; Vines, Prue	Law Students' Attitudes to Education: Pointers to Depression in the Legal Academy and the Profession	(2009) 19 *Legal Education Review* 3–40

(*Continued*)

Table 5.2 (Continued)

Year	*Author*	*Title*	*Citation*
2009	Welsman, Sandra J.	Interdisciplinary Ideas and University Law Courses – An Initial DRI Investigation, Australia	Frontiers Insight: The Frontiers Institute, 2009
2010	Butler, Des	Entry into Valhalla: Contextualising the Learning of Legal Ethics through the Use of Second Life Machinima	(2010) 20 *Legal Education Review* 85–108
2010	Castan, Melissa; Paterson, Jeannie; Richardson, Paul; Watt, Helen	Early Optimism – First-Year Law Students' Work Expectations and Aspirations	(2010) 20 *Legal Education Review* 1
2010	Corbin, Lillian; Burns, Kylie; Chrzanowski, April	If You Teach It, Will They Come? Law Students, Class Attendance and Student Engagement	(2010) 20 *Legal Education Review* 13
2010	Cowley, Jill	Confronting the Reality of Casualisation in Australia: Valuing Sessional Staff in Law Schools	(2010) 10 *Queensland University of Technology Law and Justice Journal* 27
2010	Hall, Kath; O'Brien, Molly Townes; Tang, Stephen	Developing a Professional Identity in Law School: A view from Australia	(2010) 4 *Phoenix Law Review* 21
2010	Kelk, Norm; Medlow, Sharon; Hickie, Ian	Distress and Depression among Australian Law Students: Incidence, Attitudes and the Role of Universities	(2010) 32 *Sydney Law Review* 113–122
2010	McCall, Ian	Online Enhanced Problem-Based Learning: Assessing a Blended Learning Framework	(2010) 44 *The Law Teacher* 42–58
2010	Sharp, Cassandra	'Represent a Murderer . . . I'd Never Do That!' How Students Use Stories to Link Ethical Development and Identity Construction	M. Robertson, L. Corbin, K. Tranter & F. Bartlett (eds), *The Ethics Project in Legal Education* (2011) 33–51
2011	Barnett, Eola; Baer, Roslyn	Embracing Wikipedia as a Research Tool for Law: To Wikipedia or Not to Wikipedia?	(2011) 45 *The Law Teacher* 194–213

Year	*Author*	*Title*	*Citation*
2011	Douglas, Kathy	The Teaching of ADR in Australian Law Schools: Promoting Non-adversarial Practice in Law	(2011) 22 *Australasian Dispute Resolution Journal* 49–57
2011	Hart, Caroline; Hammer, Sara; Collins, Pauline; Chardon, Toni	The Real Deal: Using Authentic Assessment to Promote Student Engagement in the First and Second Years of a Regional Law Program	(2011) 21 *Legal Education Review* 97–122
2011	Howieson, Jill	ADR Education: Creating Engagement and Increasing Mental Well-Being through an Interactive and Constructive Approach	(2011) 22 *Australasian Dispute Resolution Journal* 58–64
2011	Lester, Anthony; England, Lloyd; Antolak-Saper, Natalia	Health and Wellbeing in the First Year: The Law School Experience	(2011) 36 *Alternative Law Journal* 47–51
2011	Mascher, Sharon; Skead, Natalie	On the Record: The Trials and Tribulations of Lecture Recording in Law	(2011) 35 *University of Western Australia Law Review* 407–431
2011	O'Brien, Molly T.; Tang, Stephen; Hall, Kath	No Time to Lose: Negative Impact on Law Student Wellbeing May Begin in Year One	(2011) 2 *The International Journal of the First Year in Higher Education* 49–60
2011	O'Brien, Molly Townes; Tang, Stephen; Hall, Kath	Changing our Thinking: Empirical Research on Law Student Wellbeing, Thinking Styles and the Law Curriculum	(2011) 21 *Legal Education Review* 149
2011	Ramsay, Ian	Intensive Teaching in Law Subjects	(2011) 45 *The Law Teacher* 87–110
2011	Riley, S.; Li, G.; Parker, N. J.	Student Diversity: Widening Participation by Engaging Culturally Diverse Non-law Students in Law	In, S. Kift, M. Sanson, J. Cowley, & P. Watson (Eds.), *Excellence and Innovation in Legal Education*, Sydney, 2011, 337–362
2011	Ruyters, Michele; Douglas, Kathy; Law, Siew Fang	Blended Learning Using Role-Plays, Wikis and Blogs	(2011) 4 *Journal of Learning Design* 45–55

(*Continued*)

Table 5.2 (Continued)

Year	*Author*	*Title*	*Citation*
2012	Ailwood, Sarah; Easteal, Patricia; Sainsbury, Maree; Bartels, Lorana	Connecting Research and Teaching: A Case Study from the School of Law, University of Canberra The Teaching-Research Nexus in Law: Opportunities and Challenges	(2012) 22 *Legal Education Review* 317–338
2012	Armstrong, Susan; Sanson, Michelle	From Confusion to Confidence: Transitioning to Law School	(2012) 12 *Queensland University of Technology Law Review* 21–44
2012	Carruthers, Penny; Skead, Natalie Kym; Galloway, Kate	Teaching Skills and Outcomes in Australian Property Law Units: A Survey of Current Approaches	(2012) 12 *Queensland University of Technology Law and Justice Journal* 66–84
2012	Ferguson, Anneka; Lee, Elizabeth	Desperately Seeking – Relevant Assessment – A Case Study on the Potential for Using Online Simulated Group Bases Learning to Create Sustainable Assessment Practices	(2012) 22 *Legal Education Review* 121–146
2012	Galloway, Kate; Carruthers, Penny; Skead, Natalie Kym	Assessment in the Law School: Contemporary Approaches of Australian Property Law Teachers	(2012) 5 *Journal of the Australasian Law Teachers Association* 1–14
2012	Greaves, Kristoffer; Lynch, Julianne	Is the Lecturer in the Room – A Study of Student Satisfaction with Online Discussions in Practical Legal Training	(2012) 22 *Legal Education Review* 147–176
2012	Hammer, Sara Jeanne; Chardon, Toni; Collins, Pauline; Hart, Caroline	Legal Educators' Perceptions of Lifelong Learning: Conceptualisation and Practice	(2012) 31 *International Journal of Lifelong Education* 187–201
2012	Holmes, Vivien; Foley, Tony; Tang, Stephen; Rowe, Margie	Practising Professionalism: Observations from an Empirical Study of New Australian Lawyers	(2012) 15 *Legal Ethics* 29–55
2012	Kam, Linda; Ruyters, Michele; Coburn, Clare; Toohey, Mary	Get Real! A Case Study of Authentic Learning Activities in Legal Education	(2012) 19 *Murdoch University Law Review* 17–32

Year	*Author*	*Title*	*Citation*
2012	Larcombe, Wendy; Malkin, Ian	Identifying Students Likely to Benefit from Language Support in First Year Law	(2012) 27 *Higher Education Research & Development* 319–329
2012	Larcombe, Wendy; Malkin, Ian; Nicholson, Pip	Law Students' Motivations, Expectations and Levels of Psychological Distress: Evidence of Connections	(2012) 22 *Legal Education Review* 71–98
2012	Larcombe, Wendy; Tumbaga, Letty; Malkin, Ian; Nicholson, Penelope; Tokatlidis, Orania	Does an Improved Experience of Law School Protect Students against Depression, Anxiety and Stress? An Empirical Study of Wellbeing and the Law School Experience of LLB and JD Students	(2012) 35 *Sydney Law Review* 407–432
2012	Lo, Vai Io	Before Competition and beyond Complacency – The Internationalisation of Legal Education in Australia	(2012) 22 *Legal Education Review* 3–50
2012	Mundy, Trish Karen	'Placing' the Other: Final Year Law Students' 'Imagined' Experience of Rural and Regional Practice within the Law School Context	(2012) 2 *International Journal of Rural Law and Policy* 1
2012	Spencer, Liesel	Motivating Law Students to 'Do the Reading' Before Class: Appropriate Extrinsic and Intrinsic Motivation Tools	(2012) 5 *Journal of the Australasian Law Teachers Association* 189–205
2012	Stallman, Helen	A Qualitative Evaluation of Perceptions of the Role of Competition in the Success and Distress of Law Students	(2012) 31 *Higher Education Research & Development* 891–904
2013	Colbran, Stephen; Gilding, Anthony	E-Learning in Australian Law Schools	(2013) 23 *Legal Education Review* 201–242
2013	Douglas, Kathy	The Evolution of Lawyers' Professional Identity: The Contribution of ADR in Legal Education	(2013) 18 *Deakin Law Review* 315
2013	Evans, Adrian; Forgasz, Helen	Framing Lawyers' Choices: Factor Analysis of a Psychological Scale to Self-Assess Lawyers' Ethical Preferences	(2013) 16 *Legal Ethics* 134–161

(*Continued*)

Table 5.2 (Continued)

Year	*Author*	*Title*	*Citation*
2013	Fraser, Madeleine; MacKenzie, Joanna; Weisbrot, David; Tan, Wesley	Transition from Legal Education to Practice: Extra-Curricular Competitions Offer the Missing Link	(2013) 23 *Legal Education Review* 131–152
2013	James, Nick	'How Dare You Tell Me How to Teach!': Resistance to Educationalism within Australian Law Schools	(2013) 36 *University of New South Wales Law Journal* 779–808
2013	Knutsen, Erik S.; Rowe, Thomas, Jr; Bamford, David; Shipman, Shirley	The Teaching of Procedure Across Common Law Systems	(2013) 51 *Osgoode Hall Law Journal* 1–44
2013	Larcombe, Wendy; Fethers, Katherine	Schooling the Blues? An Investigation of Factors Associated with Psychological Distress among Law Students	(2013) 36 *University of New South Wales Law Journal* 390–436
2013	Steel, Alex	Clarifying Assessment: Developing Typologies for Forms of Assessment in Law	(2013) 6 *Journal of the Australasian Law Teachers Association* 121–132
2013	Steel, Alex; Laurens, Julian; Huggins, Anna	Class Participation as a Learning and Assessment Strategy in Law: Facilitating Students' Engagement, Skills Development and Deep Learning	(2013) 36 *University of New South Wales Law Journal* 30
2013	Waye, Vicki C.; Faulkner, Margaret	Embedding E-portfolios in a Law Program: Lessons from an Australian Law School	(2013) 61 *Journal of Legal Education* 560–584
2014	Appleby, Michael; Bourke, Judy	Promoting Law Student Mental Health Literacy and Wellbeing: A Case Study from the College of Law, Australia	(2014) 20 *International Journal of Clinical Legal Education* 461
2014	Bentley, Duncan; Squelch, Joan	Employer Perspectives on Essential Knowledge, Skills and Attributes for Law Graduates to Work in a Global Context	(2014) 24 *Legal Education Review* 93–114

Year	*Author*	*Title*	*Citation*
2014	Colbran, Stephen; Gilding, Anthony	Exploring Legal Ethics Using Student Generated Storyboards	(2014) 48 *The Law Teacher* 296–320
2014	Curró, Gina; Longo, Michael	Educating Humpty Dumpty: Statutory Interpretation in the First Year of Australian Law	(2014) 48 *The Law Teacher* 321–345
2014	Douglas, Heather; Taylor, Monica	Understanding the Power of Law: Engaging Students in Criminal Law Casework	(2014) 24 *Legal Education Review* 28–43
2014	James, Colin G.; Mahmud, Saadia	Promoting Academic Integrity in Legal Education: 'Unanswered Questions' on Disclosure	(2014) 10 *International Journal for Educational Integrity* 3–16
2014	Maharg, Paul; Nicol, Emma; others	Simulation and Technology in Legal Education: A Systematic Review and Future Research Programme	*Legal Education: Simulation in Theory and Practice*, Ashgate, 2014
2014	Rundle, Olivia	Creating a Healthy Group Work Learning Environment in Law Classes	(2014) 14 *Queensland University of Technology Law Review* 63–80
2014	Skead, Natalie Kym; Rogers, Shane	Stress, Anxiety and Depression in Law Students: How Student Behaviors Affect Student Wellbeing	(2014) 40 *Monash University Law Review* 1–24
2014	Spencer, Rachel M. A.	'First They Tell Us to Ignore Our Emotions, Then They Tell Us to Reflect': The Development of a Reflective Writing Pedagogy in Clinical Legal Education through an Analysis of Student Perceptions of Reflective Writing	(2014) 21 *International Journal of Clinical Legal Education* 1–37
2014	Steel, Alex; Huggins, Anna; Laurens, Julian	Valuable Learning, Unwelcome Assessment: What LLB and JD Students Really Think about Group Work	(2014) 36 *Sydney Law Review* 291–321
2014	Tang, Stephen; Ferguson, Anneka	The Possibility of Wellbeing: Preliminary Results from Surveys of Australian Professional Legal Education Students	(2014) 14 *Queensland University of Technology Law Review* 27–51

(*Continued*)

Table 5.2 (Continued)

Year	*Author*	*Title*	*Citation*
2014	Wardhaugh, Felicity Helen; James, Colin G.	A Client-Focused Practice: Developing and Testing Emotional Competency in Clinical Legal Interviews	(2014) 20 *International Journal of Clinical Legal Education* 633–645
2015	Bergin, Adele; Pakenham, Kenneth	Law Student Stress: Relationships between Academic Demands, Social Isolation, Career Pressure, Study/Life Imbalance and Adjustment Outcomes in Law Students	(2015) 22 *Psychiatry, Psychology and Law* 388–406
2015	Cantatore, Francina	Boosting Law Graduate Employability: Using a Pro Bono Teaching Clinic to Facilitate Experiential Learning in Commercial Law Subjects	(2015) 25 *Legal Education Review* 147–172
2015	Cockburn, Tina; Ryan, Mary	Teaching and Assessing Reflective Writing in a Large Undergraduate Core Substantive Law Unit	*Teaching Reflective Learning in Higher Education* 93–109, Springer International Publishing, 2015
2015	Curnow, Katherine	More than the Rules: Using Pleading Drafting to Develop Lawyering and Transferable Skills	(2015) 25 *Legal Education Review* 203–220
2015	Douglas, Kathy	The Role of ADR in Developing Lawyers' Practice: Lessons from Australian Legal Education	(2015) 22 *International Journal of the Legal Profession* 71–86
2015	Heath, Mary; Hewitt, Anne; Israel, Mark; Skead, Natalie	Beginning to Address the Elephant in the Classroom: Investigating and Responding to Australian Sessional Law Teachers' Unmet Professional Development Needs	(2015) 38 *University of New South Wales Law Journal* 240
2015	Hewitt, Anne	Can You Learn to Lawyer Online? A Blended Learning Environment Case Study	(2015) 49 *The Law Teacher* 92–121
2015	Holmes, Vivien	'Giving Voice to Values': Enhancing Students' Capacity to Cope with Ethical Challenges in Legal Practice	(2015) 18 *Legal Ethics* 115–137
2015	Larcombe, Wendy; Finch, Sue; Sore, Rachel	Who's Distressed – Not Only Law Students: Psychological Distress Levels in University Students across Diverse Fields of Study	(2015) 37 *Sydney Law Review* 243

Year	*Author*	*Title*	*Citation*
2015	Maguire, Amy; Young, Tamara	Indigenisation of Curricula: Current Teaching Practices in Law	(2015) 25 *Legal Education Review* 95–120
2015	Skead, Natalie K.; Rogers, Shane L.	Do Law Students Stand Apart from Other University Students in Their Quest for Mental Health: A Comparative Study on Wellbeing and Associated Behaviours in Law and Psychology Students	(2015) 42 *International Journal of Law and Psychiatry* 81–90
2015	Soh, Nerissa; Burns, Fiona; Shackel, Rita; Robinson, Bruce; Robertson, Michael; Walter, Garry	Law Student Mental Health Literacy and Distress: Finances, Accommodation and Travel Time	(2015) 25 *Legal Education Review* 29–64
2016	Colbran, Stephen; Gilding, Anthony; Colbran, Samuel	Animation and Multiple-Choice Questions as a Formative Feedback Tool for Legal Education	(2016) 51 *The Law Teacher* 249
2016	Evers, Maxine; Bourke, Judy	Resilience and Wellbeing Programmes: The Practical Legal Training Experience	*Promoting Law Student and Lawyer Well-Being in Australia and Beyond*, Ashgate (Routledge)
2016	Huggins, Anna; Steel, Alex	The Relationship between Class Participation and Law Students' Learning, Engagement and Stress: Do Demographics Matter?	*Promoting Law Student and Lawyer Well-Being in Australia and Beyond*, Ashgate (Routledge)
2016	James, Nick	Dealing with Resistance to Change by Legal Academics	*Promoting Law Student and Lawyer Well-Being in Australia and Beyond*, 204–217 Ashgate (Routledge)
2016	Kraal, Diane	Legal Teaching Methods to Diverse Student Cohorts: A Comparison between the United Kingdom, the United States, Australia and New Zealand	(2016) 47 *Cambridge Journal of Education* 1–23

(*Continued*)

Table 5.2 (Continued)

Year	*Author*	*Title*	*Citation*
2016	Larcombe, Wendy; Finch, Sue; Sore, Rachel; Murray, Christina M.; Kentish, Sandra; Mulder, Raoul A.; Lee-Stecum, Parshia; Baik, Chi; Tokatlidis, Orania; Williams, David A.	Prevalence and Socio-demographic Correlates of Psychological Distress among Students at an Australian University	(2016) 41 *Studies in Higher Education* 1074–1091
2016	McNamara, Noeleen	Authentic Assessment in Contract Law: Legal Drafting	(2016) 51 *The Law Teacher* Jan-13
2016	Skead, Natalie	Uncle Jack, Jaycee and the Equitable Doctrine of Estoppel: Using Second Life to Support the Development of Advanced Oral Communication Skills in Law Students	(2016) 50 *The Law Teacher* 230–241
2016	Skead, Natalie K.; Rogers, Shane L.	Running to Well-Being: A Comparative Study on the Impact of Exercise on the Physical and Mental Health of Law and Psychology Students	(2016) 49 *International Journal of Law and Psychiatry* 66–74
2016	Steel, Alex; Huggins, Anna	Law Student Lifestyle Pressures	*Promoting Law Student and Lawyer Well-Being in Australia and Beyond*, Ashgate (Routledge), Farnham, Surrey, 2016
2016	Wardhaugh, Felicity Helen; James, Colin G.	Enhancing Emotional Competencies with Law Students	(2016) 23 *International Journal of Clinical Legal Education* 53
2016	Williams, Brett; Sifris, Adiva; Lynch, Marty	A Psychometric Appraisal of the Jefferson Scale of Empathy Using Law Students	(2016) 9 *Psychology Research and Behavior Management* 171

6 A meta-survey of scholarship of learning and teaching in practice-based legal education

Kristoffer Greaves

I Introduction

Legal education is integral to the construction of the foundational intellectual and practical knowledge, skills, and values that qualify individuals seeking admission to the legal profession. In English common law countries, the Ormrodian conceptualisation of legal education as a continuum comprised of pre-admission academic learning and practical training, followed by post-admission supervision and continuing legal education has held fast, although its future is not certain.[1]

That uncertainty is driven in part by current technological disruptions and allied expectations or impatience regarding the time and costs associated with the qualification of individuals for professional practice and the delivery of legal services. Sullivan (author of the Carnegie Report) observes, 'recent research reveals a practice world in considerable flux. The driving imperative is to increase productivity and maximize return on investment, including the developing lawyer's considerable investment in education'.[2]

Given these expectations or impatience, students and their prospective employers do not passively accept that the content and delivery of academic and practical legal education is relevant, well adapted, and supports learning in current and future needs and contexts. By implication, it is incumbent on legal educators to be ready to account for their decisions about learning and teaching practices. In doing so, they could bring to bear their formidable capabilities for analysis and argument concerning facts and evidence.

Legal education is increasingly subject to expectations regarding its effectiveness, relevance, quality, timeliness, and cost. Justification for legal education practices should rely less on reproduction of past conventions and more on current evidence about learning professional skills and knowledge. Here, 'effectiveness' is used broadly – in respect of the achievement of specified outcomes at institutional, program, course, educational, and instructional levels – and in a social justice context, to inclusively afford equity and parity to learners who might not otherwise access legal education, and to support social and cultural diversity in the legal field. Legal education literature provides a material representation of the types of questions and methodologies adopted for learning and teaching scholarship in the field. The literature shows us what is valued as evidence to justify learning and teaching practice. By analysing this literature we can derive insights about ways in which legal education learning and teaching practices are, or are not, investigated.

This chapter describes novel bibliometric and computer-aided qualitative data analysis methods used to analyse a collection of over 780 items of legal education scholarship, with a focus on practice-based pedagogies. These methods generated insights guided by the following questions:

- What attributes of scholarship of learning and teaching (SoLT) were represented in the collection?
- What attributes of empirical research were reported in the collection?
- What were the measures for visibility and influence for this collection?

II Scholarship of learning and teaching

The approach adopted in this chapter is to focus on a specific element of SoLT (communication via publication of peer-reviewed literature) to support a discussion about scholarship of learning and teaching in practice-based legal education in the context of legal education's effectiveness and relevance. This chapter explores the attributes of empirical research and SoLT represented in a collection of peer-reviewed legal education articles. Peer-reviewed journal articles are a top-tier output in the communication dimension of Trigwell et al.'s multidimensional model for SoLT.[3] Published peer-review journal articles represent one segment of SoLT output – nevertheless they are a stable and visible data source capable of objective study and comparison.

As a baseline assumption for this study, to count as *empirical research* the SoLT output should be based on data derived from observed and measurable experience rather than opinion, belief, or pure theory. SoLT outputs would demonstrate attributes such as clearly expressed goals with methods fit for the purpose, include 'significant' results and critical reflection, and be well-presented.[4] In SoLT outputs the kinds of topics we could expect to see include discipline knowledge that teachers need to know to be able to inform learners, together with ways of representing that knowledge to expedite learners' reception and understanding.[5] However, SoLT should look beyond learners' ability to reproduce knowledge – it should also investigate ways in which to foster lifelong learning and the ability to 'extend and transform' learning in novel circumstances.[6] Pedagogical methods that underpin learners' higher-order cognitive processes, such as problem-solving, decision-making, investigation, and experimentation, are also important.[7] These topics framed the 'explicit' coding approach for identifying themes and concepts during the computer-aided qualitative data analysis of the literature collection.[8]

III Practice-based legal education

This chapter focuses on the category of pre-admission practice-based legal education, such as clinical legal education and practical legal training. Practice-based education concepts and themes were used to refine explicit coding for analysis of the literature collection.

The expression *practice-based education* is pedagogically significant and is used in the way that Higgs describes: 'practice-based education provides an approach to education that prepares students for entry to professions, disciplines or occupations'.[9] Whilst higher education study involves the pursuit and achievement of an academic award, there is also a vocational dimension within which employers and students expect that study will prepare graduates for entry into a profession.

Relevantly for legal education SoLT, the Higgs practice-based education model involves investigating pedagogical perspectives, curriculum frameworks, and practices.[10] 'Pedagogical perspectives' involve the frameworks, higher goals, contexts, understandings, about practice and education for practice – together with professional standards, values and ethics, notions of authenticity, and socialization into professional practice.[11] 'Curriculum frameworks' include the overt and covert dimensions of a program, together with the programmed and serendipitous incidents that influence a learner's learning experience.[12] 'Pedagogical practices' include different categories of simulated learning, supervised or unsupervised workplace learning experiences, and formats that include flexible, online, and distance learning, all of which can take place in face-to-face, wholly online, or blended modes.[13] Each of these concepts further informed the explicit framework for coding the literature.

IV A meta-survey and text data-mining

Peer-reviewed articles were collected and used as data for a meta-survey to gain insights about attributes of SoLT in practice-based legal education.

The descriptor, 'meta-survey' is adopted rather than 'meta-study' or 'meta-analysis'. The latter is generally identified with meta-studies of research using statistical methods (comparison of standardised effect sizes, for example).[14] Meta-analyses by Hattie and Marzano are well-known authorities in educational research and practice but appear to receive scant attention in legal education scholarship.[15] On the other hand, the use of statistical meta-analyses to inform policy and practice has been criticised because many such studies violate the statistical assumptions on which these designs depend.[16]

Peer-reviewed literature is regarded as a top-tier category output from the scholarship of learning and teaching.[17] Since Trigwell et al. published their multi-dimensional model of SoLT, other valuable scholarly outputs have emerged, such as blog posts, podcasts, and items shared on social media. The visibility of and engagement with these items can be measured and compared using 'altmetrics';[18] however, these usually depend on digital object identifier links (DOI).[19] DOIs are not yet universally adopted, so systematic measurement and comparison using altmetrics is still in its embryonic stage and not adopted here.

Using peer-reviewed literature as data relies on formalised quality controls through peer review, editorial polices and processes, and comparisons could be made using bibliometric resources. Publisher sites and databases that digitise and organise the literature expedite online searches and automate citation management. This enabled the use of computer-aided data collection and analysis software to undertake a meta-survey of a substantial corpus of literature. Criticism of the quality and fairness of the peer review model is acknowledged, but it persists as the primary practice within academia despite room for improvement.[20]

The object of text data mining is to systematically collect and analyse data from large collections of text to discern insights from quantitative and qualitative patterns and relationships.[21] The method is well adapted for undertaking literature reviews using computer-aided qualitative data analysis software.[22] The study began by concentrating on the abstracts in peer-reviewed journal articles over a five-year period (2011–2015). The initial cohort of abstracts was drawn from eight legal education journals that would be familiar to most Anglophone legal education scholars: *Journal of Legal Education; Law Teacher; International Journal of Clinical Legal Education*; *Journal of the Australasian Law Teachers Association; Legal Education Review; Clinical Law Review; International Journal of the Legal Profession*; and *Journal of Commonwealth Law and Legal Education.* Further searches expanded the collection to 101 journal titles. This was achieved by searching for relevant titles in the Australian Research Council's *Excellence for Research in Australia (ERA) 2015 Journals List* and the Australian Business Deans Council *(ABDC) Journal Quality List 2013*,[23] together with the proprietary Scopus and Web of Knowledge databases (using the phrase 'legal education' together with 'teaching' and 'learning' in English language sources, titles, and abstracts). This process caught over 900 articles – the collection was refined to 788 articles after screening for irrelevant items. Of the final collection, a small proportion (<14 per cent; 109 articles) expressly addressed 'learning'. Less than 10 per cent of the collection (78 articles) focused specifically on practice-based education areas such as clinical legal education (62) or practical legal education and training (12).

Bibliographic information, abstracts, and full texts from the collection were imported to an EndNote database using automated download mechanisms. An EndNote filter was devised to enable the export of bibliographic information to produce a dataset in spreadsheet form. This enabled rapid sorting and filtering, further screening for errors, simple queries to generate descriptive statistics, and addition of bibliometric data. The collection of 788 articles is held to be appropriately representative of the peer-reviewed literature on which to base insights and conclusions.

V Geographies

Most of the journals in the entire collection were based in the United States (56 journals), the United Kingdom (25), and Australia (11). It was observed that several law schools in the United States produce law journals that include articles addressing legal education. Smaller numbers of journal titles were based in Canada, South Africa, and Hong Kong.

The number of articles in individual journals ranged from 1 to 162. Geographically, the distribution of the number of articles was United States (328 articles), United Kingdom (278), Australia (164), South Africa (11), Canada (6), and Hong Kong (1). In each of the United States, the United Kingdom, and Australia, the articles were preponderantly sourced from three or four journals, with many of the remaining journals yielding less than ten items.

In the practice-based areas, most of the clinical legal education articles were sourced from publishers in the United Kingdom (*International Journal of Clinical Legal Education* (40)) and the United States (*Clinical Law Review* (9); *Journal of Legal Education* (4)), whereas most articles about post-graduate pre-admission practical legal training or education were sourced from Australia (*Journal of the Australasian Law Teachers Association* (5); *Legal Education Review* (3)) or the United Kingdom (*International Journal of Clinical Legal Education* (2); *The Law Teacher* (2).

VI Bibliometrics

During September 2016, the collection was subjected to bibliometric analysis using Thomson Reuters InCites Journal Citation Reports (Journal Impact Factors 2015) (JCR); Scopus Scimago Journal Rank 2015 (SJR); Google Scholar h-5 index (Google Index); and Google Scholar h-5 median (Google Median).

Bibliometric methods use measurements to study scholarly communication processes and structures.[24] SCimago Journal and Country Rank (Journal Ranking by Scopus and Elsevier),[25] and JCR[26] are proprietary bibliometric tools that automate quality rankings by reference to citation counts, journal rankings, and impact factors. Journal rankings are said to aid evaluation of journal quality by measuring citation, impact, size, and engagement of journals in a field.[27] A journal that ranks highly is held to confer prestige and value on the articles contained within, to those works that they cite, and on those in which they appear as citations.[28] Google Scholar Metrics[29] are held out as an expeditious method for scholars to gauge the visibility and influence of scholarly articles.[30]

Bibliometric tools have limitations. Databases that use parser search robots to automate collection of bibliographic information rely on technical features in texts such as file format, metadata, DOIs, and formatting of content to detect necessary information. Editorial and authorial practices in relation to these features can enhance or diminish the prospects of detection by and inclusion in bibliometric databases – consequently, an unknown number of scholarly works could be missed.[31]

Of the ten journals with the greatest number of legal education articles in the collection, the *Journal of Legal Education* was the most prolific and of the group received the top ranking in each of the indexes. Two other journals received rankings – the *Law Teacher* scored in Scopus and Google, and the *International Journal of the Legal Profession* scored in Scopus. Conversely, several journals in this group received no ranking in any index. In other words, most of the journals with the highest number of legal education articles were not ranked by measures that institutions might use to measure research and scholarship.

Re-sorting identified the ten mostly highly ranked items in each index. Of the ten items mostly highly ranked in the JCR index (scores: 1.964 to 4.736), seven were law journals each with one or two articles dealing with legal education. An interdisciplinary journal, *Psychology, Public Policy and Law*, was the most highly ranked in each index. Two other journals (psychology; education) included items focused on law or legal education. In the SJR rankings (scores: 1.189 to 5.040), of the ten most highly ranked in the list, five were law journals with one or two legal education articles. Of the remainder, three were education-focused, one was a policy journal, and the other was a psychology journal. In Google Metrics, the Google h-5 median index (scores: 32 to 81) for the ten mostly highly ranked listed five law journals each with one or two legal education articles. A mix of psychology, policy, and education journals comprised the remaining five. Of the ten most highly ranked items in Google h-5 index (scores: 31 to 81), four were law journals with one or two legal education articles. Again, the remainder were a mix of psychology, policy, and education journals.

In the practice-based legal education areas, just six of the clinical legal education and practical legal training articles were published in ranked journals – four appeared in the *Journal of Legal Education* and two in the *Law Teacher*.

In bibliometric terms, it seems that interdisciplinary journals with a small selection of academic legal education articles were stronger performers than the most prolific and more legal education–focused journals. If bibliometrics and academic publishing profiles inform decisions about recruitment, promotion, and research funding, it would be reasonable to infer that scholarly writing about legal education generally, and practice-based legal education as a subset, would not offer return on investment for academics, unless they were strategic in their choice of journal. If a strategic approach was guided by metrics alone, it is arguable that publishing in a cross- or inter-disciplinary journal outside of legal education might be considered a better investment in a wider institutional context. Those individuals whose object it is to raise the profile and standing of legal education scholarship could tactically select from the small group of ranked journals that do publish on relevant topics. If the bibliometric results were accepted, this could mean targeting selected US-based law and interdisciplinary journals. Within the confines of law and legal education, however, externally determined metrics might not be accorded as much value as other tacitly understood systems of value that are shaped by forces such as the priorities and preferences of faculty leadership groups.

In the practice-based legal education areas, the paucity of the literature might generally be attributed to the priorities and preferences of leadership groups in clinical legal education and practical legal training organisations, where the focus is on teaching legal professional knowledge and skills for the application of law in practice and there is little support for research and scholarship. The small amount of scholarly outputs from this area in the current meta-survey is consistent with insights derived from earlier research involving Australian practical legal training teachers. This disclosed that a majority of those interviewed were interested to engage with SoLT, but most of this group did not feel they had the necessary capabilities – they also lacked institutional symbolic or material supports to pursue scholarly activities.[32]

VII Qualitative insights

The qualitative investigation involved two avenues – first, to search and code the collection for attributes of empirical research usually found in learning and teaching literature. Second, to search for and code pedagogical perspectives and practices, and curriculum frameworks.[33]

The EndNote database holding the collection was imported as data into NVivo qualitative data analysis software (CAQDAS). Each text was treated as a case and linked to its bibliographic information, treated as attributes. Abstracts were treated as case memoranda and enabled faster searching of higher-level categories of information. Full-text articles were stored as searchable portable document format (PDF) files. This enabled searches of the entire collection of texts for keywords, concepts, and themes. Search results were saved and cross-referenced using framework matrices and matrix coding techniques. Sections of texts coded to specific concepts (e.g. 'experiential learning') were further analysed and coded for constituent concepts.[34] For example, 'experiential learning' could include work-integrated learning, work experience placements, clinical legal education sessions, and face-to-face or online simulations. The frequency with which concepts occurred within the collection was counted, and qualitative analysis would disclose where a concept was merely mentioned or subjected to deeper treatment in the text.

A Empirical research attributes

The collection was searched and coded for attributes of empirical research, such as specific research questions, definitions (e.g. behaviour, phenomena, population), review of literature, discussion of methodology or research design, description or justification of research methods, and critical reflection regarding the results and the work involved.

In the entire collection few of articles expressly described or problematised the methodology or methods that were adopted for the work. Quantitative methods, particularly the use of descriptive statistics, were prevalent. Low response rates were frequently a feature of reported results (an understandable problem familiar to most education researchers) – in this situation, where statistical accuracy would be difficult to establish, advanced statistical procedures were not possible and many articles relied on descriptive statistics. Sometimes articles that did report advanced statistical procedures did not discuss the assumptions underpinning them. Qualitative methodologies and methods were rarely expressly used and often confined to brief discussion of open comment responses in questionnaire results.

Literature reviews sometimes resembled an outline of legal submissions – a series of propositions supported by citations as authority (a lawyerly thing to do). It was unusual to see critical engagement or systematic review of cross-disciplinary literature on a topic – for example, examination of the strengths and weaknesses of a specific learning and teaching method across several studies and contexts. The quality of articles with cross-, multi-, or inter-disciplinary input, particularly those involving psychology, educational, technological, or sociological disciplines, appeared to benefit from outside methodological know-how.

The impression gained is that legal education researchers could benefit from broadening and deepening understanding of research paradigms (going beyond statistics), support to improve knowledge and skills for empirical research (including research paradigms, design, and methods), and that interdisciplinary collaborations expressly directed to the purpose would be fruitful.

Looking at the 78 articles dealing with the practice-based legal education areas – many of these were essentially theory- or policy-based arguments in support of a teaching method or program design. For example, several articles about clinical legal education stated the benefits of including clinical legal education in the academic legal degree. Some articles reported the implementation of a clinical legal education program in a specific location, with a description of the design and preliminary evaluation. These articles were interesting descriptive essays or personal narratives; however, they lacked several attributes of empirical research. Engagement with the literature, research design (including strategies to improve the reliability of the data), and discussion of methodology and methods, were largely absent. Few articles expressly or critically engage with methods to support student learning.

In practice-based areas, less than half of the articles expressly referred to the extant literature on a topic. Of those that did, most included statements to the effect that there was substantial literature available on a topic and would list examples – an alternative tactic involved reference to an extra-disciplinary article that included a substantial literature review. There appeared to be a sense that the literature review was a necessary burden rather than a generative scholarly activity worthy of critical engagement. There were interesting exceptions – Mkwebu, for example, reported a systematic review of clinical legal education literature for which a grounded theory method was adopted – this was atypically rigorous.[35] Spencer placed the literature at centre of her theoretical and practical analysis of reflective practice.[36] Galloway et al. explored expanding the scope of legal education literature to include grey literature and social media outputs.[37] Appleby and Bourke undertook a cross-disciplinary review of mental health literature for a case study involving promotion of mental health literacy and wellbeing for law students.[38]

Express justification for research design, methodology, or methods in the practice-based areas was rare. Again, Mkwebu was rigorous in discussing and problematising possible methodologies and in justifying the methods adopted for a systematic review of literature. Interestingly, several of the other examples involved a balance of qualitative and quantitative methodologies, with the former involving methods such as thematic data analysis, case studies, observations, auto-ethnographic reflexive writing, grounded theory techniques (explicit and emergent coding techniques), and interviews. These were in contrast with the reliance on survey questionnaires and descriptive statistics found in the wider collection – where the methods were often uncritically adopted. Similarly, several articles relied on external statistical reports and accepted the results at face value.

A recurrent trope involved observations about the need to remedy a dearth of empirical research on a topic – yet the paucity of empirical research suggests there were few scholars willing or able to undertake it. This is consistent with findings from earlier research showing that even those practice-based legal educators who were interested in pursuing SoLT research struggled with institutional symbolic and material support for the activity, or felt they were not yet capable of undertaking the work due to lack of research skills.[39]

B Practice-based education topics

This section categorises elements of the scholarly outputs with references to Higgs' model of practice-based education, namely 'pedagogical perspectives' (higher-level understandings, values, and social features), 'curriculum frameworks' (program/learning design decisions), and 'pedagogical practices' (learning and teaching methods and modes).[40]

A substantial part of the practice-based legal education collection (55 articles) involved higher-level pedagogical perspectives, particularly in respect of values and social issues. The identification of clinical legal education with social justice or access to justice was prevalent, together with awareness of social issues, social and professional understandings in historical and cultural contexts, and behavioural and social skills. Similarly, there was widespread concern about instilling appropriate professional and socially aware values and emotional intelligence through practice-based legal education – 45 articles expressly mentioned inculcation of professional and ethical values, but only a few expressly linked pedagogical practices with these.

The discussion about curriculum frameworks in the practice-based legal education collection were less about higher-level understandings of program design for learning, than advocacy for inclusion of specific pedagogical practices.[41] An exception was Leiman and Ankor's examination of the effect of graduate qualities or attributes in successful student learning outcomes, albeit primarily focused on the academic law degree.[42] Several clinical legal education articles focused on the benefits of clinical legal education's inclusion as part of the curriculum for academic law degrees to provide experiential learning and support for inculcation of core legal knowledge and skills. There appeared to be no critical discussion of curriculum frameworks specific to practical legal education or training – instead, frameworks such as Australia's competency-based standards approach seemed to be uncritically accepted.

Many articles (56) in the practice-based legal education collection touched on or were focused on pedagogical practices for learning, teaching, and assessment – most of which were focused on different methods of experiential learning (such as clinical experiences, simulations, work integrated learning or work experience placements, or service learning) or reflective practice (through reflective writing or journal keeping, peer-to-peer learning, and communities of practice). Usually these articles involved a high-level or program-level description of implementation of a pedagogical practice, with comments about student satisfaction. Explicit descriptions and evaluations of pedagogical practices and learning experiences at the educational or instructional level were omitted, as were evaluations of alignment with specified learning objectives and outcomes. Also omitted were measures for evaluation of achievement of specific learning outcomes. Perhaps this level of discussion is too 'practical' or 'educational' for publication in peer-reviewed legal education literature? However, without empirical research it is difficult to accept that individuals and organisations can account for their confidence in the reproduction of their learning and teaching methods, and the reliability of those methods for effectively producing specific learning outcomes.

VIII The wickedity

We have seen that a high proportion of journals focused on legal education do not rank highly on bibliometric measures, or at all. Also, analysis of the entire collection disclosed very few articles manifested the fundamental attributes of empirical research, and this was especially pronounced in articles dealing with practice-based legal education. This is not to ignore those few that do represent rigorous empirical research focused on learning and teaching – however, these exceptions highlight what is missing from learning and teaching scholarship in legal education and in practice-based legal education especially.

It is true that bibliometric measurements should not be the sole determinant of what constitutes quality, visible, and influential scholarship. Indeed, the situation in legal education is more complex than 'hard' sciences, and produces one example of a 'wicked problem'.[43] For example, at an institutional level bibliometrics might be utilised to rank the quality of faculties' and individual academics' outputs, and these rankings can be used for performative purposes that influence decisions about funding and access to other resources – with a flow-on consequence for the standing of those faculties and individuals within and outside of the institution. In the face of that pressure, an individual might aim to improve their prospects by submitting to journals outside of the legal education or law discipline – such as psychology, sociology, or high-ranking education research journals. If successful, those submissions could improve institutional ranking by publication in 'quality' journals. Conversely, if an individual's peers do not recognise the extra-disciplinary journal as relevant to their field, the potential for that work to influence the field might be negligible. On one recent occasion, this author observed a presentation by an institutional representative who pressed the point about the choice of 'quality' journals for publication, but was met with ridicule by the faculty audience when example journals were listed – the exemplars were meaningless to the audience, as without relevance or influence.

While it is open to scholars to strategically publish in high-ranking cross- or inter-disciplinary journals, should we not consider what we might do to raise the standing of legal education scholarship, particularly the scholarship of learning and teaching in legal education, by contributing to and uplifting the quality of our preferred journals? Arguably, this can be achieved by improving our practices and attending to the items identified in the preceding sections of this chapter. For example, we can explicitly and rigorously attend to the fundamental attributes of empirical research, including research questions, definitions, review of literature, and critical approaches to methodology or research design and methods. In undertaking literature reviews, we can more critically engage with the sources that we cite – we can evaluate the quality and influence of citations with reference to bibliometrics – however, we can also read those sources closely to distinguish between opinion and rigorous empirical research. For the latter, we can critically examine the methods, analysis and interpretation of results. We can carefully explore the use of qualitative methods to develop deeper understandings of learning and teaching in legal education, with the aim of producing highly textured insights that improve our understandings and our effectiveness as legal educators.

IX Conclusion

This chapter has used text mining, bibliometric methods, and qualitative analysis as ways of getting the 'measure' of the breadth and depth of SoLT in legal education generally, and in practice-based legal education. The approach generated an array of qualitative and quantitative insights from which it is reasonable to conclude that there is a paucity of empirical research about learning and teaching in practice-based legal education. Analysis shows SoLT does happen in practice-based legal education, although falling short of the baseline attributes for empirical research. Many of the articles focused on championing a preferred approach to practice-based education – across the pedagogical perspectives, curriculum frameworks, and pedagogical practices categories. Although there is opportunity for improvement, it is important to respect individual attempts to seriously engage with SoLT in practice-based legal education given the forces tending against it. As heterogenous acts, many of the articles can be interpreted as autoethnographic accounts – in which the author reports as a member of the research setting, making visible their material practices and theoretical understandings of practice-based legal education as social phenomena. Viewed in this way, these articles are material manifestations of the authors' 'mode of operating on the world' and as a kind of advocacy.[44] If they are bound together by any one unifying theme, it is the desire to transform or redirect the current state of things. Their works should not be disregarded or underestimated – however, the persuasive power and standing of such scholarship must be materially enhanced by rigorous empirical research in legal education SoLT if we are to raise its standing and ensure its relevance and influence for the future. The legal profession and the legal education field is experiencing great change; perhaps we are approaching a point of rupture where both interdisciplinary approaches to SoLT and rigorous empirical research can move nearer to the centre and flourish.

Notes

1 Roger Ormrod, *Report of the Committee on Legal Education* (Cmnd No. 4595, 1971) ('Ormrod').
2 William M. Sullivan, 'After Ten Years: The Carnegie Report and Contemporary Legal Education' (2018) 14 *University of Saint Thomas Law Journal* 331.
3 Keith Trigwell and others, 'Scholarship of Teaching: A Model' (2000) 19 *Higher Education Research and Development* 155.
4 Charles E. Glassick and others, Scholarship Assessed Evaluation of the Professoriate, Special Report (San Francisco, Jossey-Bass, 1997), Chapter Two 'Standards of Scholarly Work', p. 25 – note, however, that 'significant results' is not limited to statistical significance in this chapter.
5 Ernest L. Boyer, 'Highlights of the Carnegie Report: The Scholarship of Teaching from "Scholarship Reconsidered: Priorities of the Professoriate"' (1991) 39(1) *College Teaching* 11.
6 Ibid.
7 Robert J. Marzano and John S. Kendall (eds), *The New Taxonomy of Educational Objectives* (2nd edn, Corwin Press 2007).
8 Anslem L. Strauss and Juliet M. Corbin, *Basics of Qualitative Research: Grounded Theory Procedures and Techniques* (2nd edn, Sage 1990).
9 Joy Higgs, 'Practice-Based Education: Enhancing Practice and Pedagogy' (2011) Final Report for ALTC Teaching Fellowship.
10 Ibid.
11 Ibid.
12 Ibid.
13 Ibid.
14 Adrian Simpson, 'The Misdirection of Public Policy: Comparing and Combining Standardised Effect Sizes' (2017) 32 *Journal of Education Policy* 450.
15 John Hattie, 'Influences on Student Learning' (University of Auckland, 2 August 1999); Robert J. Marzano, 'A Theory-Based Meta-Analysis of Research on Instruction (Mid-continent Regional Educational Laboratory Aurora, CO 1998).
16 Simpson (n. 14).
17 Trigwell (n. 3).
18 Heather Piwowar, 'Altmetrics: Value All Research Products' (2013) 493 *Nature* 159.
19 Norman Paskin, 'Digital Object Identifier (DOI) System' (2008) 3 *Encyclopedia of Library and Information Sciences* 1586.
20 Blanca Rodríguez-Bravo and others, 'Peer review: The Experience and Views of Early Career Researchers' (2017) 30 *Learned Publishing* 269.
21 Yu-Chang Hsu, Jui-Long Hung and Yu-Hui Ching, 'Trends of Educational Technology Research: More than a Decade of International Research in Six SSCI-Indexed Refereed Journals' (2013) 61 *Educational Technology Research and Development* 685.
22 Jenine Beekhuyzen, 'Putting the Pieces of the Puzzle Together: Using Nvivo for a Literature Review' (4th QUALIT Conference Qualitative Research in IT & IT in Qualitative Research 2007).
23 Australian Research Council, 'Excellence for Research in Australia' (ERA) 2015 Journals List <www.arc.gov.au/era-2015-submitted-journal-list>, accessed 14 September 2016; Australian Business Deans Council, (ABDC) Journal Quality List <www.abdc.edu.au/pages/abdc-journal-quality-list-2013.html>, accessed 14 September 2016.
24 Christine L. Borgman and JonAthan Furner, 'Scholarly Communication and Bibliometrics' (2002) 36 *Annual Review of Information Science and Technology* 3.
25 Scimago Journal and Country Rank <www.scimagojr.com/>, accessed 10 September 2018.

26 Incites Journal Citation Reports <https://incites.thomsonreuters.com/>, accessed 10 September 2018.
27 Anonymous, 'About Journal Citation Reports' (Thomson Reuters 2012) <http://admin-apps.webofknowledge.com.ezproxy-f.deakin.edu.au/JCR/help/h_jcrabout.htm>, accessed 22 September 2014.
28 Anonymous, 'SJR (SCImago Journal Rank)' (Elsevier BV 2014) <http://help.elsevier.com/app/answers/detail/a_id/2899/p/8150/related/1/session/L2F2LzEvdGltZS8xNDExMzU0MTEzL3NpZC9JVG0xZl8ybQ%3D%3D>, accessed 22 September 2014.
29 Google Scholar Metric, <https://scholar.google.com/citations?view_op=top_venues&hl=en>, accessed 10 September 2018.
30 Anonymous, 'Google Scholar Metrics' (Google 2014) <http://scholar.google.com.au/intl/en/scholar/metrics.html>, accessed 19 September 2014.
31 Enrique Orduna-Malea, Alberto Martín-Martín and Emilio Delgado López-Cózar, 'Google Scholar as a Source for Scholarly Evaluation: A Bibliographic Review of Database Errors' (2017) 40 *Revista Española de Documentación Cientifica* 185.
32 Kristoffer Greaves, 'Australian PLT Practitioners' Engagements with Scholarship of Teaching and Learning (PhD Thesis, Deakin University 2015).
33 Higgs (n. 9).
34 See Kristoffer Greaves, 'Computer-Aided Qualitative Analysis of Social Media for Teachers and Students in Legal Education' (2016) 50 *The Law Teacher* 24, for a more detailed description of these methods.
35 Tribe Mkwebu, 'A Systematic Review of Literature on Clinical Legal Education: A Tool for Researchers in Responding to an Explosion of Clinical Scholarship' (2015) 22 *International Journal of Clinical Legal Education* 37.
36 R. Spencer, 'Holding Up the Mirror: A Theoretical and Practical Analysis of the Role of Reflection in Clinical Legal Education' (2012) 18 *International Journal of Clinical Legal Education.*
37 Kate Galloway, Kristoffer Greaves and Melissa Castan, 'Interconnectedness, Multiplexity and the Global Student: The Role of Blogging and Micro Blogging in Opening Students' Horizons' (2012) 5 *Journal of the Australasian Law Teachers Association* 177.
38 Michael Appleby and Judy Bourke, 'Promoting Law Student Mental Health Literacy and Wellbeing: A Case Study from The College of Law, Australia' (2014) 20 *International Journal of Clinical Legal Education* 38.
39 Kristoffer Greaves, 'Re-Imagining Practical Legal Training Practitioners – Soldiers for "Vocationalism", or Double Agents?' (2014) 7 *Journal of the Australasian Law Teachers Association* 101.
40 Higgs (n. 9).
41 Anneka Ferguson and Elizabeth Lee, 'Desperately Seeking . . . Relevant Assessment? A Case Study on the Potential for Using Online Simulated Group Based Learning to Create Sustainable Assessment Practices' (2012) 22 *Legal Education Review* 121.
42 Tania Leiman and Deborah Ankor, 'Are There Sign Posts at the Entry Gate? How Utilising Graduate Qualities, Threshold Learning Outcomes for Law and Inherent Course Requirements Might Impact on Satisfactory Completion of a Law Course' (2013) 6 *Journal of the Australasian Law Teachers Association* 113.
43 Judith Welch Wegner, 'Reframing Legal Education's "Wicked Problems"' (2009) 61 *Rutgers Law Review* 867.
44 Julianne Lynch and Kristoffer Greaves, 'Michel de Certeau: Research writing as an Everyday Practice' in Julianne Lynch and others (eds), *Practice Theory and Education – Diffractive Readings in Professional Practice* (Routledge 2017).

7 Towards a taxonomy of legal education research

Kate Galloway, Melissa Castan and Alex Steel

The purpose, content, and approach of legal education together create the lawyer many of our students will become. Beyond discipline knowledge, the skills and attitudes the law graduate brings to the profession find their foundation in the experiences of the student in law school. In turn, through their actions in legal practice, the law graduate-cum-lawyer turns dry words into real social structures and powers and so performs, and arguably, creates the law. From a different perspective, theories of education that are applied in law school – consciously or unconsciously – inculcate in students particular ways of engaging with the law. Such training inevitably informs approaches to legal scholarship, itself a recognised component of a functioning legal system.[1] Legal education is thus not only integral to law but might validly be seen as a constitutive part of law itself.

Legal education has long been fundamental to the development of the law and its understanding of itself. Blackstone's *Commentaries* began as university lectures, as did many of the leading treatises and textbooks. It was the process of teaching law students that sparked the impetus to catalogue and systematize the law, and then influenced practitioners and courts.[2] Legal change and development have also long been associated with law schools.[3] Much legal scholarship remains research influenced and developed within teaching environments. Community legal centres in Australia are strongly supported and developed by legal education – whether through management by law schools or through student volunteers.[4]

Similarly, when practitioners see failings in the profession, they often turn to law schools to introduce innovations to deal with the issues: three examples are increasing statutory interpretation skills,[5] developing writing programs, and addressing issues of wellbeing.[6]

Areas of law not taught in core law school subjects are seen as academic specialties (and those taught in the core subjects are seen as the expected knowledge of all lawyers), approaches to legal reasoning and research are heavily influenced by teaching methods, and the types of academics employed by law schools have a direct impact on the nature and scope of legal scholarship available to the profession. Consequently, legal education has direct impacts on how law is understood, and how the legal profession sees itself.

Because legal education is so central to the idea of law and itself a constituent part of law, the debates within law including about its purpose – positivist, doctrinal, critical, normative, and so forth – are reflected within legal education. By extension, these positions are reflected within the scholarship of legal education (SoLE), whether explicitly or implicitly: where the educational standpoint of a legal education scholar reflects their own discipline identity and commitment to the law. The positions adopted by a writer will also reflect the academic's idea of how knowledge is formed and the role of authority in society, positions that engage with broader understanding of law in society. Just as legal scholarship reflects diverse forms and perspectives, so too will SoLE. These standpoints all form part of the 'performance' of law.

This chapter first provides an overview of our project to develop a taxonomy of SoLE. The second part then articulates what is meant by legal research – itself a contested domain. We make the claim in the third part that (legal) educational research is a potentially interdisciplinary contribution to legal research. Importantly, this part spells out not only the disciplinary features of educational research, but also key education research methods. In the fourth part we extrapolate from the previous two parts to chart the likely territory of legal education research, identifying the key components of the field. We next focus on one aspect of the overarching taxonomy, exploring the dimensions of legal education themes. Finally, we draw together these frameworks to offer a means of comprehending SoLE as legal research.

I The project

The aim of the SoLE project is to recognise and chart the diversity of SoLE. In doing so, the resulting taxonomy is designed to make explicit the methods, approaches, purposes, and subjects of SoLE as a reflection of the intersection of scholars' discipline practices in both law and education, as both teachers and as researchers, as both lawyers and academics. Through description and theorization of legal education research, it substantiates the contribution of SoLE to the legal academy, and to law and legal practice, within an explicit research framework. Ultimately it aims to establish SoLE as a domain of legal research.

This chapter reports on the first stage of the SoLE taxonomy project. We take taxonomy to mean the systematic classification of areas of knowledge. Taxonomies, otherwise known as classifications, differ from inventories in that they are linked via a logical structure.[7] Library[8] and scientific[9] classification, as well as Bloom's well-known educational taxonomy, require distinct classes that are mutually exclusive, arranged in a hierarchical or other logical order and be arranged by level of complexity or detail.[10] Further, taxonomies should not merely attempt to reflect current understanding, but should draw on theoretical perspectives to provide suggestions for further research.[11] Certainly, classifications will reflect the times in which they are developed. As Mills points out, 'a modern classification of chemistry will lack a heading for alchemy'.[12] Similarly, Bloom's taxonomy has undergone further iterations in terms of the digital learning environment.[13] While representing a point in time, they should have the capacity to grow with the discipline.

This pilot phase of the project – and the subject matter of this chapter – involves the first step of labelling. In subsequent iterations of the process, we will test the relatedness of publications[14] and finally we envisage the capacity of the taxonomy to cluster publications within the layered themes, methods, and perspectives of the larger taxonomy.

Largely, and notably at this initial stage of the project, our method involves drawing on our experience as scholars in legal education to chart a prototype taxonomy. We acknowledge however, that the role of subject matter expertise is contested as a means of developing a classification. Mills, for example, argues that classification of specialist fields requires an expert classificationist.[15] Waltman and van Eck, on the other hand, acknowledge the role of subject matter experts in refining subject matter labels.[16] In light in particular of the omission of SoLE from contemporary research taxonomies such as the Australia and New Zealand Standard Research Classification,[17] and the preference for substantive legal research within the academy, we maintain that subject-matter expertise is a valid starting point for a new taxonomy.

Our first step has therefore been to anticipate what we describe as the domains of SoLE. We recognized early the combination of educational research methods, what we describe as 'perspectives' of the work, and the legal education themes per se. In other words, our hypothesised taxonomy comprises three distinct components, each of which bears its own internal structure and likely connections.

We have so far developed a prototype taxonomy by drawing on existing models of legal education,[18] and from the broader scholarship of education;[19] identifying divisions and connections between existing research and possible research suggested by the theoretical models; and arranging those divisions in ways that highlight connections and arrange the divisions from broadest to narrowest.[20]

We started with an anticipated list of perspectives and themes, drawing on our expectation of what we would find in the literature and we tested this list against a small sample of legal education literature. While our original pilot project design anticipated classification of works in the *Legal Education Review* over a decade, we have instead relied on a smaller and manageable sample of works over the two most recent editions (2016–2017). We worked individually and then together, developing a shared understanding of the likely categories and testing these against the contents of these two editions.

This exercise has resulted in a hypothesized taxonomy: a starting point for engaging in a broader and deeper examination of the literature to test the replicability of the classifications, to test and reinforce connections and divisions, and ultimately for us, to establish a connection between SoLE and legal research itself.

II Legal research

Underpinning this investigation is a fairly persistent question concerning the nature of legal research. The Council of Australian Law Deans (CALD), for example, says that 'it is not at all obvious what "legal research" comprehends'.[21] Further,

Roux also acknowledges the complexity of situating doctrinal research purely within the discipline of law. He observes, for example, that some claim that legal method is inherently interdisciplinary.[36] He concludes however, that while legal method – in the context of doctrinal research – draws on diverse analytic traditions,

> for the pure doctrinal researcher, reference to other disciplines always occurs on law's terms, with a view to improving the quality of legal doctrine. There is never any thought of subordinating the conventionally accepted reasoning techniques in the legal tradition in which they are working to the methods of another discipline.[37]

Thus, beyond doctrinal research, legal research retains a discipline-orientation regardless of the introduction of interdisciplinary methods and methodologies. Whether self-consciously interdisciplinary or not, research in the discipline of law that is a 'participant act in a particular legal system',[38] whether engaging in interdisciplinary methods or not, remains legal research.[39]

III Scholarship of legal education

The way in which we understand legal research has implications for scholars of legal education. Legal research was long seen as fundamentally about explication of legal doctrine and legal theory, and very strongly practitioner oriented.[40] Socio-legal research, where the approaches of social science research are as important as doctrinal perspectives, was often on the fringes of Australian and English research, though it has a stronger history in the United States through movements such as legal realism and law and economics.[41] More recently, socio-legal research has come to have much greater prominence, possibly through the synergy between it and grant funding – now a strategic driver of university research focus.[42] Legal education research, not having similar access to prestigious funding, has remained on the fringes.

Despite some SoLE concerning itself with the *teaching* of doctrine, its method and concerns cannot be said to be doctrinal per se. For example, such scholarship does not engage with deficiencies in the law itself.[43] Indeed, increasingly, SoLE adopts empirical and even scientific methods[44] that are obviously other than doctrinal, and outside the traditional research toolkit of the legal scholar. Consequently, and to the extent that engagement in doctrine represents legal scholarship, legal education research has to date enjoyed somewhat of an 'outsider' status within the Australian legal academy.

On the other hand, SoLE does resonate with Roux's observation of the purpose of doctrinal legal research, which seeks to

> persuade other legal professionals – fellow legal academics, practising lawyers, judges and law reformers – of the researcher's understanding of the state of the law and the seriousness of any deficiencies identified. Understood in

> this way, doctrinal research is research conducted by legal insiders for other legal insiders. It has no purpose beyond convincing other actors in the legal system of the merits of the argument made out.[45]

Rather than focusing on legal doctrine per se, legal education research seeks to improve the quality of legal education, within the law's terms of what is appropriate to serve discipline requirements of students in law, and of law graduates. The audience is inward-looking, likely to be the legal-professional community rather than educators more broadly. On this basis, scholarship in legal education performs the role of developing the practitioners who themselves will construct the law. Legal education might thus itself be seen as constructing the law.

The challenge for categorising SoLE might be better understood through appreciating its character both as legal and as educational. For example, to the extent that legal education research engages in interdisciplinary methods, Roux identifies a 'problem of belonging':

> [R]esearch . . . that attempts to integrate the internal doctrinal perspective of the trained lawyer with the external perspective of one or more other disciplines . . . [generates] a practical problem of belonging – of being forced to choose between two audiences: the legal-professional community and the wider academic community. It is also partly a philosophical problem in as much as it raises the question, common to all interdisciplinary research, of whether it is possible to participate in two different practices at the same time.[46]

Thus, for some the scholarship of legal education may be educational research: it is not 'proper law' at all. Adopting Roux's explanation, scholars in legal education face a philosophical problem of whether it is possible to be simultaneously a scholar of education and a legal scholar.[47] They face the additional problem of whether to write for a general education audience, or a legal education audience.

The characterisation of legal education research may appear a somewhat abstract problem, however it has important implications for the development of legal education, and thus, we argue, for the development of the practice of law. To the extent that discipline frameworks reject scholarship in legal education as 'outsider' research, law schools will not value it and legal academics will not research in legal education. A discipline-wide lack of engagement in the scholarship of legal education will only reinforce perceptions of its outsider status according to institutional metrics of 'quality', a point made by Bowery in the context of journal rankings.[48]

To retain a vibrant and rigorous culture of scholarship in legal education, requires institutional support. Further, law schools – and the profession – have a vested interest in high quality scholarship of legal education not only as consumers of the resulting research 'outputs', but also as stakeholders in the efficacy of legal education to serve society and the profession, while employing and advancing contemporary educational imperatives and methods. The scholarship of legal education functions at the intersection of higher education, the law school, the legal profession, the law, the community, and law students.

SoLE is thus *legal* scholarship. Its adoption of education or social science research methods occurs on law's terms. Such research is aimed at a legal audience, and it concerns the education of lawyers.

> The knowledge system to which legal researchers are contributing . . . is not the privately produced, corrigible work product of a purely academic discipline, but the state-sanctioned legal system, with its corpus of authoritative norms and its conventionally accepted ways of working with those norms.[49]

SoLE engages with those 'authoritative norms' through the lens of how best to educate those who apply them. It presents, re-presents, and adapts the modes by which new lawyers are inculcated into working with those norms. To construe SoLE as interdisciplinary implies a bifurcation of audiences where one audience is engaged in the construction of legal practitioners, and the other is concerned with education, or work, or some other discourse. We suggest that for the most part, it is more accurate to describe SoLE as legal research, incorporating diverse methods, and concerned with the education of lawyers.

IV A taxonomy of SoLE

Sitting as it does at the juncture of academia and practice, law and education, a taxonomy of SoLE would be expected to encompass diverse influences both in terms of content and in terms of method.

The aim of this undertaking is to attempt to capture these influences in a taxonomy that represents a reproducible method of describing and therefore understanding knowledge production within the sub-discipline area of legal education, and for managing that knowledge. Examination of legal education literature in terms of a taxonomy facilitates reporting, planning, and coordination,[50] to reveal trends and opportunities for new research.

The taxonomy developed here is based on three dimensions: perspectives, research method, and legal education theme – together describing the 'who', 'how', and 'what' of research. Each dimension itself comprises a classification system. We describe each in turn.

A Perspectives

The first dimension of our taxonomy we call *perspective*, addressing the 'who' and 'whom' – the authorial voice and object of the work (see Figure 7.2). Perspective addresses the subjective purpose or philosophical framework that the author adopts in their inquiry. We envisage these author perspectives as a hierarchy, reflecting a Bloom's-style evolution from lower to higher orders of

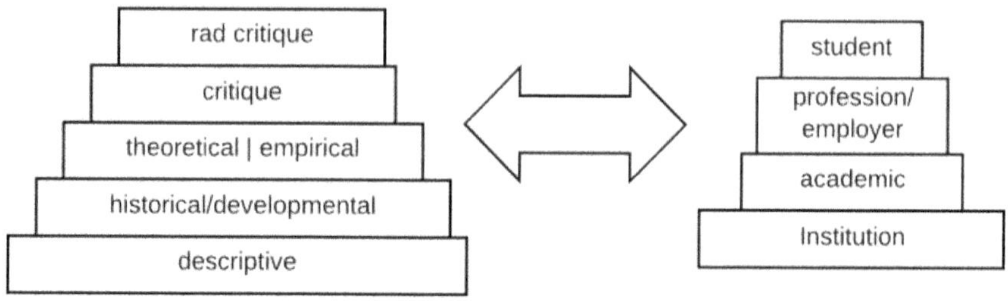

Figure 7.2 Likely Objects of Legal Education Research

abstraction. The hierarchy thus frames an author's approach to the subject matter from its description, through historical, theoretical, empirical, and critical lenses, to radical critique.

We have derived these categories as subject-matter experts, followed by refinement through testing upon a small sample of SoLE literature.[51] Some were in part informed by approaches to educational research,[52] but reflect also the diversity in legal method. This part of the classification may thus provide the potential for connection with legal research. Similarly, and as reflected in Tight's taxonomy of higher education,[53] we have identified likely objects of the research.

The hierarchical nature of this classification is based on an analytical logic, not a judgment on quality or importance. Valuable and exacting scholarly work occurs at all levels in the hierarchy, our hierarchy is intended to capture the extent to which a scholar moves outside of law's methods. We see this as important in highlighting the way SoLE interacts with other disciplines and research traditions.

Description captures the important work of describing a field of legal education, whether environmental, historical, developmental, or otherwise, and places findings in accepted approaches or categories of teaching or pedagogy.[54] In legal education such analysis would include the matching of identified approaches to law teaching or pedagogy with existing categorisations in either law teaching or teaching more generally.

Often however, research goes beyond these bounds and attempts to reorganize knowledge on a theoretical basis, or to gain new understandings on an issue by analysis of empirical findings. However, the extent to which that theory or empirical research creates new perspectives varies. Thus, the hierarchy recognises that the use of theory or empirical evidence may be an extension of a historical/developmental approach, or it may be the basis for a greater critique of the area of knowledge. The hierarchy also recognises that such critique can run within existing channels of thought, or be a radical rethinking. It is important to note, however, that the hierarchy is one of abstraction from existing knowledge and practice, not in any way a suggestion of increased scholarly merit.

Beyond the theoretical or ideological positioning of the author, we recognise that empirical or theoretical hypotheses are applied to particular subjects, whether human or institutional, concrete or abstract. We therefore suggest that the 'who' of scholarship embraces not only the authorial voice but the objects of SoLE. As noted in Figure 7.2, the categories that emerged from the pilot study are, hierarchically, the institution, the academic, the profession or employer, and the law student.

SoLE works engage with the role of the university or faculty in legal education, as well as the perspective of the academic. There is a literature concerning the relationship between the profession or employment on legal education, as well as research into the law student experience and the law student as a learner. We suggest that these may be aligned, or in tension, with authorial voice. The literature serves to reflect our interests as academics, for example, while also providing a forum for challenging institutional norms either of the university, or even of the profession. In this way we see the 'who' as connecting both the author's standpoint, as well as the object of the study.

This hierarchy again is not based on increasing merit. Instead the classification seeks to highlight the degree of indirectness to the object of legal education. That is, education is ultimately about the student and their experiences, but research into that can be mediated through analysis of the needs of the profession, the approaches of individual teachers, and broader institutional impacts on teaching and learning.

While this dimension provides information about the perspective of the research, to garner a deeper insight into the multidisciplinarity of the research requires investigation of the 'how' – that is, the research method.

B Research method

In recognition of the influence of the discipline of education upon the SoLE, we have adopted classes of educational qualitative methods to describe our second dimension: the method of inquiry.

Despite the tradition of schooling lawyers, including legal academics, in the doctrinal method, increasingly legal scholars are educated in diverse methods. This can be seen through the growing number of empirical studies in legal education research.[55] In some cases, however, it is likely that legal scholars may engage in interdisciplinary methods without a foundation knowledge of that method. Roux warns against this as an easy alternative, instead suggesting that legal scholars 'should pay rigorous attention to the conceptual frameworks and methods of all the disciplines on which they are drawing'.[56]

Yet on the other hand the rationale for the emerging field of the 'scholarship of teaching and learning' (SoTL) is that interdisciplinary scholars are not equally expert across all their fields, and consequently may need to research in teams, or recognise their developing expertise.[57] As we point out above, SoLE is also a field of research for the discipline of law and so mediates and translates between the epistemological viewpoints of various research traditions.

We chose for the starting point of our taxonomy to adopt recognised frameworks of educational research methods: naturalistic and ethnographic; historical and documentary (to which we add theoretical); surveys, longitudinal, cross-sectional, and trend studies; internet-based research and computer usage; case studies; ex post facto research; experiments, quasi-experiments, single-case research, and meta-analysis; and action research.[58]

None of these methods intersects with classical doctrinal legal research. Consequently, classification in this dimension is merely descriptive of accepted research classifications. Like education research itself, the classification is broad and catholic and open to approaches to research.

C *Legal education themes*

The third domain we describe as *themes* of legal education research. Themes relate to recognised trends in legal education research and practice – recently exemplified, for example, by the interest in student wellbeing. While some themes represent a particular period, others persist over time. These themes might be reflected in educational contexts more broadly, but the themes we focus on are emblematic of the concerns of the legal education with a view to admission to the profession.

While we initially anticipated most of the themes as subject experts – such as wellbeing, Indigenous perspectives, skills, alternative dispute resolution, internationalisation, critical thinking, work integrated learning, technology and law, gender, doctrine, and regulation – others became apparent as we tested our initial categories on the sampled articles. As we describe below, the classification of legal education themes evolved from an inventory into a true classification.

In addition to themes shared with the legal profession or specific to the law, there were some others that arose principally in the context of higher education. Notably, these include the first year experience and the student experience, as well as theories of learning. The former encompass questions of equity and diversity, but as with the latter, they also reflect explicit curricular and pedagogical (educational) imperatives. These take on a particular complexion in light of the law itself, and its practice where equity and diversity are at the forefront of concerns with progressive reform.

Through this process we labelled what we perceived to be the key themes in legal education research. The next step is classification – which we address specifically in Section V.

V Classification of legal education themes

In designing the classification, we have adapted the approach of Waltman and van Eck,[59] comprising three steps:

1 Labelling research areas;
2 Determining the relatedness of publication themes;
3 Clustering publications into research areas.

These three steps are relevant to our project in that they indicate a process for sorting a classification. Tight, for example, offers a ready-made classification of themes in higher education research.[60] However, his classification relates to higher education generally and is therefore too broad for our purposes – in particular in light of our interest in the connection with legal research. Further, he has derived two classifications, according to a survey of both journals and books separately. By contrast, we seek to derive a classification that can be applied across the literature.

While Waltman and van Eck first determine relatedness of publications followed by clustering and labelling, we have adjusted the sequence of classification stages. In common with Waltman and van Eck, our taxonomy may serve a bibliometric purpose which they identify as including 'simplify[ing] literature search, study[ing] the structure and dynamics of scientific disciplines, or to facilitate bibliometric research evaluations'.[61] However there are fundamental differences in both scope and purpose of our study.

First, unlike the sciences – the subject of Waltman and van Eck's study – law is a self-contained discipline. We have noted, however, the challenges of comprehending legal education research within the law discipline proper, and the rationale for offering a bridge between the two. While bibliometric goals will facilitate this, these are secondary to the purpose of locating the discipline context of legal education research.

Second, Waltman and van Eck dealt with a huge data set of almost ten million science publications. The field of legal education – a discrete field at that – is far smaller. While there are inevitably ways of testing the outcome of this pilot using data sets of publications globally and drawing on electronic databases using algorithmic analysis,[62] our purpose at this stage is to map likely legal education themes.

Like Waltman and van Eck, we have aimed in this method to adopt a transparent and simple system. By contrast, however, we have engaged human knowledge in our method, excluding digital solutions.[63] We envisage that our pilot program might form the basis for digital analysis at a later stage.

As described in traditional library classification, our method involves the classification of knowledge represented in the legal education literature, using logic to generate divisions. Mills suggests two principles. The first is that 'one principle of division only should be applied at a time; as a result, subclasses should be mutually exclusive'.[64] The second is that 'steps of division should be proximate – that division "should not make a leap"'.[65]

Applying these principles generates divisions in which the most general, or indeed least significant category comes first, while the most significant or focused category comes last: 'the more concrete will follow the less concrete'.[66] While library classification, for example, works through divisions, facets, subclasses, and foci,[67] we have adapted this terminology for our purposes, describing principal divisions, and facets as the most specific end point of the classification process.

As Mills points out, 'faceted classification', that is building a system of categories that recognises the faceted categories of subject matter, 'derives its facets . . . from an examination of the literature'.[68] We commenced the classification process

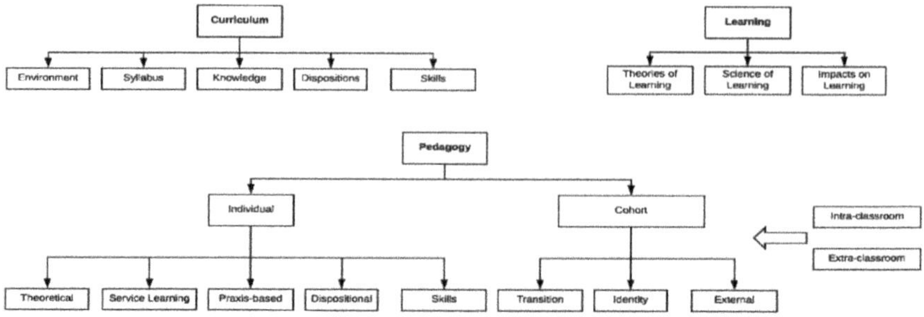

Figure 7.3 Classification of Legal Education Themes

drawing on our combined subject knowledge, anticipating the facets displayed in the literature and comparing our individually derived results. We then tested these facets against a small sample of articles in the *Legal Education Review*, over 2016–2017. We will continue to refine the themes classified in an iterative process of returning to the SoLE literature and adjusting the themes based first on the discovery of new facets of the field, and second on the relevance of any new theme to a cluster of publications. In other words, in the third stage of the project, if there is no cluster around a theme, then there is little imperative to retain it.

Through this method we have so far identified three primary divisions, and a total of 24 facets – illustrated in the diagram below. We describe the scope of these divisions in the following discussion. The first, curriculum, refers to the institutional structures, syllabus ordering and content, and the implicit and explicit aims of legal education. Second, pedagogy refers to the processes of legal education with a focus on the practices and philosophies of teachers and broader social expectations of education. Finally, learning refers to the actual internal processes of students studying law, and the external encouragements, pressures, and impacts on that learning.

A Curriculum

Curriculum is the first of three primary classifications. It addresses the various elements of the design of any program of law studies. 'We may take a curriculum in higher education to be a pedagogic vehicle for effecting changes in human beings through particular kinds of encounter with knowledge'.[69] By extension, curriculum is a prerequisite of any intentional legal education. We have drawn five secondary themes within curriculum: environment, syllabus, knowledge, dispositions, and skills.

Environment encompasses all factors that affect legal education outside of the syllabus. This includes university and government policy and politics, legislative requirements for admission, broader social factors on higher education.

Syllabus encompasses all the aspects of designing and arranging the course of studies in law, including the learning resources made available to students such as texts and digital media, assessment (including a variety of types, such as formative, summative), and learning outcomes. With syllabus we identify three key areas of research:

Knowledge relates to the content of legal education. While doctrinal research into 'the law' is primarily seen as traditional legal research, research that interrogates what content is most appropriate for achieving syllabus learning outcomes can also be seen as legal education related. It is likely to intersect with other foci such as learning engagement.

Dispositions, including research into defining the required values and self-awareness of the law student, encompasses work that engages with the construction of identity, be it as a lawyer, a law student, or a member of the profession generally. Work in this theme might take an auto-ethnographic approach, a sociological approach, or adopt reflective methodology to interrogate the nature of professional or personal identity within the legal discipline.

Skills, embracing key skills expected and required of law students and graduates, in order that they progress through their legal education and meet graduate outcomes. Work in this theme often articulates the mastery of reading for meaning, competence in communication (including oral and written manifestations of legal concepts, professional engagement and personal interactions), along with competence in collaborative work and negotiation work, and the skill of 'thinking'. By thinking we refer to the mastery of legal reasoning and analysis, which includes legal problem solving, reflective thinking, critical thinking, and creative thinking.

B Pedagogy

Pedagogy is the second of the three key classifications. 'Pedagogy may be construed as the formation of a set of principles upon which teachers can assist students in moving effectively and efficiently from a relative state of ignorance to a state of well-found knowing'.[70] It emphasises intentional strategies deployed to achieve learning beyond 'encounters with knowledge' per se.[71] Recognising the distinction between curriculum and pedagogy, in this theme we have brought together the methods of teaching in legal education and sought to draw out the different modes of engagement with the student learner. We suggest that it encompasses classroom issues (both intra- and extra-classroom), and student cohort matters. Further, we identify in the pilot project two distinct strategic approaches in pedagogy research: individual and cohort pedagogy; and a third factor we call pedagogical modalities.

The first, *individual pedagogy*, is aimed at each student individually and largely ignores broader environmental factors. While the success of such strategies may involve empirical testing across cohorts of students, that is not its starting point. Within this focus is a range of practical and theoretical approaches:

Theoretical approaches to pedagogy develop overarching philosophies to support practice. Examples include contextual theories of legal education argued for by such writers as Twining, broader liberation pedagogies, such as Friere's, and so on.

Service learning is a form of community engagement pedagogy, combining learning outcomes and community service to enhance both student development and the common benefit. Student learning then emerges by way of experience in a cycle of guided action and critical reflection, with the goal of community benefit and grounded learning based in experiential activities and meaningful motivations.

Praxis-based pedagogy research would include those forms of scholarly endeavour that seek to use teaching practice in reflective ways, and broader notions of SoTL.

Dispositional and *skills pedagogies* focus on the traditionally implicit aims of legal education – considering best to teach to 'think like a lawyer' and the teaching of ethics, ethical practice and professionalism.

The second main classification, *cohort pedagogy*, aims to identify broader cohorts and build pedagogic strategies for those groups. It addresses specific strategies to assist groups of law students that centre on a shared characteristic of that group – as opposed to strategies applied to individuals. As such we have identified three subthemes: transition, identity, and external.

Transition considers the way cohorts move into and through and beyond legal education. Such transitions include the move from secondary to tertiary studies; from non-law to law studies at a graduate level; from novice to expert in relation to individual subject areas, skills, or dispositions; or from tertiary studies into the profession.

Identity examines how cohorts of students see themselves or are seen by others and how that impacts their legal education. These can include identification in exclusive or inclusive ways, and involve intersecting identities. The theme includes research into the legal education of for example, international or domestic students, students who are the first in family to study at university, Aboriginal and Torres Strait Islander students and other ethnicities, male, female students, LGBTQI students, and examination of cohort-based diversity and inclusion pathways.

External considers the range of factors external to student's own efforts that impact on their learning. These factors can include the time demands of study, physical, and digital learning environments, the extent of learning support services, broad study stressors or events, lifestyle impacts, the market for job seekers and predicted future work environments.

In each of these subthemes, the emphasis is on pedagogical approaches to legal education that can assist these cohorts. Examination of the individual reasons for students being in transition, identifying with a particular cohort or being hindered by external factors is classified below in the learning classification, though it is recognised that a research project is likely to involve more than one classification.

In addition to these two main pedagogy classifications we recognise that pedagogical strategies often differ depending on the *modality* of teaching. To assist with identifying these modalities we suggest the following terminologies. We use the term *classroom* to denote the place of delivery. In this sense we can suggest that there are two key classifications; intra- and extra-classroom.

Intra-classroom describes the learning spaces mediated by the university, whether it be the lecture room, online learning platform, real time streaming of lectures or engagement on a specialised software platform (e.g. Second Life). This can be further sub classified into practice-oriented modes – such as simulations and mini-moots, and academic approaches that represent a traditional focus on intellectual knowledge – such as lectures, discussions, and group-work.

Extra-classroom learning spaces involve work integrated learning experiences such as internships, externships and placement programs. In addition, we include clinical and moot court programs. We acknowledge that these can sometimes occur on university premises, including in faculty-run clinics and mooting programs. But equally there are many clinical and mooting experiences that take the student beyond university-mediated spaces. In both cases, these spaces are thus differentiated in their purpose from the traditional classroom experience.

C *Learning*

This final classification captures research that examines the nature of learning in a legal context. Again, drawing both on our understanding of the field, the literature broadly, and the small sample of articles reviewed, we posit a range of approaches that are likely to fall within this classification.

Theories of learning refers to research that seeks to develop the conceptual frameworks that describe how law students process and retain knowledge during their studies at law school. Two examples of such approaches are constructivism[72] and threshold concepts.[73]

Science of learning applies research in neuroscience and psychology on how adults learn to the specific learning journeys of law students. Typically, such research is based on empirical analysis of law students undertaking discrete tasks. It may also include the application of results in non-law student cohorts to make predictions as to law student learning.

Impacts on learning researches factors that increase or decrease student learning. These effects can be both positive and negative. It is closely linked to research into the effects of curriculum and pedagogy, but also extends beyond this to include a range of factors beyond the control of universities and teachers. Such research includes work on what affects student engagement, work on student wellbeing and resilience, and into how students develop metacognition and self-management.

VI SoLE as legal research: some conclusions

The prototype taxonomy of SoLE described in this chapter makes explicit the methods, approaches, purposes and subjects of SoLE. Through describing and theorising legal education research, it establishes an explicit research framework with which to substantiate the contribution of SoLE to the legal academy.

The taxonomy categorises relationships between the who, how, and what of legal education research. The 'who' – namely the object of the research and the researcher standpoint – together evidence a connection between the legal research as generally understood, and legal education research. Perspectives adopted by the author might, for example, be expected to reflect perspectives on the law itself: a socio-legal scholar might be more likely to engage with an empirical or critical approach than a purely doctrinal scholar, for example. Further, the object of the research focusing on the student, the university, the academic, or the profession likewise articulates the connection between the legal education and its contribution to the practice of law.

In this respect, we suggest that the taxonomy provides the language with which to explain legal education research as deriving from and serving the purposes of the law and its practice.

In terms of the 'how', we suggest that the taxonomy of methods represents the increasing interdisciplinarity of legal research per se. It serves, therefore, to reinforce the connection between this development in legal scholarship and the methods of legal education research, narrowing the perceived gap between them.

Finally, the 'what' involves themes reflecting concerns within the profession per se, and with the means by which legal education inculcates the law into a new generation of lawyers. While dealing with educational themes such as 'pedagogy' and 'curriculum', the taxonomy of themes nonetheless draws on language familiar to legal scholars as the taxonomy becomes more and more precise.

Together, and when applied to legal education research, these three domains explain that research in a way that reflects concerns of legal research more widely. Integrating these dimensions represents a new picture of research that might be comprehended as a branch of legal research. The design of the taxonomy – including three domains, the descriptors within each domain, and the hierarchy within them – might also illuminate the relationship between scholars' discipline practices in law and education, as teachers and as researchers, and as lawyers and academics.

Notes

1 See, e.g., Michael Kirby, 'Welcome to Law Reviews' (2002) 26(1) *Melbourne University Law Review* 1.

2 See the review in David Sugarman, 'A Special Relationship? American Influences on English Legal Education (2011) 18(1–2) *International Journal of the Legal Profession* 7.
3 See, e.g., David Barker, *A History of Australian Legal Education* (Sydney, Federation Press, 2017).
4 See, e.g., Kingsford Legal Centre, *Community Legal Centre Guide 2016–2017* (UNSW, Sydney, 2016) <www.klc.unsw.edu.au/sites/klc.unsw.edu.au/files/2676%20CLE%20guide_WEB.pdf>.
5 Law Admissions Consultation Committee, 'Statement on Statutory Interpretation' (2010) <www.lawcouncil.asn.au/files/web-pdf/LACC%20docs/Statementon StatutoryInterpretation.pdf>.
6 See, e.g., the collaboration between major law firms and the College of Law in the Resilience@Law program <www.collaw.edu.au/learn-with-us/our-programs/practical-legal-training-programs/coursework/resilience>; Laura Helm, *Mental Health and the Legal Profession: A Preventative Strategy* (Law Institute of Victoria 2014) 16.
7 Robert M. W. Travers, 'Taxonomies of Educational Objectives and Theories of Classification' (1980) 2(2) *Educational Evaluation and Policy Analysis* 5.
8 See, e.g., J. Mills, *A Modern Outline of Library Classification* (Bombay, Asia Publishing House, 1960),
9 See, e.g., Ludo Waltman and Nees Jan van Eck, 'A New Methodology for Constructing a Publication-level Classification System of Science' (2012) 63(12) *Journal of the American Society for Information Science and Technology* 2378.
10 See, e.g., Peter W. Hill, 'Testing Hierarchy in Educational Taxonomies: A Theoretical and Empirical Investigation' (1984) 8(3) *Evaluation in Education* 179.
11 Travers (n. 7).
12 Mills (n. 8) 9.
13 See, e.g., Andrew Churches, 'Bloom's Taxonomy Blooms Digitally' (2008) 1 *Tech & Learning* 1.
14 A classification does not 'merely locate specific items but also relate[s] them helpfully': Mills (n. 8) 6.
15 Mills (n. 8) 267.
16 Waltman and van Eck (n. 9).
17 Australian Bureau of Statistics, 1297.0 – Australian and New Zealand Standard Research Classification ('ANZSRC') (2008).
18 For example, Nickolas James, *Power-Knowledge and Critique in Australian Legal Education: 1987–2003* (Queensland University of Technology, 2004) <https://eprints.qut.edu.au/15910/1/Nickolas_James_Thesis.pdf>; Sally Kift, Mark Israel and Rachael Field, 'Bachelor of Laws Learning and Teaching Academic Standards Statement' (Australian Learning and Teaching Council, 2010).
19 See, e.g., Malcolm Tight, 'Researching Higher Education' (UK, SRHE & Open University Press, 2003) who presents a taxonomy of higher education more broadly.
20 This draws on the approach in William R. Veal and James G. MaKinster, 'Pedagogical Content Knowledge Taxonomies' (1999) 3(4) *Electronic Journal of Science Education* <http://ejse.southwestern.edu/article/view/7615>, which in turn is based on the approach taken by Bloom and others; Benjamin Samuel Bloom, Committee of College and University Examiners, *Taxonomy of Educational Objectives* (New York, Longmans, Green, 1964) vol. 2.
21 Council of Australian Law Deans, 'Statement on the Nature of Legal Research' (October 2005).
22 Mathias M. Siems and Daithí Mac Síthigh, 'Mapping Legal Research' (2012) 71(3) *The Cambridge Law Journal* 651.

23 Dennis Pearce, Enid Campbell and Don Harding ('Pearce Committee'), 'Australian Law Schools: A Discipline Assessment for the Commonwealth Tertiary Education Commission' (1987) 6.
24 H. W. Arthurs, 'Law and Learning: Report to the Social Sciences and Humanities Research Council of Canada by the Consultative Group on Research and Education in Law' (Information Division, Social Sciences and Humanities Research Council of Canada, 1983).
25 Ibid., 63–71.
26 Paul Chynoweth, 'Legal Research' in Andrew Knight and Les Ruddock (eds), *Advanced Research Methods in the Built Environment* (Oxford, John Wiley and Sons, 2008) 28, 34–35.
27 Theunis Roux, 'Judging the Quality of Legal Research: A Qualified Response to the Demand for Greater Methodological Rigour' (2014) 24(1) *Legal Education Review* 177 ('Qualified Response'). Cf. some detailed exploration of research methods in, e.g., Terry Hutchinson, *Researching and Writing in Law* (2nd edn, Sydney, Thomson, 2006).
28 Theunis Robert Roux, 'The Incorporation Problem in Interdisciplinary Legal Research: Some Conceptual Issues and a Practical Illustration' (2015) 2 *Erasmus Law Review* 39 ('Incorporation Problem') 59.
29 Richard Collier, '"We're All Socio-Legal Now?" Legal Education, Scholarship and the "Global Knowledge Economy" Reflections on the UK Experience' (2004) 26(4) *Sydney Law Review* 503.
30 Kylie Burns and Terry Hutchinson, 'The Impact of "Empirical Facts" on Legal Scholarship and Legal Research Training' (2009) 42(3) *The Law Teacher* 153, 159.
31 Ibid.
32 See, e.g., Margaret Thornton, 'Inhabiting the Neoliberal University' (2014) 38 *Alternative Law Journal* 2; Margaret Thornton, 'The Demise of Diversity in Legal Education: Globalisation and the New Knowledge Economy' (2001) 8(1) *International Journal of the Legal Profession* 37; Margaret Thornton and Lucinda Shannon, '"Selling the Dream": Law School Branding and the Illusion of Choice' (2013) 23(1/2) *Legal Education Review* 249; Margaret Thornton, 'Discord in the Legal Academy: The Case of the Legal Scholar' (1994) 3 *Australian Feminist Law Journal* 53.
33 See, e.g., Sheila Slaughter and Larry L. Leslie, *Academic Capitalism: Politics, Policies, and the Entrepreneurial University* (Johns Hopkins University Press, 1997); Mary Henkel, 'Academic Values and the University as Corporate Enterprise' (1997) 51(2) *Higher Education Quarterly* 134; Kathy Bowrey, 'Audit Culture: Why Law Journals Are Ranked and What Impact This Has on the Discipline of Law Today' (2013) 23(2) *Legal Education Review* 291.
34 See, e.g., Kathy Bowery, 'Assessing Research Performance in the Discipline of Law: The Australian Experience with Research Metrics, 2006–2011' (Report to the Council of Australian Law Deans, 2012) 86 <http://cald.asn.au/assets/lists/Resources/Prof%20Kathy%20Bowrey%20Research%20Quality%20Report%20to%20CALD.pdf>.
35 Roux, 'Incorporation Problem' (n. 28).
36 See, e.g., Timothy J. Berard, 'The Relevance of the Social Sciences for Legal Education' (2009) 19(1) *Legal Education Review* 189.
37 Roux, 'Incorporation Problem' (n. 28) (footnotes omitted).
38 Ibid.
39 Similar conclusions can be drawn from the analysis in Siems and Mac Síthigh (n. 22).
40 Ibid.

41 Sugarman (n. 2).
42 See the review of this in Susan Bartie, 'The Lingering Core of Legal Scholarship' (2010) 30(3) *Legal Studies* 345.
43 Roux, 'Qualified Response' (n. 27) 178.
44 See, e.g., Wendy Larcombe and others, 'Does an Improved Experience of Law School Protect Students Against Depression, Anxiety and Stress? An Empirical Study of Wellbeing and the Law School Experience of LLB and JD Students' (2013) 35(2) *Sydney Law Review* 407.
45 Roux, 'Qualified Response' (n. 27) 178.
46 Roux, 'Incorporation Problem' (n. 28).
47 Similar issues are raised in Marilla Svinicki, 'Who Is Entitled to Do SoTL?' (2012) 6(2) *International Journal for the Scholarship of Teaching and Learning* <https://digitalcommons.georgiasouthern.edu/ij-sotl/vol6/iss2/2>.
48 Bowrey (n. 34).
49 Roux, 'Qualified Response' (n. 27).
50 See, e.g., Uber Research, 'Research Classification Approaches: Stamping or Understanding?' (11 March 2014) <www.uberresearch.com/uberresearch WP092014/wp-content/uploads/CASRAI-ReConnect-Research-Classification-1-UberResearch_March-2014.pdf>.
51 A small sample of legal education research was reviewed – namely articles published in the *Legal Education Review* 2016–2017 – to test our categories and assumptions. A deeper survey is anticipated. See Part V below.
52 See, e.g., Lawrence Manion, Louis Cohen and Keith Morrison, *Research Methods in Education* (Oxford, Routledge 2007) chs. 1, 8, who outline critical approaches as well as historical and documentary approaches, amongst others.
53 Tight (n. 19) Part II.
54 In terms of legal research outside of SoLE this could be seen as doctrinal analysis within the accepted forms of the profession. Thus an analysis that highlights overlooked precedent cases, that resolves apparent conflict in precedents in ways readily accepted by a court would fall into this level of the hierarchy.
55 See, e.g., Alex Steel "Empirical Legal Education Remark in Australia: 2000–2016" in this volume.
56 Roux, 'Qualified Response' (n. 27) 194. See also Burns and Hutchinson (n 30).
57 See, e.g., Svinicki (n. 47); Colleen Tremonte, 'Window Shopping: Fashioning a Scholarship of Interdisciplinary Teaching and Learning' (2011) 5(1) *International Journal for the Scholarship of Teaching and Learning* <https://digital commons.georgiasouthern.edu/ij-sotl/vol5/iss1/26>.
58 Manion, Cohen and Morrison (n. 52).
59 Waltman and van Eck (n. 9).
60 Tight (n. 19) 20, 43, summarising themes for journals and books respectively.
61 Waltman and van Eck (n. 9) 1.
62 See, e.g., Kristoffer Greaves, 'A Meta-survey of Scholarship of Learning and Teaching in Practice-based Legal Education' in this volume; Svinicki (n. 47).
63 Waltman and van Eck (n. 9) 2.
64 Mills (n. 8) 27.
65 Ibid., 35.
66 Ibid., 34.
67 Ibid., 15.
68 Ibid., 10.
69 Ronald Barnett, 'Knowing and Becoming in the Higher Education Curriculum' (2009) 34(4) *Studies in Higher Education* 429.
70 Ibid., 432.
71 Ibid.

72 Constructivism is grounded in psychological approached to explain how students acquire knowledge and learn the law. This puts the student at the centre of the learning process, situated as an active constructor of knowledge, rather than an acquirer of information. (Dewey, Piaget).

73 Threshold concepts are those fundamental understandings that go to the core of the body of legal knowledge. These might be exemplified by introductory concepts such as 'mens rea' or 'consideration', students must grasp these ideas so that core disciplinary knowledge of criminal law or contracts makes sense. These threshold concepts operate as a gateway that open the student to previously hidden ways of thinking.

Part III

Calls for action

8 Who controls university legal education?

The case of England and Wales

Anthony Bradney

I Introduction

> Here then [with the introduction of the Research Assessment Exercise] was a dramatic moment in the decline of donnish dominion.[1]

Over 20 years ago Elson suggested that 'the leadership of the [practicing] legal profession [in the USA needs to] . . . use their considerable authority to compel law schools to change', thereby implicitly accepting that the control of university legal education in the United States lay, at that time, in the hands of legal academics.[2] Whatever the merits of Elson's arguments, his intervention illustrates the general importance that is attached to the question of who controls university legal education. Control has both important policy consequences about the direction that such education takes as well as ethical significance, indicating who has ultimate responsibility for those consequences. In this chapter I will explore the question of who controls university legal education in England and Wales. Whilst the arguments in this chapter are limited to universities in England and Wales, the issues they raise are relevant to all other jurisdictions. However, great care is necessary when comparing university legal education in different jurisdictions, with the relationship between academics, practitioners and the state being 'a unique configuration in every country'.[3] One of the arguments put forward here is that what has happened, and is happening, in England and Wales will be of general interest even though the particulars in England and Wales are not precisely replicated elsewhere.[4]

II The legal position of universities and academics in England and Wales

Upon its face the answer to the question who controls university legal education in England and Wales is clear. Legally, universities in England and Wales are, and always have been, autonomous bodies; they are not creatures of the state. The first British university, the University of Oxford, emerged in the 13th century as a medieval corporation.[5] Similarly modern-day British universities are 'a peculiar kind of legal entity, probably best described as a corporation'.[6] With their own legal personality individual universities are free, within the limits of the law, to choose what they do. The legal position of their academic staff is a little less clear.[7] However, 'academic staff of the pre-1992 universities always enjoyed quite different terms of employment from the majority of their co-workers'.[8] Even in the present day the unusual status of academics is recognised by the fact that academic freedom in performance of their duties with respect to research and teaching is protected by statute.[9] Academics are not simply employees but are also members of their university as a corporate body.[10] The independent status of academics has led the courts to conclude that, whilst they are under a contractual duty to do research, 'preparing specific and definable scholarly papers and books, would be outside the course of the academic's employment and [as a result] he would retain copyright as the author of these works'.[11] Similarly, whilst academics are under a contractual duty to teach, allocating them wholly new teaching without consultation, even if they were qualified to do that teaching, would amount to constructive dismissal.[12] In relation to both research and teaching the courts treat academics as autonomous professionals who are employed but who are largely free to determine how they fulfil their duties.[13]

The legal status of universities and academics suggests that control of university legal education rests with universities and, perhaps, their individual academic staff. Yet, despite this relatively clear legal picture, there is a long-established and still growing literature which suggests that universities and academics no longer have the ability to determine their own direction.[14] Universities, this literature suggests, are hemmed in by regulation and universities in turn tightly control the performance of their academic staff. If this is so the answer to the question of who controls university legal education becomes more uncertain.

III Regulating universities

There are a large range of regulatory regimes that relate to universities and academics in England and Wales. Some like the Research Assessment Exercise, now the Research Excellence Framework, are long-standing.[15] Others, like the Office for Students, set up by Part 1 of the Higher Education and Research Act 2017, are very new.[16] The existence of each individual regime is pertinent for the arguments in this chapter. However also relevant is the fact of the multiplicity of the regimes. In addition to the regimes already mentioned the Quality Assurance Agency for Higher Education (QAA), Research England, the Office of the Independent Adjudicator, the Competition and Markets Authority, UK Visas and Immigration (part of the Home Office) and the Advertising Standards Authority are all part of the landscape for contemporary universities in England and Wales.[17] The Research Excellence Framework is now mirrored by the Teaching Excellence Framework.[18] The landscape sometimes changes. Thus, for example, the Office for Students and Research England recently replaced the Higher Education Funding Council for England (HEFCE) and the Office for Fair Access. However, notwithstanding such alterations, regulation itself has become a constant feature for universities in England and Wales and there is no indication that this is likely to change in the foreseeable future. When analysing the impact of this regulation in addition to the number of regulatory regimes that relate to universities, it is also necessary to consider the level of detail in those regimes. Thus, for example, despite its relatively short existence, a little more than eight months at the time of writing, the Office for Students has issued four Regulatory Notices, which are formal requirements made to universities, and 11 statements titled Regulatory Advice.[19] The content of these various documents includes, for example, references to access arrangements for students, ways of facilitating students' registration for national and local elections and how publication of numbers of university staff being paid over £100,000 per annum should be accomplished.

From the above it might seem that universities in England and Wales are now much like Gulliver bound by the Lilliputians.[20] This being so, the legal position of universities may seem to be of little moment. Consideration of the history of some of the earliest regulatory regimes however suggests a more complex story.

A The quality assurance agency

In 1997 the QAA 'was established as an independent company and registered as a charity'.[21] The Agency's remit was not wholly new in higher education in England and Wales. Polytechnics, for example, had come under the tutelage of the Council for National Academic Awards (CNAA), a body who were there to 'guarantee standards' in polytechnics and whose 'central concern was with . . . the negotiation, approval and reapproval of courses through explicit validation procedures'.[22] However polytechnics, whilst they provided higher education, were precisely not universities. Once they became universities, following the passage of the Further and Higher Education Act 1992, they ceased to come under the jurisdiction of the CNAA, which was itself abolished by the 1992 Act. Universities have long sought to maintain their autonomy from forms of external audit that were outside their control.[23] However the 1992 Act which, amongst other things set up Funding Councils for the universities, also obliged those Councils to assess the quality of education in universities and to set up bodies to advise them with respect to this.[24]

John Randall, the first chief executive of the QAA, was keen to establish its independence from universities themselves as much as from anyone else. In 1998 he wrote that 'the comfortable days are gone: the new stakeholding public no longer accepts the legitimacy of unaccountable priesthoods'.[25] In 1969 Perkins had written that '[u]niversity teaching is the key profession in the twentieth century'.[26] By 2000 Randall, writing as chief executive of the QAA, seemed to doubt whether academics were professionals. He would only go as far as saying that '[u]niversity teaching has the opportunity to demonstrate that it is worthy of recognition as a true professional activity'. Only if it did that would it have 'earned the right to play a part in the regulation of . . . [its] own activities'.[27]

That right to play a part in regulation would be earned by subscribing to the standards laid down by the QAA. Brown writes of Randall's 'enthusiastic espousal of a "tougher" regulatory regime'.[28]

B The law benchmark

One of the ways in which the QAA sought to fulfil its duties was by establishing a series of Benchmarks for each academic discipline.[29] The QAA wanted Benchmarks to 'describe the nature of study and the academic standards expected of graduates in specific subject areas. They [should] show what graduates might reasonably be expected to know, do and understand at the end of their studies'.[30] John Bell, a member of the first group to draft a Benchmark for Law, itself one of the first Benchmarks drafted, noted the potential problem with a Benchmark. A Benchmark could become a 'national curriculum . . . [something that] professionals in higher education [did not] wish to see imposed'.[31] There is no doubt that those who drafted the first Law Benchmark sought to work within the pluralistic way that law has been taught in England and Wales for many decades.[32] Nevertheless they also had to grapple with the fact that '[w]hatever its detailed content, it [a Benchmark] must, by its nature, set limits'.[33] The educational justification for some of the limits set by the first Law Benchmark was not always readily apparent. Thus, for example, the first Law Benchmark, like almost all other Benchmarks of its time, said that law graduates should have acquired teamworking skills. Whilst such skills might be useful if graduates were seen as potential employees what they had to do with knowledge of or understanding of law was less obvious. Why, on pedagogic grounds, misanthropes should be prevented from graduating in law was not made clear.[34] In this and some other respects the Law Benchmark seemed to subtly limit the autonomy of individual university law schools to decide what and how they wanted to teach.[35]

Whilst the content of the first Law Benchmark might arguably be seen as a constraint on Randall's 'unaccountable priesthood' the manner in which it was arrived at largely indicates the continuing power of that priesthood. The members of the original benchmarking group were, with one exception, legal academics.[36] In 2007, when the Law Benchmark was revised, the members of the new working group were all academics. By 2015, when the Benchmark was revised for a second time the membership of the group had somewhat altered; a much enlarged body when compared with the first two groups, it had three members who represented professional bodies for practicing lawyers and one person who was listed as an employers' representative. Three members of the QAA were also listed as members of the group. However, the 17 other members of the revising group were all from universities.[37] The priesthood dominated all three exercises.[38] Revising the Benchmark has enabled adjustments to be made which mean that the Benchmark is now even more closely aligned with actual academic practice in university law schools. Thus, for example, no mention is made of teamworking in the 2015 Law Benchmark; instead the Benchmark merely says that law schools should 'be clear with students about the benefits and limits of cooperative learning'.[39]

Even the 2015 Law Benchmark sets limits on what law schools can do. One obvious example of this is the fact that law schools are now expected to give students opportunities to discuss 'ethical questions and dilemmas that arise in law and to consider the features of ethical decision making'.[40] An academic, who looks at law from a pure doctrinal perspective, seeking to explicate rules from the internal evidence offered by precedents and statute, will not think that analysis of values falls within the purview of what they seek to do. It is this doctrinal perspective that has historically dominated law schools in England and Wales even though it does not have the same hold that it once had.[41] Given this, as a member of the 2015 working group, even though I do not think the doctrinal position is intellectually tenable, I was somewhat uncomfortable when this formulation was circulated to law schools as a draft.[42] I was, however, surprised when no law school complained about this aspect of the draft.[43] The explanation for this may lie in the comparative demise of doctrinal law with no law school feeling that it would not have academics who wished to explore these matters with students. Alternatively, it may reflect the comparative lack of interest that most academics and law schools have in the Law Benchmark.[44] Either answer suggests that whilst the Law Benchmark regulates law schools it does not do so very tightly.

C The QAA and institutional audit

The Benchmark was neither the only nor even the most important part of the QAA's proposed regulatory regime. Institutional audit and assessment were also to be part of the picture. By 1997 such interventions were not new to English and Welsh universities. For example, law schools had been one of the first subject areas which had been subject to an external audit of the quality of their teaching. In 1993 and 1994 small groups of assessors consisting of legal academics and usually one non-academic had visited each law school, looked at documentation provided by the law school and sat in on some teaching sessions. After this they then judged the law school's teaching as excellent, satisfactory or unsatisfactory and published a report on the law school. The process had been time consuming for law schools. It had produced little discernible benefit with comparison of the published reports failing to explain why some schools had been graded as excellent and others as satisfactory.[45] The experience in law schools was replicated in other disciplines. Whilst some saw merit in the assessment process others were concerned about its cost and its potential threat to academic autonomy.[46]

Previous experience in the universities of institutional audit and assessment was one of the reasons that the QAA was faced with a 'difficult inheritance' when it was first founded.[47] By 1997 universities wanted a reduction in audit. This did not seem to match John Randall's view of the QAA's role. The relationship between universities and the QAA proved to be fractious in its early years. Thus, for example, in 1998 a number of universities, including Cambridge, Newcastle and Oxford, were reported as resisting attempts by the QAA to scrutinise them.[48] In March 2001, King's College 'disowned' an adverse institutional audit report from the QAA 'claiming that the agency failed to "intellectually engage" with the college'.[49] In his 2000 essay Randall had written that '[t]he sanction of loss of funding is available if quality is found wanting'.[50] However that sanction lay with HEFCE as the funding body not with the QAA. In the same month as the Kings report was published the Board of the London School of Economics passed a motion saying that it would secede from the QAA because 'it [the QAA] infringed academic freedom, imposed its own bureaucratic and pedagogical agenda, neglected student "intellectual development" and used incompetent and unprofessional reviewers'.[51] Again in the same month the Secretary of State for Education and Employment suddenly announced, seemingly without consulting the QAA, that there was to be a 40 per cent reduction in the amount of external audit of universities by the QAA.[52] After negotiations between various parties, including the QAA, a much reduced process of audit was agreed.[53] Six months later Randall resigned from the QAA.[54] Brown has observed that after what he referred to as 'the Russell Group's putsch' 'the agency had effectively been side-lined'.[55]

Nothing in the analysis above should be taken to argue that universities or individual academics found the new QAA arrangements that were put into place to be entirely satisfactory. On the contrary it is easy to show that many academics felt that the '[e]xternal quality monitoring had become burdensome'.[56] Equally many found the resultant internal systems in their universities to be 'overly bureaucratic'.[57] Nevertheless it is hard to conclude that this history is one of audit processes simply being imposed on academics and universities. Whilst the systems, both external and internal, might constrain universities and academics and to some extent comprise their autonomy and their academic freedom universities and individual academics were part of the process, and sometimes a vital part of the process, that settled the degree of constraint and the form of compromise. As Tapper has written, commenting generally on the process of quality assurance in higher education in the United Kingdom, '[i]t seems that no regulatory authority can operate without the support of those whom it regulates'.[58]

D *The advertising standards authority*

Neither the manner in which the Law Benchmark was arrived at nor the way in which institutional audit was introduced into universities suggest that audit was simply imposed onto universities. Consideration of the work of the Advertising Standards Authority with respect to universities introduces a further layer of complexity into the relationship between universities, individual academics and audit regimes.

The Advertising Standards Authority unquestionably has a role in auditing the work of universities. Universities produce material which is subject to both the 'UK Code of Non-broadcast Advertising and Direct & Promotional Material (CAP Code)' and the 'UK Code of Broadcast Advertising (BCSAP Code)'.[59] There is a complaints system with respect to both Codes.[60] Complaints can be made by members of the public, competitors to those who have issued the advertising that is the subject of a complaint or members of a group with an 'obvious interest' in the advertising.[61]

Complaints about university advertising have usually related to claims about a university's status in relation to other universities.[62] In 2016 the ASA ruled on two complaints made about the University of Law's advertising.[63] One complaint was about the University of Law's claim that it was 'the UK's leading law school'. As is usual in such cases the ASA asked for evidence to substantiate this claim. Since it was unconvinced that readers would interpret the advertising in a way that was consistent with the evidence that the University of Law provided the ASA found against the University of Law. The second complaint was about the University of Law's claims about the salary levels that were attained by successful students. The ASA, once again, found that the evidence the University of Law supplied was not consistent with the way in which the advertising was likely to be read and so found against the University of Law. It is not, however, the way in which the ASA ruled against the University of Law that is of the greatest relevance to the arguments in this chapter; instead the most interesting matter is the identity of the complainants. One case against the University of Law was brought by a 'university law lecturer' and one by a 'retired university law professor'.

It is not entirely surprising to find complaints against universities being brought by academics. In an analysis of who complainants to the ASA are Crosier and Erdogan describe them at one point as being those who were 'well-educated, well-off, exhibited some bohemian tendencies, [and] identified with the chattering classes'.[64] Elsewhere they write that a 'psychographic profile' of complainants that they complied showed 'a clear picture of a social group not far removed from a mixture of university lecturers and the legendary "Disgusted of Tunbridge Wells"'.[65] Legal academics are not the only academics to have made complaints to the ASA. A complaint about the University of Strathclyde's claim that its physics department was 'ranked No 1 in the UK' and that it was 'number one in the UK for research in the REF 2014' was made by 'an academic'.[66] The fact that academics can and do make complaints about universities to the ASA is important when considering the ASA as a regulator of universities. The ASA itself monitors advertising and has its own compliance team.[67] It is thus an independent regulator in the same sense that, for example, the QAA is a regulator. Equally, even when it considers complaints made to it, the ASA makes its own judgements about whether or not there has been a breach of one of its codes. Nevertheless, the ASA is not just a regulator imposed on universities; it also can be and sometimes is something that individual academics use to help ensure that standards that they think are important are upheld.[68]

E *The changing role of the university?*

Regulation of the university is intimately bound up with questions about the role of the university. Thus, for example, the external audit of research in universities was first brought in at the behest of the then Conservative government in the 1980s. However, what that government sought was not simply a record of what research was being done but also reassurance that research funding was 'effectively deployed' which in turn meant that research would 'contribute more effectively to the improvement of the performance of the economy'.[69]

Successive British governments of varying political persuasions have followed the 1980s Conservative government in arguing that universities ought to direct their attention to servicing the needs of the economy in various ways. There is little to choose between the Conservative government's 1985 paper above and the then Labour government's 2009 proposition in *Higher Ambitions* that 'higher education is, and will continue to be, central to this country's economic performance in the twenty-first century'.[70] Similarly the Conservative and Liberal Democrat coalition government which followed the Labour administration said '[t]he Government believes that our universities are essential for building a strong and innovative economy. We will take action to create more college and university places, as well as help to foster stronger links between universities, colleges and industries'.[71] Its 2010 White Paper *Higher Education: Students at the Heart of the System* stated that '[o]ur reforms aim to make the English higher education system more responsive to students and employers'.[72] The argument that students are prospective employees and research should be about economic productivity is repeated in almost every government pronouncement on universities during the last three or four decades.

Yet, having noted the links that governments think there ought to be between universities and the economy, it is important not to overstate this message. *Higher Ambitions*, for example, also accepts that '[r]esearch and learning universities have intrinsic value aside from any economic considerations'.[73] *Students at the Heart of the System* says that '[h]igher education is a good thing in itself. Students may study a subject because they love it regardless of what it means for their earnings'.[74] David Willetts, the then Minister for Universities and Science, who co-authored a foreword to *Students at the Heart of the System* later wrote, in a book published after he had left office, that '[e]ducation is worthwhile in its own right, not just as a means to something else. Knowledge is better than ignorance'.[75] Nor is the acceptance of the notion of education, including higher education, as an inherent good confined to governments; it also extends to regulators. When Sir Michael Barber gave his first speech as the incoming chair of the Office for Students to Universities UK, the representative body for UK universities, he said that

> the acquisition of knowledge – for its own sake – and critical thinking capacity remain fundamental. The challenge is to engender the skills that will allow graduates to thrive in a global economy which is changing rapidly

and fundamentally and, at the same time, to engender a love of knowledge and an endless curiosity.[76]

This passage came in a section of his speech devoted to employability for students. Nonetheless the chair of the Office for Students, the regulator with statutory responsibility for the student experience, chose to assert the importance of knowledge for its own sake when making an important early speech at the beginning of his period of office. Once again examples of such beliefs and statements by regulators could be multiplied.[77] Governments and regulators strongly believe that British universities ought to service the economy but that has never been all that they believe.

IV Controlling universities?

The fact that governments and regulators have spent over three decades trying to redirect the focus of British universities to the economy is testament to the weakness of their position. Successive commentators have noted the continuing power of traditional conceptions of universities as places for the disinterested pursuit of learning and knowledge. In her study of academic identity Henkel, for example, wrote that 'liberal educational ideals still had a significant part in academic discourse'.[78] In a similar fashion, Tight contended that what he calls 'the English idea of the university remains both a coherent and highly influential model'.[79] Academics are, of course, aware that what they would like the university to be does not fit in with prevailing political mores. Bosetti and Walker observed that the ten vice chancellors that they interviewed saw this as being one of their key challenges.[80] In one sense this is neither unsurprising nor new. 'The mystery of academia . . . is how it manages to flourish in a social setting that would seemingly be hostile to its assumptions'.[81] For many in universities in England and Wales the question is how to best manage this situation. As one vice chancellor has written: '[t]o be business-like [in running a university] does not mean that we must become businesses'.[82] There are pressures upon universities and individual academics in England and Wales, as there always have been. These pressures, especially on individual academics, may be much greater now than they have been in the past.[83] However this does not mean that either universities or academics have accepted that their role should be determined by others. As Halsey suggests in the quotation at the beginning of this essay, donnish dominion may not describe the workplace for universities and academics in the modern era but servitude would not be accurate either.

V Conclusion

The sections of this chapter above demonstrate how universities and individual academics have sought to navigate an acceptable course for themselves during a period when doubts have been raised about the acceptability of academic autonomy. Opinions about how successful they have been in this will vary. Yet the fact of resistance to control cannot be denied. In this context, the position of university law schools in England and Wales becomes clear. As with their parent institutions their legal position and the reality of their everyday lives are in accord in giving them agency with respect to what they do. Exercising this agency is not necessarily easy. Others outside the university will have views about what the legal academy should do. The modern tropes of audit and accountability sit uncomfortably with the enduring professional ideals of integrity and personal responsibility.[84] Autonomy will not necessarily be welcomed.[85] Yet, of necessity, it is academics who decide what happens in the law school. Trow has distinguished the private life of a university from its public life.[86] What goes on in lectures and seminars is in the end a matter of the private life of a university, something that is determined by those who do the teaching.[87] The public life of the university, mission statements and the like, do not necessarily reflect reality.[88] How academics should use this control is not the subject of this essay. There are a range of opinions within the legal academy as to the direction that university law schools ought to take.[89] There is however one final matter that constrains the decision that legal academics make about how they exercise their control over university legal education; that is academic freedom.

Academic freedom is more properly conceptualised as an obligation than as a right. 'Professors and others who teach in universities . . . have a paradigmatic duty to discover and teach what they find important and true'.[90] The duty is personal and cannot be abandoned in favour of adherence to the views of others no matter how beguiling or forceful they are. What law schools and legal academics choose to do in legal education is a matter for them but what they choose must be what they think is important and true not what others think is important and true.[91] If they do anything else, whatever their contracts of employment say, they cease to be academics.

Notes

1 Albert Halsey, *Decline of Donnish Dominion: The British Academic Professions in the Twentieth Century* (Oxford, Clarendon Press 1992) 189.

2 John Elson, 'Why and How the Practicing Bar Must Rescue American Legal Education From the Misguided Priorities of Legal Academia' (1996–1997) 64 *Tennessee Law Review* 1135.

3 Michael Burrage, 'Practitioners, Professors and the State in France, the USA and England' in Sinclair Goodlad (ed), *Education for the Professions, Quis custodiet . . .?* (Guilford, Society for Research into Higher Education and NFER Nelson 1984) 26. See more generally Carel Stolker, *Rethinking the Law School: Education, Research, Outreach and Governance* (Cambridge, Cambridge University Press 2014) and Anthony Bradney, 'Can There Be Commensurability in Comparative Legal Education?' (2007) 1 *Canadian Legal Education Annual Review/Revue de l'enseignment de droit au Canada* 67.

4 Even university legal education in the other jurisdictions of the United Kingdom, Scotland and Northern Ireland, although very similar to that in England and Wales, has its own separate nuances. See, e.g., James Lorimer, 'The Faculty of Law' (1889) 1 *Juridical Review* 4.

5 M. B. Hackett, 'The University as a Corporate Body' in Trevor Aston (ed), *The History of the University of Oxford: Volume 1: The Early Oxford Schools* (Oxford, Clarendon Press 1984). 'Emerges' because like other early European universities it is neither possible precisely to date when it first starts or when it first becomes a corporation: see, e.g., Gaines Post, 'Parisian Masters as a Corporation, 1200–1246' (1934) *Speculum* 421–5. On the general legal position of European universities at this time see Ann Monotti and Sam Ricketson, *Universities and Intellectual Property: Ownership and Exploitation* (Oxford, Oxford University Press 2003) 20.

6 Nicola Hart, 'What Is a University as a Legal Entity?' in David Palfreyman and David Warner (eds), *Higher Education Law* (Bristol, Jordans 2002) 28.

7 The contractual position of academics provides a paradigmatic example of the conceptual problems caused by employment law jurisprudence which finds its roots the historical notion of master and servant, a somewhat implausible model for many modern workers including academics. On this problem see Jon Clarke and Lord Wedderburn, 'Modern Employment Law: Problems, Function and Policies' in Lord Wedderburn, Roy Lewis and Jon Clarke (eds), *Labour Law and Industrial Relations: Building on Kahn-Freund* (Oxford, Clarendon Press 1983) 145–52 and Otto Kahn-Freund, 'Blackstone's Neglected Child: The Contract of Employment' (1977) 93 *Law Quarterly Review* 508.

8 Dennis Farrington and David Palfreyman, *The Law of Higher Education* (2nd edn, Oxford, Oxford University Press 2012) 238.

9 Education Reform Act 1998, s. 202(2)(a).

10 See, e.g., *Thomas v University of Bradford* [1987] 2 AC 795 at 807; *R v Lord President of the Privy Council Ex Parte Page* [1991] AC 682 at 694 and *Pearce v University of Aston [No 2]* [1991] 2 All ER 469 at 473.

11 Andreas Rahmatian, 'Make the Butterflies Fly in Formation? Management of Copyright Created by Academics in UK Universities' (2014) 34 *Legal Studies* 709, 716 citing a Court of Appeal decision in *Stevenson Jordan v MacDonald and Evans* [1952] (1952) 69 RPC 10 at 18. See similarly William Cornish, 'Rights in University Innovations: The Herchel Smith Lecture for 1991' (1992) 14 *European Intellectual Property Review* 13 at 15. Cf. Monotti and Ricketson (n. 5) 273–4.

12 *Allen v Queen Mary University of London* [2016] WL 02997048 at [15]. It should be noted that this is an Employment Tribunal decision thus, even though it cites a previous tribunal decision between the same parties (*Dr JF Allen v Queen Mary University of London* [2015] WL 10990057) which makes the same finding, it has limited value as a precedent.

13 In doing this the courts' views reflect academics own conception of themselves. See, e.g., Jane Broadbent, 'If You Can't Measure It, How Can You Manage IT? Management and Governance in Higher Educational Institutions' (2007) 27 *Public Money and Management* 193 at 195 and Fiona Cownie, *Legal Academics: Culture and identities* (Oxford, Hart Publishing 2004) 105. Over half of Cownie's respondents said that autonomy was the thing that they valued most about their academic lives.

14 In relation to law schools in England and Wales see, e.g., Richard Collier, 'The Changing University and the (Legal) Academic Career – Rethinking the "Private Life" of the Law School' (2002) 22 *Legal Studies* 1; Richard Collier, 'Privatizing the University and the New Political Economy of Socio-Legal Studies: Remaking the (Legal) Academic Subject' (2013) 40 *Journal of Law and Society* 450 and Richard Collier, '"Love Law, Love Life": Neo-Liberalism, Wellbeing and Gender in the Legal Profession – The Case of the Law School' (2014) 17 *Legal Ethics* 202.

15 This form of regulation goes back to the 1980s. On the genesis of the exercise see Maurice Hogan and Stephen Hanney, *Reforming Higher Education* (London,

Jessica Kingsley 2000) 96–98. For the next iteration of the exercise see <www.ref.ac.uk/>.

16 On the Office for Students, see <www.officeforstudents.org.uk/>.

17 On these bodies see respectively <www.qaa.ac.uk/>, <https://re.ukri.org/>, <www.oiahe.org.uk/>, <www.gov.uk/government/organisations/competition-and-markets-authority>, <www.gov.uk/government/organisations/uk-visas-and-immigration> and <www.asa.org.uk/>.

18 See <www.officeforstudents.org.uk/advice-and-guidance/teaching/what-is-the-tef/>.

19 See <www.officeforstudents.org.uk/advice-and-guidance/regulation/the-regulatory-framework-for-higher-education-in-england/regulatory-notices-and-advice/>.

20 Jonathan Swift, *Gulliver's Travels* (London, JM Dent & Sons 1975) 15–16.

21 Ted Tapper, *The Governance of British Higher Education* (Dordrecht, Springer 2007) 181.

22 Harold Silver, *A Higher Education: The Council for National Academic Awards and British Higher Education* (London, The Falmer Press 1990) 8, 90.

23 Individual universities had long appointed external examiners to regulate quality but the universities determined both their appointment and what they did with their reports. Price attempts to challenge the autonomy of universities back to the Second World War: Geoffrey Price, 'The Expansion of British Universities and Their Struggle to Maintain Autonomy: 1943–46' (1978) *Minerva* 357. Goodlad goes even further back suggesting that the 'first step along a dangerous path to State control of universities was taken in a Treasury Minute of 1919 that established the University Grants Committee': Sinclair Goodlad, 'Benchmarking and Templates – Some Notes and Queries from a Sceptic' in Helen Smith, Michael Armstrong and Sally Brown (eds), *Benchmarking and Threshold Statements in Higher Education* (London, Kogan Page 1999) 72.

24 On this history see Roger Brown, *Quality Assurance in Higher Education: The UK Experience Since 1992* (London, Routledge Falmer 2004) ch. 6 and Tapper (n. 21) 167–80. For a recent description of the work of the QAA see Anthony McClaran, 'The Quality Assurance Agency' in Roger Ellis and Elaine Hogard (eds), *Handbook of Quality Assurance for University Teaching* (London, Routledge 2019).

25 Quoted in Colin Raban, 'Assurance *Versus* Enhancement: Less Is More?' (2007) 31 *Journal of Further and Higher Education* 77 at 79. On the inappropriateness of using the notion of stakeholders when analysing the work of universities see Anthony Bradney, 'Stakeholders in the University Law School: A Note in Dissent' in Fiona Cownie (ed), *Stakeholders and the University Law School* (Oxford, Hart Publishing 2010) 225.

26 Harold Perkins, *Key Profession* (New York, Augustus M. Kelley 1969) 1.

27 John Randall, 'A Profession for the New Millennium' in Peter Scott (ed.), *Higher Education Re-formed* (London, Falmer Press 2000) 168.

28 Brown (n. 24) 147.

29 On the place of benchmarks in the QAA's philosophy see Laura Bellingham, 'Quality Assurance and the Use of Subject Level Reference Points in the QAA' (2008) 14 *Quality in Higher Education* 265 at 269–74.

30 See <www.qaa.ac.uk/quality-code/subject-benchmark-statements>.

31 John Bell, 'Benchmarking; A Pedagogically Valuable Process?' (1999) 2 *Web Journal of Current Legal Issues* <www.bailii.org/uk/other/journals/WebJCLI/1999/issue2/bell2.html>. The possibility of Benchmarks becoming a national curriculum has been of general concern for academics. See, e.g., Steve Pidcock, 'What Is the Impact of Subject Benchmarking' (2006) 7 *Active Learning in Education* 111 at 117, 123 and Goodlad (n. 23) 78.

32 This has not always been the case with other benchmarks. Thus, for example, it been argued that the Economics Benchmark does not represent the full range of views about economics as an academic discipline. See, e.g., Alan Freeman, 'The Economists of Tomorrow: The Case for a Pluralist Subject Benchmark Statement for Economics' (2009) 8 *International Review of Economics* 23.

33 Anthony Bradney, 'Benchmarking: A Pedagogically Valuable Process? An Alternative View' (1992) 2 *Web Journal of Current Legal Issues* <www.bailii.org/uk/other/journals/WebJCLI/1999/issue2/bradney2.html>.

34 Ibid.

35 Benchmarks had no impact on individual academic autonomy because they described what a graduate could be expected to know because of their degree programme as a whole and do not what individual academics did in their own teaching. Of course, a problem for a law school would result if all the members of a department declined to teach in a way that was commensurate with a Benchmark's expectations.

36 The sole exception being a representative of a professional practicing body.

37 See Law Benchmark <www.qaa.ac.uk/quality-code/subject-benchmark-statements?indexCatalogue=document-search&searchQuery=Law&wordsMode=AllWords>.

38 In 1999 Brennan suggested that standards in Benchmarks might be set by those from pre-1992 rather than post-1992 universities (quoted in Brown (n. 24) 141–2). Membership of the various Law Benchmark groups does not suggest that this has been the case in Law. Nine of the academic members of the first 2000 Benchmarking group were from pre-1992 universities and four were from post-1992 universities with the chair of the group being from a pre-1992 university. However, in the second 2007 group membership was divided equally between pre and post-1992 universities with the chair being from a post-1992 university. In the third 2015 group the chair was once again from a post-1992 university and 11 of the academic members were from post-1992 universities with only six being from pre-1992 universities: Law Benchmark (n. 37).

39 Law Benchmark (n. 37) 3.2.

40 Ibid., 1.4.

41 Cownie (n. 13) 54–58.

42 On the fundamental problems inherent in the doctrinal approach see Anthony Bradney, *Conversations, Choices and Chances: The Liberal Law School in the Twenty-First Century* (Oxford, Hart Publishing 2003) 98–101.

43 This is not because law schools were unaware that the Benchmark was being reconsidered. Many responses to the consultation exercise about the draft were received.

44 In Cownie's 2004 account of the lives of legal academics no mention is made of the Law Benchmark: Cownie (n. 13). This is because none of Cownie's respondents raised the subject (personal communication from the author). Legal academics are not unusual in this respect. In a survey of academic attitudes to audit and quality assurance Cheng found that many of the academics that she interviewed across a range of disciplines were not familiar with the content of benchmarks: Ming Cheng, 'Audit Cultures and Quality Assurance Mechanisms in England: A Study of Their Perceived Impact on the Work of Academics' (2010) 15 *Teaching in Higher Education* 259 at 264.

45 See further Anthony Bradney, 'The Quality of Teaching Quality Assessment in English Law Schools' (1996) *The Law Teacher* 150. Only one law school was graded as Unsatisfactory in the exercise.

46 For an analysis of the process see Brown (n. 24) ch. 4.

47 Brown (n. 24) 118. For an assessment of the QAA's place in the politics of higher education see Anthony Bradney, 'The Quality Assurance Agency and the Politics of Audit' (2001) 28 *Journal of Law and Society* 430.

48 Tapper (n. 21) 177.
49 *Times Higher Education Supplement* (23 March 2001).
50 Randall (n. 27) 167.
51 *Times Higher Education Supplement* (23 March 2001).
52 Brown (n. 24) 131. What exactly precipitated this decision is unclear. Brown suggests that it was due to a combination of factors including lobbying by 'prominent Russell Group vice-chancellors': Brown (n. 24). Tapper suggest that whilst '[t]his may have been the case . . . [this ought to be put] in the context of the persistent and broadly-based opposition of many pre-1992 universities to the quality assurance regime from 1992 onwards': Tapper (n. 21) 184.
53 Brown (n. 24) 134.
54 Ibid., 146.
55 Ibid., 140, 147. See further David Laughton, 'Why Was the QAA Approach to Teaching Quality Assessment Rejected by Academics in UK HE? (2003) 28 *Assessment & Evaluation* 309. Randall continued his lonely campaign even after his resignation from the QAA. He concluded a 2002 article with the statement that '[f]or too long the providers of higher education have behaved like princes of all they survey. It is time for the consumer to be king': John Randall, 'Quality Assurance: Meeting the Needs of the Consumer' (2002) 56 *Higher Education Quarterly* 188 at 202. This echoes his 2000 suggestion that students were universities' 'primary client': Randall (n. 27) 165. An extensive literature on the notion of students as consumers now exists. However it is worth noting that a 2017 survey of UK undergraduates based on, amongst other things, interviews with 1,019 students found that 53 per cent of students did not see themselves as customers in relation to their university: *Education, Consumer Rights and Maintaining Trust: What Students Want from their University* (Universities UK 2017) 4, 5. See also Louise Bunce, Amy Baird and Siân Jones, 'The Student-As-Consumer Approach in Higher Education and Its Effects on Academic Performance' (2017) 42 *Studies in Higher Education* 1958, 1960–1.
56 Lee Harvey, 'A History and Critique of Quality Evaluation in the UK' (2005) 13 *Quality Assurance in Education* 263 at 271.
57 Andreas Hoecht, 'Quality Assurance in UK Higher Education: Issues of Trust, Control, Professional Autonomy and Accountability' (2006) 51 *Higher Education* 541 at 555.
58 Tapper (n. 21) 229.
59 See <www.asa.org.uk/codes-and-rulings/advertising-codes.html>.
60 See <www.asa.org.uk/make-a-complaint.html>.
61 Ibid.
62 The ASA has issued advice to universities about how they can make comparative claims in such a way as to be compliant with the ASA's Codes: see <www.asa.org.uk/advice-online/universities-comparative-claims.html>.
63 An account of the complaints and the ASA rulings is to be found at <www.asa.org.uk/rulings/the-university-of-law-ltd-and-marketing-vf-ltd-a16-346902.html>.
64 Keith Crosier and Zafer Erdogan, 'Advertising Complainants: Who and Where Are They?' (2001) 7 *Journal of Marketing Communications* 109 at 115.
65 Ibid., 118.
66 ASA Ruling on University of Strathclyde <www.asa.org.uk/rulings/university-of-strathclyde-a17-390134.html>. The complaints were upheld.
67 See <www.asa.org.uk/advice-online/universities-comparative-claims.html>.
68 On this see further Anthony Bradney, 'The Success of University Law Schools in England and Wales: Or how to fail', (2018) 52(4) *The Law Teacher* 490.
69 *The Development of Higher Education into the 1990s* (Cmnd 9524 1985) [9.1], [1.2]. For a history of early iterations of this exercise which concludes that the

exercise was ineffective in redirecting research towards the needs of the economy see Katherine Barker, 'The UK Research Assessment Exercise: The Evolution of a National Research Evaluation System' (2007) 16 *Research Evaluation* 3.
70 *Higher Ambitions: The Future of Universities in a Knowledge Economy* (Department or Business Innovation & Skills 2009) 53. *Higher Ambitions* said, amongst other things, that the Labour Government would 'ask all universities to produce a statement on how they promote student employability' at 51.
71 *The Coalition: Our Programme for Government* (Cabinet Office 2010) 31.
72 *Higher Education: Students at the Heart of the System* (2011) Cm 8122 27.
73 *Higher Ambitions* (n. 70) 41.
74 *Higher Education: Students at the Heart of the System* (n. 72) 38, 14.
75 David Willetts, *A University Education* (Oxford, Oxford University Press 2007) 122.
76 Sir Michael Barber, 'Keynote Address' (Speech to Universities UK, 23 June 2017) <www.universitiesuk.ac.uk/news/Pages/sir-michael-barber-speech-uuk-june-2017>.
77 Even John Randall wrote that students might pursue knowledge for its own sake: Randall (n. 55) 189.
78 Mary Henkel, *Academic Identities and Policy Change in Higher Education* (London, Jessica Kingsley Publishers 2000) 256.
79 Malcom Tight, *The Development of Higher Education in the United Kingdom since 1945* (Maidenhead, Society for Research into Higher Education & Open University Press 2009) 316.
80 Lynn Bosetti and Keith Walker, 'Perspectives of UK Vice-Chancellors on Leading Universities in a Knowledge-Based Economy' (2010) 64 *Higher Education Quarterly* 4 at 6.
81 William Brown, *Academic Politics* (University of Alabama, University of Alabama Press 1982) 37.
82 Gerard Pillay, 'Valuing Higher Education' (2009) 42 *Higher Education Review* 64 at 66. Elsewhere in his article Pillay writes that 'the university is among the few custodians of the quality of culture and its intellectual sustainability and depth' at 71.
83 See, e.g., Liz Morrish and Helen Saunton, 'Performance Management and the Stifling of Academic Freedom and Production' (2016) 29 *Journal of Historical Sociology* 42.
84 Cf. Michael Powers, *The Audit Society: Rituals of Verification* (Oxford, Oxford University Press 1999) and Eliot Freidson, *Professionalism: The Third Logic* (Cambridge, Polity Press 2001) ch. 9.
85 The comparative buoyancy of the job market for legal academics in England and Wales and the ease with which it is possible to commute to different universities does give legal academics more choice when deciding what conditions of employment are acceptable than is the case with many other academics.
86 Martin Trow, 'The Public and Private Lives of Higher Education' (1975) 104 *Daedalus* 365.
87 This not, of course, to deny that others both within and from outside the university may seek to influence what academics do in their teaching.
88 See, e.g., Davies and Glaister's study of such statements which finds them 'weak in application': Stuart Davies and Keith Glaister, 'Spurs to Higher Things? Mission Statements of UK Universities (1996) 50 *Higher Education Quarterly* 261 at 291.
89 Cownie (n. 13) 30–35. It is, however, clear that for those in law schools, as with the rest of the university, notions of a liberal education continue to dominate thinking: Cownie (n 13) 76–78. Academic drift, the 'tendency of institutions to aspire to and work towards higher status', is also likely to have an impact on

choices that are made: Malcom Tight, 'Theory Development and Application in Higher Education: The Case of Academic Drift' (2015) 47 *Journal of Educational Administration and History* 84 at 94.

90 Ronald Dworkin, 'A New Interpretation of Academic Freedom' in Louis Menard (ed), *The Future of Academic Freedom* (Chicago, University of Chicago Press 1996) 189.

91 See further Anthony Bradney, 'The Necessary Loneliness of Teaching (and of Being a Legal Academic)' in Bart von Klink and Ubaldus de Vries, *Academic Learning in Law: Theoretical Positions, Teaching Experiments and Learning Experiences* (Cheltenham, Edward Elgar Publishing 2016) 82–85.

9 A virtuous journey through the regulation minefield

Reflections on two decades of Australian legal education scholarship

*Sally Kift**

I Introduction

Australian legal education has much of which it is entitled to be proud. In 2019, the quality of Australian law graduates, as regards their acquisition of contemporary knowledge, skills and dispositions, is more assured than ever before. In large part, this is due to dedicated, evidence-based and research-informed enhancements to legal pedagogy over the last two decades, considerably enabled by a quantum leap in the quality of Australian higher education and teacher professionalism more generally. This is not to suggest at all that the Australian academy's learning leadership should rest easy: strident demands from the profession for more adroit responses to the training needs required by the fourth industrial revolution ('Industry 4.0'[1]) and continual claims of law school irresponsibility for producing 'too many law graduates [for] not enough jobs',[2] are not to be ignored. I simply posit that, on the whole, and without being overly complacent, we are in relatively good shape, even though some in government and the profession may choose to disagree.

This chapter will explore the rich harvest that Australian legal education scholarship continues to yield, leveraging serious national investment in pedagogical research and development over recent decades, carefully nurtured by an agentic and capable academy relentless in its pursuit of positive enhancement. We have progressed such a long way from the hard dichotomies described by Twining in 'Pericles and the Plumber'[3] – the academic isolated from the practical, theory divorced from practice, liberal education at odds with vocational training, and law sequestered from other disciplines – that it might not now be easily recalled that the case for integrating legal skills into curricula, let alone the inculcation of desirable dispositions, had to be argued long and hard before it was considered less heretical to suggest that law graduates were not well served by an exclusive, doctrinal focus on what 'lawyers need[ed] to know', without regard also to what lawyers 'need to be able to do'.[4]

The hard juxtaposition between the knowing and the doing is deeply rooted in professional regulation. Since 1982, the basis for accreditation of Australian law schools has been a list of 11 doctrinal content areas. Despite the entrenched disincentive for change that a stultifying adherence to content-based regulation might have otherwise enabled, it will be suggested that Australian legal educators have adopted a conscientious approach of 'virtuous compliance' with broader regulatory intent in order to navigate its multi-layered complexity. Such an approach has been underpinned by an explicit commitment to assuring robust graduate outcomes through the delivery of quality and contemporary curricula. While agile regulatory reform and harmonisation have remained elusive, there is now some reason for optimism that eons of intractable impasse might yet yield to productive professional-academy dialogue in response to disruptive influences, both disciplinary and other-regarding. Great care will need to be taken however to ensure that we do not mis-step, particularly given the lawyerly tendency to default to risk-adverse, inward-looking, over-prescription. But, at this point in time, like no other that has presented before, it is all for our discipline to lose should it eschew the opportunity to make bold regulatory strides towards a re-imagined, future-facing, legal education continuum.

This chapter will commence with a discussion of the context within which current regulatory discussions and assessments of legal education's fitness for purpose are taking place. Recent developments which augur well for a reduction in regulatory burden will be canvassed, and the adequacy of Australian educational assurance measures discussed. While, for the time being, it might seem that we remain trapped by the tyranny of our regulatory fragmentation, it will be suggested that there is no great need to panic. We should be calm, to use the language of war times long ago, and work hard and smart to bring the sum of our disciplinary parts to bear on a collective response; one that achieves a sustainable, fit-for-purpose legal ecosystem that is capable of weathering this and the next disruptive wave.

II Context

It is important to understand the context within which Australian legal education, as a subset of Australian higher education (HE), is currently operating and the key pedagogical, regulatory and professional drivers that have brought us to this seminal juncture.

A pivotal milestone in Australian legal education's evolution was the 2000 Australian Law Reform Commission's (ALRC) very public questioning of the fitness-for-purpose of the then (and still current) accreditation schema:[5] the 11 academic, content-focused, requirements for admission that were settled in 1982 (the 'Priestley 11'); the sequential, atomised model of academic requirements supplemented by practical legal training (PLT); and the adequacy of Australian educational assurance measures when compared with those proposed by the Bar Associations of Canada and the United States at the time.[6] In 2000, the ALRC exhorted a fundamental shift away from the 'solitary preoccupation with the detailed content of numerous bodies of substantive law, which is essentially the position taken by the "Priestley 11"'[7] towards core areas of knowledge *together with* 'the development of high level professional skills and a deep appreciation of ethical standards and professional responsibility',[8] as had occurred in other jurisdictions and professions. Since 2000, various efforts have been made to resolve aspects of these regulatory tensions, with useful contributions from both the Law Admissions Consultative Committee (LACC) and the academy, but little substantive accreditation progress has ensued. As observed in a 2014 Productivity Commission Report, LACC has found it difficult to achieve consensus among Admitting Authorities, which 'presented a reason for not re-opening [the Academic Requirements]',[9] while quite fundamentally also the relationship between the academy and the profession has been 'uneasy' over a long period,[10] with only relatively recent signs of improvement.[11]

In 2014, the Productivity Commission in its *Access to Justice Arrangements Inquiry Report* revisited the terrain and recommended that there should be 'a systemic review of the current status of the three stages of legal education (university, practical legal training and continuing professional development)'.[12] Inter alia, the Commission suggested specific consideration be had to: the role of and balance between each of those three stages; the continuing relevance of the Priestley 11 to legal practice; the 'relative merits of increased clinical legal education at the university or practical training stages of education'; and the regulatory oversight of each stage.[13] This has set the scene for the most recent regulatory manoeuvrings, which have coalesced with professional agitation to respond to Industry 4.0 disruption.

Over the same time period, the pace of change for each of legal education, HE, and the professions which both serve more broadly, has been dramatic and unrelenting. Disruption, both technical and non-technical, has been, and continues to be, ubiquitous and impacts the predictability of systematic workforce transformation.[14] In the age of Google, knowledge *acquisition* per se is not a challenge, and has long ceased to be the sole preserve of formal education; knowledge *application*, and the skills and dispositions[15] required to enable critical access, analysis, and utilisation of knowledge in context, is the future workforce holy grail.

Writing in 2004,[16] I observed that both disciplinary arms – academic and professional – had been subjected to similar disruption from an analogous range of disruptive influences. Fast forward to 2019, and these observations still hold true, even more so. Higher education, legal education, and the legal profession (as for other professions, though law has been somewhat slower to react) remain caught in the thrall of a new normal of constant change, characterised now by the term 'disruptive innovation'.[17] Specifically, both legal education and the legal services industry continue to be buffeted by waves of questioned relevance, driven by pervasive digitisation, automation and artificial intelligence, and accelerated by generational shifts, and fierce competition in a marketplace of ever-more empowered consumers. These factors have led to the pressing imperative that the next iteration of legal practice should be prepared for a 'digital, divergent and differentiated future'.[18] The unbundling of legal work and lawyer work, of legal information, knowledge and expertise[19] – forced by technological affordances, competition, affordability, and dissatisfaction with the cost inefficiencies of the 'OldLaw'[20] or 'BigLaw'[21] business models – is mirrored in the legal academy by the unbundling of almost every facet of the HE supply chain.[22] And neither academia nor the profession has any reason to be complacent as regards their staid business models and value propositions; the prime differentiator of disruptive innovation – the leveraging of technology in services and service delivery to support the practice of both HE and law – is impacting both sectors, with associated enhancements for specialisation, personalisation, accuracy and equity.

Unsurprisingly, there is no shortage of self-generated and other advice for both practitioners and academics about what to do, though it is worth noting that an agreeable amount of this commentary in law also comes with a refreshing focus on access to justice and diversity. Most recently in Australia, mirroring work done, for example, in Canada,[23] the United Kingdom,[24] the United States[25] and elsewhere, the Law Society of New South Wales (NSW) established a Commission of Inquiry into the *Future of Law and Innovation in the Profession* (FLIP), to develop its own thinking on legal practice and education in a technological world.[26] In sum, these reports have generally grappled with law-specific responses to the broader issues thrown-up by an uncertain world of future work, where different skills sets and capabilities are required for Industry 4.0 workers to thrive in technology-rich, globalised and competitive workplaces.

The world of future work: new knowledge and 21st-century skills

When the NSW FLIP Commission considered the implications of disruptive innovation for the future content of legal education in 2016, it opined:[27]

> In a changing environment, the skills and areas of knowledge likely to be of increasing importance for the graduate of the future include: technology, practice-related skills (e.g. collaboration, advocacy/negotiation skills), business skills/basic accounting and finance, project management, international and cross-border law, interdisciplinary experience, resilience, flexibility and ability to adapt to change. *Further consideration and research has been identified as being necessary to determine how these skills and knowledge areas could be taught within existing curricula.* [Emphasis added]

In the context of current accreditation requirements, how this ever-growing list of graduate requirements 'could be [validly learnt] taught [and assessed] within existing [already-crowded] curricula' by law schools and/or PLT providers, is difficult to envisage. While it might be tempting to produce a contemporary laundry list of the variously named 'enterprise skills',[28] 'work ready skills',[29] 'future skills'[30] and/or '21st-century skills'[31] now regarded as necessary to assure minimum workforce competence across a variety of skills sets such as 'values, behaviours and skills',[32] 'knowledge, abilities and characteristics'[33] and 'foundational literacies, competencies and character qualities'[34] (hereafter and compendiously '21st-century skills'), it is suggested that this is unlikely to be a productive exercise. The World Economic Forum has warned that, just as discipline-specific knowledge has a limited shelf-life, so also now there is no 'skills stability'; inevitably, expectations of skills requirements will shift because 'disruption is . . . changing the skills that employers need and shortening the shelf-life of employees' existing skill sets in the process'.[35] Perhaps it is sufficient to observe that the various reports frequently mention: problem solving; critical thinking; communication; teamwork; and creativity (all currently required in every HE course under the Australian Qualifications Framework (AQF)).[36] Reference is often also made to digital literacy; business literacy; innovative, enterprising and entrepreneurial mindsets; adaptability; leadership; resilience; and career management skills.[37] Curricular attention in Australia to these, and many of the other (currently) desirable, 21st-century skills, is either well in hand or being explored with alacrity. For the time being at least, the most recent *Australian Employer Satisfaction Survey* reports high levels of overall employer satisfaction with graduates' current skill sets as delivered by HE courseware in 2018.[38]

Another series of reports again offers various conceptualisations of, and projections for, the future world of legal work and lawyering. For example, in 2013, Frey and Osborne[39] argued that 'legal writing and truck driving will soon be automated, while persuading, for instance, will not'[40] and that while 'paralegals and legal assistants – for which computers already substitute' are vulnerable to automation:[41]

> [L]awyers, which rely on labour input from legal assistants, are in the low risk category . . . [because] engineering bottlenecks to creative and social intelligence will need to be overcome, implying that the computerisation of legal research will complement the work of lawyers in the medium term.

This analysis led Deloitte to conclude in 2016 that '[t]o date, the impact of automation within the legal sector has had a polarising effect. Lower skilled jobs, such as legal secretary, have been lost while new high-skilled roles have been created to develop and manage new technologies'.[42] Other commentators are less sanguine and forecast a far more pervasive supplanting of the professions quite broadly,[43] and of the legal profession specifically, given its hitherto resistance to commoditising legal services in order to harness the affordances and efficiencies of standardising, systemising, and packaging.[44] Most recently, it has been estimated that the tasks undertaken by solicitors changed by 23 per cent over the decade 2006–2016, as against an average change in job tasks every decade of 18 per cent.[45]

Such considerations, in tandem with the generational rise of 'millennial lawyers' who are 'not remotely as technophobic as Boomer lawyers were, and . . . won't fear technology's tendency to reduce hours',[46] have underpinned a concomitant rise of 'NewLaw'.[47] NewLaw, according to Beaton, has a 'business model [that] is the antithesis of the BigLaw model'.[48] It has been defined by Furlong and Larkan as '[a]ny strategy, structure, model, process, or way of delivering legal services that represents a significantly different approach to the creation or provision of legal services than what the legal profession has traditionally employed'.[49] It is beyond the scope of this chapter to discuss the [r]evolution of NewLaw, and the impact of its alternative provision of legal services on the legal services' ecosystem.[50] Suffice to say that NewLaw, with its harnessing of more agile business practices, disruptive technology, new fee structures, and more flexible work arrangements,[51] has had the equivalent impact on law that specialist competitors, MOOCs, micro-credentialing, and other unbundling of the education product have visited upon universities. Relevantly, and encouragingly for the future of intra-disciplinary relations, the joint onset of NewLaw, millennial lawyering and disruptive innovation has led to a new era of productive discussion now being pursued collaboratively between the practising and academic arms of the profession.

Law graduates: numbers, cost of education and employability

One consequence of both (r)evolutions – Industry 4.0 and NewLaw – has been to re-focus attention on the number of law graduates the Australian academy is producing. As this edited collection evidences, the lawyer role is changing: technology has 'removed the "grunt work" that was once a feature of entry-level positions', while 'as AI becomes easier to apply to specific tasks, there is a growing trend towards automated legal platforms that are blurring the line between the provision of legal information and the provision of legal services'.[52] And this in the context where the former prime minister of Australia had already famously warned that there were 'too many kids doing law'[53] and suggested that universities were being 'irresponsible' for continuing to enrol students in such large numbers. The prime minister might well have gone on to point out also that Bachelor of Laws (LLB) students in Australia pay disproportionally more for their university education than do many of their peers for other courses: in 2017, law students paid 84 per cent of their total course fees to be compared with, for example, a social work student, who 'would pay only 38 per cent'.[54] As the percentage of postgraduate Juris Doctor (JD) students continues to rise in Australia,[55] it is interesting to note that recent reports suggest that there is no difference between the debt payback time for a JD compared with an LLB; the payback time 'is equivalent, with tuition costs and lost income recouped four years after graduation, on average, regardless of which degree is chosen'.[56]

Considerations around the employability prospects and career needs of new law graduates are particularly keen, especially given that the Australian HE sector's graduate employment data (not to be conflated with evidence of employability) have only recently shown signs of recovery post the global financial crisis.[57] The issue here for prospective law students is that: 'A glut of graduates and game-changing digital disruption means anyone contemplating launching into a law degree faces questions to which the answers are not always easy or clear'.[58] The Council of Australian Law Deans (CALD) has attempted recently to set the record straight on the moral panic of 'irresponsible' enrolments by publishing data on law school graduate numbers and employment outcomes, drawing attention to the fact that, while all graduates might not 'be employed in the legal profession . . . the data suggests, a law degree places law graduates in good stead to secure employment across a variety of fields'.[59]

III How has Australian legal education positioned itself for a disrupted and uncertain future?

In 2016, the Boston Consulting Group and Bucerius Law School considered what this all meant for 'legal education – in law schools and firms' as follows:[60]

> Law schools, *and law firms* will have to invest in developing students' and lawyers' technical and business acumen. While law firms hire based on grades and school rankings and need lawyers trained in critical thinking and substantive law, law schools can further serve the profession by teaching students business project management, and general tech skills. To do so, schools may need to expand the mandatory curriculum beyond fields of substantive law by offering an additional course introducing case-management processes and legal technology. More specific legal-tech skills (such as database management, statistics, analytics, and digital communications) can be taught in electives and clinics throughout the course of the law degree. [Emphasis added]

Putting to one side the ramifications of this for existing course architecture, and the unwelcome spectre (again) of overcrowding the already heavily prescribed law curriculum, this passage draws attention to another issue that has eternally plagued Australian legal education: the failure to grapple with legal education and training as a continuum, a matter to which the Productivity Commission also alluded in its 2014 *Access to Justice Arrangements Inquiry Report*. This critique resonates equally in the United States: Cohen suggests that resistance to 'subsidiz[ing] on-the-job-training of law firm associates' is both an 'indictment of the Academy for its failure to produce practice-ready graduates with required skillsets and a swipe at law firms for their failure to more fully invest in associate training to drive client value'.[61] He concludes (in the American context) that a 'business as usual' approach to legal education 'no longer cuts it' and that 'Law school curricula, faculties, delivery models, and cost need a reboot'.[62]

In Australia, a strong tradition of legal scholarship and innovation over recent decades has positioned us well for our disrupted and uncertain future. Since 1989, the *Legal Education Review*[63] has been a rich repository of Australian pedagogical scholarship, supplemented by both the *Legal Education Digest* since 1992[64] and the *Australian Journal of Clinical Education* since 2016.[65] A number of Australian reviews and reports,[66] together with dedicated legal education texts,[67] have provided stocktakes and good practice disseminations at critical junctures, further incentivising learning and teaching excellence and innovation. Professional associations of dedicated legal educators offer other platforms for collaboration and sharing.[68]

A particular boon for the advancement of Australian legal education has been the funding provided by the national Office for Learning and Teaching (OLT) and its predecessors. In addition to being beneficiaries of OLT's sector-wide capability building,[69] law colleagues have featured heavily in the award of discipline-specific teaching fellowships, grants, and network funding,[70] while law also received dedicated funding for joint Discipline Scholars under a national academic standards project in 2010 (and see further below).[71] With the support of OLT investment in pedagogical research and development, a diverse array of topics has been investigated, resulting in original and critical contributions to legal pedagogical content knowledge in areas such as clinical legal education; law students' mental health and wellbeing; sessional teaching quality; internationalising law curricula; regional legal education; first year experience; capstone experiences in law; graduate professional entry; threshold concepts; law postgraduate research; and multimedia affordances. Encouragingly, and despite the demise of national enhancement funding,[72] Australian legal education continues to thrive with a number of centres[73] and blogs[74] having emerged in recent years, which have sustained and enhanced the pedagogical thought leadership for which Australia is now held in international renown.

The constancy and quality of this learning and teaching engagement has provided the robust platform on which Australian legal education is able to assure the fitness-for-contemporary purpose of its course offerings. At a different level of engagement again, and riding the current wave of engaging with 'students as partners' in their educational experience (which has been enabled in Australia by law Professor Sally Varnham's national OLT Fellowship[75]), our students and recent graduates have also been agentic in seeking to assure the quality of their legal education and managing their own law futures in tech-enabled legal workplaces.[76]

IV Legal education and Industry 4.0: some meta observations

Having canvassed these various contextual issues from a range of perspectives, what Australian legal education might take from this array of reports and contemporary commentaries may be synthesised as follows:

- *New and different learning needs.* Contemporary law graduates have broader and shifting requirements for integrated 21st-century knowledge, skills and dispositions than did their peers of previous generations. Perhaps most crucially, they should emerge from law school with a meta-cognitive commitment to lifelong learning and as self-regulating learners with a capability for evaluative judgement.[77]
- *Reconceptualised professionalism.* There is need to prepare students for New(Law) professionalism in tech-enabled legal workplaces. Obviously, the acquisition of digital literacies is critical,[78] but the ethical ambiguity inherent

in automation, and AI in particular, will place a high premium on ethical standards, moral judgment and criticality. Moreover, legal educators will need to be constantly vigilant and iteratively scanning for other desirable 21st-century skills, particularly those that are harder to automate[79] (such as, for example, emotional intelligence, interpersonal skills, human logic, creativity, inter-disciplinarity (and its enabler of collaboration skills), adaptability, resilience, design thinking, strategy, leadership, self-regulation and empathy).[80]

- *Course architecture and pedagogy.* Existing approaches to course architecture in law, as for other disciplines, require reconceptualisation. The real opportunities here are for more integrated law-with-PLT courses to breach the increasingly artificial silos of academic versus practice requirements. A fundamental reconsideration of the core and elective mix of subjects might also be undertaken, underpinned by considerations of how 'hyperspecialisation',[81] on the one hand, and/or enhanced opportunities for multi-skilling across a range of areas of expertise, on the other, might be accommodated.

  From the pedagogical perspective, contemporary understandings should be leveraged to enable better, integrative course design that delivers the quality, real-world outcomes that Industry 4.0 requires; for example – more authentic[82] and authenticated[83] assessment that demonstrates coherent, integrated learning;[84] more flexible and efficient online and blended learning delivery (mirroring technical enhancements to legal practice);[85] and clearer opportunities for (micro)credentialing and specialisation, including the recognition of other forms of learning.[86]
- *Mental health and wellbeing.* Given future workforce needs around adaptability and resilience,[87] and being cognizant of the vulnerable state of our law students' mental health, specific curriculum attention must be directed to building resilience, and assuring our students' mental health and wellbeing so that they might survive and thrive in the world of future legal work. Fortunately, Australian legal education is already well positioned to take this imperative forward.[88]
- *Agentic career self-management.* Even if we can ignore allegations of an oversupply of law graduates, as is now the case for all HE students in all disciplines, proactive attention directed to graduate employability is essential. To prepare our students for an unpredictable world of future legal work, and enable them to navigate their life, learning, and work futures with resilient agency – now characterised by iterations of careers, industries, employers, and skills requirements – will require a focus on enabling and embedding career development learning (CDL) into both core and co-curricular learning.[89]
- *Legal education continuum.* Writing in 2017 in response to the FLIP Report, the Chairman of LACC observed that it was[90]

  > [U]nrealistic to assume that law schools or PLT providers can readily include all of these proposed new requirements in their existing

> programs. Rather, we need to re-conceive legal education as a continuum, and allocate responsibilities for sequential components to other elements of the profession, after law schools and PLT providers have made their initial threshold contributions. Further, we may need to regulate each part of that continuum consistently.

> Assuring a more coherent handover from the academy to professional practice is long overdue.[91] If it ever were the case, in the context of current knowledge and skills volatility, it can now no longer be reasonable to expect that entry-level graduates will be fully formed professionals; the profession must invest and play a regulated role in post-admission capability development in the context of actual practice. Though it is beyond the scope of this chapter, the paradigm change in, and reimagining of, accreditation requirements in the context of legal Industry 4.0, must include lifelong learning engagement and training *post admission*, by way of rigorous and quality assured continuing professional development (CPD).

With these meta-observations in mind, I now turn to a consideration of how the Australian regulatory framework might support (and even encourage) a future-focused legal education agenda. In doing so, it is salutary perhaps to conclude the first half of this chapter with one final meta-reflection. The Australian legal academy has been an agentic global citizen in its sustained engagement with good pedagogical thinking and theorising nationally and internationally. We are now reaping the robust harvest of those decades of hard work and our legal education scholarship has positioned us well to embrace and advance, rather than fear, the Industry 4.0 trajectory and to contribute as equal partners to a principled regulatory response to it.

V The regulation of Australian legal education

The current regulatory framework impacting Australian legal education is distributed, complex, multilayered, and embraces both professional and HE accreditation requirements.[92] Commenting in 2014 on one law school's curriculum process, the then Chief Justice of the High Court noted the burden of academic and professional bureaucracies and said:

> In devising the new curriculum, [the university] had to navigate a number of constraints, including resources, professional accreditation – the dead hand of Priestley 11 – a couple of regulations and, of course, the managerial framework of the university itself.

Advances in regulatory harmonisation have been slow, despite the CALD calling for the 'external review, approval and accreditation processes [to be] consistent, coordinated and ideally able to be conducted by a single mechanism accepted by each relevant agency'.[93] In 2011, the Victorian Council of Legal Education (COLE) advised LACC that it would make use of independent, university-initiated, five yearly reviews of law schools for admission accreditation purposes. Subsequently, *Accreditation Standards for Australian Law Courses* were produced to enable further trials.[94] In 2018, these *Accreditation Standards* were finalised for adoption.[95]

Current regulatory framework – professional and disciplinary accreditation

From the professional accreditation perspective, regulation occurs pursuant to a range of state- and territory-based regimes, whereby local Acts of Parliament devolve accreditation of law schools and their courses to eight local Admitting Authorities. Generally, the LACC *Model Admission Rules* set out the principles to be followed in this regard. The *Rules* make reference to both the academic and PLT requirements for admission.[96] Supporting the work of Admitting Authorities, LACC's functions are 'to develop, consider and make recommendations about policies, procedures and other matters, directly or indirectly related to admission to the legal profession or to ensuring the continuing competence of its members'. LACC also provides advice to the Council of Chief Justices, which appoints the Committee's chairman and approves its annual work plan. LACC's membership includes representatives of the Admitting Authorities.[97]

LACC's predecessor first drafted the *11 Academic Requirements for Admission* in 1982.[98] Jointly with the Australasian Professional Legal Education Council (APLEC), LACC later developed the national *PLT Competency Standards for Entry-Level Lawyers*, which commenced operation in 2015.[99] As mentioned, in 2018, LACC adopted new *Accreditation Standards for Australian Law Courses*,[100] while *Uniform Standards for PLT Courses and Providers* have also been promulgated.[101] Though some law schools may disagree, LACC has consistently held the view that Admitting Authorities take a 'light touch' approach to accreditation,[102] and the 2018 *Accreditation Standards* now encourage Admitting Authorities to 'participate in, and to adapt to their purposes, accreditation and review processes undertaken by other regulators'.[103] The 2018 *Standards* are a mix of inputs and outcomes statements. For example, paragraph 4.4 '*Content of the law course*'[104] sets out in 4.4(b) '*How can a law school show that it has met this standard?*' and states that a law school needs to estimate the 'total teaching hours', whether face-to-face, online or blended, and

> (iii) if the estimated number of teaching hours for any prescribed area of knowledge is less than 36 or, if teaching hours are inappropriate, either as a measure of direct interaction in teaching that area of knowledge, or because of the teaching method used (for example, some form of digital learning or of student research), demonstrate how students will nevertheless acquire appropriate understanding and competence in that area.

The CALD has developed its own set of Standards (CALD Standards), which were adopted in November 2009 and amended in 2013 to incorporate the

Threshold Learning Outcomes for law that were developed as part of a national academic standards project ('Law TLOs' – see further below).[105] The 'primary driver' for the development of the CALD Standards was the 'shared desire to have a self-regulatory framework that would enhance the quality of all Australian law schools, for the benefit of the discipline as a whole'.[106] The CALD Standards are a mix of both minimum and aspirational standards, and of inputs and outcomes statements. Part B of the Standards establishes an independent committee – the Australian Law Schools Standards Committee (ALSSC), with both academic and professional membership – to oversight their application.[107] Section 14.2 of the CALD Standards exhorts that 'best endeavours' be made to 'coordinate any application to the Standards Committee with other relevant intra-university or externally-imposed reviews'. At the time of writing: 30 law schools have voluntarily applied for and received interim certification against the CALD Standards from ALSSC on the papers; seven did not apply;[108] and one application remains outstanding. In conducting this first round of certifications, ALSSC adopted the approach that, where the CALD Standards could be assumed to have been met under the national HE quality assurance framework, a statement by the Dean as to that compliance (and not fresh evidence of it) was sufficient.

Current regulatory framework – higher education and institutional accreditation

Since 2012, the legal framework that governs Australian HE, and legal education as a subset of it, is overseen by an independent national quality assurance and regulatory agency, the Tertiary Education Quality and Standards Agency (TEQSA). TEQSA regulates through a standards-based quality framework guided by the three principles of regulatory necessity, risk and proportionality.[109] Relevant legislative and policy instruments in this regard include

- *Tertiary Education Quality and Standards Act 2011* (TEQSA Act);
- *Higher Education Standards Framework (Threshold Standards) 2015* (HES Framework), which includes the requirement that the learning outcomes of all HE qualifications must be consistent with the relevant level classification in the *Australian Qualifications Framework* (AQF);[110]
- *Education Services for Overseas Students Act 2000* (ESOS Act);
- *National Code of Practice for Providers of Education and Training to Overseas Students 2018* (National Code 2018).

Pursuant to the TEQSA Act, universities are self-accrediting providers. Under this regime, each university also has a comprehensive array of policies and procedures that imposes a further level of regulatory detail on course constitution, approval and oversight.

As regards the link between professional and HE regulation, it is noted that the HES Framework specifically requires that the learning outcomes for each course of study 'encompass discipline-related and generic outcomes, including . . . c. knowledge and skills required for employment . . . *including those required to be eligible to seek registration to practise where applicable*' [emphasis added].[111]

VI Australian legal education: regulation and fitness-for-contemporary-purpose

Writing in the context of US legal education, Horn and Pistone claimed in 2016 that 'law schools are in crisis',[112] citing a decline in applications and the contraction of graduate employment outcomes attributed to technological disruption of the legal services' business model. They challenged US law schools' long-standing value proposition, exhorting a shift from a 'learn-to-think to a learn-to-think-and-to-practice' model,[113] and called out the signature pedagogies that had for so long been the backbone of US legal education. Specifically, issue was taken with: the common use of one summative (to be compared with formative) assessment by way of final exam; the lack of constant feedback to support learning; the slow adoption of a learning outcomes approach; failure to engage with new methods of assessment (*for* and *of* learning); the limited utilisation of blended/ online learning and modularisation; and the minimal amount of practical training.

While it is no particular cause for future complacency, in every respect Australian legal education has already embraced these pedagogical approaches, given its sustained enhancement focus of recent decades. As regards the 'learn-to-practice' dimension specifically, since the late 1990s,[114] Australian law schools have engaged in intentional, pre-PLT, curriculum design to embed and develop 'graduate attributes',[115] and employability skills as a 'subset' of them,[116] in integrated and incremental curricular approaches that have evolved in maturity over the decades since. How Australian legal education is able to lay claim to fitness-for-contemporary-purpose, and how it has managed to forestall Horn and Pistone's denunciation of 'law schools [being] in crisis', despite the regulatory minefield it traverses (even managing some regulatory harmonisation along the way), will now be discussed.

Regulatory harmonisation: law's threshold learning outcomes

A significant milestone in advancing the centrality of practice-ready graduates occurred in 2010 when the Australian Learning and Teaching Council (ALTC) oversaw the development of discipline standards under the auspices of the Learning and Teaching Academic Standards (LTAS) project.[117] Discipline Scholars were appointed across a number of broad discipline groupings to develop statements of minimum, discipline-based, academic standards – called TLOs – to harmonise the various regulatory and accreditation requirements that influenced degree content. A working definition of 'academic standards' was agreed upon for the LTAS project: 'Academic standards are learning outcomes described in terms of discipline-specific knowledge, skills and capabilities expressed as threshold learning outcomes that a graduate of any given discipline (or program) must have achieved'.[118]

Of specific significance, this exercise was conducted by way of an inclusive, iterative consultation process, with extensive engagement across each discipline's broad community of practice. In law's case, this included the judiciary, the practising profession, peak bodies (for example, LACC, CALD, Law Council of Australia (LCA), the eight Admitting Authorities, every law school, bar association and law society, the Australasian Law Teachers Association (ALTA), APLEC, the Coalition of Australian Law Administrators (COALA), the Australian and New Zealand Academic and College Law Librarians (ANZACLL), Legal Services Commissioners, a newly established Law Associate Deans Network (which, with some residual LTAS funding, became self-sustaining and is still operating), student associations, individual students, and recent graduates (including the LCA's Young Lawyers Committee). Recognising the global nature of law qualifications, specific regard was had to contemporary international benchmark statements,[119] while a Law Expert Advisory Group and a Law Discipline Reference Group were established for project oversight, both with international expert membership.

The TLOs ultimately agreed in 2010 set out the broad disciplinary consensus at that time as to what students needed to know, understand and be able to do as a result of their discipline learning, at a threshold or minimum level of achievement. Law's six TLOs for the pre-PLT AQF Levels 7 and 8 – LLB and Bachelor of Laws Honours (LLB(Hons)) degrees – were endorsed by CALD in November 2010 (LLB TLOs, set out in Appendix A).[120] TLOs for the pre-PLT JD (JD TLOs), at AQF Level 9 Master Degree (Extended), were subsequently developed and endorsed by CALD in March 2012.[121] The JD TLOs took the LLB TLOs as their starting point and adapted them to assure alignment with the increased cognitive and skilled requirements of the AQF Level 9 qualification descriptors. The TLOs are supplemented by explanatory, non-binding Notes, which provide guidance on their interpretation.[122] With their incorporation into the CALD Standards in 2013,[123] the TLOs are 'now firmly established as common and significant guiding educational principles for all pre-admission law courses'.[124]

A specific objective of the LTAS project was seek to harmonise professional accreditation and academic quality assurance requirements at the institutional and program level. It was also considered essential that the TLOs be drafted sufficiently broadly to assure flexibility as regards both their interpretation by individual law schools and to accommodate subsequent developments in contemporary legal practice. As regards the TLOs' relationship with the Priestley 11 academic requirements, the TLOs expressly include those 11 academic prerequisites for admission in TLO 1: Knowledge by requiring that graduates 'will demonstrate an understanding of a coherent body of knowledge that includes – (a) the fundamental areas of legal knowledge'. As explained in the accompanying Notes, '"fundamental areas of legal knowledge" are those that are from time to time prescribed by the relevant Australian law admitting authorities' and are 'flexible enough to allow for subsequent developments as negotiated between CALD and the law admitting authorities'.[125] In this way, at least the stasis imposed by the 1982 articulation of the Priestley 11 was not further entrenched.

As further set out in the Notes to the TLOs, in arriving at the endorsed version of each TLO, constant regard was had over the drafting process to the AQF descriptors, the CALD Standards, and the many international benchmark statements. Resources and Good Practice Guides for the implementation of the TLOs were developed and are housed on the *Legal Education Associate Deans Network* (LEAD) website.[126] In a significant advance for Australian course design, the integrative nature of professional learning outcomes was also made clear; for example:[127]

> [E]ven at the threshold level of achievement it is expected that graduates would demonstrate a broad and coherent assimilation of the TLOs across the identified knowledge and skills.
>
> For example, a graduate with an understanding of a 'coherent body of knowledge that includes . . . the fundamental areas of legal knowledge' (TLO 1: Knowledge) will frequently apply the results of legal research (TLO 4: Research skills) to demonstrate the thinking skills set out in TLO 3 (Thinking skills). Any of those TLO 3 cognitive outcomes (critical analysis, legal reasoning, creative thinking, etc) will in turn need to be communicated effectively, appropriately and persuasively in various contexts, as required by TLO 5 (Communication and collaboration), and ethically, as required by TLO 2 (Ethics and professional responsibility). Thus, within the range of diverse programs developed by the various law schools, graduates' acquisition of the TLOs will most likely be facilitated in a structured and integrated, whole-of-curriculum approach through learning, teaching and assessment.

Currency and advances in practice: HES framework

The LTAS project was commissioned by the Australian government in anticipation of new HE regulatory oversight by TEQSA as from 2012. The HES Framework, against which TEQSA regulates, provides further assurance of the pedagogical, and HE regulatory, shift to outcomes-focused curricular design, thereby endorsing the TLO approach as follows:[128] 'the expected learning outcomes for each course of study are specified, consistent with the level and field of education of the qualification awarded, and informed by national and international comparators'.

In the disruptive context of Industry 4.0, the HES Framework also explicitly requires that both course design, and its legal educator proponents, assure currency and contemporary relevance. In every respect – course content, curriculum design, pedagogy, and the purveying of it all – the requirement is to engage with current knowledge, scholarship, research and 'advances in practice'.[129] The consequence of these highlighted provisions is that, what had previously been virtuous and good practice as regards iterative disciplinary and pedagogical refresh, is now obligatory; Australian curricula must be fit-for-contemporary-purpose and assuredly address the graduate learning outcomes required for current employment and practice. Assurance of learning, based on the fostering of 'progressive and coherent achievement of expected learning outcomes throughout each course of study'[130] is now deeply embedded in our Australian curricular DNA.

Albeit with this HE regulatory nudging, our sector, and legal education swept up with it, is now leveraging the opportunity provided by the TLOs to reimagine curricula, originally 'developed at a time when content ruled', as a modern, integrative 'gestalt' that 'engage[s] students in the *practice* of the discipline'.[131] Operationalised this way, the TLOs[132]

> articulate the gestalt of each discipline in an age [of Google] when knowledge is at our fingertips. . . . So, this is our opportunity. As we grapple with the need to demonstrate the threshold learning outcomes, we must reconsider the *architecture* of our programs, which must have a structure that reflects the achievement of the outcomes rather than coverage of the knowledge domain, which is clearly impossible. It is far more possible to learn the practice of the discipline than it is to learn the *knowledge* of the discipline. This must be our focus.

Thus, the TLOs provide a cogent and contemporary response to the ALRC's 2000 exhortation to move beyond Priestley 11 *knowing* inputs to include also the disciplinary *doing* outcomes. Along the way, the TLOs have harmonised accreditation requirements – Priestley 11, HES Framework, AQF and institutional graduate attributes' statements – and forced a focus on integrative course learning *outcomes*. This latter has underpinned whole-of-course design and the delivery of constructively aligned curricula. Consequently, we now see increasingly common examples of authentic assessment for and as, as well as of, learning – a response to one of the aspects of Horn and Pistone's US critique. Specific examples of 'powerful assessments' in this regard include:[133] capstone experiences and other forms of program-level assessment;[134] ePortfolios;[135] real world, dilemma-based assessment;[136] assessments co-created between later-year students and early career graduates; real world challenges identified by industry or community partners; legal hacks and information systems design;[137] and immersive work integrated learning, clinical placements, practicum, and internships.[138] While by no means perfect or perfected, Australian legal education has been working assiduously towards assuring, as Boud and Associates have suggested, 'inclusive and trustworthy representation[s] of student achievement . . . [and] certification [that] accurately and richly portrays graduates' and students' achievements to inform future careers and learning'.[139]

Further harmonisation to reduce the regulatory burden

A further opportunity to harmonise professional and HE regulatory requirements has been presented in the TEQSA era due to the national regulator's commitment to engage with professional bodies to work towards 'complementary approach[es] to course accreditation processes and requirements' and to encourage 'alignment of professional outcomes with learning outcome requirements of the [AQF]'.[140] In this regard, TEQSA has signed Memoranda of Understanding with a number of industry and professional accreditation bodies 'to facilitate the sharing of information and reduce regulatory burden on higher education providers through joint and streamlined approaches to assessment'.[141]

In a similar vein, in 2016, Universities Australia (UA) and Professions Australia (PA) signed a *Joint Statement of Principles for Professional Accreditation* (*Joint Statement*) signalling closer collaboration between those two peak bodies and a shared 'responsibility to develop complementary approaches to course accreditation . . . [and] alignment of professional standards and the learning outcomes requirements of the Higher Education Standards Framework'.[142] The *Joint Statement* is 'well regarded by the sector . . . [and] designed to ensure that professional accreditation processes operate in a transparent, accountable, efficient, effective and fair way'.[143]

In 2017, PhillipsKPA[144] was commissioned by the federal Department of Education and Training to examine the impact of professional course accreditation practices to inform a national review by the Higher Education Standards Panel (HESP) charged with suggesting ways in which the regulatory burden on HE providers might be reduced. The HESP reported to the Minister in late 2017 with three recommendations, which have been accepted in principle and are now being progressed by TEQSA.[145] In short form, these recommendations are that[146]

- A legislated code of practice, in the form of a disallowable instrument, be developed to limit professional accreditation bodies to raising matters that are profession-specific, rather than those already assured by TEQSA against the HES Framework;
- TEQSA work with accrediting bodies to build their capacity to work more effectively and efficiently – by establishing formal guidance, participating in workshops, encouraging a focus on outcomes-based quality assurance, and promoting best practice regulation;
- A stakeholder forum be held to discuss the future of professional work and ways to further streamline accreditation.[147]

The HESP also encouraged further development of the *Joint Statement* to underpin the proposed legislative option.

Taken together, these recent initiatives have signalled a significant and positive paradigm shift in professional-HE accreditation interactions and, together with professional disruption visited by Industry 4.0, have now encouraged law's accreditation arm to move with greater determination to attempt some long overdue regulatory reform.

VII Assuring professional competence in 2019

While the PhillipsKPA Report noted that '[i]n the professional disciplines [the LTAS project] built on and has subsequently influenced the development of professional accreditation standards'[148] and had prompted a shift to learning outcomes approaches with 'less prescriptive criteria for the inputs and methods by which providers assist students to achieve learning outcomes',[149] progress in this regard in law has been slow. Despite the CALD Standards' embrace of the TLOs in 2013, and the subsequent broad engagement of law schools with the CALD Standards' interim certification process, the move to a learning outcomes focus, and the leveraging of the law TLOs, have only recently been undertaken by the LACC and its Admitting Authorities, prompted presumably by the HESP's 2017 recent recommendations.

Although in 2010 it 'seemed sensible for LACC and the Admitting Authorities to explore ways in which any discipline-specific TLOs for law might be integrated with, or complement, the existing 11 academic requirements for admission' given 'cogent reasons' for regulatory harmonisation,[150] it was ultimately decided not to proceed down that path. As the chair of LACC, Professor Clarke, has subsequently reflected[151]

> Although CALD and at least 3 admitting authorities had expressed support for the model, one admitting authority was concerned that, as TEQSA had not yet been established, it was uncertain whether and how TLOs might be changed or deployed, either in law or in other disciplines. Further, no TLOs had yet been determined for the numerous JD qualifications that had emerged. That admitting authority considered that the existing 11 academic requirements were 'necessary and sufficient' for admission purpose; and that to incorporate the TLOs would import 6 new sets of skills that were not presently required for admission. A further reason for rejecting the proposal was that many presently competent and practising lawyers could not, or were not inclined to, 'collaborate effectively'. They would thus not meet all of the TLOs, but were undoubtedly good practitioners!

The prescience of the TLOs in this latter regard specifically was acknowledged by Professor Clarke, who went on to observe:[152]

> In contrast, in 2017 the Law Society of NSW's FLIP Commission found that '[c]larity, practicality, understanding your client, being prepared to work collaboratively across disciplines and closely with the client are timeless qualities. As budgets shrink and competition grows, they are increasingly the attributes of successful lawyers of the future'.

Instead of the TLOs' regulatory integration in 2010, a limited review of the academic requirements was carried out by LACC in 2015 at the request of the Council of Chief Justices,[153] and some further work also commissioned.[154] The 2015 review resulted in no change, though critique emerged (again) that 'entry-level lawyers lacked certain knowledge and skills vital to modern legal practice'.[155]

In 2017, and following the FLIP Report, the desire to completely rethink the legal education continuum and the regulatory consequences of so doing – across the academic, PLT, pre-admission, post-admission and CPD span – led LACC to propose an 'Assuring Professional Competence' development program. A Committee chaired by the former Chief Justice of the High Court was established – the Assuring Professional Competence Committee[156] – and a plan of work proposed to develop a 'Competence Statement for Australian Legal Practitioners, as had recently been done in both England and Canada'.[157] Writing in 2017, soon after the Committee had begun its work, the LACC Chairman said that it was also proposed to develop:[158]

> (a) a Threshold Statement, derived from the Competence Statement, which entry-level lawyers would be expected to meet; and
> (b) a statement of Legal Knowledge and Skills that someone will need to acquire in order to meet the Threshold Standard.
>
> From there, it should be possible to work out where, in the continuum of legal education, the relevant knowledge and skills can best be acquired; and how compliance with the Threshold Standard can reliably be assessed.

Unfortunately, there was no funding available to pursue this ambitious scheme of work and, at the time of writing, a more modest exercise is now underway. A small Steering Committee established by LACC[159] is working with CALD to recast the Priestley 11 as learning outcomes statements, while LACC also explores 'how the TLOs and the Academic Requirements should interact and might complement one another, [given] modern law courses are required to comply with both requirements'.[160] The Steering Committee has drafted prefatory comments to make clear the relationship between the TLOs and the Priestley 11 for accreditation purposes, and has also articulated Guiding Principles for learning outcomes' development as follows: capable of replication; maintain present content and scope; indicative not prescriptive; adaptable to change; and complementary to, and compatible with, the TLOs.[161]

VIII Taking stock for an uncertain future

Looking at the 2010 TLOs through a disrupted 2019 lens, it might fairly be observed that the broadly stated TLOs have retained their relevance and continue to stand the Australian academy in good, future-proofing, stead. It is suggested that, for the 21st-century NewLawyer to enter and thrive in tech-enabled legal workplaces, they will need to: be cognisant of technology's capabilities; be able to harness those affordances appropriately; interpret and leverage the outputs delivered; and, most critically, be predisposed and ethically confident enough to challenge the propriety of such outputs. Surely this is the appropriate threshold/entry-level expectation, rather than requiring all graduates to be equipped to create the discipline's tech-enabled solutions from scratch: at entry-level, it is difficult to defend a standard requiring all graduates to be specialised and/or multi-skilled 'techno-legals'[162] who code, are data scientists, or legal solutions architects.

Returning to the TLOs, it is salutary to observe that frequently nominated 21st-century skills coalesce around many of those already commonplace in core Australian law curricula pursuant to the TLOs' synthesis of current AQF requirements[163] and university articulations of graduate attributes. Take, for example: communication (TLO 5), collaboration (TLO 5), critical thinking (TLO 3), problem solving (TLO 3), creativity (TLO 3) and self-management (TLO 6 in various of its behavioural aspects). Particularly as regards the last of these, TLO 6: Self-management allows for the development of important future work survival skills (for example, of self-agency, agentic career self-management, lifelong learning commitment, reflective capacity, emotional intelligence, resilience, and mental health and wellbeing). Many other of the (currently) desirable 21st-century skills – such as entrepreneurship, enterprise, innovation and inter-disciplinarity – are underpinned by the core thinking skills of problem solving, legal reasoning, criticality, decision-making and creativity (TLO 3: Thinking Skills, in which alternative dispute resolution already features), and are enabled by

- Well-developed interpersonal competencies (TLO 5: Communication and collaboration and TLO 6: Self-management);
- 'The intellectual and practical skills needed to identify, research, evaluate and synthesise relevant factual, legal and policy issues' (TLO 4: Research skills).

The human and relational aspects of lawyering that are less automatable (for the time being at least) also come to the fore: for example, ethical judgment in the face of techno-lawyering (TLO 2: Ethics and professional responsibility); reasoning and decision-making, strategy, and creativity (TLO 3); and social and emotional intelligence, empathy, persuasiveness, and resilience (TLOs 5 and 6). Understanding and exploiting the interrelationship and interdependency of 21st-century skills – their gestalt – is also important for their more complex Industry 4.0 application.

Finally, demands for new technology-based knowledge outcomes are able to be accommodated (as has always been the case for advances in practice), within the TLO 1: Knowledge domain: for example, blockchain and smart contracts into Contracts; automation of government decision making into Administrative Law; e-discovery into Civil Dispute Resolution; e-conveyancing into Property; and so on. Advances in automated information retrieval can take their place with the other 'intellectual and practical skills' envisaged within TLO 4: Research, while TLO 1: Knowledge also covers off on globalised legal practice for the emerging global legal community ('international and comparative contexts'), together with the entry-level practitioner's commitment to the 'principles and values of justice and of ethical practice'. Indeed, should it be the case that there are new 'fundamental areas of legal knowledge' beyond 1982's Priestley 11, such as project management, and general technical and business skills, they might similarly be incorporated under TLO 1.[164]

IX Concluding observations

This chapter has discussed how Australian legal education has continued to advance quite virtuously in the absence of professional accreditation drivers. It has presented evidence that our current educational orientations are fit-for-contemporary-purpose and has suggested that we stand up very favourably to international comparison. The law TLOs, and the legal academy's steady embrace of teaching professionalism, together with its dogged pursuit of pedagogical excellence (both theoretical and applied), have been particular enablers in this respect, while legal education in 2019 has also benefited from HE regulatory nudging since 2012. In response to the disciplinary impact of Industry 4.0's disruptive influence, I have sought to demonstrate that many, if not all, of the frequently mentioned (as currently desirable) 21st-century skills find nuanced and contemporary resonance within the TLOs' broad articulation and are able to be accommodated accordingly. Advances in practice in the knowledge domain can be incorporated more or less easily as has always been the case.

But we are in no position to rest easy. Despite our strong positioning off the back of sustained legal education research and innovation, the areas in which legal education (and subsequent training) are most vulnerable are still writ large. Chief amongst them is the urgent need to grapple with regulatory assurance of the educational continuum from pre- to post-admission, in an era of knowledge ubiquity and obsolescence, and of skills instability. It is no answer for an already over-crowded LLB/JD curriculum to be further over-loaded. It is the TLOs, I would suggest, that offer a quality assured way forward in the pre-admission regulatory space – broad and flexible, and accommodating of advances in professional and pedagogical practice. The real danger here is of regulatory mis-steps and any Australian flirtation with the recent Solicitors Regulation Authority (SRA) decision to introduce a common, mandatory professional assessment prior to admission for all prospective solicitors in England and Wales as from 2020 – the Solicitors Qualifying Examination (SQE) – is not to be encouraged.[165]

We can do better. Harmonising accreditation requirements in the spirit of the HESP recommendations will be a good start, as we settle to a serious consideration of the opportunities presented to renew our discipline and our sector. The current Priestly core/elective split must be addressed, in light of simultaneous calls for both specialisation and broadening. And course architecture must be modernised.[166] The increasingly artificial regulatory distinction between the academic and the practical training requirements requires serious re-evaluation: surely a joint LLB/JD-PLT program is the way of the future, when so much skilled acquisition is already encompassed within the current 'academic' stage. The regulatory assurance of post-admission up- and re-skilling is an obvious area for dedicated attention, though beyond the scope of this chapter to address except insofar as to observe that, if done in a principled way, pressure on pre-admission requirements would be considerably (and appropriately) relieved. If we have learnt nothing else from current disruption, it is that dedicated engagement in assured lifelong learning is now non-negotiable. What is our regulatory appetite for accommodating that new disciplinary reality? Is the practicing profession ready to acknowledge its disciplinary responsibility to step-up assurance of dynamic Industry 4.0 requirements and regulate accordingly for that, post-admission, stage of the training continuum?

Finally, and no less importantly, there are equity issues that demand our concentrated attention. Though gender parity and the attrition of women lawyers, particularly in the senior professional ranks, remain of concern for the practicing profession, in law schools across the country '66 per cent of law students are now women'[167] and have been for some years.[168] But while gender diversity might not be in question amongst law school cohorts, we have another equity and diversity issue that must be called out in the interests of our profession's future. Recent Australian research has shone a harsh light on the current inequity of access to law courses by students from low socio-economic and regional backgrounds, due to 'structural, systemic, sociocultural and personal factors that can act as barriers and enablers to high-status professions'.[169] This is a clear and ongoing challenge for our discipline to remediate as it sets its future path.

In the current environment, trying to hit the moving pedagogical target of shifting regulatory frameworks and future workforce needs with a 'tick a box' compliance mindset will not deliver graduate quality or future-proofed courses. The answer lies in conceptualising modern law curricula as a gestalt of high level outcomes; of integrated disciplinary knowledge, skills and dispositions. The academy must remain agentic and steadfast in protecting and advancing good pedagogically research and practice for an uncertain professional future, to assure our rightful contribution to the educational continuum. As legal educators, we can tie ourselves up in disciplinary knots and approach the next wave of regulatory discussions with the practising profession defensively or we can harness the good scholarship work done to date and continue on our journey of conscientious innovation and virtuous compliance. A particular, and not insubstantial, challenge will be to bring the profession with us and persuade them of, and by, our strong evidence- and research-base. But persuade them we must, for to do so is to do the right thing by our discipline, our students and their future clients, and society at large. It is also infinitely more satisfying.

As Carmen M. Garcia is quoted as saying in the ABA Commission on the Future of Legal Services:[170] 'the future will demand our full collective resources. Law students, lawyers, judges, innovators, and legal providers of all varieties will need to work collaboratively to achieve a sustainable, relevant, and valuable legal system'.

As a law Discipline Scholar who witnessed the regulatory rejection of the TLOs in 2010 because they included collaboration, the irony of a call to arms based on collaboration and joint enterprise is not lost on me. But I remain cautiously optimistic and, in the meantime, seek to hone another valuable 21st-century skill – the capability to leverage patient capital.

Appendix A

The Threshold Learning Outcomes (TLOs) for the Bachelor of Laws are as follows:[171]

- **TLO 1: Knowledge**

Graduates of the Bachelor of Laws will demonstrate an understanding of a coherent body of knowledge that includes:

(a) the fundamental areas of legal knowledge, the Australian legal system, and underlying principles and concepts, including international and comparative contexts,
(b) the broader contexts within which legal issues arise, and
(c) the principles and values of justice and of ethical practice in lawyers' roles.

- **TLO 2: Ethics and professional responsibility**

Graduates of the Bachelor of Laws will demonstrate:

(a) an understanding of approaches to ethical decision-making,
(b) an ability to recognise and reflect upon, and a developing ability to respond to, ethical issues likely to arise in professional contexts,
(c) an ability to recognise and reflect upon the professional responsibilities of lawyers in promoting justice and in service to the community, and
(d) a developing ability to exercise professional judgement.

- **TLO 3: Thinking skills**

Graduates of the Bachelor of Laws will be able to:

(a) identify and articulate legal issues,
(b) apply legal reasoning and research to generate appropriate responses to legal issues,

(c) engage in critical analysis and make a reasoned choice amongst alternatives, and
(d) think creatively in approaching legal issues and generating appropriate responses.

- **TLO 4: Research skills**

Graduates of the Bachelor of Laws will demonstrate the intellectual and practical skills needed to identify, research, evaluate and synthesise relevant factual, legal and policy issues.

- **TLO 5: Communication and collaboration**

Graduates of the Bachelor of Laws will be able to:

(a) communicate in ways that are effective, appropriate and persuasive for legal and non-legal audiences, and
(b) collaborate effectively.

- **TLO 6: Self-management**

Graduates of the Bachelor of Laws will be able to:

(a) learn and work independently, and
(b) reflect on and assess their own capabilities and performance, and make use of feedback as appropriate, to support personal and professional development.

Notes

* Professor, PFHEA FAAL; Discipline Scholar: Law; President, Australian Learning & Teaching Fellows; Visiting Professional Fellow, National Centre for Student Equity in Higher Education, Curtin University.

1 For example, Department of Industry, Innovation and Science, *Industry 4.0* <www.industry.gov.au/funding-and-incentives/manufacturing/industry-40>; Industry 4.0 describes the automation and digitisation of manufacturing, and often business generally: Mark Cotteleer and Brenna Sniderman, 'Forces of Change: Industry 4.0' (*Deloitte Insights*, 18 December 2017) <https://www2.deloitte.com/insights/us/en/focus/industry-4-0/overview.html>.

2 For example, Edmund Tadros and Katie Walsh, 'Too Many Law Graduates and Not Enough Jobs' *Australian Financial Review* (Australia, 22 October 2015 <www.afr.com/business/legal/too-many-law-graduates-and-not-enough-jobs-20151020-gkdbyx>; Emma Ryan, 'Frustration Grows over Unis "Cashing In" on Law Grad Oversupply' *Lawyers Weekly* (Australia, 20 February 2018) <www.lawyersweekly.com.au/sme-law/22768-frustration-grows-over-unis-cashing-in-on-law-grad-oversupply>.

3 William Twining, 'Pericles and the Plumber' (1967) 83 *LQ Review* 396, 421–2; Sally Kift, 'Lawyering Skills: Finding Their Place in Legal Education' (1997) *Legal Education Review* 8, 43–73.

4 David Weisbrot, 'What Lawyers Need to Know, What Lawyers Need to Be Able to Do: An Australian Experience' (2002) 1 *Journal of the Association of Legal Writing Directors* <https://papers.ssrn.com/sol3/papers.cfm?abstract_id=1095486>. See also Kift 'Lawyering Skills' (n. 3); Sharon Christensen and Sally Kift, 'Graduate Attributes and Legal Skills: Integration or Disintegration?' (2000) 11 *Legal Education Review* 20–37; Sally Kift, '21st Century Climate for Change: Curriculum Design for Quality Learning Engagement in Law' (2008) 18 *Legal Education Review* 1–30.

5 Australian Law Reform Commission, *Managing Justice: A Review of the Federal Civil Justice System* (Law Report No 89 2000) [2.21]–[2.95] <www.alrc.gov.au/report-89>.

6 Canadian Bar Association, *Systems of Civil Justice Task Force Final Report* (1996) (Ottawa: Canadian Bar Association National Task force on Systems of Civil Justice) ('CBA Task Force Report'); American Bar Association, *Legal Education and Professional Development – An Educational Continuum: Report of The Task Force on Law Schools and the Profession: Narrowing the Gap* (American Bar Association, Chicago 1992) ('MacCrate report').

7 Australian Law Reform Commission (n. 5) [2.82].

8 Ibid., recommendation 2. See also Law Admissions Consultative Committee, *Rethinking Academic Requirements for Admission* (2010) 8.2 <https://www.lawcouncil.asn.au/resources/law-admissions-consultative-committee/discussion-papers> which sets out the variety of criticisms levelled at the Priestley 11 over a sustained period.

9 Productivity Commission, *Access to Justice Arrangements Inquiry Report* (2014) 252 <www.pc.gov.au/inquiries/completed/access-justice/report>.

10 Dennis Pearce, Enid Campbell and Don Harding, *Australian Law Schools: A Discipline Assessment for the Commonwealth Tertiary Education Commission* (AGPS, Canberra 1987) ('Pearce Report') cited in Australian Law Reform Commission (n. 5) [2.75].

11 A particular milestone was the convening by the Australian Academy of Law of *The Future of Australian Legal Education Conference 2017*, which brought together judges, practitioners and educators for a landmark discussion: see <www.academyoflaw.org.au/lec2017> and Kevin Lindgren, Francois Kunc and Michael Coper (eds), *The Future of Australian Legal Education* (Thomson Reuters 2018). A current collaboration between LACC and the academy to re-draft the content of the Priestley 11 as outcomes (cf. inputs) statements has also been very positive.

12 Productivity Commission (n. 9) recommendation 7.1.

13 Ibid., recommendation 7.1.

14 See generally, World Economic Forum, *The Future of Jobs Report 2018* (2018) <http://www3.weforum.org/docs/WEF_Future_of_Jobs_2018.pdf>.

15 Also referred to as values and characteristics.

16 Sally Kift, 'A Tale of Two Sectors: Dynamic Curriculum Change for a Dynamically Changing Profession' (2004) 2(2) *Journal of Commonwealth Law and Legal Education* 5–22, 5.

17 Clayton M. Christensen and Henry J. Eyring, *The Innovative University: Changing the DNA of Higher Education from the Inside Out* (San Francisco: Jossey-Bass 2011).

18 Australasian Legal Practice Management Association, *Preparing Australasian Law Firms for a Digital, Divergent, Differentiated Future* (2015) <https://www.alpma.com.au/download-2015-alpmalexisnexis-research-report-preparing-australasian-law-firms-digital-divergent-dif>.

19 Richard Susskind, *The End of Lawyers? Rethinking the Nature of Legal Services* (Oxford University Press 2008).

20 Jordan Furlong and Sean Larkan, 'A Brief Inventory of NewLaw in Australia' *AMPLA Blog* (24 August 2014) <www.alpma.com.au/a-survival-guide-for-legal-practice-managers/inventory-of-new-law-in-Australia>.

21 George Beaton, 'Last Days of the BigLaw Business Model?' *Bigger.Better.Both? Beatoncapital* (6 September 2013) '"BigLaw" is not about big law firms. It's description of the business model used by firms generating more than 99% of law firm revenues today (that is, it excludes micro and sole practitioner 'firms' and the handful of alternative business model firms)'. See also George Beaton, 'Who Coined NewLaw?' (Blog, 8 August 2018) <https://remakinglawfirms.com/who-coined-newlaw/>.

22 Laura Czerniewicz, 'Unbundling and Rebundling Higher Education in an Age of Inequality' 53(6) *EDUCAUSE Review* (29 October 2018) <https://er.educause.edu/articles/2018/10/unbundling-and-rebundling-higher-education-in-an-age-of-inequality>.

23 Canadian Bar Association, *The Future of Legal Services in Canada: Trends and Issues* (June 2013) <www.cba.org/CBAMediaLibrary/cba_na/PDFs/CBA%20Legal%20Futures%20PDFS/trends-isssues-eng.pdf>.

24 Legal Education and Training Review, *Setting Standards: The Future of Legal Services Education and Training Regulation in England and Wales* (June 2013) ('LETR Report') <www.letr.org.uk/the-report/>; The Law Society of England and Wales, *The Future of Legal Services* (January 2016) <www.lawsociety.org.uk/support-services/research-trends/the-future-of-legal-services/>.

25 American Bar Association, *Report on the Future of Legal Services in the United States* (2016).

26 Law Society of NSW, *The Future of Law and Innovation in the Profession* (2017) ('FLIP report') <www.lawsociety.com.au/advocacy-and-resources/advocacy/flip>. See also Katie Miller, *Disruption, Innovation and Change: The Future of the Legal Profession* (Law Institute of Victoria 2015) <www.liv.asn.au/flipbooks/disruption--innovation-and-change--the-future-of-t.aspx>.

27 Law Society of NSW, 'FLIP Report' (n. 26) 6.

28 Foundation for Young Australians, *The New Work Reality* (2018) 9 <www.fya.org.au/wp-content/uploads/2018/06/FYA_TheNewWorkReality_sml.pdf>.

29 Business Council of Australia, *Future-Proof: Australia's Future Post-Secondary Education and Skills System* (2018) <https://d3n8a8pro7vhmx.cloudfront.net/bca/pages/4425/attachments/original/1543382548/LoRes-2018_BCA_EDUC_Future_Proof_WIP1A_%287%29.pdf?1543382548>.

30 Australian Industry and Skills Committee, *Future Skills and Training: A Practical Resource* (Australian Government Department of Education and Training 2016) <www.aisc.net.au/sites/aisc/files/documents/Future%20Priority%20Skills%20Resource.pdf>; AlphaBeta, *Future Skills* (2019) <www.alphabeta.com/wp-content/uploads/2019/01/google-skills-report.pdf>.

31 World Economic Forum, *New Vision for Education: Unlocking the Potential of Technology* (2015) <http://www3.weforum.org/docs/WEFUSA_NewVisionforEducation_Report2015.pdf>; World Economic Forum, *The Future of Jobs: Employment, Skills and Workforce Strategy for the Fourth Industrial Revolution* (2016) <http://www3.weforum.org/docs/WEF_Future_of_Jobs.pdf>.

32 Business Council of Australia (n. 29) 40–41.

33 AlphaBeta (n. 30) 8.

34 World Economic Forum 2015 (n. 31) 3 identifying 16 skills students require for the 21st century.

35 World Economic Forum 2016 (n. 31) 19.

36 Australian Qualifications Framework Council, *Australian Qualifications Framework* (2nd edn, 2013) <www.aqf.edu.au/sites/aqf/files/aqf-2nd-edition-january-2013.pdf>.

37 Sally Kift, 'Employability and Higher Education: Keeping Calm in the Face of Disruptive Innovation' in J. Higgs, G. Crisp and W. Letts (eds), *Education for Employability (Volume 1): Examining the Employability Agenda* (49–60) (Leiden, Netherlands: Brill Sense 2019).

38 Social Research Centre, *2018 Employer Satisfaction Survey National Report* (Quality Indicators of Learning and Teaching Survey Program 2019) <https://www.qilt.edu.au/about-this-site/employer-satisfaction>. In 2018, the overall satisfaction with graduates, as rated by their direct supervisors, was 85 per cent. Employer satisfaction with other graduate attributes was as follows: 94 per cent satisfaction with foundation skills (general literacy, numeracy and communication skills and the ability to investigate and integrate knowledge); 90 per cent satisfaction with adaptive skills (the ability to adapt and apply skills/knowledge and work independently); 89 per cent satisfaction with collaborative skills (teamwork and interpersonal skills); 94 per cent satisfaction with technical skills (application of professional and technical knowledge and standards); and 87 per cent satisfaction with employability skills (the ability to perform and innovate in the workplace).

39 Carl Benedikt Frey and Michael A. Osborne, 'The Future of Employment: How Susceptible are Jobs to Computerisation?' (September 2013) <www.oxfordmartin.ox.ac.uk/downloads/academic/The_Future_of_Employment.pdf>.

40 Ibid., 4.

41 Ibid., 41.

42 Deloitte, *Developing Legal Talent: Stepping into the Future Law Firm* (London: Deloitte LLP 2016) 4 <https://www2.deloitte.com/content/dam/Deloitte/uk/Documents/audit/deloitte-uk-developing-legal-talent-2016.pdf>.

43 Susskind (n. 19).

44 Ibid.

45 AlphaBeta (n. 30) 13.

46 Jordan Furlong, *The Rise of the Millennial Lawyer: 14 Ways a Generation Is Changing the Rules* (Lawyers on Demand 2017) 12 <www.lodlaw.com/wp-content/uploads/2017/05/Millennial-report-soft-copy.pdf>.

47 George Beaton, *NewLaw New Rules – A Conversation about the Future of the Legal Services Industry* (Smashwords 2013) <www.smashwords.com/books/view/388258>; George Beaton, 'Who Coined NewLaw?' (n. 21).

48 George Beaton, 'What Voltaire might have said about NewLaw' *Bigger.Better. Both? Beatoncapital* (18 October 2013).

49 Furlong and Larkan (n. 20).

50 See also Thomson Reuters Legal Executive Institute, Georgetown University Law Center for the Study of the Legal Profession and University of Oxford Saïd Business School *Alternative Legal Service Providers: Understanding the Growth and Benefits of These New Legal Providers* (Industry Report 2017) <https://legal.thomsonreuters.com/en/insights/reports/alternative-legal-service-provider-study-2017?gatedContent=%252Fcontent%252Fewp-marketing-websites%252Flegal%252Fgl%252Fen%252Finsights%252Freports%252Falternative-legal-service-provider-study-2017>.

51 Ilina Rejeva, 'What Is NewLaw and How It Is Changing the Legal Industry Forever!' (LegalTech, 29 April 2016) referring to virtual workspaces, fewer permanent staff and more transient 'supertemps'.

52 Chris Merrit, 'Fears of Job Losses Due to Artificial Intelligence Unfounded: LexisNexis' *The Australian* (16 November 2018) <www.theaustralian.com.au/business/legal-affairs/fears-of-job-losses-due-to-artificial-intelligence-unfounded-lexisnexis/news-story/69be7dc7e7d9b211cf54e8d0e6de00a0> citing LEXISNEXIS®, *Legal Frontiers: From AI to Ethics* (Roadshow Report 2018) <https://www.lexisnexis.com.au/en/insights-and-analysis/research-and-whitepapers/2018/legal-frontiers-ai-to-ethics>.

53 Emma Ryan (n. 2). The Productivity Commission also suggested there was an oversupply of law graduates: Productivity Commission, 'University Education,

Shifting the Dial: 5 Year Productivity Review' (Supporting Paper No 7, 2017) Box 4.2 <www.pc.gov.au/inquiries/completed/productivity-review/report/productivity-review-supporting7.pdf>.

54 ABC News, 'Fact check: Do Australian Taxpayers Subsidise over Half the Cost of Each Student's Higher Education? (16 July 2018) <www.abc.net.au/news/2017-06-14/fact-check-do-taxpayers-subsidise-over-half-higher-education/8605406>.

55 Neville Carter, 'Australian Legal Education Sector: Key Metrics' in Evin Lindgren, Francois Kunc and Michael Coper (eds), *The Future of Australian Legal Education* (Thomson Reuters 2018) citing findings from economic analyses by Ernst & Young that the proportion of JD/LLB student mix had changed significantly from 2014 (10.8 per cent JD/87.3 per cent LLB) to 2017 (16.5 per cent JD/81.8 per cent LLB).

56 Melissa Chan, 'Juris Doctor and Bachelor of Law Payback Time Both Four Years' *The Australian* (28 November 2018) <www.theaustralian.com.au/higher-education/juris-doctor-and-bachelor-of-law-payback-time-both-four-years/news-story/ea830d4fe81a0917688140fbeaaa0fbf> citing <https://postgradaustralia.com.au/>. It is also suggested here that both degrees are accorded equal weight in law firm recruitment processes.

57 Social Research Centre, 2018 Graduate Outcomes Survey: National Report (Quality Indicators for Learning and Teaching Survey Program, 2019) <https://www.qilt.edu.au/about-this-site/graduate-employment>.

58 Neil McMahon, 'Too Many Lawyers: Future-proof Your Degree' *Sydney Morning Herald* (31 July 2015) <www.smh.com.au/national/too-many-lawyers-futureproof-your-degree-20150730-ginpjh.html>; see also The College of Law, *The Legal Business Leaders Roundtable* (November 2018) <https://cdn2.hubspot.net/hubfs/3880656/assets/mlb/pdfs/The-Legal-Business-Leaders-Roundtable-Report-November-2018.pdf>.

59 Council of Australian Law Deans, *Data Regarding Law School Graduate Numbers and Outcomes* (2017) <https://cald.asn.au/wp-content/uploads/2017/11/Factsheet-Law_Students_in_Australia.pdf>. The Factsheet was updated in 2018: see Council of Australian Law Deans, *2018 Data Regarding Law School Graduate Numbers and Outcomes* (2019)

60 Christian Veith and others, *How Legal Technology Will Change the Business of Law* (The Boston Consulting Group (BCG) & Bucerius Law School 2016) 11–12 <https://docs.wixstatic.com/ugd/b30d31_7b407b2c8c6b44d697957b7fa5db48c8.pdf>. See also The Law Society of England and Wales, *Capturing Technological Innovation in Legal Services* (The Law Society of England and Wales 2017) <www.lawsociety.org.uk/support-services/research-trends/capturing-technological-innovation-report/>.

61 Mark A. Cohen, 'Who Will Train Tomorrow's Lawyers and How Will They Learn?' *Legal Mosaic* (28 September 2017). A similar point is made in Sanford Clarke, 'Regulating Admissions – Are We There Yet?' in Kevin Lindgren, Francois Kunc and Michael Coper (eds), *The Future of Australian Legal Education* (Thomson Reuters 2018).

62 Cohen (n. 61).

63 *Legal Education Review* <http://classic.austlii.edu.au/au/journals/LegEdRev/>.

64 *Legal Education Digest* <http://www6.austlii.edu.au/cgi-bin/viewdb/au/journals/LegEdDig/>.

65 *Australian Journal of Clinical Education* <https://ajce.scholasticahq.com/>.

66 For example: Pearce, Campbell and Harding, 'Pearce Report' (n. 10); Craig McInnis and Simon Marginson, *Australian Law Schools after the 1987 Pearce Report* (Australian Government Publishing Service, Canberra 1994); Australian

Law Reform Commission (n. 5); Richard Johnstone and Sumitra Vignaendra, *Learning Outcomes and Curriculum Development in Law* (Australian Universities Teaching Committee, Canberra 2003) <https://cald.asn.au/wp-content/uploads/2017/11/AUTC-Threshold-Learning-Outcomes-Report_2003_Johnstone-Vignaendra1.pdf>; Gary Davis and Susanne Owen, *Learning and Teaching in the Discipline of Law: Achieving and Sustaining Excellence in a Changed and Changing Environment* (ALTC/CALD Final Report 2009) <https://ltr.edu.au/resources/altc_LawReport.pdf>. See generally also, David Barker, *A History of Australian Legal Education* (Federation Press Sydney 2017); Kift, 'A Tale of Two Sectors: Dynamic Curriculum Change for a Dynamically Changing Profession' (n. 16) 5.

67 For example: Marlene Le Brun and Richard Johnstone, *The Quiet (R)evolution: Improving Student Learning in Law*' (Law Book Co 1994); Sally Kift and others (eds), *Excellence & Innovation in Legal Education* (LexisNexis, Sydney 2011); Paul Maharg and Caroline Maughan, *Affect and Legal Education: Emotion in Learning and Teaching the Law* (Ashgate Publishing 2011); Margaret Thornton, *Privatising the Public University: The Case of Law* (Routledge 2012).

68 For example: Australasian Law Academics Association (ALAA) (until 1 July 2019 known as the Australasian Law Teachers Association <https://www.alaa.asn.au/> and Australasian Professional Legal Education Council <https://aplec.asn.au/>.

69 See Learning & Teaching Repository <https://ltr.edu.au/>.

70 See the list in chapter 5 Appendix 1 by Alex Steel.

71 Sally Kift, Mark Israel and Rachael Field, *Bachelor of Laws Learning and Teaching Academic Standards Statement* (ALTC Learning and Teaching Academic Standards Project 2010) <http://disciplinestandards.pbworks.com/w/page/52746378/Law>.

72 Sally Kift, 'The Decline and Demise of the Commonwealth's Strategic Investment in Quality Learning and Teaching' (2016) 7(2) *Student Success* 1–9.

73 For example: Bond University's *Centre for Professional Legal Education* <https://bond.edu.au/researchers/research-strengths/university-research-centres/centre-professional-legal-education>; College of Law's *Centre of Legal Innovation* <www.cli.collaw.com/>; Griffith University's *Law Futures Centre* <www.griffith.edu.au/law-futures-centre>; UNSW's *Legal Education Research Group* <www.law.unsw.edu.au/node/52840>.

74 For example: S|M| i |L|E (Social Media in Legal Education) <https://socialmediainlegaleducation.com/>; Amicae Curiae <https://amicaecuriae.com/2013/09/27/its-more-than-the-vibe/>.

75 Sally Varnham, *Creating a National Framework for Student Partnership in University Decision-Making and Governance* (2017) <www.uts.edu.au/sites/default/files/article/downloads/Creating%20a%20National%20Framework%20for%20Student%20Partnership%20in%20University%20Decision171017.pdf>. See also <http://studentvoiceaustralia.com/>.

76 For example, the Monash University law students' publication *Techup Law* <www.monash.edu/__data/assets/pdf_file/0006/973023/TechUp-Law-Publication-Final-1.pdf>. See also resources at: Australian Law Students' Association <www.alsa.asn.au/>; Survive Law <www.survivelaw.com/>; *The Legal Forecast* <http://thelegalforecast.com/about/>.

77 Joanna Tai and others, Developing Evaluative Judgement: Enabling Students to Make Decisions about the Quality of Work (2018) 76(3) *High Education* 467–81 <https://link.springer.com/journal/10734/76/3/page/1>: 'Evaluative judgement is the capability to make decisions about the quality of work of self and others'. See also David Boud and others (eds), *Developing Evaluative*

Judgement in Higher Education: Assessment for Knowing and Producing Quality Work (Abingdon: Routledge 2018).

78 For example: Jisc, *Digital Capabilities: The 6 Elements Defined* (2015) <https://digitalcapability.jiscinvolve.org/wp/files/2015/06/1.-Digital-capabilities-6-elements.pdf>. The six elements identified are: ICT proficiency; information, data and media literacies; digital creation, problem solving and innovation; digital communication, collaboration and participation; digital learning and development; and digital identity and wellbeing.

79 For example, Adam J. Gustein and John Sviokla, '7 Skills That Aren't About to Be Automated' *Harvard Business Review* (online, July 2018) <https://hbr.org/2018/07/7-skills-that-arent-about-to-be-automated>; AlphaBeta (n. 30) 8: 'As more knowledge and abilities become codified they can be mastered by machines, leaving workers to focus on more uniquely human skills [which are the hardest for machines to replicate]'. Specifically, reference is made there to 'Characteristics [which] relate to the way we execute tasks, and include creativity, integrity, leadership, persistence, empathy, and attention to detail'.

80 For example, Quacquarelli Symonds, *The Global Skills Gap in the 21st Century* (2018) <www.qs.com/portfolio-items/the-global-skills-gap-in-the-21st-century/>, identifying that the top five most important skills for employers globally are: problem solving, teamwork, communication, adaptability, and interpersonal skills. The biggest skills gaps were to be found in the core skills of: problem solving, communication, resilience, and leadership.

81 Thomas W. Malone, Robert Laubacher and Tammy Johns, 'The Big Idea: The Age of Hyperspecialization' *Harvard Business Review* (July–August 2011) <https://hbr.org/2011/07/the-big-idea-the-age-of-hyperspecialization>.

82 For example, Margaret Bearman and others, *Guide to the Assessment Design Decisions Framework* (Australian Government Office for Learning and Teaching, September 2014) <https://ltr.edu.au/resources/ID12_2254_Dawson_Guide_2014_0.pdf>.

83 For example, Contract Cheating and Assessment Design: Exploring the Connection <https://cheatingandassessment.edu.au/>.

84 David Boud and Associates, *Assessment 2020: Seven Propositions for Assessment Reform in Higher Education* (Australian Learning and Teaching Council 2010) <www.assessmentfutures.com>.

85 For example, Mitch Parsell, *Standards for Online Education (SOE)* (Office for Learning and Teaching 2014) <https://ltr.edu.au/resources/Parsell%2C%20M_NTF_%20report_2014.pdf>.

86 Christine Ewan, *Higher Education Standards in a Disaggregated Learning Environment: Final Report* (Australian Government Office for Learning and Teaching 2016) <https://altf.org/wp-content/uploads/2016/08/Ewan_C_HESP_Fellow_Report_2016.pdf>; Beverley Oliver, *Better 21C Credentials: Evaluating the Promise, Perils and Disruptive Potential of Digital Credentials* (2016) <www.assuringgraduatecapabilities.com/uploads/4/5/0/5/45053363/better_21c_credentials.pdf>; AQF Review Panel, *Discussion Paper: Review of the Australian Qualifications Framework* (2018) <www.education.gov.au/australian-qualifications-framework-review-0>.

87 For example, Quacquarelli Symonds (n. 80).

88 Australasian Law Students' Society, *WellBeing Tips and Tricks* (2017) <https://drive.google.com/file/d/0B95-o3plGJYvWVF2ME5nZnB2cmc/view>; Council of Australian Law Deans, *Promoting Law Student Well-Being Good Practice Guidelines for Law Schools* (2014) <https://cald.asn.au/wp-content/uploads/2017/11/Promoting-Law-Student-Well-Being-Good-Practice-Guidelines-for-Law-Schools-March-2013-and-revised-September-2014.pdf>;

Rachael Field, *Promoting Law Student Well-Being Through the Curriculum* (2014) <https://ltr.edu.au/resources/Field_R_NTF_report_2014%20.pdf>; Norm Kelk and others, *Courting the Blues: Attitudes towards Depression in Australian Law Students and Lawyers* (Brain & Mind Research Institute 2009) <https://cald.asn.au/wp-content/uploads/2017/11/BMRI-Report-Courting-the-BluesLaw-Report-Website-version-4-May-091.pdf>. See also website resources at <http://wellnessforlaw.com/> (an outcome of Field's 2014 OLT Fellowship), <https://mindscount.org/> (previously Tristan Jepson Memorial Foundation) and <http://unistudentwellbeing.edu.au/>.

89 Sally Kift, 'Holistic curriculum design for employability' in J. Higgs, G. Crisp and W. Letts (eds), *Education for Employability (Volume I): The Employability Agenda* (155–164) (Leiden, Netherlands: Brill Sense 2019).

90 Clarke, (n. 61) 4.

91 The need for assurance of the legal education continuum and its staged articulation has been discussed in: Kift, '21st Century Climate for Change' (n. 4); Kift, Israel and Field (n. 71).

92 Useful discussions of current regulatory arrangements are to be found on the LACC website at <https://www.lawcouncil.asn.au/resources/law-admissions-consultative-committee> (for example, Law Admissions Consultative Committee (2010) *Background Paper on Admission Requirements* (2010) <www.lawcouncil.asn.au/files/web-pdf/LACC%20docs/Background_Paper_on_Admission_Requirements-Oct2010.rev2.pdf>). See also Alex Steel, 'Finding Ways to Quicken, Not Deaden, the Spirit of Legal Education: Reflections on Approaches to Drafting Regulatory Standards' in Kevin Lindgren, Francois Kunc and Michael Coper (eds), *The Future of Australian Legal Education* (Thomson Reuters 2018).

93 Kift, Israel and Field (n. 71) 6.

94 For a more detailed history see: Clarke (n. 61).

95 Law Admissions Consultative Committee, *Accreditation Standards for Australian Law Courses* (2018) <www.lawcouncil.asn.au/files/web-pdf/LACC%20docs/238832380_18_LACC%20-%20Standards%20for%20Accrediting%20Law%20Courses.pdf>.

96 Law Admissions Consultative Committee, *Model Admission Rules 2015* (Revised 2016) <www.lawcouncil.asn.au/files/web-pdf/LACC%20docs/212390818_9_LACC%20Model%20Admission%20Rules%202015.pdf>.

97 Law Admissions Consultative Committee, *Charter* (2010) 2.1 <www.lawcouncil.asn.au/files/web-pdf/LACC%20docs/212391469_2_LACC%20Charter%202010.pdf,>; see membership at 1. LACC is not, however, a Committee of the Council of Chief Justices.

98 Law Admissions Consultative Committee, *Prescribed Academic Areas of Knowledge* (Revised 2016) <www.lawcouncil.asn.au/files/web-pdf/LACC%20docs/249520754_2_LACC%20-%20Prescribed%20Academic%20Areas%20of%20Knowledge%20%28Revised%20December%202016%29.pdf>. In 2010, a Statement on Statutory Interpretation was developed: Law Admissions Consultative Committee, *Statement on Statutory Interpretation* (2010) <www.lawcouncil.asn.au/files/web-pdf/LACC%20docs/StatementonStatutoryInterpretation.pdf>.

99 Law Admissions Consultative Committee, *Practical Legal Training Competency Standards for Entry-Level Lawyers* (2017) <www.lawcouncil.asn.au/files/web-pdf/LACC%20docs/224336988_10_LACC%20-%20PLT.pdf>.

100 Law Admissions Consultative Committee, (n. 95).

101 Law Admissions Consultative Committee, *Uniform Standards for PLT Courses and Providers* (Amended October 2017) <www.lawcouncil.asn.au/files/web-

pdf/LACC%20docs/212001734_9_Standards%20for%20PLT%20Providers%20and%20Courses.pdf>.

102 See, e.g., Law Admissions Consultative Committee, *Submission to Productivity Commission: Draft Report on Access to Justice Arrangements* (2014) <www.lawcouncil.asn.au/files/web-pdf/LACC%20docs/2014_04_29_-_LACC_Submission_to_Productivity_Commission.pdf>.

103 Law Admissions Consultative Committee (n. 95) 3.

104 Paragraph 4.4 to the effect that the course 'includes teaching or other instruction in each of the specified elements in each of the prescribed areas of knowledge [the Priestley 11]' and meets the 'requirements of the LACC Statement on Statutory Interpretation' (additional to the Priestley 11).

105 Council of Australian Law Deans, *The CALD Standards for Australian Law Schools* (Adopted 17 November 2009 and Amended to March 2013) <https://cald.asn.au/wp-content/uploads/2017/11/CALD-Standards-As-adopted-17-November-2009-and-Amended-to-March-2013.pdf>. For a history of the development of the Standards see: *Introduction and Context to the CALD Standards for Australian Law Schools* <https://cald.asn.au/wp-content/uploads/2017/11/CALD-Standards-Introductory-Context-Statement-March-2014.pdf>.

106 *Introduction and Context to the CALD Standards for Australian Law Schools* (n. 105) 2.

107 See Michael Black, 'The CALD Standards for Australian Law Schools: much more than course content' in Kevin Lindgren, Francois Kunc and Michael Coper (eds), *The Future of Australian Legal Education* (Thomson Reuters 2018).

108 For reasons including, for example, not having yet graduated a student cohort.

109 Tertiary Education Quality and Standards Agency <www.teqsa.gov.au/>.

110 *Higher Education Standards Framework (Threshold Standards) 2015* 1.5.3 <www.legislation.gov.au/Details/F2015L01639>.

111 Ibid., 1.4.2.

112 Michael B. Horn and Michele R. Pistone, *Disrupting Law School: How Disruptive Innovation Will Revolutionize the Legal World* (Clayton Christensen Institute for Disruptive Innovation 2016) 2 <www.christenseninstitute.org/wp-content/uploads/2016/03/Disrupting-law-school.pdf>.

113 Ibid., 15.

114 Kift, 'Lawyering Skills: Finding Their Place in Legal Education' (n. 3); Christensen and Kift, 'Graduate Attributes and Legal Skills' (n. 4); Kift, '21st Century Climate for Change' (n. 4); Beverley Oliver, 'Graduate Attributes as a Focus for Institution-wide Curriculum Renewal: Innovations and Challenges' (2013) 32 *Higher Education Research & Development* 450–63; Beverley Oliver and Trina Jorre de St Jorre, 'Graduate Attributes for 2020 and Beyond: Recommendations for Australian Higher Education Providers' (2018) 37(4) *Higher Education Research & Development* 821–836.

115 See, e.g., J. Bowden and others, *Generic Capabilities of ATN University Graduates* (Australian Government Department of Education, Training and Youth Affairs 2000): Graduate attributes are the 'qualities, skills and understandings a university community agrees its students should develop during their time with the institution. These attributes include but go beyond the disciplinary expertise or technical knowledge that has traditionally formed the core of most university courses. They are qualities that also prepare graduates as agents of social good in an unknown future'.

116 Precision Consultancy, *Graduate Employability Skills* (2007) 2 <http://apo.org.au/node/1505>.

117 Australian Learning and Teaching Council, *Australian Learning and Teaching Council, Learning and Teaching Academic Standards Project Final Report* (2010) <http://pandora.nla.gov.au/pan/127341/20110608-1311/www.altc.edu.au/system/files/altc_standards.finalreport.pdf>.

118 Ibid., 11.

119 See Kift, Israel and Field (n. 71) Appendix 3 (noting that some of these international statements have been updated since 2010); American Bar Association, *Standards and Rules of Procedure for Approval of Law Schools* (2009–2010) <www.americanbar.org/content/dam/aba/publications/misc/legal_education/Standards/standardsarchive/2009_2010_standards.pdf>; American Bar Association, *Standards and Rules of Procedure for Approval of Law Schools* (2010–2011) <www.americanbar.org/content/dam/aba/publications/misc/legal_education/Standards/standardsarchive/2010_2011_standards.pdf> [See now American Bar Association, *Standards and Rules of Procedure for Approval of Law Schools* (2018–2019) <https://www.americanbar.org/groups/legal_education/resources/standards/>]; United Kingdom Quality Assurance Agency, *Subject Benchmark Statement: Law* (2007) [See now United Kingdom Quality Assurance Agency, *Subject Benchmark Statement: Law* (2015) <www.qaa.ac.uk/docs/qaa/subject-benchmark-statements/sbs-law-15.pdf?sfvrsn=ff99f781_10>]; Solictors Regulation Authority, *Joint Statement on the Completion of the Initial or Academic Stage of Training by Obtaining an Undergraduate Degree* (2002) <www.sra.org.uk/students/academic-stage-joint-statement-bsb-law-society.page>; American Bar Association, 'MacCrate Report' (n. 6); Weisbrot (n. 4); *Task Force on the Canadian Common Law Degree, Final Report* (2009) <https://flsc.ca/wp-content/uploads/2014/10/admission8.pdf>; The Law Society of Scotland, *Foundation Programme (Scottish Exempting Degree) Accreditation Guidelines for Applicants* (2010) <www.lawscot.org.uk/media/9139/foundation-programme-guidelines.pdf>; Latin America Tuning, *Subject Specific Competences: Law* (2007) <http://tuning.unideusto.org/tuningal/index.php?d=0&option=content&task=view&id=235&Itemid=265&lang=en>; European Tuning, *Generic Competences* (n.d.) <www.unideusto.org/tuningeu/competences/generic.html>; Joint Quality Initiative, *Shared 'Dublin' Descriptors for Short Cycle, First Cycle, Second Cycle and Third Cycle Awards* (2004) <www.uni-due.de/imperia/md/content/bologna/dublin_descriptors.pdf>.

120 Kift, Israel and Field (n. 71). In short form, the six TLOs are: Knowledge; Ethics and professional responsibility; Thinking skills; Research skills; Communication and collaboration; and Self-management.

121 Juris Doctor Threshold Learning Outcomes (2012) <http://disciplinestandards.pbworks.com/w/page/52746378/Law>.

122 Kift, Israel and Field (n. 71) 11.

123 Council of Australian Law Deans (n. 105).

124 Law Admissions Consultative Committee, *Specifying Learning Outcomes for Contract Law* (2018) 2 <www.lawcouncil.asn.au/files/web-pdf/LACC%20docs/252098968_6_LACC%20-%20Specifying%20Outcomes%20for%20Contract%20Law.pdf>. See also Law Admissions Consultative Committee, *Redrafting the Academic Requirements for Admission* (2019) 2 <https://www.lawcouncil.asn.au/resources/law-admissions-consultative-committee/redrafting-the-academic-requirements-for-admission>

125 Kift, Israel and Field (n. 71) 13.

126 *Legal Education Associate Deans Network* <www.lawteachnetwork.org/>.

127 Kift, Israel and Field (n. 71) 9. This conceptualisation has now been picked up in the latest LACC consideration of the TLOs: see Law Admissions

Consultative Committee, *Specifying Learning Outcomes for Contract Law* (n. 124) and Law Admissions Consultative Committee, *Redrafting the Academic Requirements for Admission* (n 124).

128 *Higher Education Standards Framework (Threshold Standards) 2015* Standard 1.4.1 <www.legislation.gov.au/Details/F2015L01639>.

129 *Higher Education Standards Framework (Threshold Standards) 2015* Standards 3.1 and 3.2 <www.legislation.gov.au/Details/F2015L01639>.

130 *Higher Education Standards Framework (Threshold Standards) 2015* Standard 3.1.3 <www.legislation.gov.au/Details/F2015L01639>.

131 Roger Hadgraft and Ian Cameron, 'Standards prompt Curriculum Reform in the age of Google' (Being TEQSA Ready 2010) <http://disciplinestandards.pbworks.com/w/file/fetch/70098293/Forum9Aug13_Pre-reading_CR_Series.pdf>.

132 Ibid.

133 Geoff Scott, *Assuring the Quality of Achievement Standards and Their Valid Assessment in Australian Higher Education* (Australian Government Department of Education and Training 2016) 24 <http://flipcurric.edu.au/sites/flipcurric/media/109.pdf>. See also resources at <http://flipcurric.edu.au/>; Shelley Kinash and others, *Global Graduate Employability Research: A Report to the Business20 Human Capital Taskforce (DRAFT)* (Paper No 100, Learning and Teaching 2014) <https://research.bond.edu.au/en/publications/global-graduate-employability-research-a-report-to-the-business20>.

134 Sally Kift and others, *Curriculum Renewal in Legal Education* (Office for Learning and Teaching 2013) <https://ltr.edu.au/resources/PP9-1374_Kift_Report_2013_1.pdf>; Nicolette Lee and Daniel Loton, 'Capstone Purposes Across Disciplines' (2019) 44(1) *Studies in Higher Education* 134–50.

135 Kift, 'Holistic curriculum design for employability' (n. 89); Vicki Waye and Margaret Faulkner, 'Embedding E-portfolios in a Law Program: Lessons from an Australian Law School' (2012) 61(4) *Journal of Legal Education* 560–84.

136 Scott (n. 133).

137 For example: Andrea Perry-Petersen and Michael Lacey, *Legal Innovation: Education in Australian Law Schools* (2018) <www.andreaperrypetersen.com.au/wp-content/uploads/2018/09/Legal-Innovation-Education-Sep-2018.pdf>; UNSW's LAWS3196/JURD7596 *Designing Technology Solutions for Access to Justice* <www.law.unsw.edu.au/form/Designing_Technology_Solutions_for_Access_to_Justice>.

138 Adrian Evans and others, *Best Practices: Australian Clinical Legal Education* (2013). The final report of the project Strengthening Australian legal education by integrating clinical experiences: identifying and supporting effective practices <https://ltr.edu.au/resources/PP10_1603_Monash_Evans_Report_2013.pdf>; Kift and others (n. 134).

139 Boud and Associates (n. 84) 3.

140 Tertiary Education Quality and Standards Agency, *Engagement with professional bodies* <www.teqsa.gov.au/engagement-professional-bodies>.

141 Ibid.

142 Universities Australia and Professions Australia, *Joint Statement of Principles for Professional Accreditation* (2016) 5 <http://www.professions.com.au/images/Joint_Statement_of_Principles_for_Professional_Accreditation_-_2016-03-09_SIGNING.pdf>.

143 Higher Education Standards Panel, *The Higher Education Standards Panel's Advice on the Impacts of Professional Accreditation in Higher Education* (2017) 2 <https://docs.education.gov.au/system/files/doc/other/higher_education_standards_panel_advice_on_professional_accreditation_0.pdf>.

144 Department of Education and Training, *Professional Accreditation: Mapping the Territory, Final Report* (February 2017) ('PhillipsKPA') <https://docs.education.gov.au/documents/professional-accreditation-mapping-territory>.
145 Higher Education Standards Panel (n. 143). See also Higher Education Standards Panel <www.education.gov.au/higher-education-standards-panel-s-advice-impacts-professional-accreditation-higher-education> and Tertiary Education Quality and Standards Agency, 'Professional Accreditation Changes Welcomed by Regulator' (28 February 2018) <www.teqsa.gov.au/latest-news/articles/professional-accreditation-changes-welcomed-regulator>.
146 Higher Education Standards Panel (n. 143).
147 An inaugural *Industry Professional Body Accreditation Forum*, convened by TEQSA, as held on 13 December 2018.
148 Department of Education and Training, PhillipsKPA (n. 144) 33–34.
149 Ibid., 5.
150 Law Admissions Consultative Committee, 'Reconciling Academic Requirements and Threshold Learning Outcomes' (Discussion Paper, June 2011) 1 <www.lawcouncil.asn.au/files/web-pdf/LACC%20docs/20110624-ReconcilingAcademicRequirementsandThresholdLearningOutcomes-DiscussionPaper.pdf>.
151 Clarke (n. 61) 4.
152 Ibid.
153 See *Review of Academic Requirements* <www.lawcouncil.asn.au/resources/law-admissions-consultative-committee/review-of-academic-requirements>.
154 See generally, Assuring Professional Competence Committee, *What We Need to Do* (2017) 3 <www.lawcouncil.asn.au/resources/law-admissions-consultative-committee/assuring-professional-competence-committee>.
155 Clarke (n. 61) 4.
156 Chaired by The Hon Robert French AC, the other members of the Committee were: Professor Sandford Clark AM (Chairman, LACC), Richard Besley (Director, Judicial Commission of Victoria), John McKenzie (NSW Legal Services Commissioner) and Professor Sally Kift (then Deputy Vice Chancellor (Academic), James Cook University).
157 Clarke (n. 61) 15.
158 Ibid.
159 Steering Committee comprised of: Associate Professor Allan Chay, Professor Sandford Clarke, Professor Sally Kift and Professor Alex Steel.
160 Law Admissions Consultative Committee, Specifying Learning Outcomes for Contract Law (n. 124) 2.
161 Ibid. See also Law Admissions Consultative Committee, *Redrafting the Academic Requirements for Admission* (n. 124).
162 George Nott, *Gilbert + Tobin's New Breed of Lawyer: The 'Techno-legal'* (March 2017) <www.computerworld.com.au/article/616030/gilbert-tobin-new-breed-lawyer-techno-legal/>.
163 Australian Qualifications Framework Council (n. 36).
164 For the sake of the record, it is noted that, at the time the TLOs were negotiated in 2010, project management, numeracy (including statistical literacy), and Indigenous perspectives, were specifically raised for TLO inclusion, but were quickly ruled out at that time by disciplinary stakeholders as not 'threshold' to LLB attainment.
165 Solicitors Regulation Authority, *Solicitors Qualifying Examination* <https://sra.org.uk/home/hot-topics/Solicitors-Qualifying-Examination.page> and Solicitors Regulation Authority, *Closed Consultations – A New Route to Qualification: The Solicitors Qualifying Examination* <https://sra.org.uk/sra/consultations/consultations-closed.page>. An 'assessment partner', Kaplan, has now been appointed to assist with the development of the SQE.

166 Christian Veith and others (n. 60).
167 See, e.g., Women Lawyers of Western Australia, *2014 20th Anniversary Review of the 1994 Chief Justice's Gender Bias Taskforce Report* (September 2014) 133 <http://www.womenscouncil.com.au/wp-content/uploads/2019/01/2014_GenderBiasReviewReport_September2014-2.pdf>. This is to be compared with 1993 when women represented 'approximately 50 per cent of students': see Australian Law Reform Commission, *Equality before the law; Women's Equality Part II* (1994) 8.7 <www.alrc.gov.au/sites/default/files/pdfs/publications/ALRC69_Pt2.pdf> citing McInnis & Marginson (1994) (n. 66) Table A5.20, 448. The ALRC went on to footnote earlier comparisons: '1984 41 per cent, 1980 33.3 per cent and 1974 21.1 per cent' citing *The Pearce Report* (1987) (n. 10) [11.7].
168 Alicia Patterson, 'Balancing Act – Women in the Law' *MLS News* (Issue 13, June 2015) <https://law.unimelb.edu.au/alumni/mls-news/issue-13-june-2015/balancing-act>.
169 Erica Southgate, *Fair Connection to Professional Careers: Understanding Social Difference and Disadvantage, Institutional Dynamics and Technological Opportunities* (NCSEHE 2017) 8 <www.ncsehe.edu.au/wp-content/uploads/2017/09/Southgate_Fair-connection-to-professional-careers.pdf>.
170 American Bar Association (n. 25) 55.
171 Kift, Israel and Field (n. 71) 10. The TLOs for the JD are comparable in scope, but pitched at the standard appropriate to AQF Level 9 Master Degree (Extended).

10 Galloping off madly in one direction

Legal education reform, the (im?)possibility of evidence-based policy making and a plea for better design thinking

Julian Webb

I Introduction

The last 30 years have seen, at least in the common law world, an unprecedented level of legal education reform activity.[1] The real impact of this on legal education and training systems is, however, sometimes hard to discern. This is not just because causal links are not straightforward, but change may be contingent on a complex range of factors.[2] The sense remains that impact is often relatively limited; although review processes may sometimes provide impetus for a new 'big idea' or core contribution, the overall effect tends to be an ironing out of creases rather than a fundamental transformation of structures.[3]

The problems of legal education reform may also be in part an instantiation of larger uncertainties around legal education regulation and policy-making. As a field of regulation, it has in many respects lagged behind other aspects of professional regulation. Often bureaucratic in form, it remains in some jurisdictions a fundamentally under-resourced and marginal activity, with regulators occupying a liminal, or in some instances even conflictual position between the state, the universities and the profession.[4] Larger structural shifts away from either state-centred regulation or professional self-regulation have left it under-theorised and under-determined, trying to define its place in an increasingly 'post-regulatory', 'polycentric' or 'de-centred' regulatory world.[5]

Research has also played an uncertain and historically undervalued role in the reform story. Although a number of reports on legal education have acknowledged the value of research, reliance thereon has often been limited, particularly with regard to core questions of pedagogy and assessment. The Ormrod[6] and ACLEC[7] Reports in the United Kingdom, for example, drew on extensive demographic and descriptive data on law schools produced by John Wilson[8] and Phil Harris,[9] however there was little in the way of pedagogic research to turn to in the 1960s, and even ACLEC failed to engage systematically with the pedagogic literature that then existed. While some reports have commissioned specific projects as a part of their remit,[10] the quality of these has also been variable.[11] The blame for this lies, I suggest, with both the academy and the profession. Historically, both have been willing to treat legal education reform as an exercise requiring little or no special expertise in either educational theory or educational research. Indeed, before the 1980s, such review processes would in any event have struggled to find much of either within legal or other professional domains.[12] Perceptions of legal research as essentially a sui generis doctrinal activity,[13] and the wider neglect of higher education as a proper subject of study, even into the 1970s,[14] would have both contributed to that, as would the constraints of resourcing already alluded to. As I shall argue in this chapter, the effects of these historical weaknesses in the research base remain a constraint on regulation and policy-making to this day.

In sum, then, reforming legal education is often a relatively thankless and insufficiently conceptualised task. Rather like turning the proverbial supertanker, it takes time and energy,[15] and a lot of distance may have to be covered before we see a change in direction. Moreover, turning a supertanker may actually be easier. In legal education policy (in contrast, hopefully, to the supertanker) it may be unclear, given the absence of sound evidence, why we are turning in the first place; who is in charge of the process; whether there is an agreed course, or even whether the manoeuvre is going to take us in the direction expected.

Why this state of affairs? Without systematic empirical research into the policy process, we can only speculate. In this chapter, I engage in such speculation. I use the current drive for a return to centralised assessment as a starting point, and a lens through which to identify and discuss a number of fundamental flaws with dominant approaches to legal education research and policy-making, including its failure to be sufficiently evidence-based. This example provides, in turn, a basis to discuss the work undertaken in the English Legal Education and Training Review (LETR),[16] which sought, in part, to reframe the process of legal education reform as one that should be more obviously research-led. I conclude the chapter with both some evaluation of the kind of evidence-based approach attempted by the LETR, and with a further (albeit synoptic) plea for re-imagining the process of legal education reform, drawing on a mix of regulatory theory and 'design thinking'. In adopting the latter term, I am not just referencing the mode(s) of user- or human-centred design process that are currently in vogue,[17] but intend more broadly to encapsulate a way of thinking and doing that focuses on design as a creative act of problem-solving and sense-making which is both concrete and abstract.[18] Good design, whether of an artefact or a complex regulatory system is fundamentally a *social learning process* that involves, in Manzini's terms, finding what an object or system *does* and what it *means* and to whom; only in this way can we hope to achieve a proper balance of function ('utility') and form ('beauty').[19]

II The debate over centralised assessment

Assessment in legal education has tended to be enacted through a mix of *distributed* and *centralised* regimes. In the common law tradition, most academic (university) systems operate on distributed principles. Universities have a high level of autonomy in selecting what and how to assess. At the vocational stage of training, however, there is greater variation. Many common law jurisdictions have moved since the 1980s from centralised, professionally controlled, assessment regimes to more distributed models.[20] In contrast, other systems have maintained or increased emphasis on centralised assessment, such as a uniform bar exam, as the primary guarantor of standards. This is the approach in many civil law systems as well as a number of mostly smaller common law jurisdictions, such as Malaysia and Singapore, though it has also long been the preferred United States model.

The move to distributed assessment in vocational education largely reflected a broadening of ambition in legal training. It can thus be closely correlated to curriculum moves that emphasised the learning of skills, and the development of 'reflective practice' capabilities, rather than 'just' developing substantive professional knowledge.[21] It also corresponded conceptually and temporally to a gradual move towards outcomes-based education (OBE) models. OBE means that curriculum and assessment are directed to the achievement of specified competences, which are framed as outcomes describing what the learner should be able to do by the end of a period of study or training. While it has its origins in developments in occupational and workplace training in the United States in the 1970s,[22] it has only relatively recently become (re-)established in US legal education.[23] By contrast, competency-based approaches have been embedded in the English and Australian vocational training systems since the 1990s, and their greater deployment in academic legal education had been pushed for example, by the Law Society's Training Framework Review in England;[24] by the Task Force on the Common Law Degree in Canada,[25] and as a matter of 'soft regulation' approved by the Council of Australian Law Deans.[26]

Part of OBE's attraction lies in its potential as a regulatory solution to consistency and quality problems that a more distributed and diversified system might create. It has the merit of simplifying the regulatory/quality assurance process. In theory, if performance of an activity can be broken down into clearly described, readily observable components, it should matter less who is teaching, or assessing whom. Moreover, by creating a standard set of outcomes for all providers, a system can also permit flexibility in learning design and delivery, while still providing some assurance of a consistent 'product'.

Strikingly, the move to OBE in legal education has not been accompanied by much substantive debate about actual and desirable assessment practices. Such neglect is not new; there are, however, signs that it is beginning to change, though not necessarily in a good way. Indeed, a new battleground may be emerging in a regulator/profession-led backlash against distributed assessment. This trend can be seen, to varying degrees and with mixed results, in initiatives across Hong Kong, Canada, the UK and, most recently, Australia.

The Hong Kong Law Society has committed itself to a move to centralised assessment since about 2013. Progress, however, has been slow, and there continues to be a real lack of certainty over whether any such assessment is intended to be an alternative to or replacement of existing (distributed) assessment required as part of the current professional legal training regime.[27] The Federation of the Law Societies of Canada has also investigated the possibility of creating a uniform national system of assessment to replace existing provincial regimes. However, after about a year of discussions with stakeholders, and some initial work on scoping and costing, the project was shelved. The primary reasons appear to be concerns over additional costs for both provincial law societies and candidates, but also technical problems in adequately accommodating variations in provincial laws, and (a lack of) capacity to centrally assess professional skills.[28]

More substantial progress has been made in the UK where the English solicitors' regulator, the Solicitors Regulation Authority (SRA) is pressing ahead with a controversial plan to introduce a two-stage centralised assessment regime, which assesses learning from across both the academic and vocational stages of training.

In part one of its Solicitors Qualifying Examination (SQE), the SRA proposes a broad knowledge assessment of law and legal processes, essentially using standardised objective (i.e. multiple choice and short answer) testing to cover-off both the existing academic and vocational compulsory subjects, which have been re-framed as a set of 'day one' outcomes.[29] Part two will comprise a practical skills assessment. Trainees will be assessed on the practical skills of interviewing and advising, writing, drafting, advocacy, negotiation and legal research. Methods of assessment will draw on the objective structured clinical examination (OSCE) model developed in medical education, but also used – seemingly successfully – by the SRA in assessing the competence of overseas lawyers seeking to transfer into the solicitors' profession.[30] Each skill will be assessed in two different practice areas, selected from civil litigation, criminal litigation, property law and practice, wills and probate, or the law of business organisations. Candidates would also be expected to deal with both contentious and non-contentious areas in the overall course of the assessments.

While the SRA model has not appreciably influenced the Law Society of Hong Kong's approach to date,[31] it does appear to have had a significant impact on the thinking of the Law Admissions Consultative Committee (LACC) in Australia. The latter's 2017 discussion paper thus proposes work on developing a 'competence statement', 'threshold standard' and a 'statement of legal knowledge and skills' akin (perhaps) to the SRA approach. It further observes:

> A major problem identified by the LETR Setting Standards report, however, was the absence of consistent assessment standards applied by 100 law schools, and of any effective and efficient means of achieving such consistency . . .
>
> A robust, credible national assessment regime at the point of commencing to practise may indirectly confer greater flexibility on providers to determine how to deliver training, education and experience that meets the required outcomes – consistently with the second element of the English LSB's statutory guidance. We will need to investigate whether it might be

possible to develop a robust and consistent professional assessment regime at the threshold of practice, following the academic Practical Legal Training and legal workplace training components of a lawyer's preparation – whether this occurs before or after admission to the profession.[32]

III What does the centralised assessment debate tell us about legal education reform?

The move to centralised assessment undoubtedly has something of an Occam's razor feel to it. It provides (on the face of it) a relatively simple response to the creation of a range of perverse systemic incentives that, as a result of neoliberal education policies, might well undermine quality. Existing reviews have not ignored these problems, though they have come up with relatively few consistent answers to them. Strikingly, academic-led processes, such as the Law Society of Scotland's redesign of its vocational stage,[33] the US Stuckey project,[34] and the LETR Report (for example) have all placed considerable emphasis on the use of process tools to assure quality and enhance consistency. These included improved use of outcomes and written standards, the development of more and better 'best practice' guidance in respect of teaching and assessment methods, use of cross-institutional assessor meetings and training, and better use of statistical tools to validate assessments. None of them felt that centralised assessment was the 'magic bullet'. This disjuncture of itself may tell us some important things about the reform process.

First, much legal education reform can be seen as a 'political' reaction to perceived and recurring crises within the policy space.[35] This sense of crisis may have relatively little to do with the performance of legal education itself. As I have observed elsewhere,[36] legal education and training reform is often driven primarily by perceived threats and challenges to the *profession*, for example over student numbers, or market, or fears about competence or probity.

The rationale behind current drives for assessment reform fits this pattern. It reflects a mix of concerns about quality, and possibly access/number control. Quality concerns are widely expressed in current regulator discourse. However, with little substantive evidence behind them, the debate proceeds on terms that are largely impressionistic and inchoate. This is not entirely surprising; 'quality' itself is something of a fugitive concept: 'an abstract notion as to which there is no objective metric for achievement'.[37] There is little doubt that (from an employer's or regulator's perspective) comparing candidates is difficult – both the massification of legal education, and the diversification of assessment approaches have made the task of comparison more onerous. Crucially, however, no serious evidence has been presented that this has resulted in a widespread failure by assessment institutions to hit a baseline standard of professional competence. Nor has any (proposed) system of centralised assessment, including the SQE, ever been properly validated against professional performance standards. It is tempting in this context to see centralised assessment as a proxy solution to what are essentially coordination and quality assurance rather than intrinsic quality problems per se.

Centralised assessment has also been frequently used by the profession as a basic mechanism for number control, and in a way that invites some scepticism regarding the profession's proclaimed role as a guardian of standards. For example, in England, the pass rate for the Law Society's Final examination rose, in the wake of the Great War's depletion of the profession, to a high of 97 per cent in 1920, only to decline again through the Depression era to a mere 54 per cent in 1939.[38] More recently, when Japan decided it needed more lawyers, it demonstrated a similar sense of expediency, relaxing the notoriously selective entrance examination to its Institute for Legal Training and Research, and exempting from it entirely the students of its new, American-style, graduate law schools.[39] Similarly, the 'recruitment crisis' of the late 1980s clearly influenced the English Law Society's decision to move away from centralised assessment in the design of its new Legal Practice Course.[40] It may be no co-incidence that centralised assessment seems attractive once more, at a point where the profession is feeling the pressure of 'oversupply'.

The relationship between issues of centralised assessment and access and diversity are complex in ways that are not always well understood in public and policy debate. Thus, one of the problems raised during the LETR was whether doubts about the comparability of graduate standards in a distributed system likely encouraged, or at least sustained, employer reliance on ascriptive, and often elitist, social and cultural assumptions, with negative consequences for the diversity of the profession. In this context, the move to centralised assessment could be seen as a levelling of the playing field.[41] But is it? In reality, much will depend on how any assessment operates, in terms both of its impact on the cost and accessibility of the assessment itself, and any necessary pre-test training,[42] and in terms of the kind of assessment instruments used. Assessment choices themselves are not neutral but may well privilege those with certain kinds of educational and cultural capital.[43] Changes to assessment also do nothing to reduce the use of other sorting mechanisms, such as unpaid internships which are, in a number of jurisdictions, a common first step on the ladder to professional employment, and yet have potentially negative effects on equality of access.[44]

Second, and relatedly, reform pressures may also be connected to attempts by the profession (or some part thereof) to preserve or extend jurisdiction. In England, for example both the 1988 Marre Report,[45] and the Law Society Training Framework Review, launched in 2001, could be seen as part of the profession's defensive response to governmental challenges to jurisdiction later enacted in the Courts and Legal Services Act 1990, and the Legal Services Act 2007.[46] Major regulatory reform may also be a cue for regulatory agencies similarly to signal jurisdiction and establish legitimacy by doing something about education and training – the lead-up to the LETR could be interpreted in this way.[47]

Third, the move to centralised assessment also provides an example of how regulation often attempts to respond to and manage systemic complexity. The (regulatory) problem with learning processes is that they are highly situated and local, and hence differentiated.[48] Such complexity is particularly apparent around assessment. As Alison Wolf has explained:

> [A]ny assessment process is complex, incremental, and, above all, judgmental. It has to be because the actual performance which one observes – directly, or in the form of artefacts – is intrinsically variable: One person's playing of a piano piece, one person's operations plan, is by definition not exactly the same as another's, and cannot be fitted mechanistically to either a written list of criteria or to an exemplar.[49]

The regulatory instinct, however, is often to simplify and to standardise, rather than design adequately complex solutions to genuinely (and often irreducibly) complex problems. There is therefore a risk of regulators turning the proverbial 'blind eye' to the fuzziness of educational outcomes, and the complexity of the judgments involved in a 'proper' assessment of competence.

As a consequence, perhaps, we also risk replacing what is important with what is readily measurable.[50] SQE may prove to be a case in point. It seems to place a premium on knowledge retention, which can be assessed relatively simply and mechanistically – over the testing of more sophisticated cognitive skills. Centralised assessment may thus also fetishise consistency at the expense of other espoused values/goals of a modern legal education system. These others might include the flexibility to respond to the needs of an increasingly varied and segmented legal services market; a capacity for innovation; the ability to increase the diversity of those qualifying for the profession, and perhaps the importance of deep learning itself.

Fourth, we (including the regulators) are undoubtedly hampered by an absence of quality research. In the absence of proper research, legal education policy falls back on a discourse of anecdote and 'common sense', creating, as in other legal policy fields, a discourse in which 'what is discussed becomes what is known. The mythology is developed and elaborated on the basis of war stories told and repeated'.[51] The answers to some quite fundamental assessment questions are still unclear: what are we *actually* measuring when we assess in law schools? Does much of our assessment practice give us meaningful measures of student learning or just lots of things that may be a good, or less good, proxy for 'real' learning? How well does our assessment correlate to notions such as professional competence? Underlying each of these are conceptually and practically difficult questions for research and research design. Assessment is, of course, not the only part of the learning process for which this is true.

Lastly, policy trends, perhaps as a consequence of limited evidence, are also quite widely mimetic. In the absence of better solutions, neighbouring systems tend to copy each other, so that all, in the words of my title, gallop off madly in one direction. The English LETR Report, discussed further in Section IV, was itself a lesson in the gravitational pull of the past. Stakeholders were almost inevitably drawn to precedent. Is the (re)turn to centralised assessment best seen in this light, as essentially no more than a change in fashion? A reminder that what was once in vogue will, after due derision as yesterday's idea and sufficient passage of time, seem à la mode again? Would a more substantive evidence base on assessment practices have made a difference to the SRA's decision-making?

IV Evidence-based policy-making and the LETR: the promise?

Evidence-led, or more commonly evidence-based policy making (EBPM) represents both a set of professional aims and aspirations for applied research, and a policy movement/rhetoric. It seeks to valorise forms of decision-making that are objectively based and transparent, or at least much less based on instinct, ideology, and tradition than more conventional policy-led policy making.[52] EBPM became something of a political mantra in the 1990s and early 2000s; while, as an aspiration, it is definitely still with us,[53] the literature has become rather more circumspect regarding its potential, particularly in areas where policy continues to be a site for the playing out of 'culture wars' rather than rational decision-making.

EBPM thus broadly interpreted is neither wholly new nor wildly objectionable. It reflects what should be a basic requirement of policy-making: the need for good data, particularly in high cost and high impact policy areas (which are also otherwise subject to ideologically driven policy interventions), like education policy, health and social welfare.[54]

Would an evidence-based approach to legal education policy-making be a possible alternative? As noted in the introduction to this chapter; few reviews have even attempted to be evidence-led. The English LETR project, in its ambition at least, sought to be the exception.

The LETR set out to be the most extensive review of English legal education since the 1971 Ormrod Report. In its design the project was conceived of as both a regulation-centric and research-led process. It thus fitted broadly within this larger discourse of EBPM, and also coincided with a drive within regulatory practice in England to develop a more nuanced and risk-based[55] approach to regulation. The latter obviously shared some of EBPM's assumptions about the importance of a reasonably robust evidence-base for regulatory decision-making.[56]

The LETR research phase itself was split into broadly two stages: an initial literature review and period of evidence-gathering, followed by more specific consultation and testing of proposals. This would then feed into the final report, which would in turn inform individual regulators' programs of work. Over a period of some 18 months, the research team completed and published an extensive thematic literature review[57] and undertook mixed-methods research into the ongoing changes in the legal services market, and their likely impact on training needs, and into user perceptions of the content, structures and design of existing education and training regimes.[58] The project published a range of working and consultation papers designed to inform stakeholders and test the climate for change.[59] It organised a substantial conference to engage stakeholders in its design work, and collaborated with the Legal Services Board in holding a number of smaller thematic seminars around the UK. In an attempt to achieve a degree of transparency and reflexivity, the team also met regularly with a large stakeholder 'steering panel'.

The result of all this endeavour was a weighty 370-page report, delivered nearly six months late, making a total of (only) 26 'high level' recommendations. The report's overarching conclusion was that there was an absence of clear or systematic evidence that the existing English system was not 'fit for purpose'. Nonetheless, it also highlighted the need to build on established strengths and address a number of important weaknesses. In so doing, the Report was, of course, framed by the regulatory backdrop of and uncertainties caused by the Legal Services Act 2007. Although the Legal Services Act 2007 had only been in force since 2010, debates about the proper form and scope of regulation were continuing as we wrote. It became clear from the evidence gathered by LETR that there was little appetite at the time for further reform to the regulatory infrastructure. Nonetheless, the relationships between frontline regulators, and the potential for and likely effects of regulatory competition and market disruption were a source of unease and created a context of unusual regulatory complexity for the Report.[60]

For this and other reasons, LETR called for specific reforms across broadly three themes: quality, accessibility and flexibility. These reflected the Report's attempt to balance, as best it could, the somewhat competing, somewhat complementary, (regulatory) calls of competition, professional independence and enhancing access/diversity.[61]

In terms of quality, the Report sought greater consistency of outcomes and assessment standards across the system. This was to be based primarily on the development or refinement of 'day one' learning outcomes for prescribed qualification routes into the regulated sector.[62] It called for greater flexibility via, again, the deployment of learning outcomes, the encouragement of integrated course-based and workplace learning, and the removal of fixed 'time served' requirements for workplace training.[63] The report also called for better internal quality assurance (i.e. within regulated organisations) and the auditing of paralegal supervision, training and development.[64] In looking at accessibility, the research identified a range of evidence demonstrating that, despite the massification of higher education, access to the traditional legal professions was becoming more socially exclusive and elitist. Increased training costs, selection biases, and recruiter reliance on unpaid internships all operated against the entry of underrepresented groups to the professions.[65] The Report sought to ameliorate their effects at particular pinch points, by providing better information on legal careers;[66] by recommending the formulation of professional standards and guidance for internships and work experience,[67] and the creation of more flexible entry and transfer points into and between professional titles.

The response to the Report has been mixed. This is hardly surprising. Aside from the fact that there was, of course, scope for legitimate critique,[68] LETR took place in an environment strongly shaped by vested interests. It was never going to please everyone (whether it actually pleased anyone may be more moot). The LETR research phase was, moreover, a restricted regulatory review of the field. This shaped both the scope and what Wegner has called the 'vantage point' of the review.[69] Those who wanted a larger policy review that addressed the *desirable* characteristics of a legal education, rather than those characteristics *necessary for professional competence*, were bound to be disappointed. For others, LETR did not sufficiently break with the status quo. Stephen Mayson, for example, has been both a cogent and trenchant critic, arguing that the Report did not take a sufficiently cross-sector view, was not forward-looking enough, and did not provide an adequate blueprint for action.[70] Methodologically too the Report has been challenged; thus, in Boon's opinion, it relied too much on the views of stakeholders rather than an analysis of (regulatory) need.[71] For Sanders, similarly, it constituted an 'incoherent mixture of normative analysis and opinion'.[72] Others still, however, have been more circumspect, recognising the Report was at least good in parts, and perhaps better than most.[73]

Whatever its strengths and weaknesses, the LETR has become a significant part of continuing national and international debate.[74] Whether, ultimately, that is for good or ill is for others to judge; but did it deliver as an exercise in EBPM for legal education and training?

V The LETR, and EBPM in legal education reform: the reality?

In its ambition to be an evidence-based review, I suggest that the LETR, if not bound to fail, was at least bound to struggle. The reasons are multiple. The first is reasonably obvious and remediable, the others less so.

First, the timescale was such as to limit its capacity to be evidence-based, or to be fleet-footed enough to change direction as the nature of problems with and gaps in the research base (or indeed larger normative problems) became more apparent. The understandable political pressure to have a report by a deadline meant that once an initial course was set, we were committed, even though this also limited our capacity for reflection and fine-tuning: the super-tanker was not for turning. It also meant that some potentially useful approaches, such as occupation-specific training needs analysis, were not feasible across the piece, particularly given other required elements of the research specification. The focus of the review was, consequently and perhaps inevitably, uneven.

The second problem was, and remains, critical and could not be remediated in any reasonable timeframe. It is difficult to be evidence-based in the relative absence of good quality research. For experienced researchers in the field, the paucity of the evidence-base was not entirely a shock. Nevertheless the LETR literature confirmed that the extent of the gaps was even greater than we had assumed. When looked at systematically and comprehensively, the state of the research was, in Paul Maharg's words 'disturbingly chaotic'.[75] There was no meaningful literature on the regulation of legal education as such. There was limited domain-specific research on OBE; 'best practice' guidance on learning and teaching was (at best) extremely patchy; much of the demographic data was dated and incomplete, and research on the smaller professions and the (apparently) growing body of unregulated providers in the English legal services market was so non-existent that we were left floundering to find a purchase on what was happening.

There was little in the way of larger scale quantitative research; existing sources of primary data were few, and much of the data that did exist could not be compared or re-purposed in a way that made it (more) relevant to our needs. We found little use by legal education researchers of experimental design; no replication studies, and no systematic reviews. While we were not against qualitative research, most studies involved one-off local projects with little evidence of follow-up or further development. Much of it was variable in quality, often with little meaningful information about methodology, and with little or no proper discussion of how observed or expressed outcomes were evaluated, including how any criteria of evaluation were agreed or validated.

Many of these evidential problems coalesced for us around the core issue of competence and its assessment. As intimated, competence has moved from being a concept that is permissibly 'fuzzy' and largely inferred from proxy measures to something which, in the modern audit society,[76] must be capable of more precise definition, and assessment. Yet our research in the field demonstrated a continuing and fundamental narrative pluralism, reflected in a proliferation of and variation between competence statements and standards, most of which have been developed, not through research, but in ways that were ad hoc, intuitive and/or mimetic of other schemas.[77] These variations would seem to reflect two important and underlying issues.

The first is the increasing difficulty of setting competences and standards for a diversified and segmented profession; as occupational segmentation increases, so the risks of over- or under-specification of competence change. The second problem is the (even) more fundamental difficulty of *articulating* standards at all.[78] This is particularly critical in professional work contexts where our description of competence cannot be contained at the level of relatively simple technical task performance. Professional work involves both substantial knowledge-based judgment (much of which would have to be inferred from task performance) and, at its core, the more 'humanistic' dimensions of communication and decision-making: for example an ability to evaluate and discuss client interests and needs in a way that requires skills of judgement, contextual understanding, emotional intelligence, and ethical evaluation.[79] The retrenchment to seemingly simple solutions, like centralised assessment, is in this context understandable, but problematic. Initiatives like the SQE or the US Bar Exam, which largely sidestep the difficulty of articulating a holistic construction of competence, and avoid setting a standard that reflects performance across the range, thereby risk marginalising these humanistic qualities of the role.[80] Whether they add thereby to both the stresses experienced by underperforming practitioners, and consumer dissatisfaction is itself a question worthy of proper consideration.

A third and inevitable problem is the effect of the natural and pragmatic limits of EBPM itself. As some critics and supporters of EBPM observe, the name itself is somewhat misleading. It may be too much to expect that regulatory or professional practice be evidence-*based* rather than evidence-*informed*.[81] What it means to be evidence-based is moreover moot. Is it the same as research-based? Few policy processes would restrict themselves in that way, even though difficult assessments of principle will arise where research conflicts with evidence from other sources.[82] Moreover, research itself will often be provisional, contradictory and fallible. Though research evidence is often paramount in the literature, it will not always, and indeed should not always prevail.[83]

Even where feasible, a rational evidence-based approach inevitably will be confronted by practical constraints imposed on it by the realities of the 'political' process. Policy constraints tend to include limited resources, entrenched commitments and positional bargaining, differing practical judgements about what can be implemented, and disagreement arising from genuinely diverse value positions.[84] The latter in particular cannot be underestimated and will include, as we saw in the LETR process, matters such as contested views of what counts as evidence, and how it should be weighed, differing views about the place of normative analysis, and arguments about the meaning, scope and relative priority of policy or regulatory objectives.[85]

While it was inevitable that proposed reform packages would be contentious and fragile, for example, in terms of opposition from affected interest groups, or the adequacy of resourcing, the lack of evidence-base added to that fragility, making some findings and recommendations highly provisional and contingent on further work and resources. As always, implementation and the will of the regulators to see things through would be critical.

Even without the limitations of the evidence-base, EBPM was never going to be the whole solution. LETR's focus on (regulatory) structure also saw to that. In short, LETR pinned its hopes on a mix of EBPM and what we have called design thinking, as necessary partners in shaping a regulatory solution.

Design thinking created an overarching framework and (normatively) served to inform both our approach to evidence gathering, and to fill some of the gaps in the evidence base. Specifically, we brought an element of design-thinking to two things; first to our formulation of the basic *functional* problem of legal education reform itself, and second to our other key question of *form:* the construction of an appropriate regulatory space for not just the co-regulation but, we argued, the *co-production* of legal education and training.

In thinking about the functional problem, we reframed legal education reform as a 'wicked' or (as we preferred) 'socially complex', problem,[86] which required, first and foremost a systemic design-based solution. This framework merits some explanation.

The concept of 'wicked problems' came out of work in the 1970s by Horst Rittel and Melvin Webber, urban planners at the University of California, Berkeley. In a landmark paper,[87] they identified a category of social planning problems that could not successfully be addressed with traditional linear, analytical problem-solving. They contrasted these 'wicked' problems that seemed resistant to resolution with 'tame' problems. Tame problems are not necessarily simple, they may be technically complicated, but within a realm of known and manageable complexity. Consequently, a tame problem can be defined and a solution identified and implemented fairly readily because 'defining a problem inherently defines a solution'.[88] Initially the wicked problem literature focused on system design problems at a relatively 'micro' level, but later work has seen the concept applied to broader and larger institutional design and social policy problems.[89]

The interest in wicked problems can be seen, in many ways, as a precursor to the growing interest in complexity in the social sciences, and the rise of complexity theory approaches to social[90] and legal/regulatory problems.[91] In preferencing the term 'socially complex problems', we sought to nod to this 'complexity turn', without necessarily committing ourselves or our readers to buy into the whole complexity of complexity theories. Nonetheless, it is significant that wicked problem and complexity approaches share a number of common assumptions. Both modalities focus on systems, which they treat as open, 'nested' (comprising layers of sub-systems) and dynamic structures,[92] and (cybernetically) as processes of communication and feedback.[93] They also see relationships amongst variables as non-linear, with consequent problems for modelling and predicting outcomes. As with the famous 'butterfly effect', small changes in local conditions may produce large differences in systemic outcomes. In the LETR Report, we translated these insights into a set of characteristics that defined legal education reform ('LER' in Table 10.1) as a socially complex problem.

Focusing on the appropriate *form* of regulatory design was also essential as a way of addressing the interplay in the legal education system between the increasing substantive complexity of legal education (reform) processes and practices, and the move signalled in the post-Legal Services Act environment towards systems of oversight that were, in conception at least, more distributed, co-regulatory and structured, in some instances, through OFR. Consequently, regulatory design in and of itself became part of the LETR's problem-solving toolkit. As we expressed it in the Literature Review:

> Design can be used to enhance [regulatory] responsibility and accountability, and extend agency . . . indeed it can do so by clearing a space, as it were, in hierarchy so that self-governance, often according to extra-legal norms, is possible in ways that it would not otherwise be within communities of practice.[94]

In sum, thinking about function and form in this way forced us to confront a number of our assumptions, our methodology, and (reflexively) came significantly to influence our recommendations for the future, but it was not enough. Why?

First, the very structure of the review was, in retrospect, probably not sufficient for the complexity of its task. Conventional problem-solving models are essentially linear, designed to work with well-defined problems that can be

Table 10.1 Legal education reform as a 'socially complex' problem (LETR Report, Table 1.1)

Characteristics of socially complex problems	*Corresponding features of LER (eg)*
There is no definitive definition of the problem	Some agreement over a need for reform, but widespread disagreement over the extent, priorities and nature of the changes required
They tend to be intractable	General lack of effect from a number of recent education and training reviews. Specific intractable problems: • Achieving consistency of standards • Reducing costs of training • Managing increasing numbers
The information needed to make sense of the problem is often ill-defined, changing and may be difficult to put into use	Currently operating in rapidly changing work and educational environments Relative lack of robust, especially longitudinal, data Costs of deriving meaningful information are relatively high
They emerge in fields where there are multiple stakeholders; limited consensus as to who the legitimate stakeholders and/or problem-solvers are, and stakeholders are likely to have different criteria of success	Large number of stakeholders, with different understandings of the problem(s), and different levels of engagement with the process Legitimacy questions exist, for example over the extent of professional and regulatory interest in the LLB Evidence of different stakeholders having different 'objectives' for the review
Every attempt at a solution matters significantly	Reform tends to be a 'one-shot' operation so relatively high risk Exacerbated by uncertainties about the new regulatory environment, and the tendency of LSET system to operate as a relatively low trust environment

divided into distinct phases (the 'waterfall' conception indicated by the stepped line in Figure 10.1). In complex problem scenarios, on the other hand, every solution that is offered exposes new features of the problem, requiring further adjustments to the potential solution(s). In essence, much more of the 'problem' becomes about *defining* the problem. Instead of a single linear process, one needs to engage in a deeply iterative and reflexive process, a multiplicity of overlapping phases in which problem understanding and solution formulation are ongoing 'conversations' and ultimately emergent qualities of the whole

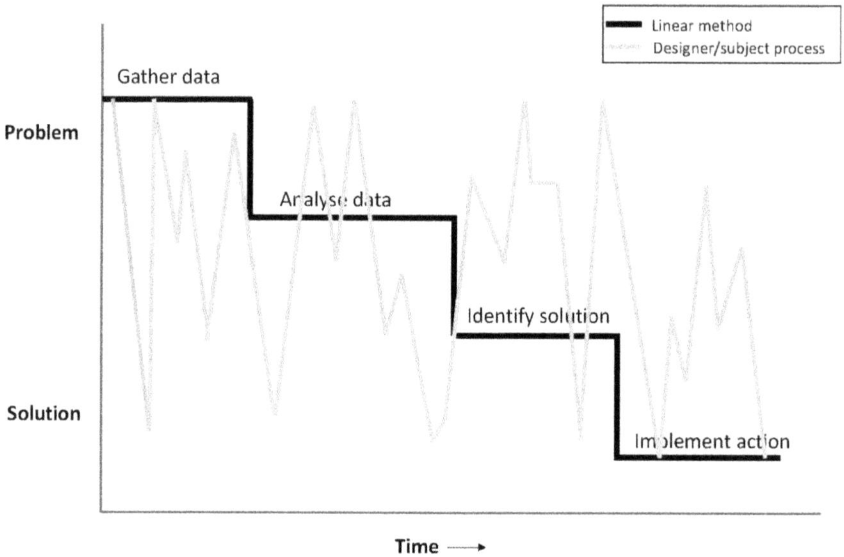

Figure 10.1 Linear versus Complex Problem-Solving (after Conklin)[95]

research process (the jagged line in Figure 10.1). Whilst we engaged in a degree of iterative research design, this insight and its consequences are far more apparent (to me at least) with the benefit of hindsight than at the point we were conducting the review. Whether such a completely iterative approach would have been feasible within the parameters set for LETR is doubtful.

Second, while the centrality of structural reform and the particular need to design for implementation and continuing support (especially support of EBPM) was clearly signalled in the report, and reflected in the recommendation for a 'Legal Education Council' as a new coordinating body,[96] we were unable to convince either the Legal Services Board or the main frontline regulators of its necessity. The speed with which this recommendation was rejected, on (unsubstantiated) resource grounds, was a major blow to the report. It effectively removed from the report much of its ability to shape the future, and made it even easier for some of the frontline regulators to tread a different path.

LETR's lack of material success in this regard may well be salutary, but the project was significant in taking thinking about the form and function of legal education reform forward. In some respects, as I have sought to show in this section, it was not clear enough in its thinking and formulation of the problems. At the risk of creating an 'ideal type', in the final section, I try to distil lessons from the LETR and the literature down into a set of principles that might better inform the regulatory review of legal education.

VI Beyond EBPM? taking system design and complexity (really) seriously: five principles

As I have sought to show, education reviews have tended to do much the same sort of thing, the same way and have generally achieved the same kind of limited results (when assessed against their own targets).

LETR was an attempt to break the mould, but it too was only partially successful. The absence of good quality evidence was only part of the problem; in both its underlying design and its delivery it failed fully to appreciate the implications of system complexity for its task. The core problem implicit in the LETR experience, I suggest, is that legal education reform processes, as currently designed, carry a relatively high intrinsic risk of failure. Specifically, failure is built into the 'one shot' reform model in two ways: (1) precisely because they are large, relatively high stakes interventions, with little evidence base and a low tolerance for failure, and (2) because they often pay insufficient attention to creating the conditions for continuing system maintenance. In short, complex systems left to their own devices tend to drift into failure.[97]

Can we reduce the risk of failure? Possibly; but, if there is never a grand solution, and problem-solving under conditions of social complexity requires the construction of uniquely engineered outcomes, this will require two things. First, an incentivisation of the necessary groundwork for reform, and, second, a different conception of the role of regulation, and of the review process itself. The following principles are therefore presented as a spur for discussion, and thinking about what it really takes to create the conditions for adequately complex legal education reform.

A Principle 1 – make regulation everyone's business

In order to counter the drift to failure, regulation must become everyone's business, not just the regulators. In the LETR report we described this in terms of the need for regulation to operate as a 'shared space':

> [A] community of educators, regulators, policy-makers and professionals working in provision of legal services, drawing information from other jurisdiction, other professions and other regulators to identify best practice in LSET [legal services education and training] and its regulation.[98]

In this regard, LETR built on insights from complexity theory and regulatory design to treat regulation as a dynamic and democratic process of co-production.[99] It implies an openness to what Maharg calls 'multiple narratives of regulation, change, standards and much else that need to be heard, analysed and acted upon'.[100] Notwithstanding the failure of Recommendation 25, I remain convinced of the importance of the shared space conception. This is only reinforced by the fact that, after some initial attempts at greater coordination following LETR, regulatory practice in England appears largely to have reverted to operating within its regulatory silos.

B Principle 2 – optimise the regulatory function

The notion of 'shared space' clearly stands as a challenge to our normal conception of regulation. As discussed at the outset of this chapter, legal education regulation has, in some respects at least, struggled to find its feet in the new world of rapidly changing legal services, and more consumerist modes of regulation. These difficulties are perhaps most apparent in the pressing need for regulation to respond to innovation challenges in legal services, and to facilitate concordant change in legal education. The American Bar Association's 2014 Task Force ably summarised the problem, thus:

> Innovation cannot come from a directive to experiment and take risks. Nor can it come simply from the removal of real or perceived barriers to innovation. Rather, it must come from a change in attitude and outlook, and from openness to learning, particularly from other fields.[101]

This, I argue, of itself implies some broadening and optimising of the regulatory function into a *design* role. This is unlikely to be achieved through traditional modes of oversight and 'command and control' regulation. The regulator needs to be both proactive and dialogical, to act as an enabler of change and quality enhancer, not just quality controller. It is a function that also requires a greater flexibility and fleetness of the regulator than we are used to, including a capacity to move between multiple modes of regulation.[102]

C Principle 3 – start with the foundations

There are two separate and related points to be made here. First, it is critical that we recognise that any review actually starts with the process of formulating the problem, not with finding the solution. To be sure, no review starts with a blank slate; the impetus will often come, as we have seen, from 'war stories' about what is not working, or other external triggers. Options in respect of regulatory models may already be closed down – in the LETR context, for example, it was clear at the outset that there was no appetite for a further substantial regulatory review, nor was a return to the former system of professional self-regulation a realistic option. But, at the same time, terms of reference or other devices are too often used to narrow the scope of enquiry, when setting the scope and nature of the enquiry is often the first real research question. Drawing on human-centred design models, rather than relying primarily on expert evaluation at this stage, reform processes might better start not just with user experience, but a more deeply embedded notion of co-design between experts and users as a way of identifying potential problems of functionality and form.[103]

Second, notwithstanding the limits of EBPM, the absence of a sound research base is a fundamental limitation. In engineering complex solutions, a good evidence base matters, not least because it should help define the scope of enquiry, and act throughout the process as an uncertainty reduction tool. As the LETR Report concluded, better and more consistent data-gathering is necessary, together with more support for legal education research in terms of funding, training and coordination.

Following from Principle 1, this should be seen as a collective responsibility, though the requirements of risk regulation arguably give the regulator a special interest in having access to the best evidence available. For this reason, and others identified under Principle 2, we argued in LETR (and still maintain)[104] that regulators have a special *primus inter pares* interest and role in relation to research and knowledge management. The regulator is appropriately placed to act as custodian, maintaining an archive of educational research and regulatory good practice, and hosting the debates around the knowledge hub or 'design lab' identified by LETR. The regulator might also have a signal role in initiating cycles of research, feedback and feedforward, and perhaps contributing to funding or other forms of research support.

D *Principle 4 – practise knowledge mobilisation, so that if we build it, they will come*

A critical issue for the success of any evidence-based policy reform is maintaining the synergy of knowledge and action: embedding evidence in practice and ensuring (changing) practice is reflected in evidence. Central to this is the ability to understand and manage the process described in the policy literature as 'knowledge brokering' or 'knowledge mobilisation' (KMb).[105] Conventionally, knowledge to action processes tend to be seen as one way: researchers disseminating work to potential users. However, this is known to be of limited effect.[106] Consequently, there is a growing interest in the impact of intermediation in the process, and a move in theory and practice to seeing the process of knowledge to action itself in relational (network) and non-linear (system) terms.[107] These approaches fit well with a view of learning, in complexity theory, as a cross-community network activity involving large numbers and intensities of interactions over time.[108] If our policy of building EBPM is to have real utility, KMb theory suggests intermediation is desirable. It adds significant value by providing knowledge translation to policy audiences, an interface (with potential for feedback and feedforward) between the creators and users of evidence, and more actively enhances access to knowledge by providing information and training to knowledge users.

In the LETR Report we saw the regulator primarily as an end user of research, and we sought to ascribe to the Legal Education Council a supporting KMb function. This arguably sits well with a risk-based regulatory approach, which sees the regulatory role move substantially away from post hoc enforcement to ex ante data gathering, provision of information and training/advice. There is, however, no reason why intermediation cannot be performed by a wholly separate knowledge broker,[109] or indeed in a distributed fashion across a network of organisations. The latter approach may have particular benefits. Reform needs its change agents and champions: what Sullivan refers to as 'institutional sites that concretely exemplify the new vision and function as exemplary centers that train and inspire reform'.[110] Research moreover also points to the importance of more systemic approaches as a mechanism for addressing the barriers of capacity and resourcing that limit sustainable knowledge mobilisation.[111]

E Principle 5 – small is beautiful

Incrementalism is not a problem; rather it often offers the better chance of a solution. Wholesale 'one shot' reforms, as we have seen are more prone to intrinsic failure and potentially may create greater risks of substantial and systemic failures in the target system. As a regulatory community, we need to work together to identify and take small risks so as to reduce the bigger systemic risks associated with either not changing, or implementing undercooked reforms. Piloting, prototyping and properly evaluating change is more easily achieved on a small scale, and needs to be encouraged and normalised through regulatory practice. This might include, for example, using 'regulatory sandbox' provisions (adopted in areas like financial services regulation)[112] that allow for experimentation that would otherwise fall outside the scope of permitted activities.

VII Conclusion

This chapter has focused on the limitations of legal education reform processes in recent decades, including their methodological and evidential limitations, under-theorised approach to the policy and regulatory process, and the potential for implementation to be undermined by stakeholders' 'political' motivations. It has identified ways in which the Legal Education and Training Review in England sought to overcome some of these challenges by reconstructing reform as both a design and evidence-based process of creating 'socially robust' solutions to complex problems. It has concluded by discussing how a more systematic deployment of principles of design thinking, supported by a more robust evidence base might potentially enhance the legal education and training sector's future capacity for better regulation and policy-making.

In their fullest manifestation the principles expressed in this chapter most likely constitute a counsel of perfection. Nonetheless, I have sought to show through the course of the chapter why some move towards such principles is desirable, if not critical, to enabling the sorts of innovation that will create novel artefacts and institutions capable of meeting the challenges of complex social and legal change. Would a process designed consistently with these principles have come out against centralised assessment? I don't know. But it would have approached the possibility of change very differently: seeking to work constructively with the grain of sector expertise, engaging critically and responsibly with the existing evidence-base, paying close attention to user experience (in other systems and jurisdictions), and undertaking piloting, and possibly even basic prototyping *before* any policy decision was made.

The discussion in this chapter may also have some particular resonance for educational practice in Australia in the light of continuing debates about standards and regulation. Funding constraints continue to limit policy work in the field. It now appears unlikely that there will be any larger-scale systematic review, as LACC has been unable to find funding to support the work of its proposed Assuring Professional Competence Committee (APCC). What will happen now, beyond a limited review of the Priestley 11, is moot, but it is hard to see where any external impetus for evidence-based reform will be found. Yet, in an increasingly complex and segmented legal services environment, questions over the appropriateness of current legal education and training are unlikely to go away. The message at least is clear. If we think evidence-based reform matters, it surely behoves the law schools collectively, not least as the profession's repository of research expertise, to take a leading and proactive role in (co-)designing the future of legal education and its regulation.

Notes

1 For an overview of the more recent activity, see Anthony Rogers, Tony Smith and Julian Webb, 'Comprehensive Review of Legal Education and Training in Hong Kong: Final Report of the Consultants' (Standing Committee on Legal Education and Training 2018) s3 <www.sclet.gov.hk/eng/publications>.

2 Stephen Daniels, William Sullivan and Martin Katz, 'Analyzing Carnegie's Reach: The Contingent Nature of Innovation' (2014) 63 *Journal of Legal Education* 586.

3 See, e.g., Rebecca C. Flanagan, 'Leveraging Academic Support Programs for Innovative Teaching Methods across the Curriculum' in David M. Moss and Debra Moss Curtis (eds), *Reforming Legal Education: Law Schools at the Crossroads* (Charlotte, NC: Information Age Pub 2012) 202; Russell G. Pearce, 'MacCrate's Missed Opportunity: The MacCrate Report's Failure to Advance Professional Values' (2003) 23 *Pace Law Review* 575; on the limited impact, beyond clinic, of the MacCrate Report, see American Bar Association, 'Legal Education and Professional Development – An Educational Continuum: Report of the Task Force on Law Schools and the Profession: Narrowing the Gap' (Chicago: American Bar Association 1992). See also Julian Webb, 'A Tale of Two Cities: Reflecting on Lord Neuberger's "Reforming Legal Education"' in Chris Ashford, Nigel Duncan and Jessica Guth (eds), *Perspectives on Legal Education: Contemporary Responses to the Lord Upjohn Lectures* (Abingdon: Routledge 2016), on the cumulative effects of the six major reviews of English legal education between 1846 and 1996.

4 See, e.g., the discussion of the Law Society of Hong Kong's role in regulation in Rogers, Smith and Webb (n. 1) s. 6.

5 Julian Webb, 'Regulating Lawyers in a Liberalized Legal Services Market: The Role of Education and Training' (2013) 24 *Stanford Law & Policy Review* 535.

6 Roger Ormrod, *Report of the Committee on Legal Education* (Cmnd No. 4595, London: HMSO 1971) ('Ormrod').

7 Lord Chancellor's Advisory Committee on Legal Education and Conduct ('ACLEC'), *First Report on Legal Education and Training* (London: ACLEC 1996).

8 John Wilson, 'A Survey of Legal Education in the United Kingdom' (1966) 9 *Journal of the Society of Public Teachers of Law* 5; John Wilson, 'A Third

Survey of University Legal Education in the United Kingdom' (1993) 13 *Legal Studies* 143.

9 Phil Harris and Martin Jones, 'A Survey of Law Schools in the United Kingdom, 1996' (1997) 31 *The Law Teacher* 38.

10 See, e.g., vol. IV of the 1987 'Pearce Report' which contains the findings of an extensive survey of law graduates commissioned for the report: Dennis Pearce, Enid Campbell and Don Harding, *Australian Law Schools: A Discipline Assessment for the Commonwealth Tertiary Education Commission* (Canberra: AGPS 1987).

11 See, e.g., Arthurs' critique of the methodological failings of the research undertaken by the Federation of Law Societies of Canada to underpin its competency framework: Harry W. Arthurs, 'The Future of Legal Education: Three Visions and a Prediction' (2014) 51 *Alberta Law Review* 705, 706–7.

12 See, e.g., Fiona Cownie and Anthony Bradney, 'An Examined Life: Research into University Legal Education in the United Kingdom and the *Journal of Law and Society*' (2017) 44 *Journal of Law and Society* 129–143.

13 See Michael Chesterman and David Weisbrot, 'Legal Scholarship in Australia' (1987) 50 *Modern Law Review* 709, 722–3; Mary Keyes and Richard Johnstone, 'Changing Legal Education: Rhetoric, Reality and Prospects for the Future' (2004) 26 *Sydney Law Review* 537, 541–2.

14 John Brennan and Ulrich Teichler, 'The Future of Higher Education and of Higher Education Research' (2008) 56 *Higher Education* 259.

15 Boon thus describes contestations over the core subjects in the UK as resembling 'trench warfare', involving 'periodic sorties by the profession, leading to skirmishes from which both sides eventually withdraw exhausted': Andrew Boon, 'Ethics in Legal Education and Training: Four Reports, Three Jurisdictions and a Prospectus' (2002) 5 *Legal Ethics* 34, 35.

16 Julian Webb and others, 'Setting Standards: The Future of Legal Services Education and Training Regulation in England and Wales' (Legal Education and Training Review 2013) ('LETR Report') <www.letr.org.uk/the-report/>.

17 Joseph Giacomin, 'What Is Human Centered Design?' (2014) 17 *The Design Journal* 606.

18 Panagiotis Louridas, 'Design as Bricolage: Anthropology Meets Design Thinking' (1999) 20 *Design Studies* 517; Ezio Manzini, *Design, When Everybody Designs: An Introduction to Design for Social Innovation* (Cambridge, MA: The MIT Press 2015) 35–37.

19 Ibid., 36, 54.

20 Solicitors Regulation Authority, *Qualification in Other Jurisdictions – International Benchmarking* (September 2016) <www.sra.org.uk/documents/SRA/research/ICLR-benchmarking.pdf>.

21 See, e.g., Neil Gold, Karl J. Mackie and William L. Twining (eds), *Learning Lawyers' Skills* (London: Butterworths in conjunction with the Commonwealth Legal Education Association 1989).

22 See notably H. R. Cort and J. L. Sammons, 'The Search for Good Lawyering: A Concept and Model of Lawyering Competencies' (1980) 29 *Cleveland State Law Review* 397.

23 See Roy T. Stuckey and others, *Best Practices for Legal Education: A Vision and a Road Map* (New York: Clinical Legal Education Association 2007); American Bar Association, 'Report and Recommendations: American Bar Association Task Force on Legal Education' (American Bar Association 2014) <www.americanbar.org/content/dam/aba/administrative/professional_responsibility/report_and_recommendations_of_aba_task_force.authcheckdam.pdf>.

24 See Andrew Boon and Julian Webb, 'Legal Education and Training in England: Back to the Future?' (2008) 58 *Journal of Legal Education* 79, 103–5.
25 Federation of Law Societies of Canada, 'Task Force on the Canadian Common Law Degree: Final Report' (October 2009) <www.slaw.ca/wp-content/uploads/2009/10/Task-Force-Final-Report.pdf>.
26 Australian Learning and Teaching Council, Bachelor of Laws: Learning and Teaching Academic Standards Statement (2010) 9 <https://cald.asn.au/wp-content/uploads/2017/11/LLB-TLOsKiftetalLTASStandardsStatement2010-TLOs-LLB2.pdf>.
27 See Rogers, Smith and Webb (n. 1) s. 6; Law Society of Hong Kong, 'Response to Standing Committee on Legal Education and Training Consultants regarding unified law school and the Common Entrance Examination ('CEE') and other recommendations' (May 2018) <www.sclet.gov.hk/eng/publications>.
28 Law Council of Australia, 'Assuring Professional Competence Committee – What We Need to Do' 5 <www.lawcouncil.asn.au/resources/law-admissions-consultative-committee/assuring-professional-competence-committee>. Development costs were estimated at C$2.8 million and the projected annual operating costs for an estimated 3,800 candidates would be C$1,725 per head.
29 The subjects are: ethics and professional conduct, business law and practice, property law, torts, criminal law and evidence, criminal litigation, civil litigation, wills and probate, taxation, contract law, trusts and equitable wrongs, constitutional law, EU law, human rights, and the English legal system.
30 See Eileen Fry, Jenny Crewe and Richard Wakeford, 'The Qualified Lawyers Transfer Scheme: Innovative Assessment Methodology and Practice in a High Stakes Professional Exam' (2012) 46 *The Law Teacher* 132; Eileen Fry, Jenny Crewe and Richard Wakeford, 'Using Multiple Choice Questions to Examine the Content of the Qualifying Law Degree Accurately and Reliably: The Experience of the Qualified Lawyers Transfer Scheme' (2013) 47 *The Law Teacher* 234.
31 Though LETR's influence on the systemic review undertaken for SCLET is more pervasive, see Rogers, Smith and Webb (n. 1) *seriatim.*
32 Assuring Professional Competence Committee (n. 28) 4, 9.
33 Paul Maharg, 'The Gordian Knot: Regulatory Relationship and Legal Education' (2017) 4 *Asian Journal of Legal Education* 79, 85–92.
34 Stuckey and others (n. 23).
35 See Richard L. Abel, '"You Never Want a Serious Crisis to Go to Waste". Reflections on the Reform of Legal Education in the US, UK, and Australia' (2015) 22 *International Journal of the Legal Profession* 3.
36 Webb (n. 3).
37 American Bar Association (n. 23) 12.
38 Richard L. Abel, *The Legal Profession in England and Wales* (Oxford: Blackwell 1988), Table 1.1.
39 Kay-Wah Chan, 'Setting the Limits: Who Controls the Size of the Legal Profession in Japan?' (2012) *International Journal of the Legal Profession* 321.
40 Andrew Boon, 'History Is Past Politics: A Critique of the Legal Skills Movement in England and Wales' (1998) 25 *Journal of Law & Society* 151, 154.
41 This has been part of the SRA's claims for the SQE, notwithstanding that its own commissioned equality impact assessment was clearly uncertain, if not ambivalent, about the diversity effects of the move to centralised assessment: see Bridge Group, 'Introduction of the Solicitors Qualifying Examination: Monitoring and Maximising Diversity' (Solicitors Regulation Authority 2017) <www.sra.org.uk/sra/policy/training-for-tomorrow/resources.page>, accessed 21 April 2018. Note also wider concerns regarding the SRA's approach to

evidence in Elaine Hall, 'Notes on the SRA Report of the Consultation on the Solicitors Qualifying Exam: "Comment Is Free, but Facts Are Sacred"' (2017) 51 *The Law Teacher* 364; Jenny Gibbons, 'Policy Recontextualisation: The Proposed Introduction of a Multiple-Choice Test for the Entry-Level Assessment of the Legal Knowledge of Prospective Solicitors in England and Wales, and the Potential Effect on University-Level Legal Education' (2017) 24 *International Journal of the Legal Profession* 227.

42 In the SQE context, while a single assessment provider has now been selected, cost questions have not yet been resolved – see Richard Simmons, 'Kaplan Get Contract to Run SRA Super-exam – but No Word yet on Cost' *The Lawyer* (1 August 2018), <www.thelawyer.com/sqe-kaplan-gets-sra-contract/>, accessed 25 September 2018.

43 Note evidence regarding the performance of minority students on the US Bar Examinations: National Conference of Bar Examiners, 'Impact of the Increase in the Passing Score on the New York Bar Examination' (New York State Board of Law Examiners, November 2006), <www.nybarexam.org/press/summary.pdf>; Stephen P. Klein and Roger Bolus, 'Minority Group Performance on the California Bar Examination' (mimeo 1987) <www.seaphe.org/pdf/past-bar-research/Minority_Group_Performance_on_the_California_Bar_Examination.pdf>.

44 See LETR Report, Recommendation 20, and (UK) All Party Parliamentary Group on Social Mobility, 'The Class Ceiling: Increasing Access to the Leading Professions' (Sutton Trust 2017) 7 <www.suttontrust.com/research-paper/class-ceiling-appg-social-mobility/>, which calls for a ban on unpaid internships in the professions.

45 The Committee on the Future of the Legal Profession, *A Time for Change* (London: Law Society/General Council of the Bar 1988).

46 See Boon (n. 15).

47 See David Edmonds, 'Training the Lawyers of the Future –A Regulator's View' (2011) 45 *The Law Teacher* 4.

48 Cp Tamsin Haggis, 'Beyond "Mutual Constitution": Looking at Learning and Context from the Perspective of Complexity Theory' in Richard Edwards, Gert Biesta and Mary Thorpe (eds), *Rethinking Contexts for Learning and Teaching: Communities, Activities and Networks* (Abingdon: Routledge 2009) 44–60.

49 Alison Wolf, 'Competence Based Assessment' in John Raven and John Stephenson (eds), *Competence in the Learning Society*, (New York: Peter Lang 2001) 453 at 466.

50 The restricted (written) formats of the US Bar Examination, for example, have long been criticised for doing insufficient to assess the range of skills required of the modern practitioner: see Stuckey (n. 23) 12–13.

51 Hazel Genn, 'Understanding Civil Justice' (1997) 50 *Current Legal Problems* 155, 169.

52 Brian W. Head, 'Reconsidering Evidence-Based Policy: Key Issues and Challenges' (2010) 29 *Policy and Society* 77.

53 Karen Chester, 'Evidence-based Policy: Missing in Action' *The Mandarin* (online) (14 December 2016) <www.themandarin.com.au/73699-evidence-based-policy-missing-action/>.

54 Note also the tendency of systems of government to use education itself as a policy tool to address intractable social problems, often with little real expectation of or criteria for success: see Daniel Tröhler, 'Educationalization of Social Problems and the Educationalization of the Modern World' in Michael A. Peters (ed), *Encyclopedia of Educational Philosophy and Theory* (Singapore: Springer 2016); David Bridges, 'Educationalisation: On the Appropriateness

of Asking Educational Institutions to Solve Social and Economic Problems' (2008) 58 *Educational Theory* 461.

55 Hutter notes that the term risk-based regulation 'embraces a very broad range of approaches' from broad frameworks of governance to highly specific quantitative approaches to the identification and assessment of risk factors: Bridget Hutter, 'The Attractions of *Risk-based Regulation*: Accounting for the Emergence of Risk Ideas in Regulation', CARR Discussion Paper 33 (London School of Economics, March 2005) <www.lse.ac.uk/accounting/Assets/CARR/documents/D-P/Disspaper33.pdf>. Educational approaches to risk regulation tend to involve more qualitative or multi-modal assessments of risk, see, e.g., the Australian Skills Quality Authority 'Regulatory Risk Framework' <www.asqa.gov.au/about/risk-based-regulation>.

56 See Adam Dodek and Emily Alderson, 'Risk Regulation for the Legal Profession' (2018) 55 *Alberta Law Review* 621; Joan Loughrey, 'Accountability and the Regulation of the Large Law Firm Lawyer' (2014) 77 *Modern Law Review* 732.

57 The Literature Review is archived at <www.letr.org.uk/literature-review/index.html>.

58 Interviews and focus groups were conducted with 307 academics, practitioners, representatives of regulatory and representative bodies, and students. An online survey obtained 1,128 responses from broadly the same groups (except regulators). The latter involved a non-randomised sample, but sample size was sufficient to satisfy basic criteria for statistical reliability: see Annex D of the Report.

59 All interim papers are archived on the LETR website at <www.letr.org.uk/briefing-and-discussion-papers/index.html>.

60 See further LETR Report, [3.49]–[3.52]. Regulation under the Legal Services Act 2007 extended to eight occupational titles (of which solicitor and barrister were just two), and to the regulation of firms or 'entities' that were licensed to undertake reserved activities potentially with various mixes of regulated, or regulated and unregulated, individuals.

61 The LETR was to an extent bounded by the regulatory objectives set down in s. 1 of the Legal Services Act 2007. These defined the functions of regulation as: (a) protecting and promoting the public interest; (b) supporting the constitutional principle of the rule of law; (c) improving access to justice; (d) protecting and promoting the interests of consumers; (e) promoting competition in the provision of [legal] services; (f) encouranging an independent, strong, diverse and effective legal profession; (g) increasing public understanding of citizen's legal rights and duties, and (h) promoting and maintaining adherence to the professional principles [laid down in the Act].

62 LETR Report, ch. 7, recommendations 1–3, 6–7, 11.

63 Ibid., recommendations 10, 12, 15.

64 Ibid., recommendation 22.

65 Ibid., [6.11]–[6.15], [6.25]–[6.34].

66 Ibid., recommendation 25.

67 LETR Report, recommendation 20.

68 For some of my own views on its limitations, see Webb (n. 3) 38 ff.

69 Judith Welch Wegner, 'The Value of Legal Education' (2015) 24 *Nottingham Law Journal* 112, 125; see also William Twining, 'Let's Talk: Framing Enquiry and Discussions about "Legal Education"' (2015) 49 *The Law Teacher* 388.

70 Stephen Mayson, 'Of Competence, Confidence and the Last Chance Saloon' in Chris Ashford, Nigel Duncan and Jessica Guth (eds), *Perspectives on Legal Education: Contemporary Responses to the Upjohn Lectures* (Abingdon: Routledge 2016) 85.

71 Andrew Boon, *The Ethics and Conduct of Lawyers in England and Wales* (3rd edn, Oxford: Hart 2014) 204–6.

72 Andrew Sanders, 'Poor Thinking, Poor Outcome? The Future of the Law Degree after the Legal Education and Training Review and the Case for Socio-Legalism' in Hilary Sommerlad and others (eds), *The Futures of Legal Education and the Legal Profession* (Oxford: Hart 2016) 152.

73 See, e.g., Graham Ferris, 'Values Ethics and Legal Ethics: The QLD and LETR Recommendations 6, 7, 10, and 11' (2014) 48 *The Law Teacher* 20; William Twining, 'Rethinking Legal Education' (2018) 52 *The Law Teacher* 241, 243 ('in many respects their review was a significant improvement on prior reports in the genre').

74 See Jane Ching and others, 'Legal Education and Training Review: A Five-Year Retro/Prospective' (2018) 52 *The Law Teacher* 384.

75 Jane Ching and others, 'An Overture for Well-Tempered Regulators: Four Variations on a LETR Theme' (2015) 49 *The Law Teacher* 143.

76 Michael Power, *The Audit Society: Rituals of Verification* (2nd edn, Oxford University Press 1999).

77 See Julian Webb and others, 'LETR Briefing Paper 1/2012: Knowledge, Skills and Attitudes Required for Practice at Present' (n.d.) <www.letr.org.uk/briefing-and-discussion-papers/index.html>.

78 Katharine Boursicot, 'Setting Standards in a Professional Higher Education Course: Defining the Concept of the Minimally Competent Student in Performance-Based Assessment at the Level of Graduation from Medical School' (2006) 60 *Higher Education Quarterly* 74.

79 See the LETR Report 'holistic' formulation at Table 4.3 and related discussion.

80 Cf. the Stuckey Report's observation that 'when objectives are not made explicit, the result is almost certainly a preoccupation with specific knowledge': Stuckey (n. 23) 43.

81 See, e.g., Philip Davies, 'What Is Evidence-Based Education?' (1999) 47 *British Journal of Educational Studies* 108; Martyn Hammersley, 'Is the Evidence-Based Practice Movement Doing More Good than Harm? Reflections on Iain Chalmers' Case for Research-Based Policy Making and Practice' (2005) 1 *Evidence & Policy* 85; Julie Nelson and Carol Campbell, 'Evidence-Informed Practice in Education: Meanings and Applications' (2017) 59 *Educational Research* 127.

82 David Byrne, 'Evidence-based: What Constitutes Valid Evidence?' in Andrew Gray and Stephen Harrison (eds), *Governing Medicine: Theory and Practice* (Open University Press 2004).

83 See further Hammersley (n. 81).

84 Head (n. 52).

85 One of the challenges for the LETR review was dealing with the breadth, overlap and potential incommensurabilities between the Legal Services Act 2007 regulatory objectives. A number of references are made to the objectives in the preparatory papers, though the final Report is perhaps light in its discussion thereof. We did attempt some deeper conceptual analysis of the objectives and their inter-relationship in an early draft of the final report, but this was dropped on the basis that it seemed to generate far more questions than answers.

86 Avoiding the terminology of 'wicked problems' was deliberate; as Peters observes: 'truly wicked problems may be relatively less common than they appear in contemporary writing in policy studies, [however] the dimensions contained in the concept may be individually useful in analysing policies': B. Guy Peters, 'What Is So Wicked about Wicked Problems? A Conceptual Analysis and a Research Program' (2017) 36 *Policy and Society* 385, 387.

87 Horst W.J. Rittel and Melvin M. Webber, 'Dilemmas in a General Theory of Planning' (1973) 4 *Policy Sciences* 155.

88 Chanpory Rith and Hugh Dubberly, 'Why Horst WJ Rittel Matters' (2007) 23 *Design Issues* 72, 73.
89 Kate Crowley and Brian W. Head, 'The Enduring Challenge of "Wicked Problems": Revisiting Rittel and Webber' (2017) 50 *Policy Sciences* 539.
90 Graham Room, *Complexity, Institutions and Public Policy: Agile Decision-Making in a Turbulent World* (Cheltenham: Edward Elgar 2011); Frederic William Hafferty and Brian Castellani, *Sociology and Complexity Science: A New Field of Inquiry* (Berlin: Springer 2009).
91 See notably J. B. Ruhl and Daniel Martin Katz, 'Measuring, Monitoring, and Managing Legal Complexity' (2015) 101 *Iowa Law Review* 191; Steven Wheatley, Jamie Murray and Thomas Webb (eds), *Complexity Theory and Law: Mapping an Emergent Jurisprudence* (Abingdon: Routledge 2018).
92 See, e.g., Rick Stephens and Michael Richey, 'Accelerating STEM Capacity: A Complex Adaptive System Perspective (2011) 100 *Journal of Engineering Education* 417, where Stephens and Richey define the higher education ecosystem as:

> Composed of systems nested within subsystems, each operating on multiple temporal scales where observable causality is often hidden . . . Changes to this system emerge through evolutionary processes and are encumbered by complex physical, behavioral, and social phenomena as well as competing interests.

93 See, e.g., Peters (n. 86); Rith and Dubberly (n. 88).
94 LETR Literature Review, ch. 3, [45].
95 E. Jeffrey Conklin, *Dialogue Mapping: Building Shared Understanding of Wicked Problems* (New York: Wiley 2006).
96 LETR Report, ch 7, recommendation 25.
97 Sidney Dekker, *Drift into Failure: From Hunting Broken Components to Understanding Complex Systems* (Farnham: Ashgate Pub 2011).
98 LETR Report, [6.158].
99 See LETR Report, [6.142]–[6.160].
100 Maharg (n. 33) 93.
101 American Bar Association (n. 23).
102 Multi-modal regulation is defined by Colin Scott as: 'mechanisms of steering – whether through hierarchy, competition, community, design or some combination thereof' cited in LETR Literature Review, ch. 3, [40].
103 Cf. Manzini (n. 18) 48–49.
104 See Ching and others (n. 74); Maharg (n. 33).
105 Amanda Cooper, 'Knowledge Mobilisation in Education across Canada: A Cross-Case Analysis of 44 Research Brokering Organisations' (2014) 10 *Evidence & Policy: A Journal of Research, Debate and Practice* 29; Vicky Ward, Allan House and Susan Hamer, 'Knowledge Brokering: The Missing Link in the Evidence to Action Chain?' (2009) 5 *Evidence & Policy: A Journal of Research, Debate and Practice* 267.
106 Jeremy Grimshaw and others, 'Toward Evidence-Based Quality Improvement: Evidence (and Its Limitations) of the Effectiveness of Guideline Dissemination and Implementation Strategies 1966–1998' (2006) 21 *Journal of General Internal Medicine* S14; Jon F. Kerner, 'Knowledge Translation versus Knowledge Integration: A "Funder's" Perspective:' (2006) 26 *Journal of Continuing Education in the Health Professions* 72.
107 Allan Best and Bev Holmes, 'Systems Thinking, Knowledge and Action: Towards Better Models and Methods' (2010) 6 *Evidence & Policy: A Journal of Research, Debate and Practice* 145; Adrian Cherney and Brian Head, 'Supporting the

Knowledge-to-Action Process: A Systems-Thinking Approach' (2011) 7 *Evidence & Policy: A Journal of Research, Debate and Practice* 471.

108 Yrjö Engeström, *Learning by Expanding: An Activity-theoretical Approach to Developmental Research* (2nd edn, Cambridge University Press 2015).

109 For example, in its work of collating and re-purposing research data into systematic reviews and providing online training, the Cochrane Collaboration (www.cochrane.org) on evidence-based medicine can be seen as performing some of these basic knowledge-brokering functions, though essentially within the uni-directional model; see the discussion in Jeremy M. Grimshaw and others, 'Knowledge for Knowledge Translation: The Role of the Cochrane Collaboration': (2006) 26 *Journal of Continuing Education in the Health Professions* 55. The nearest analogy in legal education has probably been the work of the now defunct UK Centre for Legal Education, the law subject centre of the (then) Higher Education Academy, which sought to advance effective practice in teaching and learning law, commissioned and participated in research, and also often acted in an independent expert and intermediary fashion on legal education policy matters: see Julian Webb, 'Enhancing Legal Education: The UK Experience' in Judith Brockmann, Jan-Hendrik Dietrich & Arne Pilniok (eds) *Exzellente Lehre im juristischen Studium* (Baden-Baden: Nomos Verlag 2011).

110 William M. Sullivan, 'After Ten Years: The Carnegie Report and Contemporary Legal Education' (2018) 14 *University of St Thomas Law Journal* 331, 343.

111 Cooper (n 105); Carol Campbell and others, 'Developing a Knowledge Network for Applied Education Research to Mobilise Evidence in and for Educational Practice' (2017) 59 *Educational Research* 209.

112 See Dirk A. Zetzsche and others, 'Regulating a Revolution: From Regulatory Sandboxes to Smart Regulation' (2017) *SSRN Electronic Journal* <www.ssrn.com/abstract=3018534> accessed 6 November 2018.

11 Thinking or acting like a lawyer?

What we don't know about legal education and are afraid to ask*

Carrie Menkel-Meadow

I Introduction: should we study causes of action or apps?

Thorstein Veblen, the American sociologist, wrote a hundred years ago that law schools 'belong in the modern university no more than a fencing or dancing school'.[1] This hostility to law as a subject that should be taught in a serious university came both from a desire to decrease the number of lawyers and litigation in society and a belief that certain 'skills' were not the subject of proper serious intellectual inquiry.

Fortunately for us serious legal educators, Veblen's pronouncements, although often cited in the 20th century, did not come to pass. Instead the 20th century has witnessed an expansive growth of legal education at all levels of university (and outside of university) training, including undergraduate, graduate professional and graduate academic degree programs.[2] In addition to the growth of degree and academic programs, modern legal education, beginning in the second half of the 20th century, also began to include (as medical education has for over a century) clinical training with both real and simulated clients and legal matters.[3] The practice of law itself, as well as the study of law and legal institutions, has grown from case and statutory analysis (in common law countries), and from code learning (in civil law countries) to more interdisciplinary study, including study of economics, sociology, psychology, political science and government, game theory, decision science, history, anthropology, geography and now international and comparative law or the 'globalization' of legal materials and institutions.[4] Increasingly, the professional skills (counselling, interviewing, advocacy, negotiating, mediating, drafting, decision-making) have been added to rigorous studies of constitutional law, jurisprudence, property, contract, torts, criminal and civil procedure, and legal ethics in a much more diverse set of courses and activities. Modern law schools are not only about cases, litigation and advocacy; modern lawyers are also taught to think about transaction planning, governance, counselling clients, business and social justice. Students now have some choice about what to study, instead of being required to all study the same corpus of legal materials.

This chapter reviews what I call the major 'big bang' moments of modern legal education – the addition of new subjects and methods to more conventional case study and didactic or Socratic methods of instruction. Some suggest we are in a new 'big bang' moment as technology will totally alter how law is practiced, and we use algorithms, not cases, to decide disputes and make decisions.[5] Thus, I ask here, should we be studying causes of actions and cases, or should we teaching our students to write code, and design 'apps' (applications) for smartphones and computers to deliver justice?[6] What if anything, should we be changing in modern legal education? But, I caution as well, there actually is not that much we know about how students actually learn to be lawyers and what law will look like in the modern digital age.[7] As I review a series of 'big bang' moments in legal education I will suggest some questions that should lead to more rigorous assessment of what we actually know about the effectiveness of various theories and practices of legal education and what we might usefully study in the future to test our assumptions about what makes good legal education practice. Though this essay does not take up the issues in comparative professional education, we could profitably learn from how other professions assess their educational theories and training.[8]

I have been a legal educator for over four decades, involved personally in at least ten different legal education reforms and 'movements' (clinical education, socio-legal studies, critical legal studies, legal feminism, 'outsider' jurisprudence (e.g. critical race studies), law and culture, alternative dispute resolution, legal ethics, 'problem solving' legal education, and globalization and transnational legal studies). I am now part of a group at my relatively new law school (the University of California, Irvine, which is just ten years old) that is focused on creating a 'tech and AI (artificial intelligence) justice' program. I was myself educated in the 1970s in a graduate law (Juris Doctorate) program, (after a first university sociology degree) that was classically 'Langdellian' (Socratic teaching method with mostly year-long common law subjects – property, torts, criminal procedure, civil procedure, legal writing (now called lawyering skills in most American law schools) and one innovation – labor law taught (erroneously) as a statutory course).

After law school, instead of clerking for a federal judge, I taught in and directed the University of Pennsylvania's Legal Writing and Research Program and began a career of trying to study what kinds of methods of legal education made a difference in student learning and professional aspirations and motivations. With the then Penn dean, later Harvard law professor, Bernard Wolfman, I taught a seminar on legal education, studying its history and variations in the United States and elsewhere.[9] I later edited the American *Journal of Legal Education* (2004–2009) with my colleague, and also later Harvard Law school professor, Mark Tushnet. After several years as a poverty lawyer I was one of the founding faculty of the new clinical program (the Penn Legal Assistance Program) at the University of Pennsylvania, following which I joined the then leading clinical law faculty at the University of California Los Angeles, where I was the first tenured professor of law based on both clinical and academic work.

I moved to Georgetown as an academic professor (who continued to teach clinically as well) where I was one of the founders of the modern 'alternative dispute resolution' movement, as both an academic and a practitioner. (I continue to mediate, arbitrate, consult and train judges, lawyers, diplomats and journalists). I began to teach many subjects (starting with negotiation, mediation and international dispute resolution, as well as legal ethics) in many other countries and, as of this writing, I have taught in 26 different countries. I was part of a group that founded a transnational legal education program, through Georgetown University's law school, based in London, and involving students and faculty from over 20 different law schools around the world.[10] Ten years ago I was a member of the Founding Faculty at the University of California at Irvine's new law school, founded to be a law school focused on public interest practice, which rose rapidly in the American law school rankings (currently #21 out of over 200 law schools), but is also becoming increasingly more conventional and like other law schools. I recount all this personal history to advise the reader of this essay of my considerable experience in legal education to assess my scepticism that we have or can really adequately assess the impact of all of these (and newer) attempts to reform and change the more conventional models (didactic lecture of core subjects) of legal education.

Here I present six of the 'big bangs' in modern legal education and suggest what we might need to study and research in order to assess the recent claims about (1) what is wrong with law school and (2) what might/should be changed in legal education.[11]

A Legal education = thinking like a lawyer

Unlike European and civil law countries (and the United Kingdom) where law has historically been 'learned' by traditional didactic lectures and memorization of code, in the United States we date the 'big bang' moment of legal education to the use of Christopher Columbus Langdell's (Dean of Harvard Law School 1870–1895) so-called Socratic or *case method*. The Langdellian method was based on an idea derived from the early science of German universities. Langdell believed that law, like science, could be derived from inductive observations from cases. If law students read enough cases in the same subject area they would 'induce' the applicable rules by watching them being applied by common law judges, and then could master the legal analysis skill of 'distinguishing' like cases from unlike cases. They then could turn around and use deductive arguments to apply principles derived from one case to the next one if the cases were sufficiently similar or make different arguments to show one case was, in fact, different from another and a different or 'new' rule should be used. As the method and theory behind it were very slightly modified over many years (and are still in use today in many law schools), students learned to master 'analogical' thinking by applying 'rules' to 'facts' (already 'found', as the cases studied were all appellate cases with so-called reasoned opinions.) By the time I got to law school in the 1970s, a little socio-legal studies had worked its way in as the Yale and Columbia law faculties of the 1930s added 'policy' and empirical considerations to arguments about what law should be applied.[12] The method of teaching (which can and should be de-coupled from the principle-deriving from reading appellate cases) was a professor posing hypotheticals to a room full of students (mostly men until the 1960s) and rigorously questioning students to explain their reasoning to the whole class, publicly (and famously often with their being humiliated and personally exposed in the process[13]). Langdell also introduced 'blind' or anonymous grading in law schools (often attributed to his own less privileged background when he noticed that those with wealth and resources were achieving better grades). His legacy for professional education in the United States is equalled only by the American pragmatist, John Dewey (the father of 'experiential learning' in American education[14]) as Langdell's 'case method' migrated to business and other professional schools. Students were not to engage in rote memorization but pragmatic problem solving by mastering facts and applying analysis and general principles.

Langdell's legacy[15] remains controversial. His initial idea of deriving 'scientific' legal principles did not last long, as the United States consists legally of now 50 states and 94 different federal districts, all interpreting a wide body of doctrinal law, often coming up with different legal solutions. One of our leading jurists, Supreme Court Justice Louis Brandeis, famously called it a federal system which could serve as a 'laboratory of democratic legal experimentation' with different rules being used in different states.[16]

Though the idea of scientific principles and doctrines derived by reading cases is still the core of the common law method (along with precedent in most Anglo-derived legal systems), modern legal education has moved away from the 'Socratic dialogue' in many schools (and most other countries). Professors now often 'lecture' the 'rules' and doctrines, turning what was actually quite an active, if threatening, form of education to the more passive form of students taking notes (or texting) during formal classes. One other major contribution of Langdell's method was that many students (often over 100) could be placed in the same lecture hall. High tuition dollars allowed universities to collect a lot of money and, unlike pedagogy in the science labs, law students did not need close contact with professors in this method,[17] so the law school became, for many universities, a profitable 'cash cow', often subsidizing other parts of the university.

Though the method of close questioning of a single student in front of his or now her, classmates is slowly disappearing, its intention was to demonstrate the power of analogical and rigorous thinking. Being asked how a change of facts might change the application of a particular rule, students were being asked to 'think like a lawyer', meaning learning to distinguish, with philosophically rigorous standards, what cases were 'like' each other enough to be treated the same under the law, and correspondingly, which cases, if not 'like', deserved a different rule to be applied. American law students are still told to brief cases to look at issues, rules, analysis and conclusion (IRAC) as a routinized application of this method. They are asked to analyze what facts are necessary for the 'holding' and which are only 'obiter dicta' or not essential to the court's reasoning. Most conventional American law teachers would likely still say that what they are doing is teaching students to be analytic and to 'think like a lawyer', learning how to make arguments for rules either to be applied or distinguished in particular cases.

Ironically, as I will review below, more recent applications of other fields to law, from cognitive sciences, have suggested that thinking by analogy or metaphors can, in fact, be quite 'lazy' thinking.[18] On the one hand, each problem may require its own solution and on the other, disaggregation and aggregation of 'cases' (statistical patterns) may provide a different way of analyzing and finding scientific and perhaps even legal 'truths'.

The takeaways from this 'big bang' are several:

1 Is analogical thinking the best way to learn legal doctrine?
2 Is reading appellate cases the best way to learn the 'legal rules'?
3 Is 'Socratic dialogue' a good teaching method (whether practiced in large lecture halls or more Platonically in a one on one olive grove discussion of teacher and student)?
4 Is inductive learning with lots of cases, better than a more deductive-memorization of legal rules method?
5 What happens to the variations of empirical facts in this sort of dry study of already decided cases? (Hint: read the dissents to see what other facts might have been 'found'?)

Whether practiced in its pure forms or not, many countries have now attempted to replicate American legal education (e.g. Japan, Korea, Australia, some in the UK) by instituting various forms of the Socratic method in a belief that such 'active' learning is better than the more passive form of large lecture. Do we know? Little educational research in law schools tells us much about how this method actually 'teaches' either the substantive law or how to be a good lawyer (drafter, decision-maker, counsellor or advocate).

B Critically thinking like a lawyer: the 'crits' come to law school and theory matters

In the 1970s and '80s a new political movement from the 'New Left 'challenged the orthodoxy of both elements of Langdell – the 'science' of doctrine[19] and the hierarchy of the Socratic method. Critical Legal Studies (CLS), founded as an intellectual attack on the manipulation of doctrine by the 'haves' in cases in which the law was indeterminate and could be 'argued on both sides', inspired a generation of law students and young law professors (I am of this generation) to critically examine both doctrine and teaching methods. Instead of Langdell, there was Harvard Law Professor Duncan Kennedy's *Legal Education and The Reproduction of Hierarchy*,[20] called the 'little red book' for a new group of law professors seeking to challenge traditional and capitalist doctrine, and to explore how class systems were maintained by traditional legal education. Duncan Kennedy, a brilliant and elegant teacher, taught from the back of his amphitheatre classrooms, 'deconstructing' tort, property and contract doctrine, as he encouraged students to think for themselves (as political actors, not only as lawyers) and to consider the class origins of the lawmakers (legislators, judges and executives) and whose interests they were serving in lawmaking and interpretation (railroads in the 19th century, corporations in the 20th, and autocratic and dictatorial political systems in the 21st).[21]

CLS, as an organization of politically progressive law teachers, met annually for close to 15 years and produced a vast outpouring of new scholarship and critical analysis of conventional legal doctrine,[22] coinciding with an increase in the number of women and minorities who began to enter the legal academy and frame an 'outsider jurisprudence'. What would the law look like if made by the formerly excluded women and minorities? The 'fem-crits' challenged both conventional doctrine and the masculinist models of left politics and teaching,[23] and 'critical race theorists' (African-American, then Latino, and now Asian and 'queer theory') developed their own theories of law and methods of teaching.[24] Feminists, along with other new entrants to the legal academy offered different instructional models, derived from the participatory 'women's consciousness raising' group meetings and collective organizing with 'bottom up' not top down, learning in more seminar like settings.[25] Law schools were pressured to add new courses ('Women and the Law', 'Race and the Law', 'Critical Legal Theory', and 'Queer Law') and students often created their own courses and teaching materials, aided by fellow traveling professors.

At about the same time, American legal scholarship and education was also affected by another 'big bang' intellectual movement – that of law and economics.[26] Richard Posner and a school of University of Chicago law and economics scholars argued that law could be analyzed from the perspective of how 'efficient' it was in allocating the 'transaction costs' of legal rules (the Coase theorem[27]) and maximizing wealth for the actors in any legal system. Drawing on the 'invisible hand' of Adam Smith's market-based theories, the law and economics movement drew scholars to analyze every area of law from torts, contracts, anti-trust, property, environmental law and eventually even constitutional law. One law school (George Mason) was founded to specialize in this form of analysis and many law schools developed critical masses of law and economics scholars who urged the study of both micro and macroeconomics in law schools.

In some of the major American Law Schools (Harvard, Yale, Chicago, Penn, Stanford and Berkeley), the 1980s were characterized by open political clashes of professors and students from these two 'schools' of legal thought. Appointments were hard to make and students and faculty organized protests and political actions around both internal educational issues and larger issues in the polity (originally anti-Vietnam war, civil rights, Supreme Court appointments, and even conventional political elections). For whatever reasons (some of us think the ascendancy of 'identity politics') the CLS movement ceased to have meetings (around the mid-1990s), while the Law and Economics movement was much more successful in capturing both judicial appointments for law making and interpretation (University of Chicago legal scholars Richard Posner and Frank Easterbrook among them) and forming a political action group, The Federalist Society, which, operating like a fraternity, has been able to mobilize for both professorial and judicial appointments (see recent United States judicial confirmation hearings for the Supreme Court).

Contemporaneously with the critical theory and law and economics movements, an earlier group of social scientists, some with legal educations, tried to introduce more empirical study of law into both legal scholarship and teaching methods.[28] Like the law and economics professors, socio-legal scholars developed summer programs to teach those who had been educated in conventional Langdellian methods, social science methods – quantitative and qualitative studies of the gaps between the 'law on the books' and the 'law in action'. The Law and Society Association provided a home for both legal educators and social scientists (political science, sociology, history, anthropology, psychology and some economists) to try to understand the operation of law and legal institutions 'beyond' (under, below and through) doctrine. Informed by social and political theories (Marx, Durkheim, Laura Nader, Max Weber and modern methodologists) such legal scholars sought to understand the actual effects of law on the regulated, as well as the forces which constitute lawmaking and enforcement. In some law schools, courses and seminars added empirical study to the diet of legal doctrine, but the hopes of many of us that part of legal education would necessarily include the study of statistics, quantitative methods and decision-making never really caught on except in a few places. Some socio-legal scholars challenged the claims of critical legal studies and others as not being informed by actual empirical study of the claims made.[29]

More recently, a group of legal scholars and others calling themselves 'behavioral economics' analysts have applied a variety of social and cognitive psychological studies to analysis of group behavior (not assumed to be rationally 'wealth maximizing') in corporate board governance, jury deliberations and judicial and legal decision-making, that is marred by human cognitive and social errors,[30] such as 'groupthink'.[31] This important work challenges the Langdellian ideas of the science or 'rationality' of legal rules and decision-making, but it is also derivative of some of the earlier work in socio-legal studies. Modern law school classes will now occasionally study these 'distortions' in rational legal thinking in both theoretical assumptions of human motivations and in more practical courses in advocacy, trial preparation and transaction planning, as well as corporate governance, jury decision making and negotiation behavior, among other areas.

One interesting question which has never been deeply pursued has been to understand the reasons for the relative success of law and economics in the United States, compared to CLS and the empiricism of socio-legal studies[32] in capturing legal power (through judgeships, as well as the professoriate and scholarship), perhaps because of the claims made by some, that the legal professoriate was more left, progressive and 'nihilistic'.[33]

Put together broadly (and somewhat superficially) here, the takeaways from the multiple schools of 'theory' outside of law for legal education are:

1 To what extent do we now understand that law and legal institutions are not autonomous domains, but are constituted by and constituting other social institutions?
2 Why do some theories (and schools of thought) more successfully infiltrate legal thought and education? How much explanatory purchase do different fields offer for understanding legal phenomena?
3 What fields of study, 'outside' of law, should be part of the legal curriculum? Should every lawyer be quantitatively literate (statistics, economics, policy analysis, decision making)?
4 How should we assess what basic 'ideas' or 'theories' are necessary to develop the appropriate analytic and performance skill sets for lawyers?
5 What is the political (or non-objective) content of law and legal institutions? Who is benefitted and who loses in particular legal regimes?

C 'Doing like a lawyer': experiential and clinical learning

The 1960s in the United States was a time of political activism – the civil rights movement, then the feminist movement, Earth Day and environmentalism, and later gay rights, all sparked law student activists to clamor for change in legal education, arguing that legal education should be 'relevant' to solving the nation's social and political problems. In 1969 the Ford Foundation founded the Council for Legal Education and Professional Responsibility (CLEPR) to support clinical legal education (work on real cases by law students) and to encourage the teaching of professional responsibility and ethics (more on that below). Many law schools received large grants to begin in-house clinics and hire professors (often not on the tenure track) to supervise students in poverty law matters, including class actions for employment discrimination and consumer rights, civil rights, landlord tenant, domestic relations, police abuse, welfare rights and a host of civil, and in separate clinics, criminal matters (juvenile and then some misdemeanors-later death penalty clinics were added as the American 'Innocence Project' (using DNA to exonerate erroneously convicted defendants gained prominence). The American clinical movement has probably been the most successful legal education innovation in a century. Now virtually every law school has at least one, and often more, clinical programs, focusing on either a particular subject matter (immigration, community development, criminal law, consumer rights, domestic violence, indigenous rights, environmental law, and international human rights) or a particular process (mediation, trial advocacy, legislation, policy analysis). Over the last 50 years clinical professors have published the most of any professorial legal group on pedagogy (see, e.g., *The Clinical Law Review*)[34] and also increasingly on substantive legal issues involving representation of the subordinated or least served in the legal profession.[35] The clinical movement has sparked a productive practical and scholarly debate about how best to represent the underrepresented (class actions, social movements or individual cases[36]) which has now inspired the growth of clinical education and cause lawyering around the world (see, e.g., Global Alliance for Justice Education (GAJE) <www.gaje.org>).[37]

Unlike doctrinal professors in the United States, clinical professors learned their craft – annual meetings of the clinical professoriate for decades have focused on teaching modalities of many kinds and have offered sessions of teaching, critique and feedback of teachers, modeling what supervision of student-lawyers should be. So, as a new clinical teacher in the 1970s, my classes were audio taped by my mentor and teacher, Professor Mark Spiegel,[38] and we went through each class for over a year of instruction. I learned to understand the difference between leading, directive and open questioning of students, to map teaching goals, and to develop lesson plans with students (and sometimes with clients present!). In 1978 I joined a group of innovative law professors to work with the Project for the Study and Application of Humanistic Education in Law,[39] which provided training and theories of experiential learning, applied to all law school subjects, derived from more intense relationships to law and clients from the clinical movement and studies in clinical and humanistic psychology and education theory. Since my early years as a professor, I have never taught a class that does not have some experiential component (sidebar conversations of students, role-plays and simulations, group exercises, use of other media, interviews, short 'games', practical problems and case studies to discuss, and imaginative exercises).[40]

The now robust contributions of clinical education have been to demonstrate that 'facts matter' (students are now taught fact investigation, client interviewing, deposition taking, negotiation, etc.) and that 'feelings matter' too (client counseling, the role of emotion in decision making) and a generally broader conception of what the actual practice of law is about.[41] A broader set of skills matter too, now including decision-making, problem solving, and transactional and organizational work, besides the more common conceptions of lawyer as advocate or barrister.[42] And, as a precursor to the modern clinical movement, noted Yale professors argued that legal education should be molded around the idea of creating a 'public interest profession' with legal, social and policy science as part of practical problem solving.[43]

In recent years, as law school enrollment has declined in the United States from a peak of a few years ago (following the economic recession in 2008) many law schools have redesigned their curricula to be more 'practice-ready' and professionally relevant (with critiques echoing those of Veblen that law schools have become instrumental professional and skills schools, without enough focus on the theories of justice and jurisprudence that should be taught).[44] Two states (California and New York) have mandated some minimum credits for 'experiential learning and skills training' in law school before the bar examination can be taken.[45] Most American law schools now have special deans tasked with developing and supervising courses in experiential learning, including clinics, extern and internships, simulation and skills courses within the law school, as well as supervised placements outside of law schools. The degree and type of supervision of these activities varies widely.

In other legal education developments, both Harvard and Stanford law schools, among the best in the United States, have created new programs to deepen the fields of learning and practice that young lawyers might need. Stanford offers a set of 'policy labs' and practicums in particular legal subjects in which students analyze a problem, write reports and policy recommendations and work for clients, individual and institutional, and often actually design policy and legal initiatives (in such fields as dispute system design, privacy policy, innovation and intellectual property, immigration policy, healthcare, incarceration, international law, educational policy and others.)[46] The Harvard Law School has instituted a mandatory problem solving workshop for first year students, devoted to using case studies of real problems to engage students in early multi-disciplinary and practical learning.[47]

The growth in experiential, clinical and practical training in modern American law schools has been exponential and is constantly changing. The idea is that practical training embedded inside of the law school will be deeper and richer than the 19th-century versions of apprenticeship learning in which young would-be lawyers learned their craft solely in one legal office. Students will learn about client interviewing from psychologists and social workers, statistics and quantitative analysis from social scientists, investment and development strategy from economists and financial analysts, and community organizing from community activists. Learning is intended to be rigorous, reflective and jointly academic and practical.[48]

But, questions to be studied remain:

1 Do we know that work in one practical field has carryover effects for lawyering in different fields? What is generalizable in specific clinical settings?
2 Do students learn law better when embedded in practical situations, acting, as well as studying, the law?
3 What kinds of teaching methods/supervision are optimal in such settings – should there be different kinds of teachers and teaching modalities for different kinds of learning environments?
4 How do students evaluate their clinical and practical experiences later in their years of practice?[49]
5 Is this form of 'inductive' learning better than, different from, the 'deductive' learning of conventional doctrinal education?

D 'Being' a lawyer: professional and personal responsibility and ethics

In the early 1970s, just prior to the 1972 presidential election in the United States, a group of Republican party operatives broke into Democratic headquarters and began a series of data thefts and planted political misinformation and pranks (all of this might seem quite mild, given current computer hacking and much worse). At the hearings which emerged in the United States Congress, White House Counsel John Dean produced a list of those who had been involved in the scandal and cover-up. Next to some of those names was a star. When queried about what the star signified, Mr. Dean indicated that those were lawyers who had been involved in the illegal activity.[50] The ABA responded to widespread critiques of the legal profession by requiring instruction in legal ethics and professional responsibility for all lawyers – professional responsibility is now one of the only 'required courses' in American legal education.[51]

The teaching of legal ethics and professional responsibility in American law schools has produced an important body of philosophical and practical scholarship on what it means to be a 'good' lawyer and a good person.[52] Concerns about whether 'role morality' for particular professions, such as lawyer (or soldier or executioner[53]) should differ from the morality of 'ordinary persons' has produced an important set of questions and responses.[54] These questions of whether the role of the lawyer is to be solely a 'zealous' advocate for his client or to do justice or have some responsibility for the legal system generally (or the much touted 'rule of law') or to other individuals remains a challenge, which often differs from one legal culture to another. The 'taxi-rank' rule in the English system more or less absolves barristers for any 'responsibility' for their client's actions. In the last few decades, many other legal systems have begun to regulate the legal profession, police some of its transgressions in various forms of discipline,[55] and require or encourage legal education in ethics and professional responsibility.[56]

In my own work, I combined experiential learning with socio-legal and philosophical scholarship in legal ethics to teach legal ethics with simulated ethical problems in the large law school classroom,[57] then called (before the TV show, *Law & Order*) 'ripped from the headlines!' Students enacted scenarios of a variety of ethical dilemmas facing lawyers in different contexts and then had to analyze and explain their choices to the larger class, focusing both on formal rules (ABA Model Rules of Professional Conduct and state law variations and case law) and personal conceptions of morality. My new law school at University of California Irvine now requires a full first year course on the legal profession, which attempts to teach both the formal legal ethics rules and provide instruction on the sociology of the profession so students can begin to choose their legal careers and understand the functions of different kinds of lawyers in society.[58]

As my own scholarship moved toward consideration of lawyers as problem solvers,[59] not only advocates to 'win' for clients, I taught different kinds of courses in 'alternative/appropriate dispute resolution' and sought to teach and study whether the legal culture of the legal profession could be changed from an aggressive adversarial based model to a more collaborative joint problem solving model. I also taught legal ethics in many other countries and explored whether it would be possible to develop standards of conduct and ethics in transnational and international legal settings.[60] The field of professional responsibility and legal ethics has now spawned a world-wide network of ethics professionals, not only in law but in international development and international organizational work as well,[61] suggesting that efforts to study the 'globalization of ethics' is an important topic for modern legal education.

Sadly, the modern growth of extreme nationalism and xenophobia seems to have ushered in a new 'ethical' moment in which adversarialism and self-interest seem to be gaining, not losing, ground. We are now studying how larger political developments are adversely affecting the culture of our profession.[62]

As questions to be considered in legal education research, we could be asking:

1 Does instruction in legal ethics and professional responsibility have any impact at all on actual behavior (as hoped for by the American Bar Association after Watergate; the evidence is not encouraging[63])?
2 Does instruction in legal ethics and the sociology of the profession encourage more thoughtful career choices among students?
3 Can 'legal culture' be changed through teaching and research in the world's universities and professional schools?
4 Will it ever be possible to create canons or standards of good professional and personal behavior at a global level?

E Globalization of lawyers and legal education

As this conference demonstrates, there is growing recognition that legal education is of interest globally. More and more law students all over the world are studying law not only in their own countries, but also taking semesters in other countries (the Erasmus program in Europe, many semester away exchange programs in Asia, the United States, Canada and South America) and increasing numbers of students are studying for LLMs and doctoral law degrees in countries other than their own.[64] Though for many years the 'foreign' law graduate was interested in academic credentials for careers in the professoriate, it is now clear that international study is considered important and useful for the increasing transnationalization and globalization of law practice.[65] Some would argue that legal education itself is 'converging' internationally toward a hybrid of American case and Socratic methods, with some clinical and experiential instruction, but also increasingly new methods of digital and distance learning (see #6 below), lectures and seminars in increasingly specialized areas of study (e.g. intellectual property, technology, health, venture capital and finance, international law, human rights) and the need for multiple degrees (masters in specializations, following on from first degrees).

Canada and some nations in the European Union have explored what one legal educator has called 'transsystemic legal education'[66] – the concurrent study of several different legal systems (e.g. common law and civil code (McGill), common law and indigenous law (University of Victoria)) to create 'multi-jural' law students and lawyers. Nevertheless, there are still many barriers to cross-jurisdictional practice as licensing still occurs on a national or even provincial (or state) basis.[67] So questions of how globalized legal study is being experienced by both law students and more globalized practitioners are ripe for study. Certain locuses of practice have clearly been internationalized – Big Law and the Magic Circle large law firms in the world's capitals, human rights law in both regional (Strasbourg and San Jose, Costa Rica) courts and international practice, private international arbitration, and hybrid forms of investor-state and international trade practices and legal work in the major international organizations.[68]

At the same time, critics suggest that 'convergence', if it exists in international law (and in international legal education), is a product of particular lines of influence, based on power and both the colonial and post-colonial hegemony of first the United Kingdom, and now the United States and the rest of Europe. Anthea Roberts suggests that 'international law' is not really international at all, and legal education patterns are evidence of her argument (surveying the sources of law studied in international law texts and courses in many countries).[69] In my own view, from teaching in 26 different countries, there is some diffusion of other ideas in both law making and legal education, as the field of comparative constitutional law illustrates,[70] new ideas have come from the Global 'South' (South Africa), as well as the Global 'North' (compare Canada's Charter of Freedoms to the US Bill of Rights).

In my own experience as a founding faculty member of the Centre for Transnational Legal Studies, a legal studies program of a consortium of over 20 law schools (in London, founded originally by Georgetown University and eight other law schools),[71] students studying together from many different legal systems learn that law is 'chosen' not 'given', and learn many subjects comparatively and with different teaching methods. This form of legal education is truly 'global' and international, but whether it has any lasting impact on the students who study there (and as compared to more traditional exchange programs) is not yet known.[72] Similarly, research has just begun on the impact of so many of our law schools (Australia, Canada, the United States, Singapore, Hong Kong, Paris, the UK) becoming increasingly diversified from students from other countries studying along with 'natives'. In my view, this is a positive development for diversity of the legal profession and law making, which will take decades to assess; the impact on the diversification of legal education methods is a different question.

So, as research proceeds apace on the impact of globalization on the legal profession, it will be useful to ask:

1 To what extent are national law schools now diversified in student bodies demographically?
2 To what extent does diversification of student bodies enhance, inhibit or not affect teaching modalities?
3 To what extent does the diversification of both students and faculty affect the development of new legal theories, new modes of teaching?
4 Will increased globalization of legal education have an impact on the making and enforcement of international law or the creation of transnational legal substantive orders?[73]

F The end of lawyers? Lawyers and technology

We are in the midst of the next 'big bang' moment in legal education – the use of technology to both solve legal problems and to serve as the medium of legal education. Richard Susskind (UK) has argued that the legal profession (and other professions as well)[74] will eventually be supplanted by the use of technology, forms, templates, interactive online dispute resolution, transaction planning, discovery and document management, legal filings, and even defense in certain minor criminal matters (e.g. traffic violations). Massive Online Open Courses (MOOC) and other forms of distance learning have already transformed some forms of legal education, both increasing access to legal information and formal courses and degree programs, and at the same time, frightening in-class teachers into worrying about their longevity.

Many law schools are now radically adding to or transforming their curricula to include law and technology (intellectual property, law and engineering, law and machine learning, and legal artificial intelligence), so the question may be asked, should we be teaching 'legal coding' and digital system design in law schools?[75] As I began this essay – should we be asking 'is there an APP for that?' instead of 'Is there a cause of action for that?'

In my own legal specialty of dispute resolution, we now have many forms of 'online dispute resolution',[76] including an Online Civil Court in British Columbia, online dispute resolution on e-Bay, an online divorce service in Holland, and a current proposal to put all disputes under £50,000 online in the UK,[77] and online customer service for most online purchases, as well as for disputes with governmental agencies, and most 'big box' providers of products and services.[78] Should we be teaching students how to develop, design and manage such dispute systems? Should we be teaching about or worrying about how those with little computer literacy or ability (the aged, the disabled, the poor) will access such services? Those in the field of law and technology claim that AI will be a boon to access to justice and we must reorient our teaching and training to it; others document how 'algorithmic justice' may be very dangerous (in both under and over inclusiveness in data-driven decision-making).[79]

The recent #MeToo (anti-sexual harassment) movement, making use of Twitter and other social media to aggregate and publicize legal claims has been heralded as a new form of class or aggregate justice, at the same time as others worry about such old legal concepts as due process – what kind of process will allow great variations of claims to be adjudicated in the 'court of public opinion'?[80] What will our new law students think of law as social media allow postings of 'fake news' and judgments without formal proceedings or trials? What kind of legal ethics will this 'brave new world' require?

This most recent 'big bang' moment requires some serious thinking and study. As we embark in this time of great technological change for legal education it is hard to 'skate to where the hockey puck is going, not where it has been' (as the great hockey player Wayne Gretzky has said). What legal subjects and processes will, in fact, be subject to 'techno-lawyering'? Big data and data mining will be great for eliciting patterns of behavior that can document legal and illegal activity (privacy, anti-trust, pricing and anti-competitive behavior, discrimination, insurance claims, speeding and some crimes (video cameras, etc.). Technology will be useful in litigation discovery, in document preparation,[81] and in tax filings, property filings, and some other interactions with the state (motor vehicle licenses). But, what about those legal matters that still require interpersonal interaction and human and legal judgment: immigration, family law, discrimination, individual problems that require a human listener, some cathartic response, some complex legal advice? There are many legal issues (not only complex corporate matters in bespoke legal matters, as Susskind describes them), that require personal and individual attention, not rote or 'cookie cutter' solutions. There are still many kinds of cases, (political, constitutional, challenges to government authority, interpretation of new laws) that will require reasoned precedent and judicial elaboration (at least in the common law world as we know it). How much 'code' can be written for non-legal code systems (such as most common law) remains to be seen. But, I can imagine new forms of law classes that will actually try to draft some 'artificial intelligence' statutes and forms of legal decision-making.

G *What do we not know and what should we study?*

In the hundred plus years that Langdell's case and Socratic methods have affected legal education, we have now witnessed many challenges to this conventional form of legal education (and the lecture/didactic methods in other jurisdictions). What do we actually know about the effectiveness of particular forms of legal education and what should we study? Here are a few of my own thoughts:

> Despite what Langdell argued about law and legal rules being a 'science', we know today that it is not. Law is an interpretative field- using words to define, constrain, enhance and regulate human behavior. Legal institutions try to provide certainty, but different facts require different treatment, even to achieve substantive equity. The law is not totally 'uniform' and practice is not the same for all students and all lawyers – we have too many sub-fields, specialties and law used for different purposes.

One question we might ask is 'is there still a core of subjects to be taught to all law students':

1 What is an enforceable contract? (Different in writing and online? Different in common law and civil law systems?)
2 What is a compensable injury (in tort or other legal theories, in private life, at the workplace, in public life)?
3 What is property (who got there first or some other conceptions?[82]) and how should it be allocated, regulated? What are more modern forms of property – real, personal, intellectual, and virtual?

4 How should legal disputes be resolved? (Formal procedures and courts, mediation and other forms of less brittle winner--take-all results, in person, online, focus on past facts and adjudication, or possible future relationships of parties, who should participate, only parties or others affected by dispute, e.g., environmental disputes?)
5 Who are the parties to particular legal issues or disputes? (In modern times there are almost none that are only plaintiff versus defendant – there are insurers, family members, customers, employees, always others involved in any dispute); why do we keep studying P versus D cases in our appellate casebooks?
6 How should we regulate, punish or reward lawbreakers or compliers?
7 How does the law manage new entities/ideas/products/services that were not conceived of when the legal rules were framed? (the 'no vehicles in the park' problem[83]; think 'Uber', 'Airbnb' and 'Taskrabbit').

Then, we have the complex problem of *measurement* in any evaluation of legal education:

1 *Who* are the evaluators? The students (customers); alums (with added knowledge of practice relevance of their legal educations); faculty (knowledgeable, long-term experience but conflict of interest in maintaining status quo and self-evaluation), non-legal professionals and educational evaluators?
2 *How* do people learn? Some may learn better with binary (AI, debate) methods and concepts, but many legal concepts are complex and not binary (e.g. religious freedom, gender equality, child custody, due process). Legal learning is cumulative, interpretative, involving discretion, judgment, continua and scale and based on multi-factorial 'tests' of facts applied to law. How do we accurately measure how these intangible reasoning and judgment functions are developed over time in student learning and application? Even if some legal concepts are binary; human judgment and application of rules is not.
3 *When* do we measure legal education effectiveness (a baseline of knowledge before school starts, during legal studies, after law school has been completed[84])?
4 *Who* should fund and conduct such research? In the United States the Law School Admissions Council has long funded a competitive program of sponsored research on legal education (funded by the profits made from the test (Law School Admission Test (LSAT)) and application fees administered by a central (private) body for all law schools. The American Association of Law Schools just launched a new section of Empirical Studies of Legal Education (2018) to provide a forum for exchanges of papers and research (without any funds attached). The *Journal of Legal Education* has published articles (not very much empirically reviewed) on legal education for decades without much systematic scientific replication or analysis.
5 *What* should we measure? Is the only use of effective legal education to become an effective practicing lawyer? How about legal education for

researchers, academics, government officials, business people, organizational leaders, entrepreneurs and community organizers? What should a legal education be used for?

From my own 40+ years as a legal educator, I offer my own thoughts about what a good legal education should consist of:

- A core (1–2) years of (conventional) legal thinking/training/analysis in basic legal principles, ethics, jurisprudence, history and theories of law, exposure to both general legal categories (property, contract, governance, public law, constitutional and administrative law, torts and criminal and civil procedure) and some early exposure to areas of particular interest or specialization;
- Some sequenced skills/experiential learning (research – online now, not library?), writing, interviewing clients, dispute resolution, including negotiation and mediation, advocacy, argument, litigation skills, practical problem solving and real world practicums; some technology training, uses of algorithmic models, quantitative analysis, accounting, financial literacy, and so forth;
- Some big picture (moral philosophy, theories of justice, political science, political economy, history) study of the functions, purposes, contexts and critiques of law and legal institutions;
- Some (not too much) specialization and 'deep dives' to encourage student competency and confidence in mastering at least one area of substantive law (but be careful of this, so much changes so quickly);
- Some consideration and analysis of patterns of legal change (think 'blue ocean'[85] (supplemental, additive) versus 'disruptive' changes in society and how law adapts or not).[86]

What we must remember is that law and legal education are human constructs, ever changing. Together they hope to respond to a multiplicity of human needs – providing order in society, justice, enhancement of human flourishing and new ideas, but also regulation, social control and punishment of those who commit bad acts or harm others. Legal education can be used for and by legal professionals, lawyers, judges, paralegals and others, but it is also still an excellent education for generalists, government and civic employees, business people, educators, engineers, parents and any informed citizen. Thus, legal education can be used for many things and, in my view, should not be cabined or confined to any one format. The use that humans make of law is too complex to be placed in an overly reductive education model. Yet, we should know what effects we are having in what we do and the need for rigorous research on legal education has been clearly evidenced in the wide variety of intriguing and thoughtful papers presented at this conference.

As I want to encourage as much research into what we do as I can, I conclude, as I began, with the American sociologist, Thorstein Veblen: 'the outcome of any serious research can only be to make two questions grow where only one grew before'.[87]

Notes

* This chapter is based on one of the keynote addresses presented at the University of New South Wales Conference on Research on Legal Education, December 3–5, 2017. Thanks to my hosts, Alex Steel, Ben Golder, Marina Nehme and Prue Vines and others, and fellow participants for a highly stimulating conference demonstrating great progress in legal education innovation and assessment around the world.

1 Thorstein Veblen, *The Higher Learning in America: A Memorandum on the Conduct of Universities by Businessmen* (New York, B. W. Huebsch 1918); Gilbert Geis, 'Thorstein Veblen on Legal Education' (1957) 10 *Journal of Legal Education* 62–67.

2 Robert Stevens, *Law School: Legal Education in America from the 1850s to the 1980s* (University of North Carolina Press, Chapel Hill 1983).

3 Carrie Menkel-Meadow, 'The Legacy of Clinical Education: Theories of Lawyering' (1980) 29 *Cleveland St Law Review* 555–75.

4 Carrie Menkel-Meadow, 'Why and How to Study Transnational Law' (2011) 1 *University California Irvine Law Review* 97–129.

5 Richard Susskind, *The End of Lawyers? Rethinking the Nature of Legal Services* (Oxford University Press 2008); Richard E. Susskind and Daniel Susskind, *The Future of the Professions; How Technology Will Transform the Work of Human* (Oxford University Press 2015).

6 Many law schools have already begun to do this. One of my law schools, Georgetown in Washington DC, now runs an annual 'Tech-a-thon' each year for students to design computer apps for various access to justice projects, see Iron Tech Lawyer Competition; Georgetown Law & Technology Programs, <www.georgetowntech.org>.

7 Ethan Katsh and Orna Rabinovich-Einy, *Digital Justice: Technology and the Internet of Disputes* (Oxford University Press 2017).

8 Judith Welch Wegner and others (eds), *Educating Lawyers: Preparation for the Profession of Law* (Jossey-Bass/Wiley, Plano, 2007 (known as the Carnegie Report on Legal Education)); William Sullivan, *The Power of Integrated Learning: Higher Education for Success in Life, Work and Society* (Stylus, Sterling, Virginia 2016).

9 See the only major US study of legal education at the time, Herbert Packer and Thomas Erhlich, *New Directions in Legal Education* (McGraw Hill, New York 1972).

10 Carrie Menkel-Meadow, 'Have Law Books, Computer, and Simulations – Will Travel: The Transnationalization of (Some of) the Law Professoriate' in Bryant Garth and Gregory Shaffer (eds), *The Globalization of Legal Education: A Critical Study* (forthcoming).

11 As a small sampling of recent critiques of legal education, see, e.g., Brian Tamanaha, *Failing Law Schools* (University of Chicago Press 2012); Robin West, *Teaching Law: Justice, Politics and the Demands of Professionalism* (University of Cambridge Press 2013); Elizabeth Mertz, *The Language of Law School: Learning to Think like a Lawyer* (Oxford University Press 2007); Bryant Garth, 'Crisis, Crisis Rhetoric and Competition in Legal Education: A Sociological Perspective on the (Latest) Crisis of the Legal Profession and Legal Education' (2013) 24 *Stanford Journal of Legal Policy Review* 503–32; Carrie Menkel-Meadow, 'Too Many Lawyers? or Should Lawyers Be Doing Other Things?' in Eyal Katvan and others (eds), *Too Many Lawyers? The Future of the Legal Profession* (Routledge 2017); Hilary Sommerlad and others (eds), *The Futures of Legal Education and the Legal Profession* (Hart, Oxford 2015); see an earlier set of critiques in Harry Edwards, 'The Growing Disjunction between Legal Education and the Legal Profession' (1992) 91 *Michigan Law Review* 34; Carrie Menkel-Meadow,

'Narrowing the Gap By Narrowing the Field: What's Missing From the MacCrate Report: Of Skills, Legal Science and Being A Human Being' (1994) 69 *Washington Law Review* 593.

12 John Henry Schlegel, *American Legal Realism and Empirical Social Science* (University of North Carolina Press 1995).

13 Scott Turow, *1L: An Inside Account of Life in the First Year at Harvard Law School* (Putnam, New York 1977).

14 John Dewey, *Education and Experience* (Free Press Reprint, New York 1997).

15 Thomas Grey, 'Langdell's Orthodoxy' (1983) 45 *University of Pittsburgh Law Review* 1; Bruce Kimball, 'The Langdell Problem: Historicizing the Century of Historiography' (2004) 22 *Law & History Review* 277 (reviewing the distortions and inaccuracies in Langdell's legacy as described in succeeding generations of scholars and commentators); Bruce Kimball, 'Warn Students That I Entertain Heretical Opinions Which They Are Not to Take as Law: The Inception of the Case Method Teaching in the Early Classrooms of the Early C.C. Langdell' (1999) 17 *Law & History Review* 57.

16 *New State Ice Co. v Liebmann*, 282 US 262 (1932) (dissent).

17 See John Jay Osborn, Jr, *The Paper Chase* (1972) (James Bridges, Dir Movie 1973).

18 See discussion of work of Amos Tversky in Michael Lewis, *The Undoing Project: A Friendship that Changed our Minds* (Norton, London 2016).

19 The attack on legal formalism and the 'science' of doctrine occurred in the 1930s with the legal realist assault on legal doctrine and its non-empirical assertions. Whether legal realism was also a 'political' critique of the outcomes of doctrinal analysis remains a highly debated subject, see, e.g., Lon Fuller, 'American Legal Realism' (1934) 82 *University of Pennsylvania Law Review* 429; Laura Kalman, *Legal Realism at Yale, 1927–1960* (Lawbook Exchange, New Jersey 2010).

20 Duncan Kennedy, *Legal Education and the Reproduction of Hierarchy: A Polemic Against the System* (New York University Press 2007).

21 Duncan Kennedy, 'The Structure of Blackstone's Commentaries' (1979) 28 *University of Buffalo Law Review* 205.

22 Mark Kelman, *Critical Legal Studies* (Harvard University Press 1990).

23 Carrie Menkel-Meadow, 'Feminist Legal Theory, Critical Legal Studies, and Legal Education or the "Fem-Crits" Go to Law School' (1988) 38 *Journal of Legal Education* 61.

24 Kimberle Crenshaw, Neil Gotanda and Gary Peller (eds), *Critical Race Theory: The Key Writings that Formed the Movement* (The New Press, New York 1996).

25 Carrie Menkel-Meadow, 'Women's Ways of "Knowing" Law: Feminist Legal Epistemology, Pedagogy, and Jurisprudence' in Nancy Goldberger and others (eds), *Knowledge, Difference and Power* (Basic Books, New York 1996).

26 Richard Posner, *An Economic Analysis of Law* (Aspen 1977).

27 Ronald Coase, 'The Problem of Social Cost' (1960) 3 *Journal of Law and Economics* 1–44.

28 See, e.g., Carrie Menkel-Meadow, 'Taking Law and . . . Really Seriously: Before, During and After "The Law"' (2007) 60 *Vanderbilt Law Review* 555–95.

29 Frank Munger and Carroll Seron, 'Critical Legal Studies versus Critical Legal Theory: A Comment on Method' (1984) 6 *Law & Policy* 257–97.

30 Jeffrey Rachlinski, Chris Guthrie and Andrew Wistrich, 'Blinking on the Bench: How Judges Decide Cases' (2007) 93 *Cornell Law Review* 1–43; Donald Langevoort, 'Behavioral Theories of Judgment and Decision Making in Legal Scholarship: A Literature Review' (1998) 51 *Vanderbilt Law Review* 1499; see Lewis (n. 18).

31 Cass Sunstein, 'Deliberative Trouble: Why Groups Go to Extremes' (2000) 110 *Yale Law Journal* 71.

32 Carrie Menkel-Meadow, 'Uses and Abuses of Socio-legal Studies' in Naomi Creutzfeld and others (eds), *Routledge Handbook of Sociolegal Theory and Methods* (Routledge, London 2019).
33 Paul Carrington, 'Of Law and the River' (1984) 34 *Journal of Legal Education* 222 (arguing that the 'nihilist' critical legal scholars should leave teaching in American law schools).
34 Michael Meltsner and Philip Schrag, *Reflections on Clinical Legal Education* (Northeastern Press, New Hampshire 1998).
35 See, e.g., Scott Cummings, 'Preemptive Strike: Law in the Campaign for Clean Trucks' (2015) 4 *University of California Irvine Law Review* 939; Scott Cummings, 'The Accountability Problem in Public Interest Practice: Old Paradigms and New Directions' in Lynn Mather and Leslie Levin (eds), *Lawyers In Practice: Ethical Decision Making In Context* (University of Chicago Press 2012).
36 See Gary Bellow, 'Turning Solutions into Problems: The Legal Aid Experience' (1977) 34 *NLADA Briefcase* 4; Gary Bellow and Bea Moulton, *The Lawyering Process: Materials for Clinical Instructions in Advocacy* (Foundation Press, New York 1978).
37 Austin Sarat and Stuart Scheingold, *Cause Lawyering and the State in a global Era* (Oxford University Press 2001).
38 Mark Spiegel, 'Theory and Practice in Legal Education: An Essay on Clinical Education' (1987) 34 *University of California Los Angeles Law Review* 577.
39 Jack Himmelstein and others, 'Reassessing Law Schooling: The Sterling Forest Group' (1978) 53 *New York University Law Review* 561. Inspirations for this more humanistic education were many, including the Tavistock and Esalen approaches to human potential movement 'encounter' groups and process learning.
40 Carrie Menkel-Meadow, 'Aha? Is Creativity Possible in Legal Problem Solving and Teachable in Legal Education?' (2001) 6 *Harvard Negotiation Law Review* 97–144.
41 Thomas Schaffer and James Elkins, *Legal Interviewing and Counselling in a Nutshell* (4th edn, Thomson West, Eagan, Minnesota 2005).
42 See, e.g., Paul Brest and Linda Krieger, *Problem Solving, Decision Making and Professional Judgment: A Guide for Lawyers and Policy Makers* (Oxford University Press 2010).
43 Harold Lasswell and Myres McDougal, 'Legal Education and Public Policy: Professional Training in the Public Interest' (1943) 52 *Yale Law Journal* 203.
44 See West (n 11) and for an earlier critique of the humanistic turn in clinical education see William Simon, 'Homo Psychologicus: Notes on a New Legal Formalism' (1980) 32 *Stanford Law Review* 487–559.
45 See <www.calbar.ca.gov/Portals/0/documents/bog/bot_ExecDir/STATE_BAR_TASK_FORCE_REPORT_(FINAL_AS_APPROVED_6_11_13)_062413.pdf>; <www.law360.com/articles/738717/admission-to-the-new-york-bar-just-got-harder>. The American Bar Association (ABA) standards of accreditation for American Law Schools now requires at least six units of 'experiential learning' Standard 303: CURRICULUM

(a) A law school shall offer a curriculum that requires each student to satisfactorily complete at least the following:

(3) one or more experiential course(s) totaling at least six credit hours. An experiential course must be a simulation course, a law clinic, or a field placement, as defined in Standard 304.

(b) A law school shall provide substantial opportunities to students for:

(1) law clinics or field placement(s); and
(2) student participation in pro bono legal services, including law-related public service activities. <www.americanbar.org/content/dam/aba/publications/misc/legal_education/Standards/2018-2019ABAStandardsforApprovalofLawSchools/2018-2019-aba-standards-chapter3.pdf>.

46 See Stanford 'policy labs' at <https://law.stanford.edu/education/only-at-sls/law-policy-lab/>.
47 See <https://hls.harvard.edu/dept/academics/winter-term/problem-solving-workshop/>.
48 For earlier versions of these applications in professional training, see Donald Schoen, *The Reflective Practitioner: How Professionals Think in Action* (Basic books 1984).
49 See, e.g., Frances Zemans and Victor Rosenblum, *The Making of a Public Profession* (American Bar Foundation 1981); Bryant Garth and Joanne Martin, 'The Construction of Competence' (1993) 43 *Journal of Legal Education* 469.
50 John Dean, *Blind Ambition: The White House Years* (Simon & Shuster 1976).
51 American Bar Association, Accreditation Standards, Standard 303. CURRICULUM:

(a) A law school shall offer a curriculum that requires each student to satisfactorily complete at least the following:

(1) one course of at least two credit hours in professional responsibility that includes substantial instruction in rules of professional conduct, and the values and responsibilities of the legal profession and its members; <www.americanbar.org/content/dam/aba/publications/misc/legal_education/Standards/2018-2019ABAStandardsforApprovalofLawSchools/2018-2019-aba-standards-chapter3.pdf>.

52 See, e.g., David Luban (ed), *The Good Lawyer: Lawyer's Roles and Lawyers' Ethics* (Rowman & Allanheld 1983) David Luban, *Lawyers and Justice: An Ethical Study* (Princeton 1988); Anthony Kronman, *The Lost Lawyer: Failing Ideals of the Legal Profession* (Harvard 1983).
53 Arthur Applbaum, *Ethics for Adversaries* (Princeton UP 2000).
54 Richard Wasserstrom, 'Lawyers as Professionals: Some Moral Issues' (1975) 5 *Natural Law Forum* 1–24; Stephen L. Pepper, 'The Lawyer's Amoral Role: A Defense, A Problem and Some Possibilities' (1986) *American Bar Foundation Research Journal* 613–35.
55 Richard L. Abel (ed), 'Comparative Studies of Lawyer Deviance and Discipline: Special Issue' (2012) 15 *Legal Ethics*; Carrie Menkel-Meadow, 'Private Lives and Professional Responsibilities? The Relationship of Personal Morality to Lawyering and Professional Ethics' (2001) *Pace Law Review* 365–93.
56 See, e.g., Andrew Boon, *The Ethics and Conduct of Lawyers in England and Wales* (Hart, Oxford 2005); Richard Moorhead, *Inhouse Lawyers' Ethics: Institutional Logics, Legal Risk and the Tournament of Influence* (Hart, Oxford 2018); Nigel Duncan, T*eaching Legal Ethics in the UK Workshop, City University London* (2016); Charles Sampford and Hugh Breakey, *Law, Lawyering and Legal Education: Building an Ethical Profession in a Globalizing World* (Routledge, London 2017).
57 Carrie Menkel-Meadow and Murray Schwartz, 'Teacher's Manual for Lawyers and the Legal Profession' (Bobbs Merrill 1985); see also David Papke and

others, *Law and Popular Culture: Text, Notes and Questions* (2nd edn, LexisNexis, North Carolina 2012) ch. 3.

58 Bryant Garth, Ann Southworth and Catherine Fisk, 'Some Realism About Realism in Teaching About the Legal Profession' in Stewart Macaulay, Elizabeth Mertz and Thomas W. Mitchell (eds), *The New Legal Realism: Translating Law-and-Society for Today's Legal Practice* (Oxford 2016) 74–95.

59 Carrie Menkel-Meadow, 'Toward Another View of Legal Negotiation: The Structure of Problem-Solving' (1984) 31 *University of California Los Angeles Law Review* 754–842.

60 Carrie Menkel-Meadow, 'Are Cross-Cultural Ethics Standards Possible or Desirable in International Arbitration?' in Peter Gauch, Franz Werro, Pascal Pichonnaz (eds), *Melangés en l'honneur de Pierre Tercier* (Schulthess, Geneva, Switzerland 2008).

61 See, e.g., Jean-Marc Coicaud and Daniel Warner, *Ethics and International Affairs: Extent and Limits* (United Nations University Press, Japan 2001); Galit Sarfty, *Values in Translation: Human Rights and the Culture of the World Bank* (Stanford University Press 2012).

62 See, e.g., Carrie Menkel-Meadow, 'The Culture of Negotiation: The Imprint of "Trumpism" on the Future' (2019) *Negotiation Journal* (special issue); Carrie Menkel-Meadow, 'Why We Can't "Just Get Along": Dysfunction in the Polity and Conflict Resolution and What to Do About It' (2018) *Journal Dispute Resolution* 5–25. For a study of how male aggression in negotiation has increased since the US election see Jennie Huang and Corinne Low, 'Trumping Norms: Lab Evidence on Aggressive Communications before and After the 2016 Presidential Election' (2017) 107 *American Economic Review* 120–24.

63 Richard L. Abel, *Lawyers in the Docks: Learning from Attorney Disciplinary* Proceedings (Oxford University Press 2008); Richard L. Abel, *Lawyers on Trial: Understanding Ethical Misconduct* (Oxford University Press 2010).

64 Carol Silver, 'States Side Story: I Like to Be in America: Career Paths of International LLM Students' (2012) 80 *Fordham Law Review* 2383; Bryant Garth, 'Notes Toward an Understanding of the US Market in Foreign LLM programs: From the British Empire and the Inns of Court to US LLM Programs' (2015) 22 *Indiana Journal of Law & Globalization* 62; Gail Hupper, 'Educational Ambivalence: The Rise of a Foreign Student Doctorate in Law' (2015) 49 *New England Law Review* 319; Carole Silver, 'The Variable Value of US Legal Education in the Global Legal Services Market' (2010) 24 *Georgetown Journal of Legal Ethics* 21.

65 Laurel Terry, 'The Legal World Is Flat: Globalization and its Effect on Lawyers Practicing in Non-Global Law Firms' (2008) 28 *Northwestern International Journal of Law & Business* 527; Carole Silver, 'The Case of the Foreign Lawyer: Internationalizing the US Legal Profession' (2000) 31 *Law & Policy International Business* 1093.

66 Peter Strauss, 'Transsystemia – Are We Approaching a New Langdellian Moment: Is McGill Leading the Way?' (2006) 56 *Journal of Legal Education* 161; see also University of Victoria transsystemic program in Canadian and Indigenous Law, <www.uciv.ca/law/about/indigenous/jid/index/php>.

67 Laurel S. Terry, 'The Bologna Process and its Impact in Europe: Much More than Degree Changes' (2008) 41 *Vanderbilt Journal of Transnational Law* 107; Laurel S. Terry, 'Reflections on Lawyer Mobility, Accountability, and Regulatory Systems: Has the Time Come to Talk About the Elephant in the Room?' (2013) 16 *Legal Ethics* 284.

68 Yves Dezalay and Bryant Garth (eds), *Lawyers and the Construction of Transnational Justice* (Routledge 2012); Yves Dezalay and Bryant Garth (eds), *Lawyers the Rule of Law in an Era of Globalisation* (Routledge, London 2011).

69 Anthea Roberts, *Is International Law International?* (Oxford University Press 2017). See also Fernana Nicola, 'The Global Diffusions of US Legal Thought; Changing Influence, National Security and Legal Education in Crisis' (2017).
70 Tom Ginsburg and Rosalind Dixon, *Comparative Constitutional Law* (Elgar Publication, Massachusetts 2013).
71 See <www.georgetown.law.edu/ctls>.
72 See Menkel-Meadow, 'Why and How to Study Transnational Law' (n 4); Menkel-Meadow, 'Have Law Books, Computer, and Simulations – Will Travel: The Transnationalisation of (some of) the Law Professoriate' (n. 10).
73 Terence Halliday and Gregory Shaffer (eds), *Transnational Legal Orders* (Cambridge University Press 2015).
74 Susskind and Susskind (n. 5).
75 See Mark Fenwick, Wolf Kaal and Erik Vermeulen, 'Legal Education in a Digital Age: Why Coding for Lawyers Matters' (Lex Research Topics in Corporate Law and Economics Working Paper No. 4 2018).
76 Katsh and Rabinovich-Einy (n. 7).
77 Rechtsweijzer, allowing interactive custody, spousal and child support to be negotiated online with in person counseling and mediation. As of this writing, the program has been suspended for lack of interest, see Carrie Menkel-Meadow, 'Is ODR ADR?: Reflections of an ADR Founder' (2016) 3 *International Journal of Online Dispute Resolution* 4.
78 Carrie Menkel-Meadow, 'Scripts and Playbooks: How to Negotiate With Big Bad Companies' in Andrea Kupfer Schneider and Christopher Honeyman (eds), *Negotiator's Desk Reference* (2nd edn, DRI Publicaton 2017).
79 Virginia Eubanks, *Automating Inequality: How High Tech Tools Profile, Police and Punish the Poor* (St Martins Press, New York 2018).
80 Lesley Wexler, Jennifer Robbennolt, and Colleen Murphy, '#MeToo, Time's Up, and Theories of Justice' (University of Illinois College of Law Legal Studies Research Paper No. 18–14, 6 March 2018); Vicki Schultz, 'Open Statement on Sexual Harassment From Employment Discrimination Law Scholars' (2018) 71 *Stanford Law Review*.
81 I already feel that my teaching of how to plead a proper complaint in civil procedure is vastly out of date as my state, California, now uses form complaints for many civil matters – litigants just fill out a few 'tick boxes' for basic claims. Will the 'tick box form' of legal claiming lead to a simplicity of causes of action to be realized? What about the important aspect of creative lawyering that has allowed new claims to be plead and argued for in common law systems?
82 See, e.g., *Mabo v Queensland* [1988] HCA 69 (8 December 1988); (1989) 166 CLR 186.
83 Frederick Schauer, 'A Critical Guide to Vehicles in the Park' 83 *New York University Law Review* 1109–131.
84 See the decades long study in the United States of following a cohort of law students for over a decade after completion of law school. Bryant Garth, Ronit Dinovitzer and Joyce Sterling, *After the JD Study* (American Bar Foundation 2004).
85 W. Chan Kim and Renee Mauborgne, *Blue Ocean Shift: Beyond Competing – Proven Steps to Inspire Confidence and Seize New Growth* (Hachette, New York 2017).
86 Carrie Menkel-Meadow, *Uberlaw: The Challenges of Innovation and Regulation* (Syllabus University of California Irvine Law School, Spring 2016).
87 Thorstein Veblen, The *Evolution of the Scientific Point of View* (University of California Chronicle 1908).

12 Educating for the past, the present or the future?

Tania Leiman

I Introduction

Richard Susskind posits an 'Evolution of Legal Service'[1] – from bespoke legal services to standardisation allowing for scalability, and finally to 'externalization', where commodities are offered online for fee, for free or via commons,[2] as perspective moves from 'task-based' to 'outcomes-based'.[3] If Susskind's 'Evolution of Legal Service'[4] is already taking place in the legal industry, it has not yet commenced in any real way in legal education. What if it did? What could it look like, and how would it disrupt accepted ways of doing things?[5] What might be sacrificed along the way?

This chapter will use Susskind's framework in an attempt to catalyse such thinking in the context of Australian legal education – by pushing existing boundaries, challenging existing perceptions, exploring what might be possible, and inevitably raising more questions than can yet be answered. It will begin with a lightning review of change and disruption taking place generally and in the legal sector, disruption already encountered by legal graduates now who are likely to face even further change in future. Using a recent US decision as a case study, it will explore how ethical obligations are changing as a result, imperatives which also challenge whether legal curriculum is fit for purpose in the 21st century. What is now required to develop professionals with legal knowledge and skills, who agree to be bound by accepted ethical frameworks, and who act effectively as legally literate leaders, advocates and defenders of rights responsive to society's needs? What might this mean for legal academics and educational institutions? The chapter will conclude with a challenge to re-vision legal education, and to engage with the new opportunities this presents.

II The challenge of disruption

A 'fourth industrial revolution'[6] is sweeping our world, with 'rapid advances in computing power, connectivity, mobility and data storage capacity'.[7] Data is the 'new oil'[8] and a 'new global currency'.[9] Geographic and jurisdictional boundaries begin to lose traditional meaning.[10] Emerging technologies[11] are 'fundamentally changing the way the economy and society operates',[12] disrupting how we interact and transact; the future of work itself is being re-visioned. All of this is taking place within a metanarrative of increasing geopolitical instability, rising nationalism and populism, threats to human rights, changing global demographics, resource pressures, sustainability challenges, and climate change. This 'digital age [brings] with it challenges to the rule of law that society has struggled to make sense of at every level', and 'present[s] regulatory challenges that "far outstrip our institutions' ability to keep up with them, let alone be ahead of the game"'.[13]

'Drivers of the new normal for law'[14] include competitive pressures,[15] changing business models,[16] rising customer power,[17] changing face of the profession,[18] and new ways of working.[19] Different segments of the profession are impacted differently; small or sole practices, the majority of Australian law firms,[20] face particular challenges. Extensive proprietary legal materials are available online for fee. Websites of parliaments, courts, tribunals, government agencies, public authorities, legal aid commissions, and community legal centres provide detailed legal information for no cost. Cases and journals can be searched online for free by the public.[21] Considerable legal information, including downloadable forms and precedents, is freely available on law firm websites. Online chat platforms[22] give instant access to personalised information. Some platforms replace human lawyers with chatbots[23] or other automated services. Legal procurement websites and online review functions interface with prospective clients.[24] Disputes are resolved by state operated and private online dispute resolution services.[25]

Legal technologies, too, are expanding at unprecedented levels,[26] with huge financial investment and a '484 per cent increase in the number of patents filed'[27] – 'many larger law firms now have dedicated legal technology development teams that combine legal, project management, data analytics and IT skills'.[28] Investment in AI as a legal services tool is growing.[29] Predictive analytics using big datasets are already being widely used in legal contexts such as undertaking e-discovery, legal research, and assessment of likely outcomes in litigation.[30] Algorithmic tools[31] assist bail or sentencing[32] determinations, even though one recent study has asserted it embeds racial prejudice and bias,[33] and another suggested they are 'no more accurate or fair than predictions made by people with little or no criminal justice expertise'.[34] Document analysis software can automate drafting and reviewing.[35] Taxation advice can be generated using natural language processing tools and AI.[36] Transactions may be effected using distributed ledger technology and smart contracts.[37] Artificial intelligence is used in a 'consensus accelerator' to resolve family law matters.[38] Courts[39] and other dispute resolution mechanisms[40] are changing too. Whether such AI tools may ultimately result in deskilling lawyers in negotiation and assessing strength of their client's positions, or perpetuate biases that may exist in data-driven analytics will remain to be seen.[41]

Henderson conceptualises the legal sector as three concentric circles: the innermost and smallest is the 'legal profession', and then the 'legal services industry', with the largest being 'legal industry' encompassing the other two.[42] Cohen notes:

> [L]egal practice – core differentiated knowledge, skills, and professional judgment possessed by a relatively small percentage of lawyers – is shrinking. Legal delivery – the products, tasks, competencies, technology, process, and functions that leverage and support it – is expanding.[43]

He describes a 'bifurcation' between:

> The "practice of law" and "the business of law" . . . legal delivery is no longer solely about lawyers – technologists, process and project management experts, and other service professionals and paraprofessionals are part of the legal supply chain.[44]

The latter is evidenced by the growth of in-house legal departments,[45] Big 4 consulting firms with full service legal teams[46] and claims that 'we've only begun to scratch the surface of democratising access on a business to client (B2C) level to legal services'.[47] Susskind's 'Evolution of Legal Service'[48] framework referred to above is another way of conceptualising these changes.

In a similar vein, Deloitte have predicted: 'Fewer traditional lawyers in law firms', 'a new mix of skills among elite lawyers', 'greater flexibility and mobility within the industry', 'a reformed workforce structure and alternative progression routes', and 'greater willingness to source people from other industries with non-traditional skills and training'.[49] Others are less sanguine.[50] Murray and Fortinberry claim lawyers '[cater] to the strongest of all human needs: . . . relational safety'.[51]

> There are too many specialists, . . . black-letter lawyers and . . . legal technicians. . . . What will be needed will be men and women who understand the art of listening, questioning and giving advice in a way that gives clients a sense of safety. These people will understand business and, more importantly, the psychology of running and operating a business. They will be more like advisory partners in the Big 4.[52]

As flagged earlier in this chapter, many existing legal services jobs already look and sound different.[53] New role titles include legal analyst,[54] legal project manager,[55] legal solutions architect.[56] This blurs boundaries between providing advice (externally regulated, requiring formal qualifications) and providing information (largely externally unregulated, formal qualifications not required). '[S]ophisticated infomediary business models'[57] make this line even murkier,[58] challenging the role of regulatory authorities in protecting the public.

This 'evolution of legal service' confronts us with the following questions: Is 'the very essence of the legal profession [. . .] under threat'?[59] Where does the value of lawyers lie[60] when 'both product and producer are undergoing fundamental change'?[61] What distinguishes lawyers in a legal industry replete with new business models, and transformed by technology? Initially attractive, such client-centric tools and approaches may conflict with paramount duties to the court and administration of justice owed by Australian legal practitioners.[62] As Bailes notes: 'we also cannot assume that legal technology will demonstrate fidelity to law, consider important public and legal policy questions or, as a matter of first priority, seek to preserve the authority of the courts'.[63]

What 'working practices and processes [are so] intrinsically valuable and important to retain for their own sake'?[64] These questions are particularly pressing given the breakdown of the sharp divide between regulated legal fee earners and unregulated non-fee earners in a diverse global marketplace. Legal 'practice' – those differentiated skills and expertise possessed by some lawyers – is not the same as 'the business of delivering legal services'.[65] '[T]echnology . . . is changing the economics, delivery, careers, and 'lawyers and non-lawyers' culture of the legal industry'.[66] Nevertheless fundamental questions remain. What broader role do those empowered with legal knowledge and skills have in sustaining the rule of law in our liberal democracy, supporting good government and an effective economy, while protecting those most at risk in our society?

All these imperatives now impact legal education too. What knowledge and skills are required to navigate these changes? How should these be taught, and by whom? What is the purposes of legal education, and is it being achieved? Graduates incurring considerable student debt question the value of their costly, lengthy university legal education.[67] Industry criticises universities for allowing an oversupply of law graduates 'for short term financial gain',[68] yet acknowledges that '[t]he education of the new generation is of critical importance to the entire profession'.[69] These disruptive challenges facing the legal profession underline the need for urgent re-examination of legal education in the 2020s and beyond to ensure it is fit for purpose, ethical, responsive to society's needs and able to continue to protect those most at risk. The following case study is only one example illustrating this urgency.

III Rethinking the lawyers role: a case study

The 7 August 2018 decision in *City of Rockford et al. v Mallinckrodt ARD Inc et al.*[70] ('*Mallinckrodt*') illustrates the changed reality of 21st-century legal services work. After working cooperatively on discovery 'likely involve millions of documents, the vast majority of which are stored electronically',[71] parties sought an 'Order Establishing Production Protocol For Electronically Stored Information'. Commencing with Donald Rumsfeld's classic 'known unknowns' quote,[72] the decision discussed in detail protocols for using keyword searching and technology-assisted-review (TAR) of electronically stored information (ESI). Going on to analyse whether or not 'sampling the Null set is reasonable' under the relevant rule of civil procedure requiring 'all discovery requests to be signed by at least one attorney', the decision links this to ethical obligations on lawyers for technological competence. Footnote 2 is worth reproducing:

> The Court pauses here for a moment to calm down litigators less familiar with ESI. (You know who you are.) In life, there are many things to be

> scared of, including, but not limited to, spiders, sharks, and clowns – definitely clowns, even Fizbo. ESI is not something to be scared of. The same is true for all the terms and jargon related to ESI. Discovery of ESI is still discovery, governed by the same Federal Rules of Civil Procedure as all other civil discovery. *Brown v Tellermate Holdings, Ltd.* [citation omitted] ('[T]he underlying principles governing discovery do not change just because ESI is involved'). So don't freak out. Having said that, the ethical rules now require attorneys to be competent with technologies such as ESI. ABA Model Rule 1.1, Comment 8 ('To maintain the requisite knowledge and skill, a lawyer should keep abreast of changes in the law and its practice, including the benefits and risks associated with relevant technology').

Despite claims that 'Discovery of ESI is still discovery', the judgement suggests expectations of lawyers and what they should be doing are very different now: arguably identifying new skills required, rather than simply commenting on the efficacy of new tools for use with existing skill sets. After an aside that 'the ethical rules now require attorneys to be competent with technologies such as ESI', Magistrate Johnston noted '[v]alidation and quality assurance are fundamental principles to ESI production'.[73]

Mallinckrodt thus raises the following questions for both the US and beyond: does acting ethically in this new digital environment require lawyers to have skills in ESI production, validation, quality assurance, search analysis and search design?

IV Changing obligations amid technological disruption

A *Ethical context*

If those designing search terms or tools and carrying out the electronic discovery process in *Mallinckrodt* were highly skilled data analysists or legal researchers, without legal qualifications nor admitted as legal practitioners, then their work intimately connected with litigation (determining how to undertake discovery and traditionally limited to lawyers), would have been undertaken outside traditional legal regulatory and ethical frameworks. While commentary to American Bar Association Model Rule 1.1 notes that to maintain competency, US lawyers 'should keep abreast of changes in the law and its practice, including the benefits and risks associated with relevant technology',[74] only Florida (in 2016) and North Carolina (in 2018) have mandated technology Continuing Legal Education (CLE) training for lawyers.[75] (Interestingly, the North Carolina rule gives various examples of generic technology training which do not satisfy CLE requirements[76]). This contrasts with the United Kingdom, where the Solicitor's Regulation Authority can take 'action against anyone in the firm including non-lawyer owners, managers and employees', requiring firms 'to ensure that all employees (even if non-qualified and non-fee earners) receive appropriate training' in regulatory requirements,[77] even though the mandatory UK Principles do not include reference to any explicit obligation regarding technological competence.[78] Elsewhere in North America, recent Canadian proposals recommend amendments to Ethics Rules to include:

> [5A] To maintain the required level of competence, a lawyer should develop and maintain a facility with technology relevant to the nature and area of the lawyer's practice and responsibilities. A lawyer should understand the benefits and risks associated with relevant technology, recognizing the lawyer's duty to protect confidential information.[79]

Although the *Australian Solicitors Conduct Rules*[80] are silent as to digital competency, Australian cases have highlighted that a solicitor's level of understanding and training in the use of their firm's 'computerised costing system',[81] and 'lack of expertise in tracking material on the internet'[82] may result in a finding of professional misconduct.[83] Further, obligations regarding client confidentiality may now include responsibilities regarding cybersecurity.[84] This is so even though few lawyers (and even fewer legal academics) have training in producing electronic documents to facilitate effective searches using TAR and other new tools, let alone in making decisions about which tools are most appropriate and why. Skills in collaborating effectively across disciplines will be critical to meet ethical obligations of competent legal practice, yet traditional legal curriculum rarely includes such multidisciplinary collaborative skills.

B Curriculum context

In the context of accredited Australian legal education, neither the prescribed areas of knowledge (the 'Priestleys')[85] nor the Competency Standards for Entry-Level Lawyers (the 'Competency Standards')[86] require any technological competency, let alone capacity to determine whether keyword searching or TAR is more appropriate when conducting discovery. Effective multidisciplinary collaboration is not included in the Priestleys or the Competency Standards, even though the latter indirectly may address these concerns by requiring entry level lawyers to be able to identify 'evidence needed to prove the client's case or disprove the opponent's case, according to the rules of evidence' and to identify 'various means of gathering evidence, and used at least one of them to gather evidence'.[87]

As flagged earlier in this chapter, the examples above illustrate the necessity of re-examining legal education to ensure it is fit for purpose in the digital age. Such a task must start with considering the purposes of legal education.

V The challenge for legal education – for what purpose?

What is legal education for? Is the intellectual challenge itself sufficient? Or must it develop the specific knowledge, skills and competencies necessary for admission to legal practice[88] – 'a virtual monopoly over preparation for entry into the legal profession'[89] – teaching students to 'think like lawyers'?[90] Or is it to develop transferable skills that can be used in other professional service delivery contexts? If the focus is the latter, and on teaching students to 'think critically about society and guide it productively',[91] then can this skill be effectively taught only by legal education? Perhaps the aim is to build broad legal literacy in citizens, a basic human right and an essential component of maintaining the rule of law in democratic societies in the 21st century. Grady suggests:

> Law schools should be a place to try out ideas, to innovate, to challenge, to take some risks. They should be fertile grounds for developing new ways to govern in a world where post-WWII institutions are failing. They should be ensuring that our courts are constantly behind, that our laws are years out of date when enacted, and that laws and lawyers are accessible.[92]

The question could be asked in another way: 'who legal education is helping, how and what does it mean for them?'[93] Does it help graduates get jobs, and if so, what sort of jobs? What benefits accrue to our community by investing in the legally literate leaders of tomorrow – support for civil society, its institutions and the rule of law? Does legal education increase access to justice, advocacy for the vulnerable or the voiceless?

Participation in legal education brings with it an obligation to 'provide the bedrock of a liberal, democratic society' and 'to contribute in some way to justice'.[94] Law schools have been described as 'institutions of moral purpose'[95] that face 'the dilemma of whether their primary task is training lawyers for professional practice or educating them in the discipline of law'.[96] For Levine and Pearce, 'lawyers [are] those who necessarily serve as a political leadership – or governing – class in a liberal democracy', whether they are expressly termed 'lawyers' or not.[97] Adherence by lawyers to 'principles of free access to justice and the rule of law' has been described as 'philosophical and moral positions . . . essential to the proper functioning of a legal system'.[98] Assuming then that 'human rights, the rule of law and democracy are interlinked and mutually reinforcing',[99] the knowledge of the law and the skill in using it should not be taken for granted.

The question could be reframed yet again: Do current offerings entrench a legacy of exclusivity, status, prestige and competitiveness? Is there opportunity to create an alternative legacy of inclusivity, opportunity, access to justice, innovation, entrepreneurship? If so, for whom? In today's highly competitive higher education arena, a focus on 'short-term profitability rather than long-term strategic health' (a criticism Susskind also levels at leaders in law firms)[100] might pose longer terms risks in a world where 'you don't need to finish school or study or get the paper if you are not looking for a job but instead looking to create your own opportunity'.[101] Legal tech now creates new opportunities, including for those without a law degree.

Even accepting legal education should 'focus on what lawyers need to be able to do, rather than on what lawyers need to know',[102] there is 'very little data about job prospects for law graduates'.[103] When knowledge is available in seconds via searchable databases, and answers to questions can be sourced using forms of AI, what do lawyers now need to be able to do?

A Legal education: the Australian context

More than just what happens at university, legal education at its broadest can be characterised as extending across a lifecycle: civics education in primary and secondary schools; legal studies in senior secondary school; community education; vocational paralegal, advocacy or conveyancing training; tertiary studies of law not accredited by legal admission authorities; accredited law degrees constituting academic requirements for qualification of regulated legal practice; accredited postgraduate practical legal training (PLT); postgraduate research and coursework degrees; and continuing professional development (CPD) to maintain eligibility for a practising certificate.

In the last 50 years, admission to legal practice in Australia has inevitably required successful completion of a law degree. Australian university law schools are primarily concerned with accredited law degrees, and non-accredited higher coursework and research degrees. Some have PLT components integrated within law degrees, others offer PLT separately and most offer various public CPD events for fee or free. Some also offer degrees in paralegal studies,[104] jurisprudence, socio-legal studies or teach law to students enrolled into other degrees such as accounting or commerce.

Since the 1990s, when fees were imposed for public university education, law degrees have been accredited by admitting authorities, with curricula required to include the Priestleys. Student difficulties in obtaining articles, and employer concerns that graduates needed more than academic knowledge to enter practice, led to development of postgraduate PLT courses, with national Competency Standards endorsed in 2002.[105]

From only six law schools in 1960,[106] now 'all Australian universities offer law subjects'.[107] Non-university entities[108] provide Bachelor (LLB), Juris Doctor (JD) and coursework Masters (LLM) degrees, and PLT awards. A once exclusive club is now more accessible.[109] 'Massification'[110] of tertiary education from 2008 has resulted in a much larger and a more diverse student body. LLB, JD and applied LLM studies can now be undertaken face-to-face via internal enrolment requiring attendance on campus, via blended models which require only limited physical attendance or entirely externally online. Even for internal students, most lectures are now available via live streaming or video recording, with learning resources available online via learning management systems, electronic library databases or e-books. Requirements for mandatory CPD for legal practitioners are also relatively recent, with many providers' offerings also entirely online and asynchronous.

Whether or not legal education has been successful in meeting its objectives in the past, this history does not guarantee any success will continue in a change-filled future.

B Calls for new knowledge, skills and values

In retrospect, the 'unprecedented growth and change . . . [in parallel to] the dynamic change in the legal profession' undergone by legal education during the 1990s,[111] now seems largely structural – more law schools; some universities offering PLT; some distance or online law degrees. Despite urging that 'universities 'should not teach the world as it was but as it will be',[112] little substantive change has been made to the Priestley areas of knowledge since the 1990s, with competencies largely left to PLT courses. Knowledge alone, though, is not enough.

In 2010 and 2012 respectively, Threshold Learning Outcomes (TLOs) were developed for both the Australian undergraduate law degree[113] and the Juris Doctor.[114] Only 'TLO 1: Knowledge' refers to substantive legal knowledge. TLOs 2–6 respectively refer to 'Ethics and professional responsibility'; 'Thinking skills'; 'Research Skills'; 'Communication and collaboration'; and 'Self-management'. This balance between deep discipline skill and broader professional skills is mirrored in the concept of the 'T-shaped professional' – with the vertical denoting deep disciplinary knowledge, and the horizontal denoting broader cross disciplinary transferrable skills.[115]

Training in an ambitious list of new knowledge, skills and values is now recommended[116] for inclusion within the curriculum in addition to substantive legal knowledge. This highlights a tension between expectations of deep discipline knowledge and differing demands from prospective employers and clients.[117] New skills include capacity to collaborate and apply knowledge across disciplines; 'communication/negotiation skill; empathy; creativity/innovation';[118] compassion;[119] 'social awareness' and 'social facility';[120] 'basic knowledge and skills in the areas of technology, business, data analytics and security'; 'design and e-discovery'; 'business tools and technology', and 'project management and analytics';[121] 'business skills/basic accounting and finance, project management, international and cross-border law; interdisciplinary experience; resilience; flexibility and ability to adapt to change';[122] and design thinking.[123]

The Law Society of NSW's 2017 FLIP report reflects this tension. While 'in favour of the traditional black letter law areas of knowledge and lawyer skill sets being maintained' yet it calls for a multitude of new skills and knowledge to be included in an already 'crowded curriculum'.[124]

Although PLT Competency Standards require competency in 'Ethics and Professional Responsibility', and refer to 'making applicants aware of various issues in relation to 'Resilience and well-being',[125] they do not set threshold standards for emotional intelligence (EQ) or character quotient (CQ),[126] also recently identified as necessary for new lawyers.[127] Calls to educate students not just for discipline knowledge, but broad 'top of the T' skills, competencies, 'professional identity'[128] and character formation too, may further demonstrate 'the dominance of vocationalism within contemporary legal education',[129] now with eyes firmly forward.

VI 'Tomorrow's legal education': an introduction to our future?

If Susskind's 'Evolution of Legal Service'[130] is already taking place in the legal industry, it has not yet commenced in any real way in legal education. What if it did? What could it look like, and how would it disrupt accepted ways of doing things?[131] What might be sacrificed along the way? What follows is an attempt to catalyse such thinking in an Australian context – by pushing existing boundaries, challenging existing perceptions, exploring what might be possible, inevitably raising more questions than can yet be answered.

A Bespoke, standardised or at scale

If legal education aims to equip graduates for externally regulated legal practice in an increasingly globalised market place, then bespoke, artisanal legal education may not necessarily be the best method of meeting that purpose. The quality of students' educational experiences vary significantly across and within institutions, throughout degree programs and within individual subjects themselves. On the other hand, as evidenced regularly by results of surveys evaluating teaching, students are impacted differently by different educators, course designs, learning activities and environments, with preferences varying greatly. The first steps towards standardising legal education have already taken place. The historical apprenticeship model with individual clerks serving articles has already moved to university-delivered legal education with its compulsory Priestley components. Large classes in law schools already allow for teaching at scale (although admittedly still relatively small). Private non-university providers are already using authentic assessment in simulated work environments to train law graduates in large groups during PLT. If opportunities exist for further standardisation and at even greater scale, should they be explored and by whom?

B Boundaries, mobility, uniformity

Although the Priestley areas and Competency standards are common nationally, different federal, state and territory legislative frameworks give rise to varying developments in the common law. Processes for accrediting law degrees and seeking admission differ too. Only NSW and Victoria have adopted the Legal Profession Uniform Law.[132] Despite this, students can study in one Australian jurisdiction whilst residing in another. Graduates are highly mobile across jurisdictions, and those admitted in one state often seek admission in others (and in jurisdictions outside Australia too). Does this graduate mobility reduce the need for state-specific curricula, and should there be a uniform national qualifying process.[133] What would be lost and what could be gained if a standardised approach was adopted in Australia? Would any gains outweigh those losses? This chapter does not advocate a particular course of action, but instead urges frank discussion of these issues in light of both the decreasing relevance of geographic and jurisdictional boundaries[134] and the disruptive impact of legal technology.

C *For fee, for free, open source*

Institutions set minimum thresholds for entry and requirements for the course of study that must be completed (at that institution) before academic awards will be conferred by that institution. This enables them to charge for services such as quality assurance of learning materials and verification of learning outcomes that together comprise the basis for awarding a degree. What does this mean for graduates who do not go on to traditional legal practice or even into professional services delivery? If legal education is about developing transferrable skills[135] that can be used in other contexts, then external accreditation of curricula by admitting authorities and completion of all topics comprising a degree program may not be necessary. Another barrier is the fact that limiting access to online learning resources via enrolment 'paywalls' restricts entry to legal education to those who can pay for it and wish to commit to undertaking the full program to obtain the final qualification. By contrast, many high quality public legal resources are already available online to the community for no cost via court, parliamentary, legal commission, and community legal centre websites. Additionally, massive open online courses (MOOCs) and micro-credentialing,[136] available online for free but where assessment and accreditation is still reserved for fee paying students, are examples already impacting higher education.[137] Could some or all of components of university law degrees be made available for low or no cost too.[138] If so, should they be? Why? Could such 'externalisation' increase legal literacy and skill across our communities, allowing them to make better use of legal resources that can be accessed, and increasing access to justice more broadly? In an era saturated with information and data and 'fake news', and where the justice system is inaccessible to many, equipping citizens with these skills is critical.

D *Competition, collaboration, commons*

Externalising legal education presents both opportunities and risks for educators and education providers. Academics sharing teaching material via a commons could allow for easily accessible cross fertilisation of ideas and approaches, potentially reaching a bigger audience. This might even raise the quality of legal education resources overall and tackle technological issues that may face the profession in a deeper and more meaningful way! Students might choose to mix and match offerings from multiple institutions to make up their ultimate legal qualification, making that choice based on perceptions about quality, difficulty, relevance, reputation of the individual academics involved, or links to future desired career options. If the quality of materials covering the uniform Priestleys or Competency standards could be assured (say, by reason of both internal institutional review and external accredited by admitting authorities) then why should it be necessary for students to be designated a graduate with a degree from a single institution? No incentive exists currently to adopt this approach, which strikes at the heart of competitive advantage among institutions, academic reputation and intellectual property ownership. Very cogent arguments would also no doubt be passionately advanced by curriculum designers as to the importance of scaffolding and integrating knowledge and skills within and across year levels. Yet those arguments may grow less and less convincing in light of the disruptive changes taking place in the legal services sector referred to earlier, and which change the very nature of what it is that lawyers will need to be able to do.

E *Inputs, outputs*

Time billing in the legal services sector has been under discussion for some time. Increasingly providers seek to distinguish themselves by adopting fixed-fee value-based pricing models,[139] moving away from six-minute billable units which can only be totalled when all work is complete.[140] In contrast, admission rules remain rigid in their demands and dictate 'the equivalent of at least three years full-time study of law'.[141] Whether or not PLT may be commenced during that three-year period depends on distinctions between non-integrated and integrated courses.[142] Do these requirements disproportionately value inputs of time in legal education rather than outputs? Is all of what is covered in that three years always necessary?

Other developments also prompt review of existing time requirements imposed on legal education. Conveyancers who are not legal practitioners have for many years been preparing legal documents in South Australia,[143] qualifying via an Advanced Diploma (18 months full time). Limited licence legal technicians, 'trained and licensed to advise and assist people going through divorce, child custody and other family-law matters' are now operating in the US state of Washington,[144] qualifying in shorter time than a US law degree.[145] McKenzie Friends,[146] used in the UK and Australia to assist self-represented litigants, do not require legal qualifications. Legal project managers[147] may not require all the education traditionally regarded as essential for lawyers,[148] particularly if their focus is project management, a significant discipline in its own right.[149] Education providers other than universities are already filling this space.[150] Data analysts and others similarly skilled legal workers, central to the process of the electronic discovery in *Mallinckrodt* are unlikely to have legal qualifications.

F *Just-in-case or just-in-time*

Review from another perspective brings into questions expectations regarding progression. Existing law degrees are designed as linear just-in-case three-year degrees. Regulatory authorities are increasing the amount of CPD required annually, and a proliferation of post graduate awards are offered to graduates looking to distinguish themselves from their peers. Susskind predicts 'a move from just-in-case classroom training (teaching subjects, just in case the insight provided might be needed in practice at some later stage) to just-in-time learning (interactive, multimedia tools which can supply focused and tailored training on the spot)'.[151] Both gains and losses would result from such a move, and the cries of impassioned curriculum designers can be heard ringing out again here. Nonlinear just-in-time legal education may be necessary to ensure existing lawyers regularly upskill to meet changing requirements of 21st-century practice.

G *Changing the academic's role*

Is this too an opportunity to re-envision the role of legal academics in other ways? Many legal academics have no formal training or qualifications in higher education, pedagogy or andragogy, or in online, flexible or virtual learning design or delivery. Whilst university academics are hired on the basis of their capacity as legal researchers, and universities promote the research-teaching nexus, casualization of the academic workforce to undertake front line teaching tasks has increased, as have (much contested) teaching specialist roles. Unbundling marking from other teaching tasks has been common for many years. While very legitimate concerns exist about these developments,[152] they should not obscure opportunity to consider whether legal educators can learn from the move to 'decompose', 'disaggregate' or 'unbundle'[153] the provision of legal services. What can educators do that others cannot? What tasks do legal academics do despite being overqualified for those tasks? What can others do so that legal educators don't have to?[154]

These are not necessarily comfortable questions. They confront our identities as lawyers, legal academics and legal professionals, and challenge whether they should be perpetuated. This necessarily involves drawing distinctions – who should be included within definitions of lawyer, legal professional, legal academic and law student, and who should be excluded; who should be given entry to legal education and who should be barred; and for what purpose or purposes can and should legal education be accessed. The emerging role descriptions listed above raise additional questions not only about the type of education and qualifications that will be required, but about who will have the skills and expertise to undertake that teaching. Perhaps not existing legal academics?

VII Conclusion: an imperative for change

Legal education must equip students and new graduates to face 'the reality of a more uncertain future'.[155] Seeking to justify what and how we teach because that is the way it has always been done, because it provided past positive experiences or because it has been the foundation of a successful career is no longer sufficient.[156] New demands pose new challenges, causing us to confront 'the system from which we derive our identity, sense of self, rewards and status'.[157] Self-interest should not '[blind] us to the defects in what we do'.[158] If today's legal marketplace is 'foreign to most law school faculty who are detached from the rapidly changing marketplace'[159] law schools need to act now to ensure academics are properly equipped to teach these skills.

Greenberg, Hirt and Smit issue this warning:

> Growth shifts. Accelerating disruption. A new societal deal. These are powerful forces that demand thoughtful responses and contain the seeds of extraordinary opportunity. Leaders [lawyers, law schools and legal educators] reaching for these opportunities will need to question their own assumptions and imagine new possibilities. Those who do will compete more effectively; they also will be better able to contribute to broader solutions, and ultimately to a new and more inclusive narrative of progress.[160]

Susskind describes a leading power tool manufacturer showing its executives a picture of a gleaming power drill and asking them if this is what the company sells. Most answer yes, before the company explains that what they are really selling is the neatly drilled hole in the wall, achieved by using the drill.[161] Even accepting criticisms of this analogy,[162] there is value in 'ask[ing] ourselves about the hole in the wall in the legal [education] world', rather than focusing perennially on how to make the drill better, more attractive, more effective, more efficient. What value do students and others (the community, civil society) really seek when they engage in and support legal education? It may be more than just the capacity to drill holes in the wall. Whatever is sought, it is worth scrutinising existing methods of delivering legal education to determine whether they are the best way of delivering this.

We must be prepared to 'pursue a ground-breaking agenda to meaningfully transform' the purposes for and ways in which legal education is provided, focused 'not on criticising the old, but on building the new', recognising 'that New Law is no longer the fringe of legal services, it is the future'.[163] The disruptive change we face means we must 'question [our] own assumptions and imagine new possibilities'.[164] Distinctions we have drawn in the past may no longer fit the future. We must envision legal education, not as it was in the past or even as it exists in the present, but instead as it can and must be in uncertain and disrupted future that is the 21st century. After all, what is a disruptive scourge to some may to others be salvation via the empowerment that legal knowledge, information advice and skills can bring.[165]

Notes

1 Richard Susskind, *Tomorrow's Lawyers: An Introduction to your Future* (2nd edn, Oxford: Oxford University Press 2017) 27.
2 Ibid.
3 Richard Susskind, 'AI, Work and "Outcome-thinking"' (2018) *British Academy Review* 43 <www.thebritishacademy.ac.uk/publications/british-academy-review/34/ai-work-and-outcome-thinking> accessed 20 November 2018.
4 Susskind, *Tomorrow's Lawyers* (n. 2) 27.

5 Michele R. Pistone and Michael B. Horn, 'Disrupting Law School: How Disruptive Innovation Will Revolutionize the Legal World' (*Clayton Christensen Institute for Disruptive Innovation* 2016) 112 <www.christenseninstitute.org/wp-content/uploads/2016/03/Disrupting-law-school.pdf>.

6 Klaus Schwab, *The Fourth Industrial Revolution* (Random House, New York 2016).

7 Productivity Commission, 'Digital Disruption: What Do Governments Need to Do?' (Commission Research Paper 2016) <www.pc.gov.au/news-media/pc-news/previous-editions/pc-news-november-2016/digital>.

8 Michael Haupt, '"Data is the New Oil" – A Ludicrous Proposition' (*Medium*, 2 May 2016) <https://medium.com/project-2030/data-is-the-new-oil-a-ludicrous-proposition-1d91bba4f294>, accessed 1 September 2018.

9 Javier De La Torre, 'Data Is the New Global Currency, Location the New Gold Standard' (*Geospatial World*, 2 January 2018) <www.geospatialworld.net/article/data-is-the-new-global-currency/>, accessed 1 September 2018; Natarajan Chandrasekaran, 'Is Data the New Currency?' (*World Economic Forum*, 14 August 2015). <www.weforum.org/agenda/2015/08/is-data-the-new-currency/>, accessed 1 September 2018.

10 Productivity Commission (n. 8) 1.

11 Hugh Bradlow, 'The Impact of Emerging Technologies in the Workforce of the Future' in *Australia's Future Workforce?* (Committee for Economic Development of Australia 2015) 38, 42.

12 Productivity Commission (n. 8) 14.

13 Sharon Thiruchelvam, 'Protecting the Rule of Law from Populist Threats' (*Raconteur*, 7 February 2018) <www.raconteur.net/risk-management/protecting-rule-law-populist-threats>, accessed 1 September 2018.

14 Australasian Legal Practice Management Association, 'Drivers of the New Normal in Law' (Australasian Legal Practice Management Association National Summit, Sydney, October 2013).

15 Such as international firms entering market, mergers and acquisitions, restructuring and redundancies, criticism of time unit billing and the pressure for fixed fees.

16 Such as incorporated legal practice, legal process outsourcing, online legal services, offshore legal services, control shifting to the customer, reduced customer loyalty, emphasis on value not hours spent, reduced importance of proximity of provider, price pressure and increased client expectations.

17 Such as control shifting to the customer, reduced customer loyalty, emphasis on value not hours spent, reduced importance of proximity of provider, price pressure and increased client expectations.

18 Such as dominance of female law graduates, retirement of baby boomers, managing inter-generational expectations, equity and diversity requirements and mental health challenges.

19 Such as working from anywhere, flexible hours, job sharing, rise of part-time/contract/casual labour and demands for work/life balance.

20 Law Society of New South Wales, 'National Profile of Solicitors 2016 Report' (*Urbis*, 24 August 2017) iii <www.lawsociety.com.au/sites/default/files/2018-04/NATIONAL%20PROFILE%20OF%20SOLICITORS%202016.compressed.pdf>, accessed 20 November 2018.

21 See, e.g., <https://jade.io/>, <Austlii.edu.au>, and other international databases.

22 See, e.g., Law24 <www.law24.ch/online-consultation/?lang=en>; 24Legal <http://24legal.lsc.sa.gov.au/>, both accessed 2 September 2018.

23 See, e.g., Immigration Virtual Assistant (IVA) developed by EXEO Attorneys <https://exeo.ca/>; AILIRA developed by Cartland Law <www.ailira.com/>, both accessed 2 September 2018.

24 See, e.g., FindLaw Australia <www.findlaw.com.au/find/default.aspx>; LawyerList <http://lawyerlist.com.au/>; lawtap <https://lawtap.com/au/>; Avvo <www.avvo.com/review-your-lawyer>; GoToCourt <www.gotocourt.com.au/rank-your-lawyer/>, all accessed 2 September 2018.

25 For a discussion of these see Hamish Hewitt, 'AIM-ing for the Future: Artificial Intelligence as the Mediator' (2018) *Flinders University College of Business, Government & Law Honours Dissertation* 40–48; also see Neil Rose, 'Employment Tribunals Set for Online Justice Pilot' (*Legal Futures*, 6 December 2018) <www.legalfutures.co.uk/latest-news/employment-tribunals-set-for-online-justice-pilot>, accessed 8 December 2018.

26 For a useful guide to some of these, see Daniel Linna's 'Legal Services Innovation Index' <www.legaltechinnovation.com/>, accessed 1 September 2018; In August 2017, Thomson Reuters announced '579 patents relating to new legal services technology were filed worldwide in 2016, up from just 99 patents in 2012. . . . The figures reflect the rise of alternative legal services – such as virtual law firms – and the rapid expansion of the online legal industry. This trend is in large part being driven by businesses and individuals looking beyond traditional channels for legal advice': Thomson Reuters, 'Thomson Reuters Analysis Reveals 484% Increase in New Legal Services Patents Globally as Law Firms Around the World Invest in Legal Tech' (*Thomson Reuters*, 16 August 2017) <www.thomsonreuters.com/en/press-releases/2017/august/thomson-reuters-analysis-reveals-484-percent-increase-in-new-legal-services-patents-globally.html>, accessed 1 September 2018.

27 Ibid.

28 Libby Hakim, 'The 9 Trends That Continued to Drive the Change in the Legal Sector in 2017' (*Thomson Reuters Legal Insight*, 20 November 2017) <http://insight.thomsonreuters.com.au/posts/top-9-legal-sector-trends-2017>, accessed 1 September 2018.

29 Joshua Browder developed 'robot lawyer' DoNotPay whilst still at university, but studying computer science not law. See Eleni Cresci, 'Chatbot that Overturned 160,000 Parking Fines Now Helping Refugees Claim Asylum' (*The Guardian*, 6 March 2017) <www.theguardian.com/technology/2017/mar/06/chatbot-donotpay-refugees-claim-asylum-legal-aid>,accessed 1 September 2018; Cory Doctorow, 'DoNotPay Bot Launches a Cheap Airline Ticket That Automates the Nearly Impossible Business of Getting Refunds When Prices Fall' (*Boingboing*, 14 March 2018) <https://boingboing.net/2018/03/14/code-law-norms-markets.html>, accessed 1 September 2018.

30 Jnana Settle, 'Predictive Analytics in the Legal Industry: 10 Companies to Know in 2018' (*Disruptor Daily*, 29 January 2018) <www.disruptordaily.com/predictive-analytics-legal-industry-10-companies-know-2018/> accessed 1 September 2018; see, e.g., 'Lex Machina' <https://lexmachina.com/>, accessed 1 September 2018, 'Premonition' <https://premonition.ai/>, accessed 1 September 2018 and other legal analytics services. In September 2017, Premonition issued what it claims to be the first ranking of Australian litigators based on performance metrics' with Legal Practice Intelligence noting that 'could prove to be a highly disruptive event for Australia's legal industry': Editor, 'Legal Analytics Firm, Premonition, Publishes Statistical Ranking of Australia's Top Law Firms and Barristers' (*Legal Practice Intelligence*, 7 September 2017) <www.legalpracticeintelligence.com.au/legal-analytics-firm-premoniton-publishes-statistical-ranking-of-australias-top-law-firms-and-barristers/>. Also that month, LexisNexis announced the launch of Lexis Legal Analytics, with the 'first showcase module . . . High Court Analyzer. This tool can analyse thousands of pages of High Court judgments to deliver insights into people

and their connections, legal outcomes, words and phrases judicially considered and most cited cases': Tom Lodewyke, 'LexisNexis Brings 'Cutting-edge Analytics Technologies' to Aus' (*Lawyers Weekly,* 27 September 2017) <www.lawyersweekly.com.au/biglaw/21965-lexisnexis-brings-cutting-edge-analytics-technologies-to-aus?utm_source=Lawyers%20Weekly&utm_campaign=27_09_17&utm_medium=email&utm_content=2>, accessed 1 September 2018.

31 'Equivant' <www.equivant.com/>, accessed 1 September 2018

32 *State of Wisconsin v Loomis* 881 N.W.2d 749 (Wis. 2016); 'State v Loomis: Wisconsin Supreme Court Requires Warning Before Use of Algorithmic Risk Assessments in Sentencing' (2017) 130 *Harvard Law Review* 1530.

33 Jeff Larson and others, 'How we Analysed the COMPAS Recidivism Algorithm' (*ProPublica*, 23 May 2016) <www.propublica.org/article/how-we-analyzed-the-compas-recidivism-algorithm>, accessed 1 September 2018.

34 Julia Dressel and Hany Farid, 'The Accuracy, Fairness, and Limits of Predicting Recidivism' (2018) 4(1) *Science Advances* 1.

35 See, e.g., LawGeex, 'Comparing the Performance of Artificial Intelligence to Human Lawyers in the Review of Standard Business Contracts' (LawGeex, February 2018) <www.lawgeex.com/AIvsLawyer/>, accessed 2 September 2018; LawGeex, 'The In-House Counsel's Legal Tech 2018 Buyer's Guide' (LawGeex) <www.lawgeex.com/buyersguide>; Judith Bennett and others, 'Current State of Automated Legal Advice Tools: Networked Society Institute Discussion Paper 1' (University of Melbourne, April 2018) <https://networkedsociety.unimelb.edu.au/__data/assets/pdf_file/0020/2761013/2018-NSI-CurrentStateofALAT.pdf>, accessed 1 September 2018.

36 'Artificially Intelligent Legal Information Research Assistant' <www.ailira.com/>, accessed 1 September 2018

37 Emma Ryan, 'Demand for Blockchain-competent Lawyers on the Rise' (*Lawyers Weekly,* 27 June 2018) <www.lawyersweekly.com.au/sme-law/23516-demand-for-blockchain-competent-lawyers-on-the-rise>, accessed 1 September 2018.

38 See <www.adieu.ai/start-now-lawyers/>.

39 'Civil Resolution Tribunal' <https://civilresolutionbc.ca/>, accessed 1 September 2018; Richard Susskind, @richardsusskind Tweet 9 November 2018 responding to Michael Cross, 'No Basis for Face-to-face Justice, Says Digital Court Guru Susskind' (*The Law Society Gazette*, 8 November 2018) <www.lawgazette.co.uk/practice/no-basis-for-face-to-face-justice-says-digital-court-guru-susskind/5068230.article>, accessed 9 November 2018.

40 Tyler Technologies, 'Expanding Access to Justice with Online Dispute Resolution' <www.tylertech.com/solutions-products/modria>, accessed 1 July 2018; 'Resolver' <www.resolver.co.uk/>, accessed 1 September 2018.

41 Lydia Bennett Moses, 'Artificial Intelligence in the Courts, Legal Academic and Legal Practice' (2017) 91(7) *Australian Law Journal* 561, 569–70.

42 Bill Henderson cited in Daniel Martin Katz, 'Make Law Better – The Legal Innovation Agenda in Vectors and Phases #MakeLawBetter' (FLIP Conference, Law Society of New South Wales, Sydney 2018).

43 Mark A. Cohen, 'Who Will Train Tomorrow's Lawyers and How Will They Learn?' (*Legal Mosaic*, 28 September 2017) <http://legalmosaic.com/2017/09/28/who-will-train-tomorrows-lawyers-and-how-will-they-learn/>, accessed 1 September 2018.

44 Marc Cohen, 'Legal Business Consulting: A Quick Overview of Legal Industry Change' (*Legal Mosaic*) <https://legalmosaic.com/about/>, accessed 1 September 2018.

45 Grace Ormsby, 'In-house Legal Functions on the Rise' (*Lawyers Weekly*, 23 August 2018) <www.lawyersweekly.com.au/corporate-counsel/23884-in-house-legal-functions-on-the-rise?utm_source=CorporateCounsel&utm_campaign=28_08_18&utm_medium=email&utm_content=4>, accessed 1 September 2018.

46 Sol Dolor, 'KPMG Law's New Service Helps Remake In-house Legal Departments' (*Australasian Lawyer*, 3 August 2018) <www.australasianlawyer.com.au/news/kpmg-laws-new-service-helps-remake-inhouse-legal-departments-253169.aspx>, accessed 1 September 2018; Anonymous, 'Big Four Accountancy Firm Makes Big Push into Law' (*Australasian Lawyer*, 25 September 2017) <www.australasianlawyer.com.au/news/big-four-accountancy-firm-makes-big-push-into-law-241636.aspx>, accessed 1 September 2018.

47 Tom Wilson, 'Legal Tech-Where's all the VC money?' (*techburst*, 8 November 2017) <https://techburst.io/legal-tech-wheres-all-the-vc-money-431d1aeeddd6>, accessed 1 September 2018.

48 Susskind, *Tomorrow's Lawyers* (n. 2) 27.

49 Peter Saunders, 'Developing Legal Talent: Stepping into the Future Law Firm' (*Deloitte*, February 2016) <https://www2.deloitte.com/uk/en/pages/audit/articles/developing-legal-talent.html> 16, accessed 1 September 2018.

50 See, e.g., Richard Susskind and Daniel Susskind, *The Future of the Professions* (Oxford 2015); Susskind, *Tomorrow's Lawyers* (n. 2); Tim Dunlop, *Why the Future Is Workless* (Newsouth, Sydney 2016); Alec Ross, *The Industries of the Future* (Simon & Schuster. London 2016); Paul Mason *Postcapitalism: A Guide to Our Future* (Penguin Books, London 2016); Martin Ford, '*Rise of the Robots*' (Basic Books, New York 2015); Ryan Avent, '*The Wealth of Humans: Work and its Absence in the Twenty First Century*' (Penguin Random House, New York 2016).

51 Dr Bob Murray and Dr Alicia Fortinberry, *Leading the Future: the Human Science of Law Firm Strategy and Leadership* (Ark Group, London 2016) 4.

52 Ibid., 6. Interestingly, the Big 4 accounting firms are already making a push into the legal services market: Australasian Lawyer, 'Big Four Accountancy Firm Makes Big Push into Law' (*Australasian Lawyer*, 25 September 2017) <www.australasianlawyer.com.au/news/big-four-accountancy-firm-makes-big-push-into-law-241636.aspx>, accessed 1 September 2018.

53 Artificial Lawyer, 'Legal Tech Jobs' <www.artificiallawyer.com/legal-tech-jobs/>, accessed 1 September 2018.

54 Steve Randall, 'Global Firm to Launch Alternative Legal Services Business in Australia' (*Australasian Lawyer*, 16 September 2016) <www.australasianlawyer.com.au/news/global-firm-to-launch-alternative-legal-services-business-in-australia-223460.aspx>, accessed 1 September 2018.

55 Roy Strom, 'Legal Project Managers: the New Rainmakers' (*Law.com*, 22 September 2016) <www.law.com/sites/almstaff/2016/09/22/legal-project-managers-the-new-rainmakers/>, accessed 1 September 2018; e.g., at Seyfarth & Shaw <www.seyfarth.com/DanielRaymer>, accessed 1 September 2018; e.g., at LegalVision see Head of Legal Transformation <https://legalvision.com.au/meet-our-team/thomas-kaldor/> and Legal transformation manager <https://legalvision.com.au/jobs/legalvision-legal-project-manager/>, both accessed 1 September 2018.

56 E.g., at Seyfarth & Shaw <www.seyfarth.com/KaraBrooks>, accessed 1 September 2018.

57 Judith Bennett and others (n. 36).

58 Emma Beames, 'Technology-based Legal Document Generation Services and the Regulation of Legal Practice in Australia' (2017) 42(4) *Alternative Law Journal*, 297–303.

59 Karen Barton, 'Curiosity' in Fiona Westwood And Karen Barton (eds) *The Calling of Law: The Pivotal Role of Vocational Legal education* (Taylor & Francis Group, London 2014) 4.

60 Hana Kapadia, 'In a World of Online Dispute Resolution, Why Does the UK Civil Justice System Need Lawyers?' (*Lawyer 2B*, 6 April 2017) <https://l2b.thelawyer.com/hana-kapadia-civil-justice-system-lawyers/?cmpid=l2blegb_3279497>, accessed 1 September 2018.

61 Kim Economides, 'What are Fundamental Legal Values' in Economides and others (eds) *Fundamental Values: A Volume of Essays to Commemorate the Seventy-Fifth Anniversary of the Founding of the Law School in Exeter 1923–1998* (Hart Publishing, Oxford 2000) 7.

62 *Legal Profession Uniform Law Australian Solicitors' Conduct Rules* 2015 Rule 3.1; Law Council of Australia, *Review of the Australian Solicitors' Conduct Rules*, 1 February 2018; Other jurisdiction have avoided these questions as they do not impose a paramount duty to the court to lawyers. For example, it is not included in the American Bar Association *Model Rules of Professional Conduct* <www.americanbar.org/groups/professional_responsibility/publications/model_rules_of_professional_conduct/model_rules_of_professional_conduct_table_of_contents/>.

63 Morry Bailes, 'The Law and Legal Technology – Our Changing Work Practices' (President-elect Speech, Law Council of Australia, Australian Young Lawyers' Conference, Sydney, 20 October 2017).

64 Susskind, 'AI, Work and "Outcome-thinking"' (n. 4).

65 Mark A. Cohen, 'Technology: Law's Collaborative Catalyst' (*Forbes*, 1 March 2018) <www.forbes.com/sites/markcohen1/2018/02/26/technology-laws-collaborative-catalyst/#32fc8b656952>, accessed 1 September 2018.

66 Ibid.

67 See, e.g., Amy X. Wang, 'Law School is Still Worth it – but not if You're in it for the Money' (*Quartz at Work,* 20 January 2018) <https://qz.com/work/1182346/student-debt-is-hurting-the-law-degree-but-its-still-a-good-bet/>; Isabel Dayman, 'Was Your University Degree Worth the Debt? High Paying Jobs Aren't A Sure Thing, Experts Say' (*ABC News*, 11 April 2018) <www.abc.net.au/news/2018-04-11/was-your-university-degree-worth-it/9637850>, both accessed 1 September 2018.

68 Emma Ryan, 'Universities Must Be "Held Accountable" for Law Grad Over-supply' (*Lawyers Weekly*, 14 February 2018) <www.lawyersweekly.com.au/sme-law/22737-universities-must-be-held-accountable-for-law-grad-oversupply?utm_source=LawyersWeekly&utm_campaign=14_02_18&utm_medium=email&utm_content=1>, accessed 1 September 2018.

69 Bailes (n. 64).

70 *City of Rockford et al. v Mallinckrodt ARD Inc et al.*, 17 CV 50107 (2018); *MSP Recovery Claims, Series LLC, et al. v Mallinckrodt ARD Inc.*, 18 CV 379 (2018) <www.lawsitesblog.com/wp-content/uploads/sites/509/2018/08/N.D.-Ill.-17-cv-50107-dckt-000156_000-filed-2018-08-07.pdf>, accessed 1 September 2018.

71 *Mallinckrodt* (n. 71) 2.

72 *Mallinckrodt* (n. 71) 1 citing United States Department of Defense News Briefing (12 February 2002) <http://archive.defense.gov/Transcripts/Transcript.aspx?TranscriptID=2636>, accessed 1 September 2018.

73 *Mallinckrodt* (n. 71) 6.

74 American Bar Association, 'Model Rules of Professional Conduct' (Commentary to Rule 1.1) <www.americanbar.org/groups/professional_responsibility/publications/model_rules_of_professional_conduct/rule_1_1_competence.html>, accessed 1 September 2018.

75 Robert J. Ambrogi, 'North Carolina Becomes Second State to Mandate Technology Training for Lawyers' (*Lawsites*, 5 December 2018) <www.lawsitesblog.com/2018/12/north-carolina-becomes-second-state-mandate-technology-training-lawyers.html>, accessed 8 December 2018.

76 Anonymous, 'Proposed Amendments to the Annual CLE Requirements' (Publication 27 N.C.A.C. 1D) <www.lawsitesblog.com/wp-content/uploads/sites/509/2018/12/NC-tech-rule.pdf>, accessed 7 December 2018.

77 Solicitors Regulation Authority, 'SRA handbook Version 19, Published 1 October 2017' <www.sra.org.uk/handbook/>, accessed 1 September 2018.
78 Ibid.
79 Federation of Law Societies of Canada, 'Model Code of Professional Conduct Consultation' (Consultation Report, 31 January 2017) 2 <https://flsc.ca/wp-content/uploads/2014/10/Consultation-Report-Draft-Model-Code-Amendments-for-web-Jan2017-FINAL.pdf>, accessed 1 September 2018.
80 *Legal Profession Uniform Law Australian Solicitors' Conduct Rules 2015* <www.lawcouncil.asn.au/files/web-pdf/Aus_Solicitors_Conduct_Rules.pdf>, accessed 1 September 2018.
81 *Scroope v Legal Services Commissioner* [2013] NSWCA 178, [9]; *Legal Services Commissioner v Keddie* [2012] NSWADT 106 (4 June 2012) [43], [53–54].
82 *Legal Services Commissioner v Keddie* [2012] NSWADT 106 (4 June 2012) [86].
83 Ibid.; *Scroope v Legal Services Commissioner* [2013] NSWCA 178.
84 Law Council of Australia, 'Cyber Security and Lawyers' Professional Responsibility' <http://lca.lawcouncil.asn.au/lawcouncil/cyber-precedent-risk-management/cyber-precedent-lawyers-professional-responsibility>, accessed 20 November 2018.
85 Prescribed Areas of Knowledge published by the Law Admissions Consultative Committee as Schedule 1 to the Law Admissions Consultative Committee's Uniform Admission Rules 2014 as contained in, for example, *Legal Professional Uniform Admission Rules 2015* (NSW) [Uniform Admission Rules] sch 1; *Legal Practitioners Education and Admission Council Rules 2018* (SA) [LPEAC Rules] app A.
86 Uniform Admission Rules sch 2; LPEAC Rules app B.
87 Ibid.
88 Nickolas J. James, 'More than Merely Work Ready: Vocationalism Versus Professionalism in Legal Education' 2017 (40)1 *UNSW Law Journal* 186.
89 F. Zemans and V. Rosenblum, *The Making of a Public Profession* (1981) 123 cited in David Barnhizer, 'The Purpose and Methods of American Legal Education' (Paper No. 11–205, Cleveland-Marshall Legal Studies) 13.
90 Ibid., 12.
91 Martha Nussbaum, 'Why Lawyers Need a Broad Social Education' (Speech delivered at The Future of Australian Legal Education sponsored by the Australian Academy of Law and the Australian Law Journal, Sydney, 11–13 August 2017).
92 Ken Grady, 'The Confusion of Legal Education' (*The Algorithmic Society,* 28 July 2017) <https://medium.com/the-algorithmic-society/the-confusion-of-legal-education-5032efc6cb61>, accessed 1 September 2018.
93 Susskind *Tomorrow's Lawyers* (n. 2) 44.
94 Barton (n. 60) 5–6.
95 Sandford D. Clark, 'Regulating Admissions – Are We there Yet?' (Speech delivered at The Future of Australian Legal Education sponsored by the Australian Academy of Law and the Australian Law Journal, Sydney, August 2017).
96 Ibid; Lloyd England, *A Basic Legal Education – A Basic Human Right?* (2 June 2017) <https://ssrn.com/abstract=3036739> accessed 1 September 2018; The Report of the Committee on Legal Education of the Indian Law Institute's All India Law Conference (1958) 1 cited in A.M Varkey, 'Learning Objectives of Legal Education in India: A Critique' (1991) XV *Cochin University Law Review* 444, 448; S.O Akindipe, 'An Appraisal of the Objectives of Legal Education' <www.nigerianlawguru.com/articles/general/AN%20APPRAISAL%20OF%20THE%20OBJECTIVES%20OF%20LEGAL%20EDUCATION.pdf>, accessed 1 September 2018.

97 Samuel J. Levine and Russell G. Pearce, 'Rethinking the Legal Reform Agenda: Will Raising the Standards for Bar Admission Promote or Undermine Democracy, Human Rights, and Rule of Law?' (2009) 44(4) *Fordham Law Review* 1635, 1637.

98 John Flood in Fiona Westwood & Karen Barton (eds), *The Calling of Law: The Pivotal Role of Vocational Legal Education* (Taylor & Francis Group, London 2014) 5.

99 United Nations, Resolution adopted by the General Assembly, 67/1. Declaration of the High-level Meeting of the General Assembly on the Rule of Law at the National and International Levels <www.un.org/ruleoflaw/files/A-RES-67-1.pdf>, accessed 2 September 2018.

100 Susskind, *Tomorrow's* Lawyers (n. 2) 31.

101 Muhammad Yunus, 'Zero Poverty, Zero Unemployment and Zero Carbon Emissions – Is it Possible for South Australia' (Speech delivered at Flinders University, 22 March 2018); Also see Muhammad Yunus, *A World of Three Zeroes* (Scribe, Melbourne 2017) 70.

102 James (n. 89) 188–9.

103 Council of Australian Law Deans (CALD), 'Factsheet: Data Regarding Law School Graduate Numbers and Outcomes' (November 2016) <http://cald.asn.au/assets/lists/Education/Factsheet- Law_Students_in_Australia.pdf>, accessed 4 January 2017. In 2018, CALD is exploring gathering further data.

104 See, e.g., University of New England, 'Legal and Paralegal Studies' <https://studyat.une.edu.au/cl-landing-digital-2018-tri3/legal-studies-157PF-13737J.html?gclid=CjwKCAjw8ajcBRBSEiwAsSky_ZGUddJAr5TrJqIoikl37o2aIJMAgt3CLfcHaw47K5GYp2HQADYBOxoC6YsQAvD_BwE&gclsrc=aw.ds>, accessed 2 September 2018; Southern Cross University, 'Associate Degree in Law (Paralegal Studies)' www.scu.edu.au/study-at-scu/courses/associate-degree-in-law-paralegal-studies-2206351/>; see, e.g., University of New England, 'Diploma in Prosecution and Advocacy' <https://my.une.edu.au/courses/courses/DPA>, accessed 2 September 2018.

105 Uniform Admission Rules sch 2; LPEAC Rules app B, 1.

106 David Weisbrot, 'Recent Statistical Trends in Australian Legal Education' (1990–91) 2(1) *Legal Education Review* 219.

107 Gwilym Croucher and Peter Woelert, 'How Australia Got So Many Law Schools' (2018) *Pursuit* <https://pursuit.unimelb.edu.au/articles/how-australia-got-so-many-law-schools>, accessed 9 November 2018.

108 See, e.g., undergraduate provider Sydney City School of Law Top Education Institute; and post graduate practical legal training providers The College of Law <www.collaw.edu.au/>, accessed 1 September 2018; Leo Cussen Centre for Law <www.leocussen.edu.au/>, accessed 1 September 2018; Law Society of South Australia <www.lawsocietysa.asn.au/LSSA/Students/GDLP.aspx>, accessed 1 September 2018.

109 Weisbrot (n 107); for a discussion more generally see Danny Iny, *Leveraged Learning* <https://leveragedlearningbook.com/chapters/introduction/>, accessed 8 December 2018.

110 Denise Bradley and others, *Review of Australian Higher Education*, Final report (2008).

111 Australian Law Reform Commission, *Managing Justice: A Review of the Federal Civil Justice System* (ALRC Report 89) 120 <www.alrc.gov.au/sites/default/files/pdfs/publications/ALRC89.pdf>, accessed 1 September 2018.

112 Gerlind Wisskirchen and others, 'Artificial Intelligence and Robotics and Their Impact on the Workplace' (IBA Global Employment Institute, April 2017) 24 <www.ibanet.org/Article/NewDetail.aspx?ArticleUid=012A3473-007F-4519-827C-7DA56D7E3509>, accessed 1 September 2018.

113 Sally Kift, Mark Israel and Rachael Field, 'Bachelor of Laws Learning and Teaching Academic Standards Statement December 2010' (Australian Learning and Teaching Council 2010).

114 Council of Australian Law Deans, 'Juris Doctor Threshold Learning Outcomes' <https://cald.asn.au/wp-content/uploads/2017/11/Threhold-Learning-Outcomes-JD.pdf>, accessed 1 September 2018.

115 'First mentioned by David Guest in a 1991 [newspaper] article discussing the future of computer jobs, and then championed by Tim Brown, CEO of IDEO design firm, as an approach to hiring the right talent in order to build interdisciplinary teams that can come together to create new ideas': Maria Doyle, 'Why Engineers Need to Develop T shaped skill' (PTC) <www.ptc.com/en/product-lifecycle-report/why-engineers-need-to-develop-t-shaped-skills>, accessed 1 September 2018.

116 See, e.g., Law Society of NSW, '2017 FLIP Report: Future Of Law and Innovation in the Profession' <www.lawsociety.com.au/sites/default/files/2018-03/1272952.pdf>; Law Society of WA, 'The Future of the Legal Profession' (Report 2017) <www.lawsocietywa.asn.au/wp-content/uploads/2015/10/2017DEC12-Law-Society-Future-of-the-Legal-Profession.pdf>; Singapore Academy of Law, 'Future Law Innovation Programme' <www.flip.org.sg/>; Law Society of England and Wales, 'The Future of Legal Services' (2016) <www.lawsociety.org.uk/support-services/research-trends/the-future-of-legal-services/>; Canadian Bar Association, 'Futures: Transforming the Delivery of Legal Services in Canada' (2014) <www.cba.org/CBAMediaLibrary/cba_na/PDFs/CBA%20Legal%20Futures%20PDFS/trends-isssues-eng.pdf>; International Bar Association, 'Task Force on the Future of Legal Services' <www.ibanet.org/Task-Force-on-the-Future-of-Legal-Services.aspx#undefined>; Pistone and Horn (n 5); Alli Gerkman and Logan Cornett, 'Foundations for Practice: The Whole Lawyer and the Character Quotient' (*The Institute for the Advancement of the American Legal System* 2016) <http://iaals.du.edu/sites/default/files/reports/foundations_for_practice_whole_lawyer_character_quotient.pdf>, all accessed 1 September 2018.

117 M. Weir, 'The Dissonance between Law School Academics and Practitioners – The Why the How the Where to Now' (1993) 9 *Queensland University of Technology Law Journal* 143, 143 citing F. Allen, 'The Causes of Popular Dissatisfaction with Legal Education' (1976) 62 *ABAJ* 447, 449.

118 Rainmaking Oasis, 'The T-Shaped Professional: Talent Needed for Future' (Rainmaking Oasis Inc 2014) <https://pbs.twimg.com/media/CmO0h0qWgAA5dr6.jpg>, accessed 1 September 2018.

119 See, e.g., Paul Bloom, *Against Empathy: The Case for Rational Compassion* and the transcript of his interview on 4 January 2017 on CBC Radio's The Current with Anna Maria Tremonti: 'Against Empathy: Yale Psychology Professor Says Too Much Emotion Leads to Bad Moral Decisions' <www.cbc.ca/radio/thecurrent/the-current-for-january-4-2017-1.3919635/january-4-2017-full-episode-transcript-1.3921463#segment2>, accessed 1 September 2018.

120 See, e.g., Daniel Goleman, *Social Intelligence: The New Science of Human Relationships* (Arrow Books, London 2007) 84.

121 R. Amani Smathers, 'The 21st Century T-Shaped Lawyer' (2014) 40(4) *Law Practice Magazine*.

122 Law Society of NSW FLIP Report (n. 117) 6.

123 See, e.g., Margaret Hagan of the Legal Design Lab based at Stanford Law School, <www.legaltechdesign.com/>, accessed 1 September 2017.

124 Law Society of NSW FLIP Report (n. 117) 77.

125 See, e.g., Uniform Admission Rules sch 2, LPEAC Rules app B.

126 Gerkman and Cornett (n. 116) 1.

127 Ibid; James (n. 89).
128 James (n. 89) 205, and more generally at 200–5.
129 James (n. 89) 186.
130 Susskind, *Tomorrow's Lawyers* (n. 2) 27.
131 Pistone and Horn (n. 6).
132 *Legal Profession Uniform Law 2014* (NSW); *Legal Profession Uniform Law Application Act 2014 (Vic).*
133 This is particularly in light of the Solicitors Qualifying Examination to come in effect in the UK in 2020. See Solicitors Regulation Authority, 'Solicitors Qualifying Examination' <www.sra.org.uk/sra/policy/sqe.page>, accessed 1 September 2018, and State Bar exams in the US.
134 Productivity Commission (n. 8).
135 Such as critical analysis, problem solving, logic, constructing persuasive and coherent arguments.
136 See, e.g., Patti Dyur and Gabrielle L. Kindstrom, 'Perceptions and Use of Digital Badges for Professional Learning Development in Higher Education' (2017) (61(4) *TechTrends* 386–92 <https://link.springer.com/article/10.1007/s11528-017-0168-2> accessed 1 September 2018.
137 'The impact of this trend is magnified in South Asia, where the rising student population is challenging education providers to pioneer non-traditional avenues of credentialing': Johnson, L. Adams Becker and others, 'NMC Horizon Report: 2016 Higher Education Edition' (Austin Texas: the New Media Consortium 2016) 11.
138 Susskind, *Tomorrow's Lawyers* (n. 2) 31.
139 John Chisholm Consulting, 'Value Based Pricing' <https://chisconsult.com/value-based-pricing/>; Utpal M. Dholakia, 'A Quick Guide to Value Based Pricing' (*Harvard Business Review*, 9 August 2016) <https://hbr.org/2016/08/a-quick-guide-to-value-based-pricing>, both accessed 1 September 2018.
140 Susskind, *Tomorrow's Lawyers* (n 2) 126; '[h]ourly billing will fade away in the 2020s as the dominant charging mechanism': CommBank Legal Market Pulse, (August 2017) 15 <www.commbank.com.au/content/dam/commbank/corporate/pds/commbank-legal-market-pulse-Aug-2017.pdf>, accessed 1 September 2018.
141 See, e.g., Law Admissions Consultative Committee's Uniform Admission Rules 2014 as contained in, for example, Uniform Admission Rules; LPEAC Rules Rule 7(1)(a). The CALD standards refer to 'at least three years, or six semesters, of full-time study of law': Council of Australian Law Deans, 'The CALD Standards for Australian Law Schools: As Adopted 17 November 2009 and Amended to March 2013', cl 2.4.1 <http://cald.asn.au/assets/lists/Education/CALD%20Standards%20As%20adopted%2017%20November%202009%20and%20Amended%20to%20March%202013%5b1%5d.pdf>.
142 LPEAC Rules app B Rule 3.2.
143 South Australian Government, *Engaging Professionals: Conveyancers* <www.sa.gov.au/topics/planning-and-property/buying-a-home-or-property/engaging-professionals/conveyancers>, accessed 1 September 2018.
144 Washington State Bar Association, *Limited Licence Legal Technician Program* (2017) <www.wsba.org/licensing-and-lawyer-conduct/limited-licenses/legal-technicians>; Mary Juetten, 'The Limited License Legal Technician Is the Way of the Future of Law' (*ABA Journal*, 8 December 2017) <www.abajournal.com/news/article/the_limited_license_legal_technician_story_start_with_why>, both accessed 1 September 2018.
145 Interestingly, the core education requirements include a course entitled 'Law office procedures/technology' which covers material including 'Legal Software

for the Office/Trial Software', 'e-filing', 'protection of confidential information/records – hard copy and electronic (e-discovery)' – topics far less likely to be covered in Australian law degrees or PLT: Washington State Bar Association, 'Core Education Requirements'<www.wsba.org/docs/default-source/licensing/lllt/core-education-requirements.pdf?sfvrsn=224706f1_0>, accessed 1 September 2018.

146 *McKenzie v McKenzie* (1970) 3 WLR 472; *R v Leicester City Justices* (1991) 3 WLR 368.

147 Therese Linton, *Taking It Step by Step: Why Legal Project Management (LPM) Matters* (The Law Society of New South Wales) <www.lawsociety.com.au/ForSolictors/CareerHub/LearningDevelopment/Postgraduate/Articles/Takingitstepbystep/index.htm>; International Institute of Legal Project Management, 'Legal Project Management and its Importance to Law Schools' (May 2017) <www.iilpm.com/legal-project-management-importance-law-schools/>, accessed 1 September 2018.

148 Mark A. Cohen, 'The Reluctant Rise of Project Management in Law' (*Legal Mosaic*, 24 March 2015) <http://legalmosaic.com/2015/03/24/reluctant-rise-project-management-law/#>, accessed 1 September 2018.

149 Susskind, *Tomorrow's Lawyers* (n 2) 35.

150 E.g., Business Education Institute <www.bei.edu.au/legal-pm/^$>; LPM Institute <https://lpminstitute.net/>.

151 Susskind, *Tomorrow's Lawyers* (n. 2) 48.

152 Megan Kimber, 'The Tenured "Core" and the Tenuous "Periphery": The Casualisation of Academic Work in Australian Universities' (2003) 25(1) *Journal of Higher Education Policy and Management* 41–50; The excellent SmartCasual online professional development modules resources are a very useful and timely response to the reality of this trend in legal education – Smart Casual <https://smartlawteacher.org/>.

153 Susskind, *Tomorrow's Lawyers* (n. 2) 33.

154 The new online JD at Flinders University is one example of beginning to explore positive ways in which the academic role can be disaggregated. The Flinders JD adopts a problem-based-learning (PBL) pedagogy across all topics. Teaching is a team-based endeavour: some staff have roles as discipline experts, problem designers or resource curators; other staff focus on design and delivery of the learning management system across all topics, or oversee student engagement in the topic tasks, or take pastoral responsibility for student progress and wellbeing, or respond to administrative queries.

155 Robert Size, 'Taking Advantage of Advances in Technology to Enhance the Rule of Law' (2017) 91(7) *Australian Law Journal* 575.

156 As Michael Kirby has cautioned: 'There is a natural tendency in human affairs to think that the familiar is good; that the well-established is better; and that the training that produced a person as estimable as oneself, is best of all. It is important that practitioners of the law should resist such thinking': Michael Kirby, 'Online Legal Education in Australia: The New CQU Law Degree' (2011) 34 *Australian Bar Review* 237, 237.

157 Barnhizer (n. 90) 2.

158 Ibid.

159 Cohen (n. 444); Barnhizer (n. 90).

160 Ezra Greenberg, Martin Hirt, and Sven Smit, 'The Global Forces Inspiring a New Narrative of Progress' (*McKinsey Quarterly*, April 2017) <www.mckinsey.com/business-functions/strategy-and-corporate-finance/our-insights/the-global-forces-inspiring-a-new-narrative-of-progress?cid=other-eml-alt-mkq-mck-oth-1704&hlkid=f0e28348b>.

161 Susskind, *Tomorrow's Lawyers* (n. 2) 188–9.

162 Bennett Moses takes issue with this analogy, arguing that 'it assumes that technologies, including artificial intelligence, can offer the same "hole in the wall" as legal practitioners, academics and judges. That is not always the case when viewed from the perspective of clients, law students and society at large': Bennett Moses (n. 423) 568.
163 Andrew Mellett, 'Legal Transformation: The New Playbook' (*Lawyers Weekly*, 29 August 2017) <www.lawyersweekly.com.au/corporate-counsel/21772-legal-transformation-the-new-playbook>.
164 Greenberg, Hirt and Smit (n. 161).
165 Susskind, *Tomorrow's Lawyers* (n. 2) 44.

13 Prometheus, Sisyphus, Themis

Three futures for legal education research

Paul Maharg

I Introduction[1]

To think independently of any relationship is not to think at all.[2]

Legal education research takes many forms: discourse analyses, jurisprudential studies, histories of institutions and movements, studies of educational interventions, empirical studies, theoretical studies and much else. Being a synthetic discipline, comprising at the very least law and education, such variety is to be expected and indeed welcomed. But there are infrastructural problems arising from our research practices. Legal education research focuses predominantly on single empirical projects and theory/practice/policy research. The field as a whole therefore develops haphazardly; there is little attempt to map it by various means and identify gaps in the literature, little co-ordination of research initiatives between academy and regulators on a sustained basis. There is a significant lack of longitudinal studies, very few ongoing and sustained data studies, no meta-reviews. Almost no systematic reviews of research literature are produced, few policy paper series, little in the way of a stream of historical literature on legal education that feeds into current developments and future innovation. Such lack of organisation and the thin historical awareness that it gives rise to, I argue here, constitutes a bar to the development of a rich legal educational research paradigm, and affects our ability to generate, curate and argue from evidence-based data and a richer jurisprudential context.

II The two David Hamiltons: interdisciplinary historical understanding and legal education

Let us begin not with legal education but with education. During the mid-1980s the Department of Education at the University of Glasgow, where I was working as a tutorial assistant in various arts departments, obtained funding to develop what was then an interesting and unusual project. Concerned about the low number of applications from lower socioeconomic classes to the university from Glasgow, the department sought and obtained funding to set up an outreach project to encourage applications from what was then termed areas of priority treatment (APTs) – housing zones of multiple deprivation. The project was called 'The University and its Ways'. Of its type, it was a precursor to other similar projects, 'Pathways to Higher Education' and such like.[3] The final word in the title was deliberately ambiguous: it referred to routes into the university, other than the usual routes via school grades. Pupils at schools in APTs were invited to join a summer school lasting around two months, during which they could choose classes from a variety of subjects. If they completed the courses, they could be given access to university, even if they had insufficient or no higher grade examination results.[4] The project as a whole was directed by Dr David Hamilton, who organized outreach information visits to schools, organized the substantive classes (largely in arts and social sciences, but in sciences as well as law), and who developed evaluative instruments. His organizational skills and his intellectual vision for the educational project gave it vibrancy and longevity.

But the project title also referred to the social and cultural ways of higher education (HE). As many educationalists and educational historians have pointed out, arts and social science curricula at school and at university discriminates against students from lower socioeconomic classes who do not have privileged access at home, in schools and elsewhere to the cultural capital prized in universities and often made available to their middle-class peers.[5]

The project therefore held a mandatory class that focused on analyzing the social and cultural aspects of university life and study that students from APTs may find alienating and difficult.[6] The class was designed to assist students from lower socioeconomic groups not just to cope with study skills in first year, but how to act and find their voices in situations where they may have felt disadvantaged by other students' backgrounds.[7] It lasted almost the entire two months, small group teaching was the norm, and we focused on topics such as research and academic reading (reading with purpose, notating, discriminating argument, building one's own argument, integrating prescribed and independent reading), cultural discourse, writing, analysis, tutorial discourse analysis, dealing with academic staff, coping with feedback or the lack of it, developing the ability to plan academic study, dealing with feelings of alienation, inferiority and humiliation and, integrating without losing identity or voice. Some classes of those students were the most inspirational I have taught in HE. School pupils who would otherwise have had no opportunity to attend university went on to complete degrees; and to see them grow in confidence and maturity over a short period of time was remarkable. And they did so in relation to each other, forming a community and network that sustained at least some of them.[8]

From those classes I learned important lessons about induction and teaching writing. First, students no matter what their backgrounds arrived as already highly literate, highly skilled persons – HE literacies were just others to be learned. Second, students did not proceed from basic to higher skills in an orderly direction. Learning was much more unordered, personal, task- and person-based, not class-based. Third, transfer of learning was difficult: from one genre to another, and from the context of The University and its Ways itself to the context of first year essay and exam writing. Transfer needed constant practice, from induction to first year, and from first year back to induction. Fourth, many of these personal experiences were confirmed by the contemporary literature on composition.[9]

Down the corridor from David was another Dr David Hamilton. He was about to publish a book on the history and culture of the curriculum, titled *Towards a Theory of Schooling*.[10] A considerable part of it was devoted to historical investigations of educational ideas such as 'class', 'course', 'curriculum', via a methodology that entailed historical exploration of the concepts. Two examples give a sense of its argument. Hamilton analysed the concept of *curriculum*, noting that it was first used in English in the records of the University of Glasgow, in 1633. He glossed its use by the innovator Andrew Melville, whose intention was to create a specifically Calvinist mode of learning, in which structures Ramist techniques of highly formalized teaching were deployed. In that knowledge architecture 'the "whole life" of each student was to be rendered open to teacher supervision'.[11] As Hamilton put it:

> First came the introduction of class divisions and closer pupil surveillance; and second came the refinement of pedagogic content and methods. The net result, however, was cumulative: teaching and learning became, for good or ill, more open to external scrutiny and control.[12]

The second example is the word *classroom*. According to the Oxford English Dictionary it was first recorded in minutes of a meeting of the faculty of Glasgow University, discussing the conversion of a 'chamber' (living quarters) into a 'class room' for the teaching and learning of civil law.[13] For Hamilton the terminology is indicative of a change in fundamental educational practice – 'the ultimate victory of group-based pedagogies over the more individualized forms of teaching and learning that had been dominant in earlier times'.[14] He traces the shift at Glasgow central to the bodies of educational thought being developed by Adam Smith, Robert Owen, David Stow and others.[15] Hamilton notes how the word described a space where a different pedagogy could be developed around sympathy and emulation (as self-esteem and self-improvement), not emulation and competition (as rivalry and conflict). This was explored in Smith's *The Theory of Moral Sentiments*, where sympathy is an ethical and social bond, aligned to the philosopher Francis Hutcheson's concept of the moral sense faculty, itself akin to an aesthetic sense. This was taken up by other local but nationally influential educationalists in and around Glasgow, such as David Stow and Robert Owen.[16]

I read the book and was influenced by many of its approaches, but above all by its understanding of education as stratigraphy, an archaeology of ideas. Hamilton's historical discourse analysis draws on generations of bibliographies into medieval, renaissance and modern universities. His work is an example of multi-disciplines brought together to work on a project of recovery but also re-interpretation. In the process, he began to link together the weaknesses in educational research, which led to common (mis-)interpretations of educational concepts, encouraged at least in part by the shape of academic discourses or lenses by which we understand the past. Hamilton recalls how '[s]lowly [he] began to appreciate that the weak sense of history shown by classroom researchers was matched only by the weak sense of the classroom shown by educational historians'.[17] Only later did I begin to appreciate how this applies to legal education. There are legal historians, and (many fewer) legal educational historians. There are legal educators and legal educationalists, and the weakness of the two sets of analysts matches the other, like a rhetorical zeugma, in the way that Hamilton describes. We shall explore this idea further below.

For now, though, it is important to observe that this weakness goes to the heart of one of the most profound debates in western and northern education systems in the last millennium, no matter the level of schooling or the discipline involved. Hamilton describes it as a tension between two arguments. On the one hand educationalists argue that 'schools merely "reproduce" predetermined social structures', while on the other there are those who argue that schools 'can shake themselves free of social structure and become autonomous sites of educational innovation'.[18] The first position sees 'pedagogic change' as originating outside of school, while the second argues that change 'stems from the ability of teachers to construct new educational relationships within the status quo'.[19] Hamilton situates himself differently, arguing that such positions set up a dualism where '"school in society" is reconceptualised as "school and society"'.[20] Hamilton argues for a different standpoint – 'that schooling and society must be examined in terms of the reciprocal relationships that hold them together across time and space'.[21]

At this point Hamilton's argument becomes reflexive. If schooling and society must be examined in these terms, then so too must education itself as a discipline. Here he draws a distinction between 'theorists of schooling' and 'theorists of education', citing the rise of the latter with the emergence of disciplines such as sociology, psychology, cognition and the like. The former use school innovations 'as a means of co-opting teachers, learners, taxpayers (etc) to a state-sponsored model of the future'.[22] As a result, 'the pedagogical delivery system is not so much re-examined as retuned. [. . .] School reform becomes a permanent solution. Yet, in the process, deliverance is reduced to delivery'. Hamilton characterizes this as a form of 'technocratic thinking'. By contrast theorists of education are those who draw upon education's disciplinary sisters, who think and work beyond the values of state, and for whom learners and teachers are both the subject and the active media of schooling. It is an argument that has been taken up by others, notably Lawrence Stenhouse, the progressive educational movement in the United States in the early 20th century and later in English school education in the post-WWII period.[23]

I would argue that programmes such as The University and its Ways are essential to create diversity and social mobility in HE, and we need many more such outreach programmes that paid attention to identity and voice in community and the necessity to work with what some such as Gergen have identified as the relational turn in education and philosophy. But alone this is insufficient. We also need theoretical and historical awareness in order to interpret how we are who we think we are. The second David reveals interlocking concepts and systems of education that while apparently opening opportunity for students also constrains them, and reflexively reveals the gap between pedagogic discourse and classroom reality in schools and HE.[24] While wholly different in their methods, the two Davids' projects dovetailed with each other. In the structure and content of The University and its Ways, there was awareness of how hegemonic cultures constrain students from certain socioeconomic groupings, and from racialized cultures; and how they needed support not just at induction but throughout their academic and indeed early professional careers. Had there been more focus on such support, the results of the project could have contributed to a dynamic shift for social change, identity and mobility in HE.[25]

Much of this argument applies to legal education. If we are to consider how the reciprocal relationships between legal education and society affect law schools then we must have the breadth of vision that brings together time and space, theory and history. This is not an argument for *grands récits* but for the analysis of *petits récits* and how they construct, consolidate and render inarguable the hegemonic and the status quo in legal education. We also need spaces where such researches and practices are brought together so that they are accessible to anyone wishing to read and learn from it. Currently, this space does not exist in any jurisdiction.

Nowhere is this more apparent than in the history of technology in legal education.

III Techne and forgetfulness

If we understand technology in the widest sense to mean the use of any material object or cultural arrangement then perhaps the first point we should make about technology in legal education is that it is, comparatively speaking, historyless.[26] There is no general history of technology in our discipline. Rather remarkably, neither is there a history of the most prominent technologies in use today, namely digital technologies.

This is in contrast to education generally, where the material culture of education has long been of interest to historians of education. In the last three decades or so there has flourished a stream of research that uncovers the material of educational practices in locales globally.[27] Our understanding of how physical technologies – classrooms, writing tools, digital databases, for example – affect what might be termed conceptual technologies – teaching, timetables, forms of assessment – are key to our understanding of the culture of education we inhabit today.

Does it matter that we have a weak sense of our history? Surely the avalanche of digital technologies sweep away all prior analogue analogies and metaphors? I would strongly disagree. As I argue elsewhere, the research literature on media transformation reveals the extent to which innovators depend upon the cognitive categories associated with the older media within which meaning is communicated, and migrate them over time to the affordances of a new media.[28] Margaret Smith, for instance, showed that the common understanding among researchers that printers of early books in the 15th century simply copied manuscripts because they wanted to preserve the uniqueness of the manuscript for economic reasons or because it was simply the only literate form available, was simplistic. By examining the relationship in detail she concluded that printed books did not imitate but *emulated* manuscripts, and largely for genre reasons.[29]

What we see in this and many other examples is not a sudden switch, manuscript to book, but printers, publishers, authors and readers making incremental shifts from one communications platform to another. It is nothing less than the gradual emergence of new media objects, cultures, economies out of the old; and in that change lies the transformational intermediation of media and knowledge migration.[30]

The same is true of legal education within digital media, but in a very much more compressed timescale. Take the example of digitally recorded lectures, which is rapidly becoming a norm for many institutions, though inconceivable two or three decades ago. The literature on this is sophisticated and growing.[31] Over a decade ago, Patricia McKellar and I carried out a study of the implementation of recorded lectures that replaced two face-to-face lecture series in civil and criminal law.[32] They were developed for a professional legal education programme called the Diploma in Legal Practice.[33] The results in general showed that students were very much in favour of the innovation; and that they made considerable shifts in their learning habits and practices, negotiating the changes on a personal level. One of the interesting themes was the effect of webcasts upon the emergence and construction of personal knowledge. More specifically in the context of this chapter how is it that a new form of media representation of knowledge, a webcast, can bring about the emergence of learning?

In the interviews and logs it was clear that there were many habits and forms of learning that were adapted from earlier patterns, in which students negotiated the still relatively new forms of data presentation that they encountered, and the following are examples of some of them. In pilots, students told us clear navigation down to the most granulated concepts, definitions, questions and back up again (rather like the rhetorical Jacob's ladder, beloved of medieval rhetoricians) was absolutely critical; and we built that into the software, using maps of webcast nodes, as well as a linear index of links to the webcasts all of which were brief (most less than 15 minutes in length). For updating the law we used jump-cuts where possible – again, an ancient rhetorical device, and, arguably, practised visually in 13th-century glossed manuscripts.[34]

Several students commented on their use of the webcast as an aural mnemonic. They simply listened to the webcast as a podcast while travelling or in the house, and used it as a revision tool by speeding up the speaking pace of the presenter. On the subject of writing up or typing up notes, webcast note-taking was always going to be very different process from taking notes at lectures. The procedures that students adopted varied from traditional pen-and-paper solutions and approaches to more electronic dialoguing with the on-screen resources.[35]

> When I did the first few I was writing absolutely everything out and I hadn't really – because quite a lot of people [in the computer lab] were looking at the screen and were writing down what was on the screen and working their notes around that. I wasn't doing that I was writing everything out and that took ages. So it was like well I'll just write down what's on the screen and then write my own notes.

All students were glad of the printout resources that were available. However one student commented that the presence of more bullet point slides in the Civil webcasts than in the Criminal webcasts made her study pattern less not more effective:

> In [the Civil webcast environment] I just became very passive [. . .] because it was all very much in front of me. But in [the Criminal webcast environment] I was very active about taking notes and if I had missed a few words I went back and made sure I had exactly what he was saying, so I have quite comprehensive notes for that.

The same student commented on the effect that the bulleted style of information summary had on her note-taking method:

> Maybe it's just me, but I found it quite hard to work from the PowerPoint slide presentation that was on the lecture slides. It highlights what [the presenter] was just saying – so it is quite difficult then to think back and think, what context was it in, or what was the first part of that sentence or what was the last few words of the sentence. There was one point where I thought, I can't remember if that flows on from the thing above so I started to draw arrows on to it to make sure that I knew the sentence was one and it flowed rather than thinking of things as distinct parts as bullet points.

Such detailed experiential comment was invaluable to us for design of the webcast environment. Forms of presentation seemed, for some students at least, to induce less not more engagement. Giving students the opportunity to print three-to-a-page 'slides' with five blank lines opposite each bordered slide made it more, not less, difficult for some students to form knowledge objects of legal argument.[36] This print format also forced students to take notes in a way that marginalised their own notes while foregrounding the presenter's notes. Ideally, we needed a design in which students could print out the information in a form that suited their own unique forms of note-taking; or better still, assist them to take online notes with visualisers and applications that supported legal argumentation, then choose for themselves which methods they used. We also wanted to enhance agency by developing ways in which students could share their notes with each other, ask questions to tutors and keep a bank of the answers. Such methods would, in Hamilton's terms above, move from delivery to deliverance. But our research project had to end before we were able to build that functionality (which was a considerable coding task) into the environment, and test it with students.

Much has been made more recently of webcasts and recorded lectures as being supplementary of face-to-face lectures. But if lectures are abolished as they were in our project and replaced with webcasts, then they become something quite different, a study environment online that affects conventional forms of teaching, assessment, the organisation of curriculum and administration of syllabus. And though they seem to be information-push environments, they can also stimulate collaborative working. Recall that the student above only altered her technique of note taking by observing others. This is an example of what Edwards and D'Arcy called 'relational agency' – not simply collaborative action on an object but 'the capacity to recognize and use the support of others in order to transform the object', and there were other examples of that happening in our research.[37] Note too, that certain forms of information presentation assisted or baffled learners – at a granular level, we discovered, the relations between digital text, image, context and concept required much more investigation.

Since this research (well over a decade ago), there has been little detailed empirical research into law students' use of such environments. There is, to be sure, much more research generally on how students use online study environments including lecture recordings and webcasts; but almost none specific to law. And the vast majority of webcasting that occurs happens not as carefully constructed learning environments, but as capture of live lectures. Moreover the technologies by which such capture is created, and the e-learning middleware environments such as Articulate or Echo360 by which the majority of video, audio and textual and other resources are designed and created are now provided by digital education corporations. The means of digital production thus lie increasingly in their hands, and less in the hands of law schools, individual faculty or students.

More recently, the subject of webcasting and more particularly the capture of live lectures has presented new issues for faculty. At the 2018 British and Irish Law Education Technology Association (BILETA) conference in Aberdeen, concerns were raised about the use of such recordings by institutions, in particular the mandated capture of lectures and their mandatory use by institutions, for example their possible use during strike action by faculty. There are also other concerns arising from the surveillance culture that is part of lecture capture, and the role that data protection and Article 8 privacy rights may play in offering faculty remedies for the re-use of lectures without consent in such circumstances. In the recent case of *Antović and Mirković v Montenegro*[38] the European Court of Human Rights decided that a breach of Article 8 had occurred when lectures were re-used during strike action without a lecturer's consent, but the majority opinion was a narrow one.[39] The majority judgments reflected the extent to which, in Europe at least and perhaps in other jurisdictions too, the legal arguments centre upon a change of purpose in the way that the recordings are deployed from that for which they were originally created (i.e. a shift from educational design – increasing accessibility for students, or improving learning – to use as strike cover). As a result, the BILETA Executive is currently drawing up guidelines for a Teaching Recording Policy, which will sit alongside recently updated UK Joint Information Systems Committee (JISC) guidelines.[40]

What this case study demonstrates is the extent to which a new technology, a digital video presentation of legal data, is still emergent, still in the process of being shaped by technologists, designers and HE institution, but increasingly by corporations. That process by which over the last two decades law schools have gradually lost agency in the technological choices that they make as they bend to the pressures of the corporatized marketplace, is one of many narratives that needs to be researched and brought to light. As a result there are changes to student learning practices and to faculty workplace practices that require much more research, analysis and comment than has hitherto been produced in legal education. We also need to know under which conditions the published general guidelines on the use of webcasts and recorded lectures apply specifically to law as a discipline, and where they do not.[41] Other narratives matter too. There are intersecting narratives between education, cultural commentary, jurisprudential critique and technological analysis – for example the links between jurisprudential analysis and the place of technological and educational theory in legal education; or the effects of a networked society in an information age upon the deep educational structures of legal knowledge, legal reasoning and the learning and application of both in our curricula.[42]

And yet, while these narratives grow in profusion all around us, and we are living through transformations as profound as any in the past such as the scholarly revolution of the 13th century, the moveable print revolution of the 15th century, the industrial print revolution of the 19th century, we cannot represent or interrogate them for ourselves and for others with the sophistication that they merit. To be sure, there are many isolated accounts of projects, pilots and developments in articles, book chapters and books; but no histories, one updated bibliography, few policy papers, no map of interdisciplinary analyses of the field and only a single systematic summary of the research covering a fraction of the field.[43]

Not only are there no histories of the changes we undergo: we have no central records of the technologies that have been in use in our legal curricula. In no jurisdiction is there a detailed record and archive of digital technologies, nor a history of their development and use across jurisdictions. Even the primary texts are disappearing. Webcasts that need close interrogation are dependent on software, operating systems and hosting servers that have brief lives of less than a decade; digital textual formats online, perhaps even less. The detailed, meticulous research carried out by Margaret Smith on the textual practices of publishers in their migration from manuscript to printed book cannot be carried out on early digital texts, because they no longer exist.[44] They are constantly evolving, and because we have little sense of how they are used by learners, in that chartless, unanalysed becoming, we have become amnesiac and inarticulate about our use of digital technology.

As a result, the research literature that does exist on technology and legal education lacks the quality and rigour that we need to understand the field and to guide our practices. Hamilton's perception of a 'weak sense of history shown by classroom researchers' applies here, and is matched by a 'weak sense of the [legal educational] classroom shown by educational historians'. Lacking strong models and evidence bases, our understanding of the power of digital in legal learning is too easily captured by slicker, more apparently persuasive discourses such as those around digital natives, disruption, artificial intelligence, and practice-ready law students. It also cannot function as a strong challenge to the hegemony of the status quo in the legal academy: innovation too easily withers as digital methods are co-opted into versions of 20th-century curricula, aspects of which would not look out of place in a 19th-century classroom.[45] The dovetailing of theory and practice, the two David Hamiltons, cannot easily be accomplished in such a context.

What is true *in extremis* about digital technology can also be said to be true about legal education more generally. In England the Legal Education and Training Review was tasked inter alia to create a literature review on nine topics in professional legal education stretching back over 40 years.[46] We reported on poor or non-existent data, on research that was not sufficiently robust in methods, on the lack of research organisation and, since our remit was to take into account other jurisdictions, we could see the same was true there. Apart from the project carried out by the UK Centre for Legal Education around 2009 to create a taxonomy of legal education, there has been few sustained, longitudinal attempts to map the field. In short, there is little to guide our thinking about the historical moment we find ourselves in, and less to shape our thinking about the future.

IV Three rival futures of legal education research: Prometheus, Sisyphus, Themis

If we turn our gaze to a sister discipline, medical education, we see quite a different landscape. There are professional bodies such as the Accreditation Council for Graduate Medical Education (ACGME) in the United States, and the Association for Medical Educators in Europe (AMEE), originally a European now a global organization.[47] AMEE has a global conference, an initiative to promote teaching alongside research as a measure of excellence (called ASPIRE), is a founder member of the Best Evidence Medical Education Collaboration (BEME), its members produce AMEE Guides to key topics and issues in medical education (121 to date), it offers Essential Skills in Medical Education (ESME) courses and accreditation, and through MedEdWorld offers a platform and international network for medical schools and others to share expertise and collaborate with each other.

An organization such as AMEE could not exist without extensive funding (based largely on individual and institutional subscriptions); but even more essential is the commitment to produce research for the benefit of the community – a quality that is emphasized strongly on many AMEE webpages. Also binding the community together are shared research methodologies with, at their core, a scientific bias that reflects medical research. The statistical basis to much of medical education stems of course from educators' training in basic science and medical science. But this bias is also contested within the field by those sub-disciplines such as medical humanities that adopt quite different approaches to medical education, and where views on, for example standardization within assessments, are quite different to those who hold to a more scientific approach. AMEE accommodates and encourages these debates.

There is much that we legal educators can learn from medical education and its organization and community focus. The method of research review is fundamental to the way medical education organizes its research – not just meta-reviews that rely on statistical content, but systematic summaries of research, policy summaries, analyses of prior research, educational debates, and much else.[48] These research genres are forms of reflection upon the corpus of research and they are essential not just for educators in the discipline, both newcomers and experienced practitioners, but also for others such as accreditors, regulators, policymakers and those in other disciplines seeking to understand key issues and methods in medical education.

Such research mapping takes place in disciplines other than medical and science education, for example education itself, where it is essential to the formation of theory as well as practice. Indeed it would not have been possible for David Hamilton to have written a theoretical text on the history and cultures of northern and western schooling and curriculum without the research summaries, bibliographies and other research tools that he relied upon. To have done this for legal education, and particularly in the modern period, would have been even more difficult, not just because of the weaknesses that he identifies, but because the secondary organization of research is simply not present for researchers in the field.

It is time we took steps to remedy the situation. And it is in this respect that some of us are putting together an initiative we have called the Themis project. It is an online space for collaborative, cross-disciplinary, inter-jurisdictional research into legal education and the profession. It will have the capacity to host original research but also systematic reviews of the changing profession and market for legal services, and developments, theory and practice in legal education and training. It will develop research training resources. It will create syntheses of research – for example on the research into the consequences for legal education of regulatory, organizational or technological changes in legal services. Regular updating of research into regulatory literatures, to take another example, would be invaluable to legal education regulators and accreditors globally. The project will be capable of databanking for evidence-based policy-making. We plan to develop a platform for Working Paper Series, Systematic Review Series and Methods Series, all open-access. Medical education organisations such as AMEE will be models for us, but our methods will of course be adapted to our own discipline; and we shall use open source referencing tools where possible to build libraries of research materials.[49]

These proposals are innovative in that they attempt to provide a platform for the organization of our practices, our theory and our research worldwide. They are an attempt to create a community of jurisdictional initiatives that brings us together globally – a network of networks.[50] In this sense they attempt to change the narrative of our research; and they can be represented in narrative, too. We often see our research role as Promethean – to uncover new knowledge, to make it available for the benefit of others, as Prometheus brought the gift of fire to humankind. But Prometheus, a Titan, is an isolated figure; there is no community in the core mythos around him, and he pays a heavy price for his actions. Moreover his actions are isolated – there is no community action around them. Contrast him with the figure of another Titan, Themis, the goddess of custom and order, achieved through her daughters *Eunomia*, law's order, *Dīke*, justice, and *Eirēnē*, peace, and, with her prophetic skill, a sometime oracle at Delphi. Community, and the processes that bring about and sustain community, are central to her *mythos*. And in final contrast to the creative, isolated Prometheus and the community and order of Themis is the isolated, repetitious labour undergone in an ever-present punishment by Sisyphus, a clever and deceitful mortal.[51]

These three contrasting figures hold many contrasting and yet interlocking narratives for us. The Promethean and Sisyphean stories are pathologies, extremes of their type to be sure; but creativity and idealism, habit and repetition are core to much legal education research. Indeed the figures are dark and disturbing mirror images of each other: the idealism of Prometheus, the deceitfulness of Sisyphus, the similar endless torments to which they are condemned by their actions. Prometheus often seems to exist outside historical lifeworld, an atomistic figure; but bring him closer to our lives and we can see the compulsion to be original, unique, new, forced upon us systemically by research managers and audits, and by governmental policies and strategies, of which the REF 2020 in the UK and ERA in Australia are only two examples. No place here in the assessment of research items for the careful tending of scholarship: all must be innovative thought, radical world-beating invention. In the process we carry out far too much repetitious, Sisyphean work in our research that could be made much more productive were we to carry it out not just for ourselves and our individual Promethean research projects, but for the sake of the wider community – a Themistic approach from which we would all benefit.

Themis represents that relational turn, embodied in the project work of the first David described above, and in the analyses of schooling by the second David. The Themis project is an attempt to bring about a sense of order and community in legal education research that other disciplines such as medical education have well understood and enacted in their work. Themis thus represents an impulse to order that is for the good of the community, for order of any kind is impossible without memory and without histories and the interpretive, reflexive turn that such narratives bring – qualities that, as we saw in the field of our historyless *techne*, are urgently required. Themis brings to our research, too, the resonance of communitarian values, and a belief that by organizing our past work we may be able to better understand the present, and gaze further into the future.

Notes

1 This chapter is a version of the plenary address given to the UNSW Legal Education Research Conference, held December 2017. My grateful thanks to Alex Steel and the Conference Committee for the invitation to speak at the conference.

2 Kenneth J. Gergen, *Relational Being: Beyond Self and Community* (Oxford University Press, New York 2009) 366.

3 See, e.g., the High Scope method of pre-school education, one of the first major studies of transition into an educational system, and itself the product of a long tradition in US education stretching back into the 19th century, and including the educational practices and philosophies of John Dewey and Jane Addams. Scheinhart and Weikart note in the early studies a turn from a pre-occupation with IQ to 'a broader perspective on young people's experience in school and community': see Lawrence J. Schweinhart and David P. Weikart, 'The High/Scope Perry Preschool Study. Implications for Early Childhood Care and Education' (2008) 7 *Prevention in Human Services* 109, 110. The literature on transitions from school to university, within university and from higher education (HE) to the world of employment beyond was really only beginning to be published at this period. Tinto's Model of Institutional Departure was one of the key early models. See Vincent Tinto and John Cullen, *Dropout in Higher Education: A Review and Theoretical Synthesis of Recent Research* (Columbia University Press 1973). Others such as Yorke pointed to the higher rate of withdrawal by students from low socioeconomic groupings, mature students and disabled students. See Mantz Yorke, *Leaving Early: Undergraduate Non-Completion in Higher Education* (1st edn, Routledge, Abingdon-on-Thames 1999).

4 Highers are the Scots equivalent of English A-levels for entrance to HE. They are normally studied in fifth year in secondary school, with more advanced grading now available in sixth year at Advanced Higher level (which is generally regarded as a qualification beyond A-level in complexity and sophistication).

5 And by cultural capital I mean in the broadest sense the deep learning of certain views of history, art, social practices, nationhood, politics and economics. See, e.g., Henry A. Giroux, 'Liberal Arts Education and the Struggle for Public Life: Dreaming about Democracy' (1990) 89 *South Atlantic Quarterly* 113. This includes the development of attitudes in learners regarding new knowledge and its integration that require, as Barnett has pointed out, a degree of epistemic flexibility. See Ronald Barnett, 'Conditions of Flexibility. Securing a More Responsive Higher Education System' (The Higher Education Academy 2014). Flexibility and transition, both highly Brunerian in focus, were important to us teaching on the programme. See, e.g., Jerome Bruner, 'The New Educational Technology' (1962) 6 *American Behavioral Scientist* 5.

6 There is extensive work on this. See, e.g., David Harvie, 'Alienation, Class and Enclosure in UK Universities' (2000) 24 *Capital & Class* 103; Rolf Becker and Anna E. Hecken, 'Why Are Working-Class Children Diverted from

Universities? – An Empirical Assessment of the Diversion Thesis' (2009) 25 *European Sociological Review* 233. For theoretical work, see Giroux (n. 5).

7 First year was the crux, particularly the period several months in. During this transition Whittaker noted the need for a range of support that was not just academic but also social and personal, and this was out of experience too, in following up with those students who did withdraw in first year – Ruth Whittaker, 'Quality Enhancement Themes: The First Year Experience. Transition to and during the First Year' (Quality Assurance Agency for Higher Education 2008). Yorke points out that 'roughly two thirds of premature departures take place in, or at the end of, the first year of full-time study in the UK': Yorke (n. 3) 37.

8 On relational agency, see especially Anne Edwards and Carmen D'Arcy, 'Relational Agency and Disposition in Sociocultural Accounts of Learning to Teach' (2004) 56 *Educational Review* 147. Edwards acknowledges her work is based upon the foundational work of Gergen.

9 Sylvia Scribner and Michael Cole, *The Psychology of Literacy* (Harvard University Press 1981). David Bartholomae, *Facts, Artifacts, and Counterfacts: Theory and Method for a Reading and Writing Course* (Heinemann, London 1986). Linda Flower, 'Detection, Diagnosis, and the Strategies of Revision' (1986) 37 *College Composition and Communication* 16.

10 See David Hamilton, *Towards a Theory of Schooling* (1st edn, Routledge, Abingdon-on-Thames 2014). The book was first published in 1989.

11 Ibid., 49.

12 Ibid.

13 Ibid., 76.

14 Ibid., 77.

15 The context of Adam Smith's professorial lectures in Glasgow University, including those on jurisprudence, are adduced by Hamilton. In a forthcoming book on modernising legal education my chapter describes a similar movement from a different perspective, citing the valuable work of the legal historian John Cairns on 18th-century legal educators such as Adam Smith and Henry Home, Lord Kames. Smith's new definition of rhetoric, expanding from the classical tradition of persuasive eloquence to treat of all forms of contemporary communication, was critical to the new rhetoric. See Paul Maharg, 'Same as It Ever Was? Second Modernity, Technocracy and the Design of Digital Legal Education' in Catrina Denvir (ed), *Modernising Legal Education* (forthcoming, Cambridge University Press, Cambridge 2019).

16 Thus Hamilton observes how Smith's arguments 'in favour of natural liberty and against artificial restraint' gave legitimacy to disrupt the traditional practices of mercantile and craft guilds. See Hamilton (n. 10) 78. Among them was James Watt, whose work on steam engines required the development of specialist skills in measurement and instrument-building that simply could not be accommodated by the then current craft guilds such as the Hammermen.

17 Hamilton (n. 10) 2.

18 Ibid., 150.

19 Ibid.

20 Ibid., 151.

21 Ibid.

22 Ibid., 153.

23 Lawrence Stenhouse, *Authority, Education and Emancipation* (Heinemann Educational Publishers, London 1983). There are many still unrecognised influences and connections between radical theorists of learning across related disciplines. Cole, an extraordinarily interdisciplinary researcher in reading and writing, has written on the parallels between Dewey and his circle and sociocultural theorists. See Michael Cole, *Cultural Psychology: A Once and Future Discipline* (New edn,

Harvard University Press 1998). See also the conceptual treatment of literacy in media literacy (James Paul Gee, *Teaching, Learning, Literacy in Our High-Risk High-Tech World: A Framework for Becoming Human* (Teachers' College Press, New York 2017); the work of the New London Group in Henry Jenkins, *Convergence Culture: Where Old and New Media Collide* (Rev edn, NYU Press 2008) and multimodality theory in Gunther Kress, *Multimodality: Exploring Contemporary Methods of Communication* (1st ed, Routledge, London 2009). See also the passage of ideas regarding networks between complexity theory and cyber-economics and network economics in Gregory Bateson, *Steps to an Ecology of Mind: Collected Essays in Anthropology, Psychiatry, Evolution, and Epistemology* (University of Chicago Press 2000); Yochai Benkler, *The Wealth of Networks: How Social Production Transforms Markets and Freedom* (Yale University Press 2007); and between cyber-ethnology and ethnology see, e.g., Tom Boellstorff, *Coming of Age in Second Life: An Anthropologist Explores the Virtually Human* (Rev edn, Princeton University Press 2015). Note the reference in Boellstorff's title to Margaret Mead's famous anthropological study, *Coming of Age in Samoa: A Psychological Study of Primitive Youth for Western Civilisation*, where the subtitles after the caesura of the colon tell us much about the differences between digital and pre-digital ethnology.

24 He references the work of scholars such as Anthony Grafton and Lisa Jardine in textual and humanities studies. Grafton and Jardine point to the capacity for humanist education to teach 'a properly docile attitude towards authority', an authority that comprised 'closed governing elites, hereditary offices and strenuous efforts to close off debate on vital political and social questions'. They observe that it is only from the Enlightenment onwards that there develops a rhetoric of liberation and liberal values applied to humanist education. See Hamilton (n. 10) 51; Anthony Grafton and Jardine, *From Humanism to the Humanities* (Harvard University Press 1986) xiv.

25 To be fair to The University and its Ways, project funding was directed only at induction activities, and not for substantial ongoing support either during subsequent university years or in early professional careers. Dr David Hamilton, the project director, was instrumental in organising what support could be arranged, given tight budgetary constraints.

26 My wide definition of technology is in part a social constructionist view; but also a common account of the term in the literature of new media. See Lisa Gitelman, *Always Already New: Media, History, and the Data of Culture* (MIT Press, Cambridge MASS 2008).

27 See, e.g., Annemarieke Willemsen, *Back to the Schoolyard: The Daily Practice of Medieval and Renaissance Education* (1st edn, Brepols NV, Turnhout 2008); Ian Grosvenor (ed), *Silences & Images: The Social History of the Classroom* (1st edn, Peter Lang AG, Pieterlen 1999).

28 See Paul Maharg, *Transforming Legal Education: Learning and Teaching the Law in the Early Twenty-First Century* (Routledge, London 2016).

29 Ibid., 120–1; Margaret M. Smith, 'The Design Relationship between the Manuscript and the Incunable' in Robert Myers and Michael Harris (eds), *A Millennium of the Book: Production, Design and Illustration in Manuscript and Print 900–1900* (St Paul's Bibliographies, London 1994).

30 An example from 16th-century legal education in the Netherlands is discussed in Paul Maharg, 'Disintermediation' (2016) 50 *The Law Teacher* 114.

31 See, e.g., Husam Aldamen, Rajab Al-Esmail and Janice Hollindale, 'Does Lecture Capturing Impact Student Performance and Attendance in an Introductory Accounting Course?' (2015) 24 *Accounting Education* 291; Jared Danielson and others, 'Is the Effectiveness of Lecture Capture Related to Teaching Approach or Content Type?' (2014) 72 *Computers & Education* 121; Martin R. Edwards

and Michael E. Clinton, 'A Study Exploring the Impact of Lecture Capture Availability and Lecture Capture Usage on Student Attendance and Attainment' (*Higher Education* 2018) https://doi.org/10.1007/s10734-018-0275-9; Johanna Inman and Simuelle Myers, 'Now Streaming: Strategies That Improve Video Lectures' (2018) IDEA Paper 68/2018 www.ideaedu.org/Portals/0/Uploads/Documents/IDEA%20Papers/IDEA%20Papers/PaperIDEA_68.pdf; Frances V. O'Callaghan and others, 'The Use of Lecture Recordings in Higher Education: A Review of Institutional, Student, and Lecturer Issues' (2017) 22 *Education and Information Technologies* 399.

32 There are of course many forms of recorded lectures, either visual and aural or simply aural, as podcasts. They are frequently recordings of live lectures posted in a variety of formats on the web in institutional VLEs. Our study, described below, entailed a different approach, recording a talking head, and splicing that with bullet-point summaries, texts, cases, legislation, handbooks and much else. The environment was thus much more of a planned study environment. It was designed and built by the technology team in the Learning Technologies Development Unit in the Glasgow Graduate School of Law, later maintained by Strathclyde Law School.

33 Now titled the Diploma in Professional Legal Practice, and part of the Professional Education and Training programme of the Law Society of Scotland. Our research, carried out in 2004, aimed to discover:

- The variation in student learning
- The quality of student learning

on the two procedural courses. The aims were of course influenced by the project methodology, which was phenomenographic in design. We tracked variation and quality in learning using the following instruments:

- Selection of 14 students to track closely throughout the year (11 completed the project);
- Students filled in and submitted weekly logs when they used the webcast resources;
- Focus group discussion late in semester one;
- Individual interviews in early/mid semester two and post-examination;
- Questionnaire issued to the group of 11 students;
- End-of-year evaluation data derived from whole-year cohort.

Over 100 pages of qualitative data were collected and qualitative responses were arrayed in a thematic coding-frame by two raters, with relatively high inter-rater reliability. Results and discussions were published in Patricia McKellar and Paul Maharg, 'Virtual Learning Environents: The Alternative to the Box under the Bed' (2005) 39 *The Law Teacher* 43, and in Maharg (n. 17) ch. 9.

34 For a description and examples of video jump-cuts, see www.youtube.com/watch?v=p2BqEvoiX04. A glossed manuscript often comprised a two-column *textura* sited centrally but often around a third of the way down a page. It was surrounded by glosses, a collection of short, dense, highly abbreviated explicatory passages, often attributed to scholars by initials. These comments were not fixed, and of course the gloss invited further gloss. They tended to be in slow flux, as rebuttals of earlier comments gained ground in a scholarly community, and one gloss might replace another. What we have, in effect, are slo-mo versions of the video jump-cut.

35 In this sense the students were moving, in Laurillard's learning types, between acquisition of knowledge, inquiry and production (of notes, knowledge objects, and the like). See Diana Laurillard, *Rethinking University Teaching: A Conversational Framework for the Effective Use of Learning Technologies* (2nd edn,

Routledge, London 2001). In our design we followed the research on notetaking, e.g., Kenneth A. Kiewra, 'Notetaking and Review: The Research and Its Implications' (1987) 16 *Instructional Science* 233.

36 Noel Entwistle and Ference Marton, 'Knowledge Objects: Understandings Constituted through Intensive Academic Study' (1994) 64 *British Journal of Educational Psychology* 161.

37 Edwards and D'Arcy (n. 8) 150. Edwards derives the concept in part from Gergen's account of relational being.

38 Application no. 70838/13, 28 November 2017; [2017] ECHR 365.

39 For detailed comment see Lilian Edwards, Laura Martin and Tristan Henderson, 'Employee Surveillance: The Road to Surveillance Is Paved with Good Intentions' <https://papers.ssrn.com/sol3/papers.cfm?abstract_id=3234382>.

40 The UK JISC Guidelines are available at <www.jisc.ac.uk/guides/recording-lectures-legal-considerations>. It is indicative of the interest in these issues now, in the light of recent extended strike action during 2018 by staff on the subject of USS pensions, that these guidelines were last updated in July 2010.

41 Hilary Putnam has pointed out Dewey's insistence that 'by creating new observation-concepts we "institute" new data'. This is true of the emergence of new forms of academic media convergence, and our relationships with them. See Hilary Putnam, Ruth Anna Putnam and David Macarthur, *Pragmatism as a Way of Life: The Lasting Legacy of William James and John Dewey* (Harvard University Press 2017).

42 The jurisprudential debates regarding technology and legal education are central to our theory and practice, for regulators as well as educators, and take in figures as different as Bruner and Manuel Castells, *The Power of Identity: The Information Age – Economy, Society, and Culture: 2* (2nd edn, Wiley-Blackwell, Hoboken 2009). For discussion of the regulatory context, see Paul Maharg, 'Shared Space: Regulation, Technology and Legal Education in a Global Context' (2015) 6 *European Journal of Law and Technology* <http://ejlt.org/index.php/ejlt/>.

43 For the updated bibliography, see Pearl Goldman, 'Legal Education and Technology II: An Annotated Bibliography' (2008) 100 *Law Library Journal* 415. For the systematic summary see Paul Maharg and Emma Nicol, 'Simulation and Technology in Legal Education: A Systematic Review and Future Research Programme' in Richard Grimes, Edward Phillips and Caroline Strevens (eds), *Legal Education: Simulation in Theory and Practice* (Ashgate Publishing, Farnham 2014). BILETA made an early attempt to map the field, but this was discontinued. See the following three BILETA Reports: British and Irish Law Education Technology Association, 'Inquiry into the Provision of Information Technology in the UK Law Schools' (University of Warwick 1991); British and Irish Legal Education Technology Association, 'Information Technology for UK Law Schools: The Second of Law Schools in the United Kingdom, 2004' (BILETA 1996); Phil Harris and Sarah Beinart, 'A Survey of Law Schools in the United Kingdom, 2004' (2005) 39 *The Law Teacher* 299.

44 For Smith's work see endnotes 15 and 16 above.

45 See, e.g., Jos Boys' perceptive comment that applications such as a learning management system were 'taking hold precisely because it enables institutions to avoid difficult questions about how they organise themselves': Jos Boys, 'Managed Learning Environments, Joined up Systems and the Problems of Organisational Change' (2002) JISC Report, 21 <www.tinyurl.com/2bpofr>, accessed 11 November 2018.

46 Julian Webb and others, 'Setting Standards. The Future of Legal Services Education and Training Regulation in England and Wales' (SRA, BSB, IPS 2013) <http://letr.org.uk>. Our review was 299 pages in length and drew upon a cited reference database of over 2,000 items in Zotero. The review and the reference

database was made public online at our project website, <http://letr.org.uk/literature-review/index.html>, but five years later, and contrary to our request, the references have not been updated by the regulators who instructed the Review.

47 'ACGME Home' <www.acgme.org/>, accessed 16 September 2018; 'An International Association For Medical Education – AMEE' <https://amee.org/home>, accessed 16 September 2018.

48 See, e.g., Adam Cheng and others, 'Using the METRICS Model for Defining Routes to Scholarship in Healthcare Simulation' (2018) 40 *Medical Teacher* 652. In this article the authors applied a new model of scholarship that described seven patterns of scholarship, and applied this to a dataset of 432 articles on simulation from four established journals in the field of healthcare simulation. The resulting array enabled the researchers to map the forms of research used in the field, the gaps, and in the case of two authors, how the patterns that emerged 'would influence their approach to future scholarly activities'.

49 Project documentation on file with Maharg. By the time of publication of this book our website should be publicly available.

50 They are however supplemental to the arguments and outcomes of the Nuffield Inquiry on Empirical Legal Research in England. See Hazel Genn, 'Nuffield Inquiry on Empirical Legal Research – Law in the Real World | Nuffield Foundation' (*Nuffield Foundation* 2006) <www.nuffieldfoundation.org/nuffield-inquiry-empirical-legal-research-law-real-world>, accessed 15 September 2018.

51 The figures of Prometheus and Sisyphus figure more prominently in northern and western literature than Themis, who is of course represented as the blind figure of Justice and thus associated with courts, litigation and punishment rather than the original and much more sophisticated qualities of her mythic origins. Shelley's long poem 'Prometheus Unbound' is an example of Promethean literature; while the Scots poet Robert Garioch writes a portrait of Sisyphus as a working-class man (who himself nudges the boulder at the top of the hill and follows it down to begin again, 'shair of his cheque at the month's end'), while Carole Ann Duffy gives us a scathing portrait of Sisyphus as a workaholic husband in Mrs Sisyphus. See Robin Fulton (ed), *Robert Garioch: Collected Poems* (Polygon, Edinburgh 2004); Carol Ann Duffy, *The World's Wife* (Reprints edition, Picador, London 2010).

Index

Note: Page numbers in italic indicate a figure and page numbers in bold indicate a table on the corresponding page.

For Product Safety Concerns and Information please contact our EU representative GPSR@taylorandfrancis.com
Taylor & Francis Verlag GmbH, Kaufingerstraße 24, 80331 München, Germany

www.ingramcontent.com/pod-product-compliance
Ingram Content Group UK Ltd.
Pitfield, Milton Keynes, MK11 3LW, UK
UKHW022013180926
475701UK00003B/344
9781032240503